C. S. Lewis and the
Craft of Communication

"I envy Dr. Beebe because he has learned from C. S. Lewis what it is like to be able to say exactly what he means. But I'm getting beyond the envy, thanks to Dr. Beebe's *C. S. Lewis and the Craft of Communication*. He wants us to be as clear in what we say, as in what we hear. And his book provides us with a framework and advice for how to do this well. Both men use these rules: 'Always prefer the plain direct word to the long, vague one. Don't implement promises, but keep them.' 'Never use abstract nouns when concrete ones will do.' 'If you mean, "More people died" don't say "Mortality rose." ' "

—Walter Hooper, former secretary to C. S. Lewis, Literary Advisor of the C. S. Lewis Estate, and author of *C. S. Lewis: A Companion and Guide*

"Steven A. Beebe reveals that nobody can fully appreciate the genius of Lewis without seeing the brilliance of Lewis's skill as a communicator. If you are going to learn about government you would like to have Abraham Lincoln at your elbow. If you want to learn about leadership, who would not love to tag along with Sir Winston Churchill? If you want to learn about American football, John Madden is the man to guide you.... When it comes to communication, Beebe is the one to facilitate the process of learning. Furthermore, when Beebe turns his attention to C. S. Lewis, the combination is unbeatable: Lewis the master communicator, and Beebe the master teacher."

—Jerry Root, Professor, Wheaton College, Wheaton, Illinois, and co-author of *The Quotable C. S. Lewis*

"C. S. Lewis continues to enchant readers worldwide, in part because of *what* he said but also because of *how* he said it. This important book offers clear and surprisingly practical insight into a truly remarkable communicator. It is profound without being ponderous; it is useful without being formulaic. I learned a great deal in these pages, and I look forward to reading it again and again. I give it my highest recommendation."

—Diana Pavlac Glyer, Professor, The Honors College, Azusa Pacific University, and author of *Bandersnatch* and *The Company They Keep: C. S. Lewis and J.R.R. Tolkien as Writers in Community*

"Here indeed we find a great treasure; in the beautifully conceived carefully written pages of this book, Steven A. Beebe has brilliantly answered a question readers have long felt but perhaps never formed: How did Lewis communicate so clearly? Bringing to bear a lifetime of distinguished scholarship and decades of keenly insightful thinking about Lewis, Beebe has created an indispensable aid not only for lovers of Lewis but for all who would communicate clearly themselves."

—Andrew Lazo, an independent scholar and speaker on C. S. Lewis, editor of "Early Prose Joy," Lewis's groundbreaking first spiritual autobiography, and co-editor, *Mere Christians: Inspiring Stores of Encounters with C. S. Lewis*

"C. S. Lewis understood the theory and practice of the medieval trivium (grammar, dialectic, rhetoric) better than anyone in his generation, but far too little attention has been given to his extraordinary skill as a communicator. Steven A. Beebe brings to this gap in scholarship his own formidable experience and expertise as a professor of communication, and also a keen personal enthusiasm. The result is a thoughtful, insightful, delightful book that informs, instructs and illuminates."

—Michael Ward, Senior Research Fellow, University of Oxford, co-editor of *The Cambridge Companion to C. S. Lewis*, and author of *Planet Narnia* and *The Narnia Code*

"Who better to write the book on C. S. Lewis and the craft of communication than one of the foremost professors of communication in the world—Steven A. Beebe, who also happens to be a Lewis enthusiast? This book is a must-read for all who study the craft of communication, for all communicators who want to improve their art-form, and for all lovers of C. S. Lewis and his work. Even the latter are bound to learn something new from this book, since it is brimming over with insightful analysis. Beebe writes in a style as clear as water from a fresh, mountain spring, in a manner as engaging as a man on his knees with a ring in his hand, occasionally with a gentle humor befitting a Garrison Keillor, and always with the academic finesse of a bookworm in the bowels of the Bodleian Library. Bravo!"

—Will Vaus, author of *Mere Theology: A Guide to the Thought of C. S. Lewis*

"In exploring what made C. S. Lewis a master communicator, Steven A. Beebe has fine-tuned the Lewis biography with a wealth of freshly discovered details on the man and his writings. The combination of precise reasoning and an expansive imagination continues to make the Oxford don a compelling author. Through understanding better the communication principles Lewis followed, readers are invited to follow suit and become more effective communicators themselves."

—Bruce R. Johnson, General Editor of *Sehnsucht: The C. S. Lewis Journal*

"Throughout his life C. S. Lewis thought much about how to speak and how to write, always seeking a human touch. Steven A. Beebe's book is also based on a lifetime's reflection, with the grateful acknowledgment of many insights from Lewis's life, thinking and imagination. As with Lewis, Beebe's love of the gift of language that all humans share is the foundation for truly understanding the important craft of communication. His book, in a unique manner, provides a rich portrait of many aspects of Lewis which, in their diversity, prove to be connected in a wholesome and attractive way."

—Colin Duriez, author of *C. S. Lewis: A Biography of Friendship*

"If you have long loved C. S. Lewis—Christian apologist, children's book author, Oxford and Cambridge scholar—viewing Lewis through the lens of what he can teach us about human communication is likely a new experience. Beebe's decades of Lewis scholarship and teaching from a communication standpoint has led to this singular contribution that expands our understanding of and appreciation for Lewis. For those who aspire to teach students about Lewis's power to move people through his written and oral communication, we now have the perfect primer."

—*Diana K. Ivy, Professor of Communication Studies, Texas A & M University—Corpus Christi*

"Lewis, a communicator? If you think about it, of course. This makes sense to us intuitively, for how could Lewis such a good writer without knowing how to communicate to a reading audience? In *C. S. Lewis and the Craft of Communication*, we read the fascinating story of Steven A. Beebe discovering a lost manuscript, or at least thought to be lost, the manuscript on communication that Lewis and Tolkien talked about writing together. The book never happened, but the reasons why help us understand both Lewis and Tolkien. More importantly, throughout Dr. Beebe's book, we read about the development of C. S. Lewis the communicator, whose facility in language and English literature, along with many other factors, led to the making of the twentieth century's most famous Christian writer, and communicator, topics of interest to any communicator."

—Joel Heck, Professor, Concordia University Texas,
and author of *Irrigating Deserts: C. S. Lewis on Education*

"When you write a book about how effective C. S. Lewis was at communicating, then your presentation better be interesting and engaging to the reader. Beebe definitely delivers in this work! Those who know little more than his stories about Narnia will learn the breadth and range Lewis had in his other writings (and places where he spoke). If you are well versed in what Lewis wrote, then you'll have a clearer picture of why you enjoy his writings so much. Individuals with only an interest in communication, and caring little about Lewis, will walk away with a better understanding of how to communicate effectively and find they enjoyed learning about Lewis along the way.

The way Beebe organizes his book and presents it in his chapters is both entertaining and educational. I remember coming across a writer, in my field of professional counseling years ago, who for the first time gave me this experience. Each chapter of the book offered an overview of what was going to be presented, laid it out and then provided a summary without making me feel like I was being talked down to. Beebe lays out five principles gleaned from his obvious knowledge of Lewis's vast works and clearly backs them up. Then in the final chapter of his book, you are given practical ways to put into practice what you've learned. It is a delightful read that is clearly presented and surely a work that stands out in the crowded field of books related to Lewis."

—William O'Flaherty, author of *The Misquotable C. S. Lewis* and
C. S. Lewis Goes to Hell and host of the podcast *All About Jack*

C. S. Lewis and the
Craft of Communication

This book is part of the Peter Lang Media and Communication list.
Every volume is peer reviewed and meets
the highest quality standards for content and production.

PETER LANG
New York • Bern • Berlin
Brussels • Vienna • Oxford • Warsaw

Steven A. Beebe

C. S. Lewis and the
Craft of Communication

Foreword by Jerry Root

PETER LANG
New York • Bern • Berlin
Brussels • Vienna • Oxford • Warsaw

Library of Congress Cataloging-in-Publication Data
Names: Beebe, Steven A., author.
Title: C. S. Lewis and the craft of communication / Steven A. Beebe.
Description: New York: Peter Lang, 2020.
Includes bibliographical references and index.
Identifiers: LCCN 2019045758 (print) | LCCN 2019045759 (ebook)
ISBN 978-1-4331-7233-5 (hardback: alk. paper)
ISBN 978-1-4331-7234-2 (paperback: alk. paper) | ISBN 978-1-4331-7235-9 (ebook pdf)
ISBN 978-1-4331-7236-6 (epub) | ISBN 978-1-4331-7237-3 (mobi)
Subjects: LCSH: Lewis, C. S. (Clive Staples),
1898–1963—Knowledge—Communication. | Communication. | Written
communication. | Authorship. | Interpersonal communication.
Classification: LCC PR6023.E926 Z5856 2020 (print) |
LCC PR6023.E926 (ebook) | DDC 823/.912—dc23
LC record available at https://lccn.loc.gov/2019045758
LC ebook record available at https://lccn.loc.gov/2019045759
DOI 10.3726/b15950

Bibliographic information published by **Die Deutsche Nationalbibliothek**.
Die Deutsche Nationalbibliothek lists this publication in the "Deutsche
Nationalbibliografie"; detailed bibliographic data are available
on the Internet at http://dnb.d-nb.de/.

© 2020 Peter Lang Publishing, Inc., New York
29 Broadway, 18th floor, New York, NY 10006
www.peterlang.com

Printed in the United States of America

To my family, for their love and encouragement, and to C. S. Lewis, for teaching me lessons about communication and The Source of all Joy.

Contents

Foreword

When the Nobel Prize winning poet, Seamus Heaney, came to the door of The Kilns, C. S. Lewis's home in Oxford, he shouted, "I want to see the house where the Irishman lived!" Heaney grew up in North Ireland not all that far from where Lewis was raised. Ireland is a country that seems to have a disproportionate number of great writers, given the comparatively small population. Lewis thought it was in the genes to be a communicator. He once wrote, "I am an Irishman and a congenital rhetorician"[1] Perhaps that is it. The Irish are simply great at communication, and there is nothing more to it: great storytellers; great at spinning a yarn, and great at holding the attention of an audience. Perhaps it is something in the water. Perhaps, it is the island's unique combination of extraordinary beauty. The landscapes take one's breath away. However, the beauty also coexists with the history of a people who have endured centuries of suffering. Beauty and sorrow weave the texture unique to Irish literature. Is this what Lewis had in mind when he connected his rhetorical skill to his being Irish? Whatever the case, Lewis was a brilliant communicator.

Professor Steven Beebe reveals that nobody can fully appreciate the genius of Lewis without seeing the brilliance of Lewis's skill as a communicator. Lewis's scholarly books like *The Allegory of Love* and *English Literature in the Sixteenth Century: Excluding Drama* are masterpieces for their ability to follow a narrative thread through such a wide fabric of material. They hold a reader's attention for their clarity, their imaginative depiction, and their delightful winsomeness. He was certainly a master communicator as an academic. Furthermore, *The Chronicles of Narnia* are stories admitted into the very canons of classical children's literature, next to likes of Lewis Carroll's *Alice in Wonderland*, Kenneth Grahame's *The Wind in the Willows*, the Brothers Grimm, and Hans Christian Anderson. Lewis the master communicator could tell a story to delight the hearts of children. His storytelling skills also classify his science fiction among some of the best of that genre, such as Ray Bradbury and Isaac Asimov. How was it possible that he could communicate with such skill across such wide territory?

Lewis was also a scintillating debater. As the first president of the Oxford Socratic Club, he became what Oxford Philosopher Austin Farrer called "Oxford's Bonny Fighter." Lewis could stand on his own two feet and debate the best minds in Britain during the 1940s to mid-1950s. Nevertheless, his communication skills were not limited merely to oral communication; he was also highly capable when it came to debating in print. His dispute with Professor E. M. W Tillyard in *The Personal Heresy* is a noteworthy model of academic engagement. There are no *ad hominem* arguments in the book, no straw man arguments, virtually no informal fallacies to be found in the entire volume—just the arguments of two men who knew how to communicate effectively. He could preach too. I knew a woman who was present at St. Mary's, the University Church at Oxford when Lewis delivered his sermon, "The Weight of Glory." She said the pews were crammed full and the students filled all the floor space as well. Furthermore, his skill as a communicator was not reserved for public or formal occasions. I once received a letter from Lewis's fellow Inkling, the Chaucer scholar Nevill Coghill, in which he said that as a conversationalist, Lewis was "a splendid talker, a lot like Dr. Johnson in bulk as well as in wit and learning." It does not stop there; Lewis was also a disciplined letter writer. He said he answered all of his mail. And the letters were full of wisdom and insight. Consequently, those who received letters from him saved them. As a result, there are eight volumes of collected correspondence. He wrote to fellow academics, he wrote to friends, he wrote to readers of his books, he wrote thoughtful letters to children, with no sign of condescension. His letters are pithy and thought provoking; some are clearly pastoral and full of spiritual direction. It is not merely that he wrote letters, but that the range of topics he discusses is encyclopedic.

Lewis was a master communicator on every imaginable level. Was it simply because he was Irish? I doubt it. He certainly was gifted, and honed his gifts to a well-practiced skill. We may never be the communicator Lewis was; even so, there is much one can learn from him if attentive to his craft, and willing to cultivate the discipline to develop the skill. If this is the reader's interest, then a guide would be helpful. And I can think of no greater guide to define and clarify those elements that made Lewis a master communicator than Professor Steve Beebe. Dr. Beebe was the chairperson of one of the nation's largest communication departments at Texas State University, in San Marcos, Texas. Arguably, he has authored as many college and university textbooks on communication as anybody. Furthermore, he was president of the National Communication Association, the largest academic association for communicators in the world. Their annual meetings each year are where the experts in communication go to learn from one another. If you are going to learn about government you would like to have Abraham Lincoln at your elbow. If you want to learn about leadership, who would not love to tag along with Sir Winston Churchill? If you want to learn about American football, John Madden is the man to guide you. If you want to learn about art, Makoto Fujimura would be a great guide. For acting, Kenneth Branagh or Mark Rylands are the ones to seek out. When it comes to communication, Steve Beebe is the one to facilitate the process of learning. Furthermore, when Beebe turns his attention to C. S. Lewis, the combination is unbeatable: Lewis the master communicator, and Beebe the master teacher.

Not all of us will become communicators like Lewis; not all of us can teach like Beebe; but all of us can grow in skill. As Beebe reminds us, communication is audience centered. A good communicator speaking truth always gives hope to his or her audience. Professor Beebe gives double the hope. First, he points us to Lewis, whose written and oral communication is flush with hope. Furthermore, I know firsthand that Dr. Beebe is also a man whose insights and instruction breathe hope. When I sat for my doctoral defense at the Oxford Center for Mission Studies in Oxford, England, Steve Beebe was by my side. He was one of two supervisors who walked me through the seventh draft and the eight revision of my dissertation. I was nervous. He was confident. He knew his stuff and knew he had instructed me well. The topic was Lewis. He was my guide. I passed. It was a thrill. May you sense something of that thrill with Beebe at your elbow, guiding you through the corpus of Lewis as he teaches you about Lewis the master communicator.

Jerry Root, Ph.D.
Professor, Wheaton College

Note

1. C. S. Lewis, Letter to Eliza Marian Butler, September 25, 1940. *The Collected Letters of C. S. Lewis Volume II: Books, Broadcasts, and the War* 1931–1949. ed. Walter Hooper (San Francisco: Harper San Francisco, 2004), 444.

Preface

I had my "Indiana Jones" moment of discovery while watching my clothes tumble in a laundromat dryer in San Marcos, Texas. Several years before my laundry insight, in Oxford University's 400-year-old Bodleian Library, I had stumbled on an unpublished, unidentified partial book manuscript by author C. S. Lewis. But at the time I first read it, I didn't know its significance. Seven years later, in a single "Eureka!" laundromat moment, I realized what I had discovered. I had found a manuscript whose existence was doubted by most Lewis scholars: the opening pages of a planned collaboration between Lewis and *The Lord of the Rings* author J. R. R. Tolkien. Who would have thought that a laundry epiphany would solve a decades-old literary mystery involving two of the twentieth century's most famous authors? The contents of that manuscript provided just the evidence I needed that C. S. Lewis was, among his many talents, also a communication professor. Discovering that manuscript provided the principal impetus for this book.

Communication is my life. I have spent more than forty years as a communication professor and author and co-author of several widely-used communication college textbooks.[2] I have also had the privilege of serving as president of the National Communication Association, the largest academic professional association of communication educators and scholars in the world. Yet discovering Lewis and

Tolkien's ideas about language and human nature was like finding the wardrobe door into some of the most important lessons I have ever learned about communication. This book includes those lessons.

At the time I found the manuscript I was relatively new to C. S. Lewis studies. I had not read *The Chronicles of Narnia* until I was in my 40s. In fact, I had not read a single word of Lewis until I spent Trinity Term 1993 in Oxford as a visiting scholar, attached to Wolfson College and the Department of Experimental Psychology.

While I was in Oxford, given that the city is where Lewis lived, studied and taught, I thought it would be a good place to learn about him. I picked up a biography of Lewis by A. N. Wilson, straightforwardly titled, *C. S. Lewis: A Biography.* I later learned that Wilson's biography, although engagingly written, was controversial among Lewis scholars for including several errors, over-speculating about Lewis's personal life, and being too "Freudian" in its analysis of Lewis's relationships.[3] Unaware at the time that the biography had been criticized by many Lewis scholars for inaccuracies, I nonetheless found Lewis's life fascinating. The basic information in the book is true. I learned that Lewis was raised a Christian, then became an atheist, and then, in his late 20s and early 30s, slowly converted to Christianity, seeing it as the best way to make sense out of life. I also learned about Lewis's marriage (twice) to Jewish and former communist and atheist Joy Davidman.[4]

After reading about Lewis and then returning home to Texas to see the movie *Shadowlands*, a film about the romance between Lewis and Davidman, which had been filmed during the time we were in Oxford (my wife, two sons, and I are in one of the crowd scenes), I was motivated to learn more about Lewis. I began reading his work more systematically, attending weekend seminars in nearby Austin and San Antonio, and eventually joining a Lewis discussion group in Austin. Those monthly meetings were like taking a five-year graduate seminar in C. S. Lewis. There I met and learned from distinguished Lewis scholars such as Dr. Joel Heck, who wrote the well-received *Irrigating Deserts: C. S. Lewis on Education*, and Dr. George Musacchio, author of *C. S. Lewis, Man & Writer*. These individuals were generous in sharing their insights about Lewis, as well as patient with me and others who did not have their depth of understanding. As I more systematically studied Lewis, I became aware of his frequent references to language, meaning, communication, and words. As a communication professor, I recognized a number of insightful communication ideas embedded in his works. I thought it might be interesting to see if I could learn more about Lewis's perspective on communication.

With my emerging fascination with C. S. Lewis, I returned to Oxford in 2002 on a second sabbatical from Texas State University. I wanted to read original, handwritten C. S. Lewis manuscripts in Oxford University's centuries-old Bodleian Library. I enjoyed leisurely leafing through manuscript pages that Lewis's pen had touched. Lewis was ahead of the sustainability curve, as he would re-use paper and often write on the back of old manuscripts. Among my favorite documents are Lewis essays written on the back of student papers that had been corrected in a firm hand by his friend J. R. R. Tolkien.

As a communication professor, I was interested in what Lewis thought about language, meaning, and communication, but also in *how* he thought about these topics. I wondered if I could glean new insights into what the ancient Roman rhetoricians called *invention*: how Lewis's thoughts emerged and took shape. Could looking at his original manuscripts help me better understand him as a thinker, author, and speaker? I hoped so.

Upon returning my first batch of Lewis manuscripts to the library staff, I ordered a notebook described in the Lewis manuscript catalogue as a collection of miscellaneous notes and scraps. If you are granted access to the holdings at the Bodleian Library (requiring that you swear a centuries-old oath that you will not "kindle a fire" in the library), you first complete a form to request a book or manuscript from the archives, and then wait a few hours (or sometimes a day or more) to retrieve what was ordered. Since the Bodleian is a non-lending library, books and manuscripts are under tight security and read in special reading rooms; even the Queen cannot take a book out of the library! (Other monarchs have tried, with no success.) When the manuscript I had requested arrived in the reading room, it was a somewhat worn and slightly frayed, small, orange-covered paper notebook. I smiled when I saw that Lewis had penciled the word "SCRAPS" in capital letters on the outside cover.

The Lewis catalogue had accurately described the little notebook as containing drafts of Lewis's ideas on a variety of topics. Other researchers had read these scraps before I did—it is quite famous because its pages include one of the only existing fragment drafts for *The Chronicles of Narnia* held in the Bodleian Library. Early ideas for *The Magician's Nephew* can be found beginning on page 9. This early fragment of *The Magician's Nephew* is called "The Lefay Manuscript" because of a character named Mrs. Lefay that appears in the story.[5]

It was on the first page of the notebook—actually the first page when I turned the book upside down and read it back to front—where I read the words, "In a book like this it might be expected that we should begin with the origins of language ..."[6] I froze. I held my breath. "What's this?" Having already read the manuscript of *Studies in Words*, I knew that it did not start this way. I knew immediately that these words were important. What I did not realize at the time was that they were the beginning of a planned collaborative book with none other than J. R. R. Tolkien. In fact, I was slow to make the connection. Very slow. It took *seven years* for my laundry room insight to occur. The manuscript I was reading was intended to be a collaboration between Lewis and Tolkien that scholars had assumed was never started.

Because Lewis's handwriting is sometimes difficult to read (my friend and Lewis scholar Charlie Starr labels Lewis's handwriting "villainous"),[7] I had actually hoped the manuscript was already published. I scoured his published works, searching for it. And given that this was the beginning of a book about language and meaning, a topic right up my alley, I was keenly interested to find out what he had to say on this topic. Because of my impatience, I did not want to spend time trying to decode Lewis's penmanship; I wanted to get on with reading what he wrote, to learn his communication insights.

No luck in finding the book in print. I was disappointed because that meant I would have to decipher Lewis's "villainous" handwriting myself.[8] But my research did uncover references to the manuscript. It was catalogued by Lewis manuscript curator, Dr. Judith Priestman. Walter Hooper, Lewis's former secretary, editor, and literary executor, made a brief reference to the little notebook in his book *Past Watchful Dragons*, describing it as a manuscript about "English literature" and even suggesting that Lewis saved the little notebook of miscellaneous ideas because of the "English literature" essay.[9]

Because some of the handwriting was challenging to read, three years after first seeing the manuscript, I received special permission from the library (thanks to Walter Hooper, the original depositor of the manuscript) to make a photocopy. Walter and I met in 2002; he invited me to his home for tea, and we have been friends ever since. Being able to take a photocopy of the manuscript back to Texas was a great help in scrutinizing the scribbles I could not quite decipher. With the photocopied manuscript in hand, Hooper, who came to Texas State University to give a lecture five years after I started decoding the manuscript, helped me figure out a few additional illegible words. Another good friend and prominent Lewis scholar, Dr. Michael Ward, who also guest lectured at Texas State (and is the author of the groundbreaking books *Planet Narnia* and *The Narnia Code*) kindly helped me decipher a few remaining puzzling words. But even after painstakingly transcribing the manuscript, I still did not realize that it was the beginning of the book he had planned to write with Tolkien. It would take me a couple more years to connect those literary dots.

When I left Oxford to return to Texas after this second sabbatical, I did not fully understand the significance of what I had found, but I did have a bolstered belief that Lewis was interested in communication. Based on the content of the manuscript, I proposed an honors course at Texas State called "C. S. Lewis: Chronicles of a Master Communicator." My colleagues in the Honors College liked the idea. The course filled on the first day it was available to students, and more students wanted to enroll; I soon had more than 70 students on a waiting list hoping to take the course. I learned that C. S. Lewis generates interest. In addition to teaching a Lewis course on the Texas State campus, I also started teaching the course during the summer at Oxford University for Texas State students.

When in Oxford, I rarely held class in one of the well-appointed Victorian seminar rooms in St. Hilda's College, Oxford, where we were based. Instead, we used the city of Oxford as our educational canvas. (St. Hilda's College was the site of a famous debate between C. S. Lewis and philosopher Elizabeth Anscombe held on February 2, 1948).[10] We took walking tours of notable Lewis sites, including the numerous pubs he and his fellow Inklings used as locations for their literary conversations. For example, the day we talked about Lewis and interpersonal relationships, we held class in the room in the Eastgate Hotel, where some claim Lewis initially met his wife Joy. We visited his home, "The Kilns," toured University College, where Lewis was a student (and where President Bill Clinton later studied as a Rhodes scholar), and spent an afternoon at Magdalen College, the Oxford college where Lewis taught from 1925 to 1954. A highlight for many students (and for me) was the Bodleian Library, where they saw original Lewis manuscripts, including his own hand-drawn map of Narnia and, of course, the orange-colored paper notebook labeled "SCRAPS."

Despite the success of the Honors course, and although I had received encouragement and interest from many people to pursue investigating Lewis from a communication angle, some of my communication faculty colleagues from my home department were at first less impressed. On my annual faculty evaluations, written anonymously, I would find such occasional comments as: "Why is he making his hobby about C. S. Lewis into a communication class?" Or "Not really much information to justify teaching a communication class focused on Lewis." And even "Beebe is just using his interest in Oxford as an excuse to teach a course about Lewis." Well, it was true that I had a passionate interest in the City of Oxford and Oxford University. And it was also true that I found C. S. Lewis intriguing—not just because of what he wrote, but because his own life story captivated me. Yet I also firmly believed that Lewis had something to say about human communication.

Despite the collegial criticism, I forged ahead and continued to teach the Honors class about Lewis. Although I still did not comprehend what that manuscript was, its content formed a key part of the information I shared with my students about Lewis and communication. In the manuscript fragment, Lewis develops an interesting definition of language, a definition I have not seen in any of his other published works. He further presents a thoughtful discussion of the nature of meaning, including how we derive meaning from language. (These ideas will be discussed in Chapter 5.) What is most interesting to me, as a professor of communication, is Lewis's focus on the *oral* nature of language. Each of his examples and illustrations are about *spoken* rather than written language—unusual since he specialized in sixteenth century English literature and spent so much of his time writing.

Earlier on the morning of my laundromat epiphany, as my wife Sue and I left our house because our home washing machine had broken, I had randomly grabbed a book from my bookshelf—*The Company They Keep,* by Diana Pavlac Glyer—to help pass the time. It is a well-researched and masterfully written book that I had read a couple of years prior, but I thought I would re-read it.[11] Glyer's book chronicles the relationships among the Inklings, a group of Christian writers who met together weekly in Oxford, England, beginning in the 1930s and continuing for several decades. Glyer was so thorough that she read all 365 books written by Inklings authors, in order to better understand their collaborative alchemy. The two lead Inklings were C. S. Lewis and J. R. R. Tolkien. As Glyer has documented, the Inklings served as resonators, collaborators, opponents, and editors for one another's writing.[12] Tolkien read part of *The Hobbit* to the group, as well as chapter installments of *The Lord of the Rings*. Lewis read serialized portions of his first science fiction book, *Out of the Silent Planet,*[13] along with many other now-classic works.

My wife Sue and I were both reading silently as our clothes tumbled in the laundromat dryer on that bleak March Saturday afternoon. It was only when I came to page 146 of Glyer's summary of Lewis and Tolkien's planned collaboration about a book called *Language and Human Nature* that it hit me.[14] Like rusty tumblers of a combination lock clicking into place, I suddenly recognized what I had meticulously transcribed those past seven years: Lewis's opening chapter of *Language and Human Nature*! I paused. I set the book down. I looked up. My eyes widened. I smiled broadly and much too loudly blurted, "I KNOW WHAT IT IS!" My wife, used to my non-sequiturs, and looking only slightly embarrassed, coolly deadpanned, "What *what* is?" To the bewilderment of fellow laundry patrons mindlessly folding their clothes, I ear-splittingly burbled, "I KNOW

WHAT THE LEWIS MANSUCRIPT IS! IT'S THE BEGINNING OF THE BOOK LEWIS WAS PLANNING TO WRITE WITH J. R. R. TOLKIEN!"

All the scholars who were aware of the planned Lewis-Tolkien collaboration had concluded that the book was likely never started and certainly never completed. Although the publisher announced the Lewis-Tolkien book as forthcoming in 1949, Tolkien seems never to have started work on the project. According to a November 29, 1944, letter J. R. R. Tolkien wrote to his son Christopher, Tolkien and Lewis were "to begin to consider writing a book in collaboration on 'Language' (Nature, Origins, Functions)."[15] Perhaps Tolkien would like to have written the book but simply was too busy or distracted working on *The Lord of the Rings* and a myriad of other projects. At any rate, Tolkien seemed to recognize that he had more ideas than time; after telling Christopher about the planned book about language with Lewis, he wrote, "Would [that] there were time for all these projects!"[16] In conversations I have had with J. R. R. Tolkien's daughter, Priscilla, she does not recall seeing her father work on the planned Lewis and Tolkien book.

In a 1950 letter to a friend, Lewis confided his own doubts that the book with Tolkien would ever be written. He added a few unflattering remarks about Tolkien's procrastinating writing habits and then added in exasperation, "My book with Professor Tolkien—any book in collaboration with that great but dilatory and unmethodical man—is dated, I fear to appear on the Greek Kalends!"[17] Walter Hooper, who expertly edited the Lewis letters for publication, provides a footnote to explain that "Augustus [and apparently Lewis] used 'on the Greek Kalends' for 'Never.'"[18]

So why did this manuscript fragment survive, while drafts of other manuscripts, including manuscripts of *The Chronicles of Narnia*, did not? Lewis himself wondered, "Is there a discovered law by which important manuscripts survive and unimportant perish? Do you ever turn out an old drawer (say, at the breakup of your father's house) without wondering at the survival of trivial documents and the disappearance of those which everyone would have thought worth preservation?"[19] Hooper speculates, "This one survived because the notebook in which it was written contains notes on English literature that Lewis made a point of preserving."[20]

After experiencing my laundry eureka moment, and having other Lewis scholars confirm my conclusion, I sent a manuscript detailing my claim that this was the collaborative Lewis-Tolkien book to *SEVEN*, the premier journal of C. S. Lewis studies published by the Marion E. Wade Center. I received a polite response from the editor indicating that there was a publishing backlog; it could be up to nine months before I would hear back from them. So I waited. But not for long. I received an email the next week confirming that my find was important and informing me that my manuscript was accepted.[21] I have had many publication acceptance letters, but this notice was the most thrilling of my career! Once I had strong corroboration that the manuscript fragment was indeed *Language and Human Nature*, my university disseminated a news release about the discovery, and newspapers and blogs around the world picked up the story. When I was in Oxford later in the summer, I was invited to participate in a couple of BBC radio interviews describing my discovery. The interview with BBC Ireland seemed especially apropos, given that Lewis was born in Belfast.

Although Lewis once described himself in a letter to his father as "a born rhetorician … I love to 'ride like a cork on the ocean of eloquence,'"[22] there is no evidence that he ever explicitly referred to his professional expertise as including "communication," "speech," or "rhetoric." This book, however, suggests that C. S. Lewis *should* be considered for his knowledge, insight, and expertise as a communication scholar. His life's work, what he wrote about, as well as his application of communication principles, provides evidence of his communication expertise.

C. S. Lewis and the Craft of Communication is not only about C. S. Lewis and his communication principles and practices. It is also about *you*. My hope is that this book will facilitate your learning lessons from Lewis about how *you* can enhance *your* skill as a communicator. Chapter 9, "How to Communicate Like C. S. Lewis," offers several specific applications about communication competencies inspired by what Lewis said about communication.

Lewis was a quintessential educator who would want his lessons about communication to endure. On describing the role of a good teacher, Lewis wrote, "The task of the modern educator is not to cut down jungles, but to irrigate deserts."[23] This book is written to irrigate your understanding of communication. By better understanding Lewis's principles of communication, each of us can learn strategies to enhance our own ability to write, speak, and relate to others so that we, too, can become master communicators.

Steven Beebe
San Marcos, Texas

Notes

2. For example, see: Steven A. Beebe and Susan J. Beebe, *Public Speaking: An Audience-Centered Approach* 11th edition (Boston: Pearson, 2021); Steven A. Beebe, Susan J. Beebe and Diana K. Ivy, *Communication: Principles for a Lifetime* 7th edition

(Boston: Pearson, 2019); Steven A. Beebe and John T. Masterson, *Communicating in Small Groups: Principles and Practices* 12th edition (Boston: Pearson, 2021); Steven A. Beebe, Susan J. Beebe and Mark V. Redmond, *Interpersonal Communication: Relating to Others* 9th edition (Boston: Pearson, 2020); Steven A. Beebe and Timothy P. Mottet, *Business and Professional Communication: Principles and Skills for Leadership* 3rd edition (Boston: Pearson, 2016); Steven A. Beebe, Timothy P. Mottet and K. David Roach, *Training and Development: Communicating for Success* 2nd edition (Boston: Pearson, 2014).

3. See: Kathryn Lindskoog, "A. N. Wilson Errata," Into the Wardrobe: A C. S. Lewis Website. http://cslewis.drzeus.net/papers/wilson-errata/ Accessed April 21, 2017; Arend Smilde, "Sweetly Poisonous in a Welcome Way: Reflections on a Definitive Biography," Lewisana.NIL http://lewisiana.nl/definitivebiography/ Accessed April 21, 2017; Bruce L. Edwards, "A Review of A. N. Wilson's *C. S. Lewis: A Biography*," http://personal.bgsu.edu/~edwards/Wilson.html Accessed April 21, 2017.

4. See: Abigail Santamaria, *Joy: Poet, Seeker, and the Woman Who Captivated C. S. Lewis* (Boston: Houghton Mifflin Harcourt, 2015).

5. "The Lefay Manuscript" fragment is published in: Walter Hooper, *Past Watchful Dragons: A Guide to C. S. Lewis's Chronicles of Narnia* (Glasgow: Collins, 1979).

6. See: Steven A. Beebe, "C. S. Lewis on Language and Meaning: Manuscript Fragment Identified," *VII: An Anglo-American Literary Review* 27 (2010): 7–24.

7. Charlie W. Starr, "Villainous Handwriting": A Chronological Study of C. S. Lewis's Script*, VII: Journal of the Marion E. Wade Center* 33 (2016): 73–94.

8. For an excellent overview of Lewis's handwriting and how it has evolved over the years and how the dates of a Lewis manuscript can be determined based on his handwriting see: Starr, "Villainous Handwriting."

9. Walter Hooper, *Past Watchful Dragons: A Guide to C. S. Lewis's Chronicles of Narnia* (Glasgow: Collins, 1979), 56.

10. See: Elizabeth Anscome, "C. S. Lewis's Rewrite of Chapter III of Miracles," M. Roger White, Judith Wolfe and Brendan N. Wolfe ed. "*C. S. Lewis & His Circle: Essays and Memoirs from the Oxford C. S. Lewis Society* (Oxford: Oxford University Press, 2015), 15–23.

11. Diana. P. Glyer, *The Company They Keep: C. S. Lewis and J. R. R. Tolkien as Writers in Community* (Kent: Kent State University Press, 2007).

12. Glyer, *The Company They Keep.*

13. Colin Duriez, *The Oxford Inklings: Lewis, Tolkien and Their Circle* (Oxford: Lion Hudson, 2015), 78.

14. Glyer, *The Company They Keep*, 146.

15. J. R. R. Tolkien, Letter to Christopher Tolkien, November 29, 1944, *Letters of J. R. R. Tolkien,* ed. Humphrey Carpenter with Christopher Tolkien (London: George Allen & Unwin, 1981), 105.

16. Tolkien, *Letters*, 105.

17. C. S. Lewis, Letter to Sister Penelope, January 12, 1950, *The Collected Letters of C. S. Lewis, Vol. III: Narnia, Cambridge, and Joy 1950–1963*, ed. Walter Hooper (San Francisco: Harper San Francisco, 2007), 6.

18. Lewis, *Collected Letters III*, 6.

19. C. S. Lewis, *Fern Seed and Elephants: And Other Essays on Christianity*, ed. Walter Hooper (London: Collins, Fontana, 1975), 58.

20. Walter Hooper, *Past Watchful Dragons*, 56.

21. Beebe, "C. S. Lewis on Language and Meaning; C. S. Lewis," *Language and Human Nature, VII: An Anglo-American Literary Review* 27 (2010), 15.

22. C. S. Lewis, Letter to Albert Lewis, July 29, 1927, *Collected Letters, Vol. I: Family Letters 1905–1931*, ed. Walter Hooper (San Francisco: Harper San Francisco, 2004), 713.

23. C. S. Lewis, *The Abolition of Man: Reflections on Education with Special Reference to the Teaching of English in the Upper Forms of Schools* (London: Oxford University Press, 1943), 9.

Acknowledgements

This book has been an important part of my life for more than a decade. I have many people to thank for their encouragement, ideas, support, and suggestions.

Several people spent many hours reading the manuscript and offered detailed comments, affirmations, corrections, and suggestions. Although all errors are mine, I benefited from the generous offering of wise counsel from many people: Diana Ivy (the first person I trusted to read this book offered unswerving encouragement), Joel Heck (whose knowledge of Lewis was invaluable), Jerry Root (a master communicator and Lewis scholar), Michael Ward (whose knowledge of Lewis is unbounded), Andrew Lazo (who has a considerable gift with words), Will Vaus (who helped me fine-tune my ideas), Karen Black (an astonishingly gifted proofreader), Greg Anderson (who was especially helpful with Chapter 6), William O'Flaherty (who helped confirm the validity of my Lewis quotes) and Susan Beebe (editor extraordinaire) each offered invaluable comments, critiques, and encouragement after carefully reading drafts of the manuscript. Thank you for the countless ways you made this a better book.

Several Oxford friends offered support, ideas, encouragement and a listening ear as I've developed ideas for the book.

- Walter Hooper, a dear friend and the pre-eminent C. S. Lewis scholar in the world, offered enthusiastic encouragement, ideas, support, suggestions, inspiration, loan of manuscripts, and Lewis handwriting expertise. Thank you, Walter, for being such an important friend and inspiration to me.
- Priscilla Tolkien, a good and wise friend, offered her support, insights, and much appreciated encouragement.
- Jacob Imam is a good friend and brilliant scholar who offered generous support for my work both in Oxford and during happy visits to Texas.
- Colin Duriez, an outstanding C. S. Lewis scholar, offered valued advice and encouragement.
- Jill and Peter Collett, and their talented daughters Clemi and Katie, are cherished friends I've known for more than a quarter of a century. They offered ongoing love, support and enthusiastic encouragement during many visits to our beloved Oxford.

I owe much to many C. S. Lewis scholars for their ideas, information, and meticulous scholarship that appear in endnotes in this book and helped shape many of the ideas presented. Special thanks go to the following scholars:

- Terry Lindvall and his excellent dissertation *C. S. Lewis' Theory of Communication* was invaluable in helping me clarify my ideas about Lewis and communication.
- Greg Anderson provided friendship, joyful conversations, time in London hunting for Lewis first editions, and brilliant published scholarship about C. S. Lewis and rhetoric.
- Diana Pavlac Glyer provided support, encouragement, and outstanding scholarship that helped me solve a decades-old literary mystery. She is a role model for all Lewis scholars.
- The late Bruce Edwards offered his friendship, rich conversation, and outstanding published Lewis scholarship. I miss him and his enthusiastic support.
- Don King helped interpret Lewis's handwriting, confirmed my discovery of C. S. Lewis poems, and offered much appreciated encouragement and support.
- Charlie Starr provided invaluable help in interpreting Lewis's handwriting and offering support and encouragement.
- Andrew Lazo, who, in addition to carefully reading the manuscript, spent time with me in golden hours of friendship chasing after Lewis life details.

- Jerry Root, who not only read the manuscript, provided copious notes, and wrote the masterful Foreword, but was transformational in helping me develop as a Lewis researcher. I will always be grateful for his enduring friendship, love, and presence in my life.

I thank my editor at Peter Lang, Erika Hendrix, for her support of this project, excellent suggestions, and skilled editorial guidance.

The staff at the University of Oxford Bodleian Library provided outstanding support and expertise. Specifically, I thank:

- Judith Priestman, librarian and curator of Lewis manuscripts and papers, provided professional support and encouragement. Her personal presentation of original Lewis manuscripts was always a highlight for me and my students who visited the Bodleian Library.
- Collin Harris, who provided a cheerful presence in the Modern Papers Reading Room, and who always offered words of encouragement and professional acumen.

Members of the Austin C. S. Lewis Society were kind, generous, patient, and encouraging as I participated in their monthly meetings for more than half a decade.

- Margaret and Johnny Humphreys were especially generous in providing the initial funds for a C. S. Lewis workshop that lead to the founding of the Austin C. S. Lewis Reading Group. Their friendship, and their son Paul's taking my Oxford Lewis class, are treasured memories.
- Joel Heck and George Musacchio are outstanding Lewis scholars and educators who were like graduate faculty who patiently and skillfully helped me develop my ideas.
- Larry Linnenschmitd is a good friend and an avid Lewis reader, whose invitation to participate in a radio conversation on his program not only was fun, but also helped me develop my ideas about Lewis and communication.

Several dear friends offered excellent advice and encouragement just when I needed it:

- Mike Hennessey, a valued friend and eminent academic scholar and educator, proposed the title that you read on the cover of this book.
- Lancia Smith, who skillfully took my author photo, illuminates beauty with her gifts of friendship, wisdom, and encouragement.

- Ron and Judy Brown are long-time cherished friends who offer love and encouragement and were members of the travel group that let me commandeer the tour bus, with the unforgettable help of our Irish-ballad-singing bus driver Kevin Clancy, to make an unplanned stop during our Belfast, Ireland, tour to see Lewis's childhood home, "Little Lea."

I thank the many students who have taken my C. S. Lewis course, both on the Texas State University campus and at Oxford University. Your enthusiasm, curiosity, and passion for learning about C. S. Lewis provided the perfect educational pasture that helped me irrigate my ideas. I especially thank my former Oxford C. S. Lewis student and beloved nephew Luke Adam Dye, dubbed "The Magician's Nephew," who read the manuscript and offers love and enthusiasm cheering on his uncle.

Several colleagues—no, friends—including Tom Willett, John Masterson, Thompson Biggers, Deborah Uecker, Richard Cheatham, Tim Mottet, Rick Gonzalez, John Fleming, Phil Salem, Cookie Salem, Lee Williams, Cathy Fleuriet, Sue Stewart, Marian Houser, Erik Timmerman, Maureen Keeley, Sue Hall, and Bob Hannah, offered much encouragement and support on this journey.

To my beloved family, wife Sue, son Matt, daughter-in-law Kara, granddaughter Mary, son Mark, and daughter-in-law Amanda: Thank you for the two C. S. Lewis games you invented that made my work more joyful. Game one: Taking bets as to what time of the day I will first mention C. S. Lewis. Game two: If a member of my family is within earshot and they hear me mention Lewis's name, with just an ever-so-slight eye roll, they murmur "glug glug" and then mime taking a drink. Thank you for your abiding love, good humor, and unswerving support.

Finally, extra-special thanks go to my life editor-in-chief, frequent co-author, former college debate partner, fellow music-major-turned-communication major, personal grammar queen, life partner, and best friend, Sue. Sue was the last person who read the book before publication; her editing skills are simply the best I've encountered during the 50 years I've known her. Her "life music" is the soundtrack of my life. This book would not have been possible without her.

1

The Case for C. S. Lewis as Master Communicator

"I have an idea of what is good and bad language ... Language is an instrument of communication. The language which can with the greatest ease make the finest and most numerous distinctions of meaning is best."[1]

- C. S. Lewis

"Be sure you know the meaning (or meanings) of every word you use."[2]

- C. S. Lewis

One of the first things I give my students when I teach my course, "C. S. Lewis: Chronicles of a Master Communicator," is the final examination; it appears on the last page of the syllabus. I realize that it is unusual to give the students the final exam questions early, especially on the first day of class. But giving students their final exam on day one helps them know what to look for as they begin to examine Lewis as communicator. (Education, I believe, should not be a game of "Guess what I want you to learn," but rather, a guided conversation with clear goals and objectives.) The final exam consists of two questions that form the overarching goals of the course:

1. What *communication principles* did C. S. Lewis discuss, either implicitly or explicitly, in his works?

2. What *techniques of effective communication* did Lewis use in his writing and speaking that contributed to his success as an author and speaker?

Underlying these two questions is a claim that informs the premise of this book: *C. S. Lewis was one of the most effective communicators of the twentieth century as evidenced by his continued popularity.* So, in effect, by writing this book I am taking my own final exam.

Lewis was a master communication craftsperson. He was also a mere communicator. As in the title of one of his most widely read books, *Mere Christianity*, *mere* means *essential, absolute* or, as derived from the Middle English use of the word, *pure*.[3] (Lewis was not the first to use the phrase "Mere Christianity." Richard Baxter, a seventeenth-century Puritan, used those words to avoid denominational labels when describing Christians.)[4] C. S. Lewis was a masterful, "pure communicator" who also wrote about essential principles of communication. This book makes the case that C. S. Lewis knew, discussed, and used effective principles of communication; his application of those principles explains, in part, his enduring success as an author, speaker, and broadcaster.

Being a skilled communication craftsperson does not mean he was a perfect communicator. Lewis sometimes made tactical errors. He misread his audience on rare occasions, and by his own admission, he was not always skilled at appealing to the emotions of his listeners or readers.[5] Yet he learned from his experiences and drew upon a comprehensive set of principles about language, meaning, and communication to become one of the twentieth Century's most celebrated authors and speakers. He was not only a Christian apologist, literary scholar, and prolific author of both fiction and non-fiction, he was an accomplished communication practitioner who modeled what he said about communication.

The assumption that C. S. Lewis was a master at crafting enduring communication messages is supported by three arguments. First, Lewis was and continues to be an astoundingly popular author. People bought his books during his lifetime, and since his death more than five decades ago, his book sales continue to be strong. Both Samuel Joeckel's book *The C. S. Lewis Phenomenon* and Stephanie Derrick's book *The Fame of C. S. Lewis* document the continuing popularity of Lewis studies, an especially thriving industry in the U.S., with more books about C. S. Lewis published each year.[6]

A second argument to support his legacy as a communicator is that, in addition to continued popular success, Lewis has garnered considerable professional accolades. He earned his living teaching, writing, and speaking. His scholarly books remain required reading in many English department graduate programs that focus on literary criticism and English literature of the sixteenth century. Besides inclusion on undergraduate and graduate student reading lists, Lewis and his works remain a popular topic for doctoral dissertations, master's theses, and other academic research and scholarly inquiry.

Finally, both Lewis's continued popularity and professional contributions and influence support the third and most important argument for the "master communication craftsperson" label—Lewis embedded lessons about how to communicate effectively throughout his works. In addition to *being* an effective communicator, he also *wrote about* principles and strategies for communicating well. Many authors are popular, and a few also have impressive professional credentials, but only a select handful devote considerable attention to teaching others how to be effective communicators. Lewis was a professor of communication.

This chapter makes the case that C. S. Lewis *should* be the focus of a book about communication. He was prolific and endures as a multi-million-book popular author. Colleges and universities continue to assign his work; scholars continue to mine it for his insights about literature and language. And he often wrote about how to be an effective communicator. His spoken and written messages not only model communication principles, but also offer numerous prescriptions for communication effectiveness. Let's explore these three reasons in more detail.

A Popular Communicator

Lewis sells. Millions of copies of his books are in print, with millions of new readers throughout the world discovering his writing each year. Although it is always challenging to identify the precise number of books Lewis has sold (a challenge both because the number keeps growing larger every year and because publishers typically keep that information proprietary), even modest estimates provide evidence of his astounding popularity. One source suggests that the Narnia books have sold more than 100 million copies.[7] Michael Maudlin, an editor of HarperCollins's *C. S. Lewis Bible*, made this observation in 2011: "I would say in the last 10 years C. S. Lewis has sold more books than any other 10-year span since he started publishing."[8] Maudlin added, "He's not only not declining, he is in the sweet spot."[9] His book sales have continued to be strong moving into the third decade of the 21st Century. Lewis scholar James Como notes, "Since his death in November 1963, sales of his books have increased six-fold (with several titles selling more than one million copies per year in some twenty languages)."[10] Estimates of Lewis's total book sales range from 150 to 200 million copies.[11]

There is substantial evidence that Lewis's books are not only widely read, but also widely celebrated. Both Lewis's fiction and non-fiction continue to make the "100 top book lists" of best-selling and most influential books of the twentieth century.

- A 2019 survey from the United Kingdom (UK) rated *The Lion, the Witch and the Wardrobe* the number one ranked "favorite book" of UK readers.[12]
- In the fall of 2018 the Public Broadcasting System (PBS) used a national (U.S.) survey to identify the 100 best novels ever written. During an eight-week period, PBS then asked people to nominate their most favorite book. *The Chronicles of Narnia* series was voted number nine on the list of 100.[13]
- According to a panel organized by the editor of the *National Review*, Lewis's *Abolition of Man* was ranked seventh; in a "top book" list prepared by Intercollegiate Studies, it was ranked second.[14]
- A survey of the most read Christian writers suggests that Lewis continues to appeal to a wide variety of readers from various denominational perspectives.[15] Among mainline Protestants, Lewis's books were ranked sixth in popularity.[16] According to the same poll, they were ranked eighth by conservative clergy and eleventh among Catholic priests.[17]
- The widely-read Christian magazine, *Christianity Today*, ranked *Mere Christianity* as the *best* book about Christianity of the twentieth century.[18]

Mere Christianity has influenced many notable people, including Thomas Monaghan, founder of Domino's Pizza, and Francis Collins, an award-winning scientist known for his leadership in the Human Genome Project and Director of the National Institutes of Health.[19] Both have credited Lewis with their conversion to Christianity.[20] The late Charles Colson, former counsel to President Nixon, who served seven months in prison for obstruction of justice associated with the Watergate scandal and later established a nationally-recognized prison ministry, credits Lewis with changing his life: "I opened *Mere Christianity* and found myself … face-to-face with an intellect so disciplined, so lucid, so relentlessly logical that I was glad I never had to face him in a court of law."[21] In describing Lewis's style Colson wrote, "Lewis' words seemed to pound straight at me."[22] He later added that Lewis's words, "ripped through the protective armor in which I had unknowingly encased myself for forty-one years."[23] The number of people who have become Christians or had their Christian faith strengthened due to Lewis's writings is surely in the millions.[24]

Lewis is internationally popular. His books have been translated into 47 languages.[25] Visitors from around the world visit his home, The Kilns, located about three miles from the center of Oxford. Lewis-themed stained-glass windows can be found not only in his home church in Headington Quarry, near Oxford, but also in St. Luke's Episcopal church in Monrovia, California, and St. David's Church, in Denton, Texas.

Not everyone, however, is enamored with treating Lewis as "St. Jack."[26] (Lewis preferred to be called Jack). Lewis biographer A. N. Wilson finds the stained-glass window treatment unnecessarily over the top. Wilson's biography delves into Lewis's psychological motivations and peccadillos—something Lewis would have disdained and several Lewis scholars have refuted.[27] Lewis undoubtedly would not have approved of the numerous other biographies that have sought to provide "back stage" perceptions of him. Subscribing to "new criticism," the theory that dominated mid-twentieth-century literary criticism, Lewis thought considering the personality and backstory of an author to be unnecessary and unhelpful when seeking to interpret what the author wrote.[28] Lewis's sentiment: Just study the work, not the personal indulgences of the author.

Why does Lewis remain a best-selling author with a long list of popular titles? Books with Christian themes do not typically make *The New York Times* bestseller list. What did Lewis *do* that made his message so accessible? Some writers point to his liberal use of literary tropes such as metaphor and analogy. Others attribute his popularity to his clarity of expression.[29] Lewis scholar Terry Lindvall suggest that one of the reasons Lewis remains popular is because of his keen sense of humor.[30] Lewis loved to laugh and those who knew him attest to his jovial sense of fun and good humor that sparkles through his writing. Lewis's popularity is most likely the result of multiple principles and practices, among which is his ability *to communicate*—to forge a relationship between author and reader. The chapters ahead provide a detailed, panoramic look at his ability to communicate.

Lewis did not have to wait until he died to be famous. Britons readily recognized his voice in the 1940s because of his successful broadcast talks.[31] His series of 15-minute BBC radio broadcasts began on August 6, 1941, at 7:45 P.M., and continued at regular intervals for more than two years to a war-weary Britain. His first talk had an audience of 560,000 people; his second talk, a week later, had more than 1.7 million listeners—triple his first night's broadcast.[32] Although his biggest audience on a radio call-in program called *Brains Trust* had an audience of more than 5 million listeners, they did not hear Lewis at his best. It was one of his performances during which he gave long-winded, tedious answers, not always on point; he was not well received by many in this particular listening audience.[33]

But despite an occasional misstep, he consistently connected to his readers and listeners.

Lewis thought that after his death his popularity would decline and his book sales would decline as well, eventually dwindling to zero. Walter Hooper, Lewis's secretary during the last summer of Lewis's life, recalls a specific conversation with Lewis in which he expressed certainty his book sales would taper off after his death. Lewis was concerned about income for his brother, Warren (called "Warnie"), and worried that Warnie would have no substantial income beyond his small pension.[34] But Lewis need not have worried. His book sales have continued to flourish, in part because Hooper agreed to edit an existing manuscript, resulting in a "new" book, if the publisher would also re-publish two out-of-print books.[35] Because of this shrewd deal, all of Lewis's books continue to be in print. C. S. Lewis remains famous—more so in the U.S. than where he lived and taught in England, in part because his Christian message resonates with Americans more than it does in a less demonstrably Christian England.[36]

Although not as widely heralded in England, Lewis was memorialized on the 50th anniversary of his death with a stone in the floor of Poets' Corner in Westminster Abbey.[37] Chiseled on the stone is one of his most quoted sentences: "I believe in Christianity as I believe that the Sun has risen not only because I see it but because by it I see everything else."[38] The thousands who congregated there on November 22, 2013, heard former Archbishop of Canterbury, the Right Reverend Rowan Williams, deliver a memorial sermon focused on Lewis's skilled use of language.[39]

In addition to his book sales, Lewis's popularity as a communicator is further evidenced by his continued focal point as a subject of reading groups and Lewis societies. If you want to join a Lewis reading group, there is probably one near you. By one count more than 500 Lewis societies exist in the U.S.[40] The C. S. Lewis Society that meets in Oxford during term time will welcome you, should you happen to be in Oxford on a Tuesday—the day the Inklings, the famed literary group, would meet at The Eagle and Child pub just a few doors from where the Lewis Society meets in the St. Giles area of Oxford. The book *C. S. Lewis & His Circle* is a collection of essays presented to the society over the years, including several by people who knew Lewis well.[41] Google "C. S. Lewis" and you will find numerous websites, such as *Into the Wardrobe,* that feature his works and provide a virtual Lewis society. Both the stage play *Shadowlands* and the 1993 movie chronicle the intriguing love story between Lewis and the woman he married (twice),[42] Joy Davidman, bringing the Lewis-Davidman story to millions. Several of Lewis's Narnia Chronicles (*The Lion, the Witch and the Wardrobe*; *The Voyage of the Dawn*

Treader; Prince Caspian; and The Silver Chair) have been made into movies (with varying critical acclaim). Yet *The Lion, the Witch and the Wardrobe* set box office records when it debuted in 2005; with world-wide box office receipts of more than one billion dollars, it is the highest grossing Christian-themed movie ever made. More Narnia movies are in the works, as well as a movie chronicling the friendship of Lewis and Tolkien.[43]

Students are eager to learn from Lewis's ideas. One of the most popular courses at Harvard University, taught by Dr. Armand Nicholi, examines the dramatically contrasting life philosophies of Lewis and Psychologist Sigmund Freud. Nicholi's best-selling book *A Question of God* and the nationally broadcast PBS special and DVD of the same name brought an examination of Lewis's ideas to millions of readers and viewers.[44] The creatively conceived play *Freud's Last Session* imagines a conversation between Lewis and Freud in 1939—late in Freud's life and just when Lewis was coming into his own as a writer. The crackling dialogue may be fiction (although there are direct quotations from both men's writings), but the play is a riveting and insightful drama that enjoyed positive reviews and broke box office records in New York and several U.S. national tours. *The Most Reluctant Convert*, a one-man play about Lewis's conversion starring Max McClean as Lewis, toured the U.S. and appeared on Broadway in New York to packed houses for months. Lewis's ideas and his life story continue to generate interest in various forms—from traditional academic classes to Broadway performances.

What additional evidence documents Lewis's popularity? His readers' responses. In his book *An Experiment in Criticism*, Lewis suggests that among the best ways to assess a literary work is to consider the impact the work has on those who read it. The impact of Lewis's own body of written and spoken communication, based on the responses of his readers, has been significant. Lewis's work has inspired institutes, societies, and artistic projects. Three C. S. Lewis academic institutes specifically feature his work and champion his legacy. The C. S. Lewis Foundation, based in Redlands, California, which owns Lewis's home, The Kilns, in Oxford, is actively working to establish a C. S. Lewis liberal arts college. The proposed college would be based on a Great Books foundation to mirror Lewis's wide-ranging knowledge in and application of the liberal arts and sciences.

And finally, C. S. Lewis has become a ubiquitous presence in American pulpits. In summarizing Lewis's impact, one could argue that he is the third most quoted person in Sunday morning sermons, right behind Jesus and the Apostle Paul. Given his continued popularity, it is worthwhile to investigate his communication strategies that contribute to his popularity.

A Professional Communicator

C. S. Lewis earned his living teaching, writing and speaking: He was a professional communicator. The study of words and meaning was central to Lewis's professional life. Not only do C. S. Lewis's books remain popular, but he also enjoys a formidable professional reputation. He was and remains a respected scholar and literary historian. Literary scholar Doris Myers argues that Lewis should be recognized for his expertise primarily as a literary scholar, concluding, "It is literary craftsmanship, after all, that will ensure for Lewis a permanent place in the canon."[45] As a literary scholar, Lewis was interested in the nature of language and how to use language effectively to connect with readers and listeners. As a Christian apologist, he was renowned for his rhetorical prowess. Lewis, who liked to talk, wrote in a letter to E. M. Butler, "I am also an Irishman and a congenital rhetorician."[46] That even in this lighthearted comment he identified himself as a rhetorician is notable. It was integral to his identify.

C. S. Lewis's intellect is reflected in his highly-lauded professional achievements. He was one of the few people in the twentieth century to win a triple first at Oxford University, comparable to being *Summa Cum Laude* (with highest honors) in Latin and Greek (Classical Honor Mods), philosophy (called "Greats"), and English literature. His 1922 first degree in Classics included two curricular elements, the first part consisting of Latin and Greek and the second part, "Greats," focusing on philosophy. His second degree, just one year later in 1923, in English language and literature, was the most practical; it enhanced his employability as a tutor. Language and literature were to remain the focus of his academic work for the rest of his life. His scholarly books *The Allegory of Love, A Preface to Paradise Lost, English Literature in the Sixteenth Century: Excluding Drama,* and *The Discarded Image* remain required reading in graduate English literature programs. Lewis was clearly a scholar interested in the rhetorical impact of words and their meaning.

Lewis was prolific. He wrote or contributed to 37 books during his lifetime (with several books and essays published after his death).[47] He also wrote dozens of essays, many first delivered as lectures, that are also still in print.[48] If you go into a bookstore and ask where most authors' books may be found, you will be directed to a specific shelf or department. But go into a contemporary bookstore and ask, "Where are books by C. S. Lewis?" and you will be directed to several different shelves. His Narnia books can be found in the children's section, his Ransom trilogy (*Out of the Silent Planet, Perelandra* [recently performed as an opera], and *That Hideous Strength*) are housed in science fiction. His academic works are often found in the literary criticism section. Of course, several books are housed in the theology or Christian section. His novel *Till We Have Faces* is in fiction and literature. His published poetry books, including the book originally published under the pseudonym Clive Hamilton, are found in the poetry section. Although *The Abolition of Man* is often found in the Religion section, given its content it could be catalogued in philosophy. Lewis scholars Jerry Root and Mark Neal count 17 different literary genres in which Lewis wrote: apologetics, auto-biography, educational philosophy, essays, fairy stories, journals, letters, literary criticism, literary history, lyric poetry, narrative poetry, novels, religious devotion, satire, science fiction, short stories, and translations.[49] The argument for Lewis as a master communication craftsperson rests not only on his productivity and popularity, but also on his genre-spanning professional presence throughout a bookstore.

Besides Lewis's considerable professional and popular works, his skill as a communicator is evident in the thousands of letters he wrote. He considered writing responses to his letters both a burden and a responsibility, and he would respond to anyone who wrote to him. He believed that if he was sharing infor-mation with his readers and listeners and they responded to him with a letter, it was his obligation to acknowledge their response. With the help of his brother Warnie, Lewis would dedicate a portion of most workdays to answering letters. Lewis's close friend Owen Barfield observed, "Lewis used to sit down and answer his letters, which became very numerous indeed, either before or immediately after breakfast."[50] Some of his responses were quite brief, but others were full of detailed explanations, heart-felt empathic response, or advice.

The massive three-volume publication of his letters, masterfully edited by Walter Hooper, fills 4,000 pages.[51] Estimates for the number of Lewis letters range from 10,000 to 14,000.[52] New discoveries of Lewis letters continue to emerge. For example, I own a short note Lewis wrote to Nobel Laureate Jacques Lucien Monod, thanking Monod for a letter extoling Lewis's literary contributions; the letter does not appear in any published collection. The skillfully edited book *Let-ters to Children*, compiled by Lyle Dorsett and Marjorie Lamp Mead, showcases Lewis's tenderness, sensitivity, and clarity in responding to the hundreds of letters he received from his younger fans.[53] *Letters to an American Lady* includes the cor-respondence of Lewis to a woman known only as Mary in the book, who is now known to be Mary Willis Shelburne, then a widow from Washington, DC.[54] Such letters provide a record of Lewis's stalwart, faithful friendship. (Lewis eventually provided a monthly stipend for Mary from royalties of his books published in the U.S.) Letters to his life-long friend and confidant Arthur Greeves published in *They Stand Together*[55] and correspondence (originally written in Latin) to Don Giovanni Calabria[56] also are compiled in separate published collections. Sheldon Vanauken's autobiographical book *A Severe Mercy* describes the author's friendship among himself, his wife Jean (called Davy) and C. S. Lewis; several letters between Lewis and Vanauken are included in the book.[57]

So we have a record of not only Lewis's "front stage" polished, professional communication with his readers and academic colleagues, but also his "back stage" communication with countless individuals, which he would never have imagined would be read by others. Such an extensive 360-degree view of an author is not available for many other communicators. With today's reliance on ephemeral, often-deleted electronic messages, we may no longer have such permanent records of an author's public and private communication. Although Lewis's letters did not have the benefit of careful editing by proofreaders (he sometimes struggled with spelling), Lewis letters provide a rich and comprehensive basis for analysis.

A Professor of Communication

C. S. Lewis was often introduced at speaking events or described on the dust jackets of his books as "Professor Lewis." It was only during the last nine years of his life, however, that he officially acquired the title "professor," a prestigious rank bestowed by British colleges and universities on a select few. When at Magdalen College in Oxford, Lewis lost the election for Professor of Poetry to Cecil Day-Lewis (father of Oscar-winning actor Daniel Day-Lewis) in 1951. But three years later, in recognition of his academic accomplishments, he was appointed Chair of Medieval and Renaissance Literature at Cambridge, a position that also included the coveted title *Professor*. Lewis was well qualified for his professorial rank. Although he did not hold an earned doctorate, he had received honorary doctorates from several universities.[58] His triple first honors at Oxford, along with his voluminous output as an author and scholar, and his skill as a tutor and lecturer, had firmly established his academic credentials. C. S. Lewis clearly deserved the title *Professor*.

But what did he profess? Lewis's title was Professor of Medieval and Renaissance Literature, yet he had eclectic academic interests in a variety of subjects. As noted earlier, his formal education included not only classical Greek and Roman literature, typical curricular components of an Oxford education, but also philosophy and English literature. His lectures at his first teaching position for University College focused on philosophy. His writing reflects his diverse interests and broad scope of knowledge, including an interest in words, language, meaning, and philology; this book suggests that in addition to his other diverse academic interests, he was a professor of *communication*.

To make the case that Lewis should be embraced for his knowledge of human communication, it helpful to know how the communication discipline and Lewis's interests intersect. The central focus of the communication discipline, according to former National Communication Association president David Zarefsky, is the study of the relationship between messages and people.[59] Meaning, messages, and the importance of language are also consistent and pervasive themes running throughout Lewis's professional work. As this book documents, Lewis possessed a sophisticated understanding of the nature of meaning and the centrality of using language to develop human connections.

The communication discipline is interdisciplinary; it embraces several academic traditions, some as ancient as the study of rhetoric, and others more contemporary, including social media and critical cultural theory. Mirroring the multifaceted nature of the communication discipline, Lewis, too, had interdisciplinary interests; his study and writing ventured into literature, literary history, theology, psychology, philosophy and other topics found in both the humanities and social sciences. An essay or lecture about education and Natural Law blossomed into a multi-part lecture series that continues to be required reading in philosophy classes: *The Abolition of Man*.[60] Lewis's writing reflects his own interdisciplinary approach to whatever topic or issue he is exploring. Ideas emanating from philosophy, literature, theology, and literary criticism are sprinkled throughout his writing and speaking.

The National Communication Association, the oldest and largest national professional academic communication association, defines communication as "how people use messages to generate meanings within and across various contexts" and "the discipline that studies all forms, modes, media, and consequences of communication through humanistic, social scientific, and aesthetic inquiry."[61] The U.S. Department of Education defines the academic domain of communication as including "instruction in the theory and practice of interpersonal, group, organizational, professional, and intercultural communication; speaking and listening; verbal and nonverbal interaction; rhetorical theory and criticism; performance studies; argumentation and persuasion; technologically mediated communication; popular culture; and various contextual applications."[62] C. S. Lewis was not just mildly interested in these topics, he had insightful and detailed observations about the theory and practice of human communication.

The growth of the contemporary communication discipline parallels C. S. Lewis's growing interest in language, words, and meaning. The academic discipline of communication studies has most fully developed in the United States in the years since World War II, as evidenced by the plethora of organized departments and schools of communication established in that interim. There were no U.S. departments of "speech" in 1900.[63] By 1930 (the same time Lewis was coming into his own as a tutor at Magdalen College, Oxford), a survey of selected U. S. institutions found more than 25 U.S. departments that included the word "speech" in their titles.[64] As Lewis's career began to soar, a 1948 survey reported 256 U. S. colleges and universities that included the word "speech" in a department title; 51 were titled "speech and drama," 18, "public speaking," 48, "English and speech," and 5, "communication."[65] Today there are approximately 2,000 U.S. colleges, universities and community colleges that include a study of what used to be encompassed by the word "speech" or "public speaking" and what today is more often labeled "communication" or "communication studies."[66]

There are several reasons to consider C.S. Lewis a *communication* educator and scholar—a *Professor of Communication*. First, applications of communication ideas and principles, as well as explicit observations about words, meaning, messages and human behavior, can be found in virtually everything he wrote. C. S. Lewis was a meta-communicator. He communicated about communication; he wrote about the process of writing and speaking. His principles of how to communicate well are found in many of his works. Although some well-known authors write about the writing process (such as Stephen King[67]), only a handful of celebrated and prolific writers have described in such considerable detail how they developed their communication craft. Lewis's title "Communication Professor" is appropriate because of the number of words he devoted to writing about how he communicated. His former student V. Brown Patterson noted that Lewis "loved to talk about the sheer mechanics of turning thoughts into sentences."[68] Had Lewis been only a popular author, or only a successful writer and teacher, this book probably would not have been written. But he made copious comments about the communication process. In addition to being an effective communicator, Lewis also discussed *how* to be an effective communicator. The chapters ahead, especially chapters four–eight, document the numerous principles, suggestions, and observations that he had about the human communication process.

A second reason to consider Lewis a professor of communication is that communication studies scholars historically tend to emphasize oral communication. Lewis was interested in writing and *speaking*, both in theory and in application; he gave special attention to the oral nature of messages. Lewis's academic training focused on English literature and the written word, but there is evidence Lewis was especially interested in oral communication, as evidenced by his definition of language as "spoken language."[69] Reflecting Lewis's holistic interest in communication and supporting his Professor of Communication title, he was interested in both.

Lewis was a skilled writer *and speaker*. Gervase Mathew, who for nine years coordinated his lectures for the English faculty with Lewis, confirms, "His influence on his contemporaries was at least as much as orator as writer."[70] In response to suggestions that Lewis thought lectures and tutorials a waste of his valuable time, Mathew vehemently disagreed: "No travesty could be further from the truth."[71] In describing Lewis's oratorical skills, Mathew notes,

> He took a vivid, perhaps rather sporting, interest in the numbers who came to him, and he was depressed when he failed to repeat his Oxford triumphs at Cambridge. At times he lectured from skeleton notes, at times from a written text; on occasion he improvised; it was hard to tell which method he was following. But always he forged a personal link with those who heard him.[72]

Lewis liked a good-sized audience. He was a popular lecturer who often had standing-room only audiences.

In addition to the evidence that he often wrote about communication and had a keen interest in oral communication, a third and final reason to consider Lewis as a Professor of Communication is that he applied communication principles to several communication contexts, including interpersonal and small group communication. He was a "catholic communicator" in the sense that he was interested in a variety of communication contexts and genres, from friendship to classical rhetoric.

Interpersonal communication is defined as a "distinctive, transactional form of human communication involving mutual influence, usually for the purpose of managing relationships."[73] The study of human relationships is at the heart of the interpersonal communication context. C. S. Lewis was clearly interested in the quality of interpersonal relationships. Several of his books, including *The Four Loves, Till We Have Faces, The Screwtape Letters*, and all three of the books in his Ransom trilogy (*Out of the Silent Planet, Perelandra*, and *That Hideous Strength*) include both implicit and explicit observations about the nature and importance of human relationships.

He not only wrote about interpersonal communication topics, but also loved the joy of just visiting with his friends. Lewis was known to close friends as a marvelous conversationalist with a wonderful sense of humor. His good friend Owen

Barfield describes how Lewis liked to tease by playing insulting word games with his friends:

> It was much more like a 'language game,' particularly so in the case of sarcasm. There the object of the game was to come as near as possible to formulating an insult as if it were intended, while at the same time choosing one which would be particularly telling if it were. He once carried this so far, or I was so stupid, that I thought it was *meant*; and, for a time after that (but this was rather in correspondence than in conversation) we would preface with a solemn rubric to the effect that "this is a joke."[74]

Lewis seemed to take pleasure from the joy of conversation with his friends. Walter Hooper appreciatively recalls, "C. S. Lewis was the best listener I have ever talked with in my life. He was actually very interested in what you had to say."[75]

In addition to interpersonal communication, Lewis made astute observations about small group communication, defined as "communication among a small group of people who share a common purpose, who feel a sense of belonging to the group, and who exert influence on one another."[76] The dynamics of what causes groups to form, stay together, and accomplish specific tasks through communication, are key elements of group communication study. As with applications of interpersonal communication, Lewis was ahead of his time when discussing group interaction. Although books with "group discussion" in the title were published in the 1930s, group communication textbooks that referenced social-psychological dynamics of groups emerged only after Lewis's death.[77]

In noting a standard observation of contemporary group communication textbooks, Lewis knew that "Two heads are better than one, not because either is infallible, but because they are unlikely to go wrong in the same direction."[78] For Lewis, friendship among a group of people, in contrast to friendship between only two people, adds a new dynamic to the relationships. The 1945 loss of his friend Charles Williams gave Lewis insights about the collaborative nature of friendship. As Lewis put it, "[I]f, of three friends (A, B, and C), A should die, then B loses not only A but 'A's B."[79] Lewis understood the dynamic of group interaction and the influence of individual members on the group. He adds, "In each of my friends there is something that only some other friend can fully bring out. By myself I am not large enough to call the whole man into activity; I want other lights than my own to show all his facets."[80] The loss of his dear friend Williams (friend A) meant that he also lost observing the rich interaction between Williams and J. R. R. Tolkien (friend B). Without using the term *synergy* or referring to systems theory, Lewis illustrated a sophisticated understanding of group dynamics.

His address "Membership," given to the Society of St. Alban and St. Sergius in February 1945, is chock full of observations about the nature of groups, societies, organizations, and communities. For example, he makes a comparison between group membership and family membership with this observation:

> How true membership in a body differs from inclusion in a collective may be seen in the structure of a family. The grandfather, the parents, the grown-up son, the child, the dog, and the cat are true members (in the organic sense) precisely because they are not members or units of a homogeneous class. They are not interchangeable.[81]

Although he doesn't use contemporary communication terminology, he goes on to describe the nature and function of roles, norms, and other classic group communication variables. Diana Pavlac Glyer's award-winning book *Bandersnatch: C. S. Lewis, J. R. R. Tolkien and the Creative Collaboration of the Inklings*, masterfully describes how the Inklings literary group illustrates principles and practices of group communication and collaboration.[82] C. S. Lewis was interested in more than speaking and writing; he was also a keen observer of communication in several contexts.

Applications of communication ideas and principles, as well as explicit observations about words, meaning, messages, and human behavior, can be found in virtually everything he wrote, especially his scholarly publications such as *A Preface to Paradise Lost*. His friends and colleagues, J. R. R. Tolkien and Owen Barfield, were both celebrated philologists and Lewis was a philological scholar in his own right. Lewis wrote, "This book has grown out of a practice which was at first my necessity and later my hobby; whether at last it has attained the dignity of a study others must decide."[83] This thesis sentence from *Studies in Words,* published in 1960 that evolved from a lecture series titled "Some Difficult Words," offers evidence of Lewis's life-long love of language and how words affect and reflect human nature.[84] Lewis believed that through language we articulate our longing for joy and acknowledge objective truth. Therefore, a prime argument for viewing Lewis as a communication professor is both his "necessity" and "hobby" of thinking and writing about language and meaning.

Although Lewis wrote about words, meaning, and messages, he did not set out to develop a theory of communication. As noted earlier, it is unlikely that he studied contemporary communication theory—an area of study that has more fully blossomed in academia since his death in 1963. Lewis was known for applying principles rather than proposing new theories. Rhetorical scholar James Como suggests that when studying rhetoric, "[Lewis] had no grand theories and did not follow schools or invent intricate methodologies."[85] In fact, Como argues that Lewis "did not lend himself to rhetorical theory with the same characteristic thoroughness that marked his other reading."[86] Rhetorical scholar Greg Anderson chronicles Lewis's rhetorical roots and reaches this conclusion: "The extant evidence shows that Lewis did take rhetoric seriously as a student but even more so as a young don."[87] Anderson additionally notes, "His focus was not so much on classical as on medieval and even modern rhetoricians."[88] Regardless of the extent of his academic interest in and study of rhetoric, Lewis could have had little formal training in communication as presented in contemporary departments of communication studies.[89] Yet Lewis was keenly interested in Communication Studies from the perspective of meaning, the nature of words, and the function of language.

If we were to enter a classroom with Lewis as our communication professor, we might not be immediately impressed, at least by his appearance. William Griffin describes Lewis as an unassuming persona: "[He was] something of an Everyman in that he was just a bloke."[90] He apparently didn't look like a university don. Griffin continues,

> Some thought he looked like a farmer, and he certainly enjoyed a ploughman's lunch as much as the next fellow, especially with a pint of cider or a bottle of stout … at The Trout, a public house near Oxford. But he was just one of the millions, trying to make his own spiritual way, and it was well known that he was not the best map-reader in his brigade.[91]

Based on photos and descriptions of those who knew Lewis during his years as a Fellow at Magdalen, he was slightly overweight and balding, with a ruddy complexion. Walter Hooper described him as just under 6 feet tall.[92] Lewis usually dressed in baggy flannel pants and an old elbow-patched tweed jacket. (Some wondered if he only owned one jacket.) One of his students described him as "verging on the shabby."[93]

Just as Lewis was not a fashion icon, he was not always a perfect communicator. Even though he was valued as a friend and listener, at times he was perceived as distant and aloof.[94] He was also known to sometimes withhold affection from those who sought a closer relationship with him. For example, his strained relationship with his father, as acknowledged in his autobiography *Surprised by Joy*, does not always reflect positively on his family communication skills.[95] There were clearly times his father wanted a closer relationship with Lewis, but Lewis kept his distance. To be fair, there were also times when Lewis sought greater intimacy with his father and his father did not reciprocate, such as the time after Lewis was wounded in World War I and his father did not come visit him as Lewis request-ed. He sometimes felt his father was more a caricature of a father, acting the part of an irascible and eccentric parent rather than providing genuine support and af-fection.[96] Reflecting Lewis's impatience with his father's inelegance and irritability, Lewis scholar Crystal Hurd suggests Lewis had "a straightforward and down-to-earth condemnation of the 'pseudo'—the shoddy and the insincere" in reference to his relationship with his father.[97] Consequently, Lewis did not always evidence warm, supportive communication responses from or to his father.

It was not just with his father; there is evidence that he could be less than im-mediate with his students—some describing him as being belligerent at times.[98] As a tutor he was occasionally perceived as a bully because of his perhaps too enthusiastic application of his debating skills. He famously did not respond charitably to John Betjeman, a student of Lewis's who eventually became the beloved Poet Laureate of England. He found Betjeman immature, unprepared, and non-responsive.[99] Rather than modeling grace and an understanding of how students can often be impertinent, Lewis's verbal and nonverbal behavior did not always demonstrate grace. I once met an elderly couple in Oxford who had both been tutored by Lewis. They said that although they thought Lewis was brilliant, he could be tediously exacting as a tutor and sometimes unnecessarily harsh with students—although, they added, only with those whom he thought could take pointed criticism. So perhaps Lewis thought Betjeman could take his criticism.

George Bailey, an American student of Lewis's, observed that as a tutor Lewis was "interesting, colourful and lively" but then added, "but he was not a good teacher."[100] Bailey's personal perception was that "Lewis lacked the warmth to fire his students with enthusiasm."[101] In addition, Lewis apparently sometimes couldn't figure out who was who. Bailey notes, "Lewis consistently mistook me for Geoff Dutton, an Australian and an excellent student, and Dutton for me."[102] Yet Bailey found a benefit in the mislabeling: "For three years I basked in my misgiven status of a talented dominionite while Dutton groaned in durance vile as the only American in the college—if not, indeed, in the university—with the temerity to read English."[103] Bailey added, "Lewis credited Dutton's performances to me and penalized Dutton for mine."[104]

A few colleagues not in his inner circle reportedly perceived Lewis as im-personal. Lewis researcher Stephanie Derrick, after reviewing Lewis's percep-tion among some of his colleagues, concluded that Lewis could sometimes be "a divisive person in the cultural life of his peers."[105] She explains his sometimes "negative critiques" from his colleagues "in light of Lewis's persona of aggressive bravado and his platform as someone who looked back, to the authorities and sensibilities of a past age."[106] Although, it should be noted, Derrick's description of Lewis has not been uniformly supported by other Lewis scholars. Lewis author and scholar James Spencer notes, "Derrick's insinuations are poorly supported by a fair reading of Lewis' voluminous correspondence, the common witness of a wide range of his friends and even critical biographers …"[107]

Yet one former Lewis student confirms Derrick's conclusions about his relationship with his colleagues. George Bailey concludes, "Lewis was not popular among his fellow dons. My impression was that he kept almost as aloof from dons as from undergraduates."[108] Although Bailey suggests the underlying reason for the perception of relational coolness may have been jealousy and the fact that Lewis wrote books about Christianity: "The lack of rapport between Lewis and the dons at Magdalen, on their side, was due not only to their envy of his fame but also to their distaste of the nature of his fame …"[109] Bailey speculates, "As popularizer of Christian dogma, Lewis was embarrassing to the academic community."[110]

Lewis's friend Own Barfield noted that when Lewis was ready to end a conversation he would betray his boredom nonverbally. Barfield notes, "For casual acquaintances he had a peculiarly, perhaps deliberately, expressionless stare to show when the limit had been reached."[111] Famed zoologist Desmond Morris, who attended Magdalen College in Oxford and occasionally saw Lewis in the dining hall, told me Lewis could be standoffish and difficult to get to know well, often keeping to himself.[112]

Lewis also sometimes exhibited unusual, norm-violating, abrupt leave-taking cues. As reported in detailed notes, while meeting with some academics and publishers in the summer of 1955 at the Eastgate Hotel in Oxford about the possibility of Lewis serving as editor of a book series, Lewis was described as cordial, pleasant, and engaged in the conversation. Geoffrey Shepherd, a member of the editorial board for a publication for which they wanted Lewis to serve as General Editor, summarized the conversation as follows: "… we found ourselves talking about Tolkien and fairy stories and ancient Egyptians. We got rather noisy too and I saw a pale-faced solitary drinkers pressed back all round the sides of the room as if they were expecting an explosion."[113] While in the middle of the conversation Shepherd noted, "… then suddenly at five to one CS stood up, wrapped himself up, shook hands and suddenly shot off like a cork out of a bottle."[114] When it was time for Lewis to leave there was no pleasantries or dithering. Lewis simply left. Lewis had the same exiting approach when ending his academic lectures. Often, at the conclusion of an academic talk he would edge toward the door, pick up his hat and coat, and, while delivering his closing line, leave the lecture hall thus concluding the lecture and avoiding any questions or post-lecture conversations.[115]

It is easy for books about Lewis to be labeled mere hagiography, providing praise and adulation without noting his faults. Although Lewis was popular, professional, and professor of communication principles, he was also very human. He did not always demonstrate effective communication applications with his family, students, or some of his acquaintances. Yet perhaps his authentic struggles and challenges in his own personal and professional life helped him empathically connect with those who heard his lectures and broadcasts or read his works. C. S. Lewis was not a perfect communicator. In part because of his own grappling with the challenges of making human connections, he understood and applied principles of human communication that help explain his popularity, prolific output, and professional acumen.

HI TEA: A Preview of Lewis's Communication Lessons

In the next chapter we will look more closely at Lewis's life to provide a context for understanding Lewis as communicator. Many of his early experiences were traumatic. The death of his mother when he was nine, the series of inept boarding schools he attended, and his brief, harrowing foray into World War I were life-challenging experiences that influenced both the content of his messages and the way he connected to others. He knew pain and thus he could write about its problem. He observed grief yet wrote about Joy surprising him. Perhaps it is his own, sometimes eccentric but always interesting, life that continues to add to his mystique. Lewis lived a compartmentalized life in the sense that few people saw the "complete Lewis." He had secrets. He kept his marriage to Joy Davidman hidden from his friend J. R. R. Tolkien for a period of time. Michael Ward develops the widely-supported theory of Lewis's compartmentalization based on the fact that Lewis embedded a theme within *The Chronicles of Narnia*. Lewis, argues Ward, wanted to make this hidden theme implicit to all and explicit to none.[116] C. S. Lewis remains both enigmatic as well as a focal point of interest, in part because of his multifaceted life experiences. Although it is true that Lewis's *writing* evidence common themes, as a *person* Lewis was sometimes secretive and complicated.

As his popularity as an author continues unabated, C. S. Lewis remains a person of great interest. Original Lewis letters are in high demand. (A one-page Lewis letter sold at auction in London in 2018 for $5,700. Another two-sided letter, written in 1952, is for sale with a suggested price of $46,000.)[117] A first edition of some of his harder-to-find books can sell for tens of thousands of dollars.[118] But the question many continue to ask is "Why?" Why do people continue to be enamored with his work? And more to the point of this book: What makes Lewis a successful communicator as evidenced by his continued book sales? What did he know about the craft of communication? What were his techniques of connecting to readers and, through his radio broadcasts and lectures, listeners?

Although many excellent biographies about Lewis exist, none comprehensively explore how Lewis's life experiences shaped his *communication* principles and practices.[119] The discipline of communication encompasses a wide array of concepts, variables and skills. Specifically, communication is the process of making sense out of the world and sharing that sense with others by creating meaning through the use of verbal and nonverbal messages.[120]

There have been excellent summaries of selected elements of Lewis as communicator, but they typically focus on either his speaking skill, writing skill, or rhetorical applications. The book *C. S. Lewis: Speaker and Teacher,* published in 1971 edited by Carolyn Keefe, presents a clear description of his speaking skills from those who heard him (including a detailed analysis of his voice), but it does not highlight his overarching *communication* principles.[121] Others have written about his literary skill or his rhetorical insights.[122] Gary Tandy's well-written book *The Rhetoric of Certitude: C. S. Lewis's Nonfiction Prose*[123] offers considerable insight about Lewis as rhetorician, as does James Como's excellent *Branches to Heaven: The Geniuses of C. S. Lewis.*[124] Lewis scholar Greg Anderson's insightful essay "A Most Potent Rhetoric: C. S. Lewis Congenital Rhetorician" is a *tour de force* describing Lewis's rhetorical gifts.[125] Another well-researched book, *C. S. Lewis and the Art of Writing* by Corey Latta, describes Lewis's skill as an author.[126] Yet little has been written about his overall approach to and application of communication principles. One exception is the comprehensive doctoral dissertation by Terry Lindvall that provides an excellent summary of Lewis's observations about communication from a broad perspective.[127] My efforts here are to draw upon these excellent previous summaries, as well as Lewis's own work, to present a comprehensive discussion of Lewis as *communicator,* not just as rhetorician, teacher, broadcaster, or speaker. My goal is to highlight Lewis's mere (essential) communication principles that help explain his popularity and continued presence in so many academic and literary genres, including communication. Although Lewis did offer explicit advice about writing and communication, including the unfinished *Language and Human Nature* that he planned to write with J. R. R. Tolkien, he did not develop a cogent set of principles in any single work. The principles presented here are not explicitly articulated by Lewis as his "five principles of communication." Nevertheless, his insights into and applications of principles of effective communication found throughout his work make the identification of these principles possible. Before highlighting each principle in a separate chapter, we begin by providing background information about his life and "big ideas."

Chapter 2 explores more fully how Lewis's life experiences shaped his communication talents. In order to be an effective communicator, it is imperative to have something to say. Chapter 3 examines the major themes and big ideas in Lewis's works. Owen Barfield, Lewis's friend, financial executor, and fellow Inkling, noted that all of Lewis's key themes were present in whatever Lewis wrote.[128] So it is important to understand these ideas to appreciate his ability to communicate them.

After the opening chapters provide background and set the stage for a discussion of Lewis's key communication ideas, chapters four-eight then present five core principles, one for each chapter, that constitute the essence of Lewis's understanding of communication. Each of the five principles can be cogently summarized with one word: Holistic (Chapter 4), Intentional (Chapter 5), Transpositional (Chapter 6), Evocative (Chapter 7), Audience (Chapter 8) which form the acronym HI TEA. Here's a preview of these five principles that provide the core concepts of Lewis's communication ideas.

Effective Communicators Are Holistic

The first communication principle describes Lewis's holistic communication strategies. To be holistic is to be all-encompassing, drawing upon several elements to create an integrated, comprehensive approach to communicating with others. Lewis was a holistic communicator in that his messages appealed to both the eye and the ear; his written messages were not only designed to be read (an appeal to the eye) but also to have an auditory quality (an appeal to the ear), as reflected in his practice of speaking the words aloud as he wrote.

In addition, Lewis was holistic in that he integrated reasoning—the process of using evidence to reach a conclusion, with creative applications of his rich imagination to express his ideas. The nature of his subject matter made his ideas difficult to document with tangible, or observable evidence. Lewis sought to provide evidence for the nature of God, affirm the underlying logic of Christianity, while inviting his readers and listeners to use their own powers of reasoning to reach a conclusion. He constructed arguments either inductively (from specific examples to a general conclusion) or deductively (arguing from a general, assumed-to-be-true premise to reach a specific conclusion). Many of his readers appreciate his logical, structured way of clarifying murky or mysterious ideas. Lewis was holistic in that in addition to, and often simultaneously, he would spark the imagination with images, analogies, metaphors, and stories. It was his skilled use of *both* strategies that made him a holistic communicator.

Besides appealing to the eye and the ear, as well as reason and imagination, Lewis drew upon skills in persuasion (rhetoric), debate (dialectic), and romantic ideals (the poetic) to communicate his ideas and message. His apologetic works were unabashedly persuasive; he used his debating skills to refute the ideas of others in support of his own. He would also use language poetically to appeal to his reader's and listener's sense of aesthetics. Chapter 4 uses Lewis's own words as examples of his holistic communication strategies to look both "at" and "along" what he describes.[129]

Effective Communicators Are Intentional

The second principle posits that Lewis was an intentional communicator. To be intentional is to be mindful, purposeful, and aware of the communication goals and objectives to be accomplished. Lewis was intentional in that he planned his messages for maximum clarity and persuasive effect—he used the writing process to help sharpen his ideas and communication goals. Pre-writing activities, taking walks and being a voluminous reader, helped him think about what he was going to say before he said it. His communication objective, although sometimes intentionally but subversively masked from the reader until just the right moment, was always clear to Lewis. He knew where he was leading his readers. Lewis's letters and occasional diary entries modeled his journalistic skill of clear and memorable description. Lewis does not wander aimlessly—even though as a reader you may, at times, not know exactly where he is or where he is leading you, he knows. His books, essays, lectures, stories and poems focused on illuminating a specific idea linked to a precise purpose.

Clarity was an important communication goal for Lewis, whether writing a novel or helping a student express his or her ideas in a tutorial. A specific strategy for being clear is to use precisely the correct word. Having the command of a large vocabulary gave Lewis the ability to use just the right word rather than needing to pile on unneeded words. Brevity was more than the soul of wit; it was his pathway to clarity. Lewis marshalled words to achieve a memorable style. Chapter 5 describes Lewis's principle of intentionality.

Effective Communicators Are Transpositional

The third principle is that of transposition. Lewis described this unique communication concept in a sermon published as delivered at Mansfield College, Oxford University, in June 1944. To transpose is to *transform* something from one level to another. *Transpose* is a musical term. To transpose from one musical key to another is to play the same tune written in, for example, the key of D down a whole tone to the key of C. All notes in both the melody and harmony are played, or transposed, to a different key. Transposition for Lewis was always a process of going from the higher to the lower. As he described the process, transposition is moving from a richer, more-detailed, more-colorful, multidimensional experience to a less-rich, less-detailed but nonetheless accurate explanation in an attempt to communicate (or transpose). He sought a way to illustrate how an ineffable emotion could more easily be understood by someone. Some experiences, especially emotional ones, are simply too rich, "high," inexplicable, or foreign to the experiences of others, to adequately describe. "Symbolism," wrote Lewis to Sister Penelope in a March 25, 1943 letter, "exists precisely for the purpose of conveying to the imagination what the intellect is not ready for."[130] Transposition is a communication process that uses similes and metaphors—especially visual metaphors—to express emotional ideas that the "intellect is not ready for."[131]

How do you describe the emotional impact of Grand Canyon to someone who is blind? How do you express the joy experienced when listening to Beethoven's Ninth Symphony to someone who is deaf? In each instance one would transpose—use a means of communication with which the listener is familiar—to describe a richer ("higher") experience that is completely foreign and unobtainable. Metaphor, simile, and allegory are key communication strategies to express the inexpressible. The story of the incarnation, suggests Lewis, is a classic example of the metaphorical process of transposition when myth became fact.

Effective communicators are able to select symbols, images, metaphors, or make other comparisons to clarify that which is difficult to explain prosaically. The principle of transposition makes the ineffable effable, the murky clear, and the difficult-to-comprehend more easily grasped. Lewis was a master of this technique often relying on visual metaphor, comparisons, "supposals," and other tropes to express complex or hard-to-explain ideas. Chapter 6 describes the process of transposition in detail and uses Lewis's own words and examples to illustrate the concept.

Effective Communicators Are Evocative

The fourth communication principle, that effective communicators are evocative, involves getting messages out of the reader or listener, stimulating both their hearts and minds to help them discover meaning. To evoke is to elicit, awaken, arouse, induce, and stimulate. C. S. Lewis used a variety of communication techniques to evoke images and emotions from his readers and listeners. Lewis knew that people are more likely to believe "data" drawn from their personal experiences, rather than to rely on the descriptions of others. Chapter 7 discusses Lewis's methods for evoking a response, especially an emotional response, from his readers and listeners.

How does Lewis evoke emotional meaning? He describes a situation for the reader or listener rather than tells someone how to feel. The key to evoking a response is not to *tell* someone what to feel, but to paint a picture with words so that the reader or listener experiences his or her own emotional reaction. Lewis once suggested that he didn't consider himself effective at making strong, explicit emotional appeals to listeners, such as making an emotion-infused, impassioned plea to persuade others.[132] He would not, he said, be good at using strong emotional appeals to make successful "alter calls" in a religious service.[133] He did, however, effectively describe emotion-evoking situations by telling stories, using illustrations, and creating visual metaphors that resulted strong emotional responses from his readers and listeners. His best-selling Narnia series is successful, in large part, because it connects emotionally with readers. Lewis called the evocation of emotional response a "surprisingness." The story of Aslan and other characters does more than tell a tale; it creates an emotional response that we want to experience again and again as we re-read the Narnia books.

When reading a book a second time we already know what will happen in the story; we re-read to experience the emotion of the story. We re-read a book or may see a favorite movie again and again not to be surprised by what will happen, but to evoke an emotional response to the story. Lewis suggested that an author or speaker should not tell someone what to feel, but rather, set the stage and create a scene that evokes a response.

Effective Communicators Are Audience Centered

Finally, Lewis was focused on his audience. To be audience centered is to know that ultimately it is the reader or listener who will make sense out of any message that is crafted. People who heard Lewis on the radio when he was delivering his

Broadcast Talks attended to his message because he had a gift for making a direct connection with the listener. Readers find, too, a personal quality in his ability to connect to the reader. His journey from being raised a Christian, to becoming an atheist during his adolescence and young adulthood, and then returning to belief in God and ultimately a strong Christian belief in his 30s, gave him insight into the skeptical audience he was often trying to reach. Chad Walsh, one of the first scholars to study Lewis and his work aptly subtitled his book about Lewis *Apostle to the Skeptics*. Walsh knew that Lewis's message was designed to reach those who may have doubt and uncertainties, who may need their faith bolstered. That audience remains wide and vast, as do Lewis readers.

Mere Christianity was and remains popular because of Lewis's ability to keep his audience (his reader, or in the case of his broadcast talks, his listener) in his mind's eye. How does Lewis develop an author-listener relationship? He offers this pithy communication advice in his essay "Christian Apologetics" when he proclaims, "We must learn the language of our audience."[134] As noted earlier, Lewis was not attempting to write the final word about Christianity but to provide an open invitation, especially for those who already believed in Christianity, to explore their beliefs more deeply. After delivering one of his early Broadcast Talks, he wrote to a friend with this assessment of his audience: "I assumed last night that I was talking to those who already believed. If I'd been speaking to those who didn't, of course everything I'd said would have been different."[135]

As you read the writing of C. S. Lewis, HI TEA (Holistic, Intentional, Transpositional, Evocative, Audience Centered) offers a framework for explaining why his message resonates with such power for so many people. Having high tea (literally) with Lewis who loved tea (he liked the Typhoo brand), liberally sweetened with several spoons of sugar, would have been a delight. He told Walter Hooper, "You can't get a cup of tea large enough or a book long enough to suit me."[136] Those who had that pleasure of having tea with Lewis speak of those cherished moments as indelibly memorable. Lewis was not only a scintillating conversationalist but an especially attentive listener. But since we cannot visit with Lewis personally, we can glean from his writing and speaking how he would have communicated (HI TEA) with us over a nice "cuppa" and a biscuit.

When C. S. Lewis died, on the same day at almost the same hour as President John F. Kennedy—November 22, 1963, he left a legacy that continues to inform, persuade, and inspire. This book argues that Lewis's continued popularity, professional acumen, and his skill as a Professor of Communication stem in large part from an application of his principles and practices as a communicator. In a nutshell, C. S. Lewis *holistically* and *intentionally* crafted strategies to *transpose* his ideas and *evoke* appropriate emotions from his readers and listeners while keeping his focus on the most important aspect of communication—the *audience*.

Notes

1. C. S. Lewis, *Studies in Words* (Cambridge: Cambridge University Press, 1960), 6.
2. C. S. Lewis, Letter to Thomasine, December 14, 1959, *Collected Letters III*, 1108.
3. See: Mark A. Pike, *Mere Education: C. S. Lewis as Ethical Teacher for Our Time* (Cambridge, England: Lutterworth Press, 2013); N. H. Keeble, "C. S. Lewis, Richard Baxter, and 'Mere Christianity,'" in *Christianity and Literature* 30, 3 (Spring 1981): 27–44.
4. Richard Baxter, *Church History of the Government of Bishops*, 1680. Also see, Keeble, "C. S. Lewis, Richard Baxter, and 'Mere Christianity,'" 27–44.
5. For a detailed discussion of some of Lewis's communication miss-steps see: Bruce R. Johnson, "C. S. Lewis and the BBC's Brains Trust: A Study in Resiliency," *VII: An Anglo-American Literary Review* 30 (2013): 67–92.
6. Stephanie L. Derrick, *The Fame of C. S. Lewis: A Controversialist's Reception in Britain and America* (Oxford: Oxford University Press, 2018); Samuel Joeckel, *The C. S. Lewis Phenomenon* (Mercer: Mercer University Press, 2013).
7. Greg Albrecht, "The Enduring Legacy of C. S. Lewis," *Plain Truth Magazine* (Summer 2012).
8. As quoted in: Mark Oppenheimer, "C. S. Lewis's Legacy Lives on, and Not Just through the Wardrobe," *The New York Times* (March 5, 2011), A18.
9. Oppenheimer, "C. S. Lewis's Legacy."
10. James T. Como, *Remembering C. S. Lewis* (San Francisco: Ignatius Press, 2005), 33.
11. Como, *Remembering C. S. Lewis*. Also see: Steven Erlanger, "The Chronicles of C. S. Lewis Lead to Poet's Corner," *The New York Times* (November 20, 2013). https://www.nytimes.com/2013/11/21/books/the-chronicles-of-c-s-lewis-lead-to-poets-corner.html, accessed February 3, 2019.
12. *The Daily Mail*, London, England "The Lion the Witch and the Wardrobe Is Voted UK's Favorite Book," (August 7, 2019). https://www.dailymail.co.uk/news/article-7335205/The-Lion-Witch-Wardrobe-voted-UKs-favourite-book.html?fbclid=I-wAR1pNubfey5DCIloCjGViPtK1Y3n4JGNrOfzN_AQUvpJYo4CM8Gx0PwxcTg
13. *The Great American Read* https://www.pbs.org/the-great-american-read/home/ accessed February 4, 2019.
14. Thomas M. Lessl, "The Legacy of C. S. Lewis and the Prospect of Religious Rhetoric," *Journal of Communication and Religion* 27, 1 (2004): 117–137.
15. David Briggs, "Henri Nouwen Tops Clergy's Reading Lists," *Atlanta Journal-Constitution* (October 4, 2003). http://www.freerepublic.com/focus/f-religion/995088/posts accessed August 26, 2019.

16. Briggs, "Henri Nouwen."

17. Briggs, "Henri Nouwen."

18. *Christianity Today*, "Books of the Century" (April 24, 2000). https://www.christianitytoday.com/ct/2000/april24/5.92.html

19. See: Joseph Pearce, *Monaghan: A Life* (Charlotte: TAN Books, 2016); Francis S. Collins, *The Language of God: A Scientist Presents Evidence for B*elief (New York: Free Press, 2006).

20. *Christianity Today*, "Books of the Century."

21. Charles W. Colson, *Born Again* (Grand Rapids, MI: Chosen Books, 1976), 130.

22. Colson, *Born Again*, 130.

23. Charles W. Colson, "The Conversion of a Skeptic," *Mere Christians: Inspiring Stories of Encounters with C. S. Lewis*, ed. Mary Anne Phemister and Andrew Lazo (Friendswood: Bold Vision Books, 2017), 93.

24. See: Phemister and Lazo, *Mere Christians*.

25. See: Albrecht, "The Enduring Legacy of C. S. Lewis."

26. For a discussion of less flattering perceptions of C. S. Lewis see: Stephanie L. Derrick, Chapter 2 "Lewis Among His Peers: Oxbridge, c.1930s–1950s," *The Fame of C. S. Lewis: A Controversialist's Reception in Britain and America* (Oxford: Oxford University Press, 2018), 46–78. For a refutation of Derrick's conclusions see: Andrew J. Spence, *A Book Review from Books at a Glance*, Review published, April 29, 2019. https://www.booksataglance.com/book-reviews/the-fame-of-c-s-lewis-a-controversialists-reception-in-britain-and-america-by-stephanie-derrick/ Accessed June 17, 2019.

27. See: Kathryn Lindskoog, "A. N. Wilson Errata," *Into the Wardrobe: A C. S. Lewis Website.* http://cslewis.drzeus.net/papers/wilson-errata/ Accessed April 21, 2017; Arend Smilde, "Sweetly Poisonous in a Welcome Way: Reflections on a Definitive Biography," *Lewisana.NIL* http://lewisiana.nl/definitivebiography/ Accessed April 21, 2017; Bruce L. Edwards, "A Review of A. N. Wilson," *C. S. Lewis: A Biography*, http://personal.bgsu.edu/~edwards/Wilson.html Accessed April 21, 2017.

28. See: "New Criticism," *Poetry Foundation*, www.poetryfoundation.org, 2016.

29. See: George M. Marsden. *C. S. Lewis's Mere Christianity: A Biography* (Princeton: Princeton University Press, 2016).

30. Terry Lindvall, *Surprised by Laughter: The Comic World of C. S. Lewis* (Nashville, Tennessee, Thomas Nelson, 1996).

31. See: Kathryn Lindskoog, *Sleuthing C. S. Lewis: More Light in the Shadowlands* (Mercer University Press, 2001), 1.

32. Bruce R. Johnson, "C. S. Lewis and the BBC's Brains Trust: A Study in Resiliency," *VII: An Anglo-American Literary Review* 30 (2013): 67–92.

33. Johnson, "Brains Trust."

34. Walter Hooper, "Remembering C. S. Lewis," *C. S. Lewis at Poets' Corner*, ed. Michael Ward and Peter Williams (Eugene: Cascade Books, 2016), 228.

35. Hooper, "Remembering C. S. Lewis."

36. Membership in the Church of England dropped to 14 percent in 2018 down from 31 percent in 2002. Regular attendance in Britain fell by 15 percent from 2007 to 2017. See: Megan Specia, "English Cathedrals Offer More Than Exalted Architecture. But Mini Golf?" *New York Times* (August 14, 2019), A 7.

37. Ward and Williams, *C. S. Lewis at Poets' Corner*.

38. C. S. Lewis, "Is Theology Poetry," *They Asked for a Paper* (London: Geoffrey Bles, 1962), 165.

39. Rowan Williams, "Address to Commemorate Lewis in Poet's Corner, Westminster Abbey," November 22, 2013 http://www.lewisiana.nl/poetscorner/

40. For a summary of Lewis's continued popularity see: Samuel Joeckel, *The C. S. Lewis Phenomenon* (Mercer: Mercer University Press, 2013).

41. M. Roger White, Judith Wolfe and Brendan N. Wolfe ed. *C. S. Lewis & His Circle: Essays and Memoirs from the Oxford C. S. Lewis Society* (Oxford: Oxford University Press, 2015).

42. Lewis married Joy in a civil ceremony in 1956. It was a "technical" marriage so that she could use Lewis's citizenship to remain in England. They were married the next year by an Anglican Priest after Joy discovered she had cancer and Lewis discovered that she really did love Joy.

43. Nellie Andreeva, "Netflix to Develop 'The Chronicles of Narnia' TV Series & Films," *Deadline Hollywood*, October 3, 2018 https://deadline.com/2018/10/netflix-the-chronicles-of-narnia-tv-series-and-films-eone-1202475272/ accessed February 4, 2019; Tolkien & Lewis Movie in Development, IMDb, https://www.imdb.com/title/tt3230774/ accessed February 4, 2019. The Tolkien and Lewis movie has been in development for several years.

44. Armand Nicholi, *The Question of God: C. S. Lewis and Sigmund Freud Debate God, Love, Sex and the Meaning of Life* (New York: Free Press, 2003).

45. Doris T. Myers, *C. S. Lewis in Context* (Kent: The Kent State University Press, 1994), xvi.

46. C. S. Lewis, *Collected Letters II*, 444.

47. The precise count of C. S. Lewis books vary given that several books, essay collections and poetry collections were published posthumously. See: Jerry Root and Mark Neal, *The Surprising Imagination of C. S. Lewis: An Introduction* (Nashville: Abingdon Press, 2015).

48. For collection of essays that began as oral presentations see: C. S. Lewis, *They Asked for a Paper* (London: Geoffrey Bles, 1962).

49. Root and Neal, *The Surprising Imagination of C. S. Lewis*.

50. Owen Barfield, "C. S. Lewis in Conversation," *Owen Barfield on C. S. Lewis*, ed. G. B. Tennyson (San Rafael: The Barfield Press in association with Wesleyan University Press, 1989), 38.

51. C. S. Lewis, *Collected Letters, Vol. I: Family Letters 1905–1931*, ed. Walter Hooper (San Francisco: Harper San Francisco, 2004); C. S. Lewis, *The Collected Letters of*

C. S. Lewis Vol. II: Books, Broadcasts, and the War 1931–1949, ed. Walter Hooper (London: HarperCollins, 2004); C. S. Lewis, *Collected Letters, Vol. III: Narnia, Cambridge, and Joy 1950–1963*, ed. Walter Hooper (San Francisco: Harper San Francisco, 2007).

52. Don King, "Writing Tips from Lewis and Tolkien (King and Poe)," Podcast May 18, 2017, *All About Jack: A C. S. Lewis Podcast*, hosted by William O'Flaherty.

53. C. S. Lewis, *C. S. Lewis' Letters to Children*, ed. Lyle Dorsett and Marjorie Lamp Mead. (New York: Scribner, 1996). A recent collection of 29 letters to children, many of them included in *C. S. Lewis' Letters to Children*, was listed for sale by the rare book dealer Peter Harrington, London for $260,000. See: Peter Harrington, Catalogue 160 (January 2020).

54. C. S. Lewis, *Letters to an American Lady* (Grand Rapids: Eerdmans, 1967).

55. C. S. Lewis, *They Stand Together: The Letters of C. S. Lewis to Arthur Greeves (1914–1963)*, ed. Walter Hooper (London: Collins, 1979).

56. C. S. Lewis and Don Giovanni Calabria, *The Latin Letters of C. S. Lewis*, ed. Martin Moynihan (South Bend: St. Augustine's Press, 1998).

57. Sheldon Vanauken, *A Severe Mercy* (New York: Harper & Row, 1980).

58. Lewis's honorary degrees include Doctor of Divinity from the University of St. Andrews (1946), Doctor of Letters from Laval University (1952), Doctor of Literature from the University of Manchester (1959), a Doctorate from the University of Dijon (1962), and a Doctorate from the University of Lyon (1963).

59. David Zarefsky, "The State of the Communication Discipline," Address presented to the National Communication Association (San Francisco, November 14, 2010).

60. C. S. Lewis, *The Abolition of Man: Reflections on Education with Special Reference to the Teaching of English in the Upper Forms of Schools* (London: Oxford University Press, 1943).

61. The National Communication website, natcom.org Accessed April 17, 2019.

62. United States Department of Education, *Classification of Instructional Programs* (Washington D.C., 2000).

63. D. K. Smith, "Origin and Development of Departments of Speech," *History of Speech Education in America: Background Studies*, ed. K. R. Wallace (New York: Appleton-Century-Crofts, 1954), 447.

64. Smith "Origin and Development," 462.

65. Smith "Origin and Development," 462.

66. Everett M. Rogers, *A History of Communication Study: A Biographical Approach* (New York: The Free Press, 1997).

67. Stephen King, *On Writing: 10th Anniversary Edition: A Memoir of the Craft* (New York: Scribner, 2010).

68. W. Brown Patterson, "C. S. Lewis: Personal Reflections," *C. S. Lewis Remembered: Collected Reflections of Students, Friends & Colleagues*, ed. Harry Lee Poe and Rebecca Whitten Poe (Grand Rapids: Zondervan, 2006), 90.

69. C. S. Lewis, *Language and Human Nature, VII: An Anglo-American Literary Review* 27 (2010): 25–28.

70. Gervase Matthew, "Orator," *C. S. Lewis at the Breakfast Table*, ed. James Como (San Diego: A Harvest Book Harcourt Brace and Company, 1992), 96.

71. Matthew, "Orator," 97.

72. Matthew, "Orator," 97.

73. Steven A. Beebe, Susan J. Beebe and Mark V. Redmond, *Interpersonal Communication: Relating to Others* 9th edition (New York: Pearson, 2020), 3.

74. Owen Barfield, "C. S. Lewis in Conversation," *Owen Barfield on C. S. Lewis*, ed. G. B. Tennyson (San Rafael: The Barfield Press, 1989), 34.

75. Walter Hooper, personal conversation, July 14, 2002.

76. Steven A. Beebe and John T. Masterson, *Communicating in Small Groups: Principles and Practices* 12th edition (New York: Pearson, 2021).

77. See: Steven A. Beebe and John T. Masterson, *Communicating in Small Groups: Principles and Practices* 12th edition (Boston: Pearson, 2021).

78. C. S. Lewis, "On the Reading of Old Books," *God in the Dock: Essays on Theology*, ed. Walter Hooper (London: Collins, 1979), 202

79. C. S. Lewis, *The Four Loves* (New York: Harcourt Brace Jovanovitch, 1960), 78.

80. Lewis, *The Four Loves*, 78.

81. C. S. Lewis, "Membership," *Transposition and Other Addresses* (London: Geoffrey Bles, 1949), 37.

82. Diana Pavlac Glyer, *Bandersnatch* (Kent: Kent State University Press, 2015).

83. C. S. Lewis, *Studies in Words* (Cambridge: Cambridge University Press, 1960), 6.

84. See: Alan Jacobs, *The Narnian: The Life and Imagination of C. S. Lewis* (San Francisco: HarperSanFrancisco, 2005), 283.

85. James Como, *Branches to Heaven: The Geniuses of C. S. Lewis* (Dallas: Spence Publishing Company, 1998), 119.

86. Como, *Branches*, 27.

87. Greg M. Anderson, "A Most Potent Rhetoric: C. S. Lewis, 'Congenital Rhetorician'," *C. S. Lewis: Life, Works, and Legacy*, ed. Bruce L. Edwards (Wesport: Praeger Perspectives, 2007), 196.

88. Greg M. Anderson, "A Most Potent Rhetoric," 196.

89. Greg M. Anderson, "A Most Potent Rhetoric," 196.

90. William Griffin, *C. S. Lewis: Spirituality for Mere Christians* (New York: The Crossroad Publishing Company, 1998), 16.

91. Griffin, *Spirituality for Mere Christians*, 16.

92. Walter Hooper, interview by Steven A. Beebe, (Oxford, England, June 25, 2015).

93. Phillip Zaleski and Carol Zaleski, *The Fellowship: The Literary Lives of the Inklings*, ed. J. R. R. Tolkien, C. S. Lewis, Owen Barfield and Charles Williams (New York: Farrar, Straus and Giroux, 2015).

94. Stephanie L. Derrick, Chapter 2 "Lewis Among His Peers: Oxbridge, c. 1930s–1950s" in *The Fame of C. S. Lewis: A Controversialist's Reception in Britain and America* (Oxford: Oxford University Press, 2018), 46–78.

95. Also see: Crystal Hurd, "*The Padaita Pie*: Reflections on Albert Lewis," *VII: Journal of the Marion E. Wade Center*, 32 (2015), 47–58.

96. Hurd, "Reflections on Albert Lewis," 47.

97. Hurd, "Reflections on Albert Lewis," 47.

98. *See:* Norman Bradshaw, "Impressions of a Pupil," *In Search of C. S. Lewis*, ed. Stephen Schofield (London: Bridge Logos, 1983), 18.

99. John Betjeman, Letter to C. S. Lewis, December 13, 1939, *John Betjeman Letters, Volume One; 1926 to 1951*, ed. Candida Lycett Green (London: Methuen, 2006), 250–253.

100. George Bailey, "In the University," *C. S. Lewis Speaker & Teacher*, ed. Carolyn Keefe (London: Hodder and Stoughton, 1971), 114.

101. Bailey, "In the University," 114.

102. Bailey, "In the University," 115.

103. Bailey, "In the University," 115.

104. Bailey, "In the University," 115.

105. Stephanie L. Derrick, *The Fame of C. S. Lewis: A Controversialist's Reception in Britain and America* (Oxford: Oxford University Press, 2018), 76.

106. Derrick, *The Fame of C. S. Lewis*, 76.

107. See: Andrew J. Spence, *A Book Review from Books at a Glance*, Review published, April 29, 2019. https://www.booksataglance.com/book-reviews/the-fame-of-c-s-lewis-a-controversialists-reception-in-britain-and-america-by-stephanie-derrick/ Accessed June 17, 2019.

108. Bailey, "In the University," 120.

109. Bailey, "In the University," 120.

110. Bailey, "In the University," 120.

111. Owen Barfield, "C. S. Lewis in Conversation," *Owen Barfield on C. S. Lewis*, ed. G. B. Tennyson (San Rafael: The Barfield Press, 1989), 32.

112. Personal conversation with Desmond Morris, Oxford, England (July 17, 2011).

113. Geoffrey Shepherd, undated personal meeting notes in author's possession summarizing a meeting with C. S. Lewis, Derek Brewer, and Shepherd to "Mr. Murby" circa summer 1955 to seek Lewis's permission to be the General Editor for Thomas *Nelson's Medieval and Renaissance Library*.

114. Shepherd, meeting notes.

115. See: Roger Lancelyn Green and Walter Hooper, *C. S. Lewis: A Biography* (New York: HarperCollins, 1974) as published in Walter Hooper, "The Discarded Image: An Introduction to Medieval and Renaissance Literature (1964)," *C. S. Lewis: Companion and Guide* (San Francisco: HarperCollins, 1996), 525.

116. Michael Ward, *Planet Narnia: The Seven Heavens in the Imagination of C. S. Lewis* (Oxford: Oxford University Press, 2008); Also see: Michael Ward, *The Narnia Code: C. S. Lewis and the Secret of the Seven Heavens* (Carol Stream, IL: Tyndale House Publishers, 2010).

117. BBC News, C. S. Lewis Letters Sells for 4,600 pounds [$5,700] at Auction. http://www.bbc.com/news/uk-england-gloucestershire-30531079. Accessed April 17, 2017. In 2019, ABE books listed a C. S. Lewis letter for sale at $46,000 on their abebooks.com.

118. Edwin W. Brown with Dan Hamilton, *In Pursuit of C. S. Lewis: Adventures in Collecting His Works* (Bloomington: Author-House), 206.

119. Excellent C. S. Lewis biographies include: George Sayer, *Jack: A Life of C. S. Lewis* (Wheaton: Crossway Books, 1994); Alister McGrath, *C. S. Lewis: A Life* (Carol Stream: Tyndale House Publishers Inc., 2013); Roger Lancelyn Green and Walter Hooper. *C. S. Lewis: A Biography* (London: HarperCollins, 2002); Alan Jacobs, *The Narnian: The Life and Imagination of C. S. Lewis* (New York: HarperCollins, 2008); Devin Brown, *A Life Observed: A Spiritual Biography of C. S. Lewis* (Ada: Brazos Press, 2013).

120. Steven A. Beebe, Susan J. Beebe and Diana K. Ivy, *Communication: Principles for a Lifetime* (Boston: Pearson, 2019), 7.

121. Caroline Keefe, *C. S. Lewis: Speaker and Teacher* (Michigan: Zondervan, 1971).

122. Terry Lindvall. *C. S. Lewis' Theory of Communication*. Unpublished doctoral dissertation University of Southern California (1980). Dr. Lindvall's insightful and comprehensive work was especially helpful to me as I developed my own thoughts about Lewis and communication. Also see: Gary L. Tandy, *The Rhetoric of Certitude: C. S. Lewis's Nonfiction Prose* (Kent: Kent State University Press, 2009). Another excellent resource that was especially influential to my thinking: Greg M. Anderson, "A Most Potent Rhetoric: C. S. Lewis, 'Congenital Rhetorician'," *C. S. Lewis: Life, Works, and Legacy*, ed. Bruce L. Edwards (Westport: Praeger Perspectives, 2007), 195–228; Also see: James Como, *Branches to Heaven: The Geniuses of C. S. Lewis* (Dallas: Spence Publishing Company, 1998).

123. Gary L. Tandy, *The Rhetoric of Certitude: C. S. Lewis's Nonfiction Prose* (Kent: Kent State University Press, 2009).

124. Como, *Branches to Heaven*.

125. Greg M. Anderson, "A Most Potent Rhetoric."

126. Corey Latta, *C. S. Lewis and the Art of Writing: What the Essayist, Poet, Novelist, Literary Critic, Apologist, Memoirist, Theologian Teaches Us about the Life and Craft of Writing* (Eugene: Wipf and Stock, 2016).

127. Terry Lindvall, *C. S. Lewis' Theory of Communication*.

128. Owen Barfield, "Owen Barfield on C. S. Lewis." ed. G. B. Tennyson (Middletown: Wesleyan University Press, 1989 and San Rafael: Sophia Perennis, The Barfield Press, 2006), 121–122.

129. For a description of Lewis's argument to look holistically at and along what is observed see: C. S. Lewis. "Mediation in a Toolshed," *God in the Dock* (Grand Rapids: Eerdmans, 1970), 212.

130. C. S. Lewis, Letter to Sister Penelope CSMV, March 25, 1943, *Collected Letters. II*, 565.

131. Lewis, Sister Penelope, *Collected Letters II*, 565.

132. See: Johnson, "C. S. Lewis and the BBC's Brains Trust," 67–92.

133. Johnson, "C. S. Lewis and the BBC's Brain's Trust," 67–92.

134. C. S. Lewis, "Christian Apologetics," *God in the Dock*, ed. Walter Hooper (Grand Rapids: Eerdmans, 1970), 96.

135. C. S. Lewis, Letter to Patricia Thomson, December 8, 1941, *The Collected Letters of C. S. Lewis Vol. II: Books, Broadcasts, and the War 1931-1949*, ed. Walter Hooper (London: HarperCollins, 2004), 499–500.

136. C. S. Lewis, as quoted by Walter Hooper, "Preface," *Of Other Worlds: Essays and Stories* (London: Geoffrey Bles, 1966), v.

2

The Making of a Master Communicator

"[T]he only thing of any importance (if that is) about me is what I have to say ... I can't abide the idea that a man's books should be "set in their biographical context" and if I had some rare information about the private life of Shakespeare or Dante I'd throw it in the fire, tell no one, and re-read their works. All this biographical interest is only a device for indulging in gossip as an excuse for not reading what the chaps say, [which] is their only real claim on our attention. (I here resist a wild impulse to invent some really exciting background—that I am an illegitimate son of Edward VII, married to a chimpanzee, was rescued from the practice of magic by a Russian monk, and always eat eggs with the shells on.)"[1]

- C. S. Lewis

"In his rooms in the New Building ... I found a medium-size, rather stout, ruddy-faced man with a fine, large head (what the Germans call a 'Charakterkopf'), and a booming voice much given to what someone once called 'rhetorical guffawing' ('Ho, ho, ho, so you think Milton was ascetic, do you? Ho, ho! You are quite wrong there!'). Lewis looked—and often acted—like the book description of Friar Tuck. His general manner was pronouncedly and—it often seemed—deliberately hearty. But he displayed no heartiness during my first interview with him. Just as I was about to take my leave, Lewis said to me: 'Are you aware, sir, that your fly is open?' My surprise was so great that it precluded embarrassment: "If I had been, sir, I should never admit it.' "[2]

- George Bailey

"I'm tall, fat, rather bald, red-faced, double-chinned, black-haired, have a deep voice, and wear glasses for reading."[3]

- C. S. Lewis

C. S. Lewis would not have approved of this chapter. In fact, he would have hated it. He did not think it was helpful to delve into the personal background, especially the personality, of an author to understand the author's work. His point: If you want to interpret someone's work, just read what he or she has written; the writing should stand on its own merits. Echoing excerpts from the letter that opens this chapter ("[T]he only thing of any importance (if that is) about me is what I have to say")[4] is Lewis's contribution to *The Personal Heresy,* published in 1939 and written in point-counter-point with Milton scholar E. M. W. Tillyard. It was one of Lewis's few co-authored works.[5] (Tillyard's first name was Eustace; although Lewis had great respect for Tillyard, some speculate he was the namesake of Eustace Clarence Scrub, a sometimes-obnoxious character featured in *The Voyage of the Dawn Treader* and *The Silver Chair.*) In contrast to Lewis, Tillyard's belief is that all poetry is about the poet's state of mind.[6] Tillyard argues that to interpret any text, including Milton's *Paradise Lost,* insightfully and accurately, the reader must see the work as an expression of Milton's personality.[7] The fact that this chapter appears in this book reflects a nod toward Tillyard's argument; understanding the background, experiences, and personality of an author *can* help put a work, or in this case, a communicator, in context.

Lewis, on the other hand, maintained that the poet's personality and personal life are superfluous: "I … maintain that when we read poetry as poetry should be read, we have before us no representation which claims to be the poet, and frequently no representation of a *man*, a *character*, or a *personality* at all."[8] In other words, let the work speak for itself, or as Lewis put it: "I look with his eyes, not at him."[9] Lewis added, "The poet is not a man who asks me to look at *him*; he is a man who says 'look at that' and points; the more I follow the pointing of his finger the less I can possibly see of him."[10]

Although Lewis and Tillyard were primarily debating the merits of delving into an author's background in reference to poetry, Lewis felt the argument applied to *all* literary genres. He wanted the reader's gaze to be directed toward what the author wrote, rather than at the author's psychological profile or family. However, although Lewis disapproved of biographical criticism as a means of interpreting a literary work, the fact that he wrote and published his autobiography in response to those who wanted to learn more about his journey to faith, suggests that he was not completely against providing context for the development of an author's ideas.

Many of Lewis's writings included autobiographical elements. Lewis appears as a character in *The Great Divorce.* Glimpses of Lewis as the patient emerge in *The Screwtape Letters. The Four Loves* includes many personal reflections from the author. Lewis's personal experiences echo through *The Chronicles of Narnia*. His trio of science fiction books and his novel *Till We Have Faces* also reference Lewisian life elements. Lewis certainly used his own personal experiences to illustrate his ideas, both in his fiction and his non-fiction. But Lewis was not against placing the development of a work in context only so long as such commentary didn't impinge on how the work was *interpreted*. He would nonetheless argue that the written or spoken word should stand on its own.

Notwithstanding Lewis's contempt for looking at the personality of an author to help better understand the author's meaning, this chapter identifies factors that helped to make C. S. Lewis one of the most popular communicators about Christian theology in the twentieth century. Of the many influences on Lewis as a communicator, chronicled here are seven influences that include his (1) family, (2) education (including his friendship with Arthur Greeves), (3) WWI experiences, (4) "adopted mother" Mrs. Moore, (5) friend and colleague J. R. R. Tolkien, (6) conversion, and (7) late-in-life marriage to Joy Davidman.

His Family: Flora, Albert, and Warnie

When Clive Staples Lewis was born in Belfast, Ireland, on Tuesday, November 29, 1898, his parents, Flora and Albert Lewis, and his two-and-a-half-year older brother Warnie, lived in the Dundela section of Belfast. Although 47 Dundela Village is the address listed in most Lewis biographies, census records document that the address was actually 21 Dundela Village. At any rate, neither dwelling still stands.

Our early relationships with our parents and siblings (if we have them) provide seminal life experiences that influence how we express ourselves to others. Lewis was no exception. His parents and brother Warnie, as well as the boys' nurse, Lizzie Endicott, were foundational to who Lewis was, how he related to others, and who he would become, including his skill as a communicator. As Lewis scholar Jerry Root observed, "Certainly, there were early formative experiences that shaped Lewis as a rhetorician. He was raised in an environment where a rhetorical approach to life was as native to him as the Irish air he breathed."[11]

Lewis's mother Flora had a quick mind and a talent for mathematics—a skill that was apparently not hereditary since Lewis struggled with math and made miserable math scores on the entrance exam to Oxford University. Had it not been for Lewis joining the Army in 1917, which allowed him to bypass the math examination, he never would have been admitted.

Lewis adored his mother. By every indication she was patient, and kind, and loved spending time with both her sons Clive and Warren. Her patience and indulgence are evident from the account that one day four-year-old Clive decided that his name would be "Jacksie" and thereafter simply would not respond to any other name.[12] Jacksie was soon shortened to Jacks and eventually reduced to Jack—the name his closest friends, family, and colleagues called him for the rest of his life.[13]

Flora loved to read and modeled this pleasure that was to fill Lewis's time when he was not writing or interacting with others. She enjoyed her children and encouraged their innate abilities to express themselves. In a letter to her husband Albert, who was away at the time, she described how Clive would stand on top of a piano stool and imitate others, an early foray into public speaking.[14] Lewis biographer and former student George Sayer interprets the scene as "revealing his precociousness and an early talent for mimicry."[15] Lewis's public presentation proclivities were thus evident early on.

In addition to Flora, Lizzie Endicott and Warnie were important early influences in Lewis's life. He wrote that, as well as "good parents, good food, and a garden (which then seemed large) to play in, I began life with two other blessings. One was our nurse, Lizzie Endicott ... The other blessing was my brother."[16] Lewis describes Lizzie as someone "in whom even the exacting memory of childhood can discover no flaw—nothing but kindness, gaiety, and good sense."[17] Flora did not spend much time reading to her children or teaching them classic tales and nursery rhymes; those tasks fell to Lizzie. His nurse was affectionate and nurturing, comforting him when there were frightening storms at night and especially attentive when Jack was ill.[18] In short, Lizzie joined Flora at the center of young Jack's universe.

Warnie was a constant companion and confidant, and would remain so throughout Lewis's life. Jack and Warnie enjoyed reading, making up stories, and joyful, childhood play—activities that nurtured both of their imaginations. Lewis describes Warnie affectionately: "Though three years my senior, he never seemed to be an elder brother; we were allies, not to say confederates, from the first."[19] Thus from his earliest years Lewis learned the importance of having empathic listeners.

While his mother Flora was cool, nurturing, and rational, Lewis's father, Albert James Lewis (1863–1929), was irascible and quick to express emotion when he became impatient or upset.[20] Sayer suggests that Lewis inherited his talent for using words well and structuring logical arguments from Albert, whose speeches showed an authentic "rhetorical gift" and who "spoke in admirably rhythmic sentences, was shrewd in his attack on his opponents, convincing in his show of moderation, and above all, had the gift of presenting a complex argument in convincingly simple terms. Both his sons inherited the gift of simple exposition."[21] Albert joined the Belmont Literary Society in 1881, where he was considered one of the best speakers in the society.[22] Yet while Albert Lewis had the gift of speaking, his communication skills did not transfer to interpersonal interactions with his sons. His strong personality, emotional outbursts, and temper, as well as frequent trips resulting in absences from home, made him a less nurturing presence than Flora and Lizzie.

Warnie would muse in later years that "some awareness of my father's smothering tendency to dominate life and especially the conversation of his household is necessary to an understanding of Jack's mind and life."[23] Lewis himself seemed to understand that he inherited his rhetorical talents from his father. Regarding his father's approach to reprimanding his sons, Lewis recalls, "He therefore relied wholly on his tongue as the instrument of domestic discipline. And here that fatal bent towards dramatization and rhetoric (I speak of it the more freely since I inherit it) …"[24] Lewis notes in his autobiography *Surprised by Joy* that his father had "a fine presence, a resonant voice, great quickness of mind, eloquence, and memory."[25] He adds that Albert "was found of oratory and had himself spoken on political platforms in England as a young man; if he had had independent means he would certainly have aimed at a political career."[26] Lewis also says that his father "was fond of poetry provided it had elements of rhetoric or pathos, or both …"[27]

Although he seemed to admire some of his father's rhetorical attributes, Lewis was not always laudatory of his father's approach to communication. In *Surprised by Joy* Lewis writes that his father provided "simile piled on simile, rhetorical question on rhetorical question, the flash of an orator's eye and the thundercloud of an orator's brow …"[28] And although a hallmark of Lewis's communication is his ability to connect with his audience, whether through the written word or during a lecture or sermon, he apparently did not learn this skill from his father. Lewis recalled that when his father disciplined him, Albert "forgot not only the offense but the capacities of his audience. All the resources of his immense vocabulary were poured forth."[29]

Both Jack and Warnie sometimes wearied of their father's presence and intrusion. Lewis describes one occasion with too much togetherness with his father as unnecessarily stressful:

> For the whole rest of the day, whether sitting or walking, we were inseparable; and the speech (you see that it could hardly be called conversation), the speech

with its cross-purposes, with its tone (inevitably) always set by him, continued intermittently till bedtime … It was extraordinarily tiring.[30]

For most of Lewis's life, the relationship between himself and his father would remain strained. In an essay titled, "The Failure to Communicate: The Communicative Relationship Between C. S. Lewis and his Father,"[31] Michael McCray writes, "It is ironic that Jack Lewis, one of the most effective communicators of this century, and Albert Lewis, an eloquent court solicitor and pubic speaker known for his gift of simple exposition, struggled in their own communicative relationship."[32]

Then, in 1908, Lewis's childhood took a dramatic turn for the worse. Lewis writes, "There came a night when I was ill and crying both with headache and toothache and distressed because my mother did not come to me. That was because she was ill too …"[33] Flora's illness proved to be terminal cancer. After writing a passage in his autobiography extoling the virtues of a life of books and nurturing, Lewis says, "I cannot be absolutely sure whether the things I have just been speaking of happened before or after the great loss which befell our family and to which I must now turn."[34] The "great loss" was his mother's death. He describes in detail the heartbreaking scene when he was taken into the bedroom "… where my mother lay dead; as they said, 'to see her.' In reality, as I at once knew, 'to see it.' There was nothing that a grown-up would call disfigurement—except for that total disfigurement which is death itself. Grief was overwhelmed in terror."[35] This previous sentence from his autobiography, published in 1955, foreshadowed another famous sentence, the opening line in his book *A Grief Observed*: "No one ever told me that grief felt so like fear."[36]

Lewis also echoes his mother's death in *The Magician's Nephew*, where he depicts a poignant scene where Digory's mother is dying and he feels helpless that he has no powers to stop it.[37] Lewis wrote clearly and eloquently about pain, grief, loss, and longing because he experienced all of these feelings. He learned how to communicate about these universal emotions and experiences not by dictating how someone should feel, but by describing the situation and letting the reader bring her or his own experience to the scene.

Lewis reflects that when his mother died, "all settled happiness, all that was tranquil and reliable, disappeared from my life."[38] Not only had Albert lost his wife, but also his own father earlier in the same year. And just ten days after Flora died, Albert's brother Joseph died. With so much sadness in his life, Albert knew that he could not fulfill both the role of mother and father to Jack. With Warnie already at boarding school, it seemed an obvious and simple solution: Send Jack to boarding school with Warnie.

The Education of a Master Communicator

C. S. Lewis's education could be described as having a disastrous beginning with a glorious conclusion, punctuated by unevenness in educational quality. His education had really begun at home. He refers frequently in his autobiography to "Little Lea," (formally known as Leeborough) the grand Belfast home into which the family had moved from Dundela Village in 1905, with its cozy little "end room" where he and Warnie would read, dream, and play. Little Lea was almost like another character in his life. Biographer A. N. Wilson notes that "In memory, [Jack and Warnie] returned to it again and again …"[39] With books stuffed in shelves and stacked throughout, the home had space to let imagination soar.

Lewis's parents, Albert and Flora, had also contributed to their young son's education. Although Lewis had a sometimes challenging relationship with his father, he also picked up on his father's rhetorical skills, as well as his impressive memory.[40] Lewis himself had a photographic (eidetic) memory that was to be a significant intellectual asset as both student and scholar. If not his math skills, his powers of logic had been passed on from his mother Flora, who had also started Lewis in Latin and French. Learning and mastering languages was a talent that further contributed to his academic and communication talents.

Before he could get to his ultimate educational experience at Oxford, however, he would attend four boarding schools, some better than others, before benefitting from the life-shaping instruction of William T. Kirkpatrick, tutor to both his father and Warnie.

Boarding Schools

The worst was to be first. Following his mother's death in August 1908, Jack was sent to Wynyard School, in Watford, Hertfordshire, England. Because Warnie was already attending Wynyard, it seemed the logical choice. But it was a bad choice. Wynyard was a dreadful school. The headmaster, Rev. Robert Capron (whom the boys nicknamed "Oldie") would sometimes mercilessly beat students for being unprepared.[41] Capron was later declared insane. Jack's educational experience became even more unpleasant when, after his first year, he felt abandoned by his brother; Warnie left Wynyard to attend school in Malvern. After much pleading, Jack convinced his father to let him come home. Albert acquiesced and placed Jack in Campbell College, a fifteen-minute walk from the Lewis home in Belfast. Yet that brief matriculation may have helped shape Lewis's love of language. Lewis biographer Alan Jacobs noted that when enrolled at Campbell

College, even for the one semester, "Jack became acquainted, perhaps for the first time, with the power of poetic language, especially the rhythm and propulsion it can give to a story."[42]

After only about three months at Campbell, Jack enrolled in Cherbourg House in Malvern, England, in January of 1911. One benefit of Cherbourg House was its being almost next door to Malvern College, where Warnie was now a pupil. Jack demonstrated promise at Cherbourg House, which was the first place where he received a consistent and proper formal education.

Jack Lewis joined his brother at Malvern College in the summer of 1913 to prepare for taking the entrance exams for university. In later years, Jack and Warnie agreed to disagree about the educational quality at Malvern College. Warnie thought that the education was quite good, but Jack was less impressed. The different recollections may have been due to their differing levels of enjoyment of athletic events. As in many boarding schools, to be part of the accepted social circle, participating in college sports teams was a must. For Jack it was a must not. While Warnie enjoyed sports, Jack did not like sports or most games. But he did like speaking and oral reading.

Friend and biographer George Sayer reports that as an adult, Lewis enjoyed good animated conversations. "How I like talking!"[43] Sayer quotes Lewis as saying. This love for communication was nurtured at Malvern, where he found a role model in, and received direct instruction from, influential teacher Harry Wakelyn Smith, affectionately dubbed "Smewgy" by his students. Smewgy had a considerable dramatic flair for reading poetry. In him, Jack found someone who would develop his interest in words, language, and even performance. Smewgy taught Lewis two key communication skills: first, to analyze the grammar and syntax of a poem, and second, to read poetry with a focus on the sounds and rhythms of the poem. Sayer adds, "Although he [Lewis] did not have Smewgy's lovely musical voice and could not read romantic poetry with Smewgy's power to enchant, Jack excelled in reading heroic verse and such poetry as Milton's that required a grand style."[44] Lewis biographer Harry Poe, who also noted the importance of Lewis's love of poetry in shaping his writing "voice" noted, "Jack was learning not merely to read the lines of poetry but also to hear them ringing in his ears even when reading silently."[45]

Lewis's talent for holding an audience with his speaking perhaps began with Smewgy's attention to not only the substance of a message, but also its sound. It was also at Malvern where Lewis developed a keen interest in Northernness—his fascination with Norse mythology. In addition to Norse mythology, Lewis was captivated by the Arthur Rackham illustrations of Wagner's opera *Der Ring des Nibelungen*, inspiring a life-long love of Wagner's music.

Arthur Greeves: First Friend and Intimate Confidant

It was during Lewis's time at Malvern College that he met Arthur Greeves, a trusted confidant who had a personal influence on Lewis's experiential insights about the nature of friendship and interpersonal communication. Greeves lived just across the street from Lewis when the Lewis family moved to Little Lea in 1905, although the boys did not meet until 1914, when Greeves was home, ill, and confined to his room. When at last they did meet, they immediately discovered that they had a mutual love of Norse mythology and developed a close, personal friendship that would last for Lewis's entire life. Lewis wrote more letters to Greeves than to anyone else, and Greeves was one of Lewis's most loyal "audiences" and confidants. Lewis suggests that their compatible differences enriched their friendship:

> Though my friendship with Arthur began from an identity of taste on a particular point [Norse mythology], we were sufficiently different to help one another. His home-life was almost the opposite of mine. His parents were members of the Plymouth Brothers, and he was the youngest of a large family; his home nevertheless, was almost as silent as ours was noisy ...[46]

Lewis describes Greeves as a "First Friend"—someone whom Lewis describes as an "alter ego, the man who first reveals to you that you are not alone in the world by turning out (beyond hope) to share all your most secret delights."[47] Lewis further adds, "There is nothing to be overcome in making him your friend; he and you join like rain-drops on a window."[48] Lewis's close friendship with Greeves provided a comfortable "backstage" relationship in which Lewis could be his uncensored self and fearlessly propose kernels of new ideas that eventually grew into books, lectures, and essays. Although Greeves was gay and never married, no evidence suggests that his sexual orientation was an obstacle in his and Lewis's life-long relationship.[49] Lewis remained loyal to his trusted friend and exchanged letters with him (although there were sometimes long gaps between letters over the course of their friendship) until the last few weeks of Lewis's life.

In *The Four Loves*, Lewis describes the nature of friendship. He may have had Greeves in mind when he wrote, "Friendship arises out of mere Companionship when two or more of the companions discover that they have in common some insight or interest or even taste which the others do not share and which, till that moment, each believed to be his own unique treasure (or burden)."[50] Perhaps recalling when he and Arthur first met and both discovered their mutual interest in Norse mythology, Lewis adds, "The typical expression of opening Friendship would be something like, 'What? You too? I thought I was the only one.' "[51]

The correspondence between Arthur and Jack has been compiled in a book edited by Walter Hooper, aptly titled *They Stand Together*. Lewis used the phrase "they stand together" to describe the importance of friendship in several of his works, including both his autobiography *Surprised by Joy* and *The Four Loves*. Effective communicators need attentive sounding boards, safe places to try out new lines of thought, honest editors, and trusted confidants to share and develop ideas. Arthur was such a loyal friend to Jack. The two stood together their entire lives.

The Great Knock

Lewis's four boarding schools, woeful Wynyard, close-by Campbell, challenging Cherbourg, and memorable Malvern, helped prepare him for the educational experience that tapped his true intellectual potential—his tutelage with William T. Kirkpatrick, also known as "the Great Knock." Kirkpatrick had also been Lewis's father Albert's tutor, as well as Warnie's tutor. Arriving in Surrey on September 19, 1914, and residing with Mr. and Mrs. Kirkpatrick, Lewis quickly discovered that "The Great Knock" lived up to his name by boldly inflicting his logical and analytical skills on others. September 19 was a significant date in C. S. Lewis's life. It was not only the date he met "The Great Knock," but the date on which, seventeen years later, he would have a late-night conversation with Hugo Dyson and J. R. R. Tolkien that appeared to be the final push to Lewis's believing in Christianity—what he eventually called "the true myth."[52]

Lewis learned an important lesson about language, meaning, and inference during an early interaction with Kirkpatrick, whom he describes as being "over six feet tall, very shabbily dressed (like a gardener, I thought), lean as a rake, and immensely muscular ... he wore moustache and side whiskers with a clean-shaven chin like the Emperor Franz Joseph."[53] Shortly after meeting Kirkpatrick, when riding in a carriage toward his new home, fifteen-year-old Lewis tried to make polite conversation. He writes in his autobiography, published on September 19, 1955 (another important September 19th), about his expectations for the landscape in Surrey: "I had been told that Surrey was 'suburban', and the landscape that actually flitted past the windows astonished me."[54] He casually mentioned to Kirkpatrick that the countryside of Surrey seemed wilder than he had expected. Lewis writes of Kirkpatrick's startling retort: " 'Stop!' Shouted Kirk with a suddenness that made me jump. 'What do you mean by wildness and what grounds had you for not expecting it?' I replied I don't know what ... As answer after answer was torn to shreds it at last dawned upon me that he really wanted to know."[55] Lewis had learned an important lesson: Words have power to describe or to reveal a lack of understanding. This first, memorable, impromptu tutorial was a lesson in both language and logic. Lewis found in Kirkpatrick a teacher who would scrutinize every sentence for its logical construction—both in use of words and in how that sentence would add to the larger argument. Lewis later noted in his autobiography that "the most casual remark was taken as a summons to disputation."[56] He says of his training in logic and argumentation by Kirkpatrick, "If ever a man came near to being a purely logical entity that man was Kirk."[57]

Lewis's time with Kirkpatrick was a turning point in his education. It was here in Surrey that Lewis learned the importance of precise communication. The Great Knock wrote to Albert Lewis in January 1915 that his son "was born with the literary temperament … By an unerring instinct he detects first rate quality in literary workmanship, and the second rate does not interest him in any way."[58] Lewis loved having the attention and being pushed to excel. Learning from Kirkpatrick, says Lewis, was like "red beef and strong beer"—substantial and stout. It was on this foundation of logic, languages, and literature that Lewis polished his communication gifts. "Here was a man," Lewis says, "who thought not about you but about what you said."[59]

Lewis's Oxford education would certainly refine and add to his intellectual and rhetorical competencies, but without Kirkpatrick, it is questionable that Lewis would have become the communicator readers know today. Although Lewis thought orators Demosthenes and Cicero were "The Two Great Bores," he nonetheless fine-tuned his dialectical and rhetorical skills.[60] Lewis acknowledges both Smewgy and Kirk for their skill in speaking, analytical thinking, and writing: "Smewgy and Kirk were my two greatest teachers. Roughly, one might say (in medieval language) that Smewgy taught me Grammar and Rhetoric and Kirk taught me Dialectic."[61] Dialectic is the study and practice of argument and debate. From the Great Knock, Lewis learned to focus on the essence of what a book had to say. At the heart of Kirkpatrick's educational mission was to provide Lewis with a firm grounding in the liberal arts and, through the use of the Socratic question and answer teaching method, the development of his critical thinking skills. As Lewis reflected, "If Kirk's ruthless dialectic had been merely a pedagogic instrument I might have resented it."[62] In a letter referring to Kirkpatrick Lewis notes, "A pure agnostic is a fine thing. I have known only one and he was the man who taught me how to think."[63]

Lewis also valued his education from The Great Knock in challenging ideas. In *The Personal Heresy* Lewis observed, "We have both [Lewis and co-author E. M.

W. Tillyard] learnt our dialectic in rough academic arena where knocks that would frighten the London literary coteries are given and taken in good part."[64] Rather than intimidate, the metaphorical "great knocks" Lewis received from Kirkpatrick helped to prepare him for the next phase of his education. Kirkpatrick clearly saw Lewis's ability to think and communicate well. By the winter of 1916, Lewis was ready to seek an Oxford education.

Oxford and the Dreaming Spires

Lewis traveled to Oxford for the first time on December 5, 1916, to take his exam to be considered for a scholarship. Although not his first choice, University College, one of the oldest Colleges at Oxford, offered him a scholarship on December 13, 1916, and he enrolled in University College in April 1917. But he still had not passed Responsions, the Oxford University entrance exam dubbed the "little go," because it was an exam that required a prospective student to respond (hence the term *responsions*) to moderately easy questions from experts. It may have been called the "little go" but it was "no go" for Lewis because he failed the math portion of the exam. Lewis's talents lay in working with words, not numbers. Nonetheless, University College honored its scholarship offer on the assumption that he would eventually pass the required exam.

In May 1917, just a few weeks after "coming up" to Oxford, Lewis joined the Officers' Training Corps. (When accepted to Oxford one "came up"; if asked to leave one was "sent down.") It was because he served in the military that he was ultimately not required to complete and pass Responsions—a good thing because he might never have been admitted to Oxford otherwise.

It was at Oxford that Lewis's academic talents flourished, and his intellectual refinement at the hand of Kirkpatrick came to fruition. Lewis's rooms at University College were in the Front Quad, Number 5, accessed through staircase number 12. He had a lovely view overlooking the Radcliffe Quad.[65] He was an excellent student.[66] And he loved Oxford.

At Oxford, Lewis first studied Classical Honour Moderations—Greek and Latin. Lewis excelled. He then studied what was known as "Greats," which included ancient history and philosophy, as well as classical rhetoric and poetics (orators and poets). Lewis also read Homer, Demosthenes, Cicero, Virgil, Euripides, Sophocles, and Aeschylus as an Oxford student.[67] Throughout his life, Lewis drew upon his early training in logic and his love of romance and story to enhance his communication talents.

But it is the classical roots of communication and rhetoric that Lewis would come to know best. During his pre-Oxford education Lewis wrote to his father, "In Greek we have begun Demosthenes. Of course oratory is not a sort of literature that I appreciate or understand in any language, so that I am hardly qualified to express an opinion on our friend with the mouthful of pebbles."[68] Even though Lewis had pronounced Demosthenes as one of the two "great bores" he also noted, "However, compared with Cicero, he strikes me as a man with something to say, intent only upon saying it clearly and shortly."[69] Lewis became well versed in the classical approaches to words and meaning. Lewis scholar Bruce Edwards concludes, "Lewis understood 'rhetoric' in its traditional classical and medieval sense—a compendium of verbal tools that assisted and equipped an artist or essayist with strategies to communicate truth more memorably, and, ultimately, to express difficult ideas more accessibly ..."[70] Edwards adds that through Lewis's study of rhetoric he was able "... to appeal to the imagination with greater aplomb and delight."[71]

As Lewis charted his educational course, especially attracted to the study of ideas, language, and literature, his academic experiences were abruptly interrupted by experiences that, although rarely explicitly discussed, were not far from the surface of his writing and thinking—World War I.

The Great War

Lewis seldom talked about or wrote about his war experience with anyone. He did describe some of his army experiences in his chapter "Guns and Good Company," in *Surprised by Joy*, but he did not make explicit links between his war experiences and the ideas that would illuminate his speaking and writing.[72] A case could be made that his military experience was not a major factor shaping his professional life. Yet in his book *A Morning After War: C. S. Lewis and WWI*, K. J. Gilchrist argues that although Lewis made little direct or even indirect reference to his brief war experience (he was in combat for less than three months), his war experience had a profound effect on him and his writing.[73] Gilchrist noted, "C. S. Lewis once explained that communication requires a listener not only to hear a message and understand what has been said but also requires the listener to understand what has not been said."[74] Gilchrist concludes, "Understanding what has not been said has been much of the difficulty in understanding Lewis's service in the First World War."[75]

Given Lewis's disdain for subjectivism, he would likely refute Gilchrist by cautioning him to avoid "reading between the lines."[76] In commenting about the interpretation of scripture, Lewis noted, "These men ask me to believe they can read between the lines of the old texts; the evidence is their obvious inability to read (in any sense worth discussing) the lines themselves. They claim to see fern-seeds and can't see an elephant ten yards away in broad daylight."[77] Lewis scholar Jerry Root notes, "It was this ... practice of reading between the lines that led Lewis to question some of the work done by the higher critics of Scripture."[78]

Even if one heeds Lewis's caution about "reading between the lines," serving in the trenches in World War I was undoubtedly an indelible experience that gave Lewis seminal insights about war, death, pain, suffering, and loss—topics of Lewis's books, essays, and stories. As Gilchrist cogently describes, "As an adult, he was first a soldier; as a writer, first a war poet; as an adherent to reasoned beliefs, first an atheist."[79] Here again, however, Lewis might caution against "The Personal Heresy" by suggesting that we look at what he actually wrote rather than trying to "read between the lines" to identify and attribute meaning to pieces of his past when interpreting his work.

When Lewis arrived in Oxford to start his studies at University College he volunteered to train with the university Officers' Training Corps (OTC). Owing his education to England could have been one motivation for patriotically deciding to enlist in the Army. The purpose of the OTC, according to the *Oxford University Handbook*, was to "give an opportunity to undergraduates to offer their services to the Country in the simplest and most practical way during peace, and to provide officers for His Majesty's Army (Regular and Territorial) from this University in time of national emergency."[80] Lewis spent only a few weeks in his rooms at University College before he was shuttled off to a dreary room in Keble College to fulfill his OTC commitments. (With its angular exterior brick façade, Keble College remains one of the most architecturally distinctive of Oxford's 39 colleges.) With the war at full tilt, officers were needed, and Lewis's past and present educational experience made an OTC member a prime candidate for leadership.

Although he did not directly discuss his war experiences in his writing, his military and battlefield encounters were perhaps his inspiration for discussing pain and the nature of hell in *The Great Divorce*, *The Screwtape Letters*, and other essays and poems. Lewis's first book, *Spirits in Bondage*, published under the pseudonym Clive Hamilton in 1919—the year he returned to Oxford—includes allusions to dark and troublesome events in WWI.[81] Although his war experiences cast shadows over his early 20s, it was his connection with one soldier who was to become his friend, which had an influence on him for the rest of his life.

Mrs. Moore and Lewis's Audience

Lewis first mentions his friend "Paddy" Moore (Edward Francis Courtenay Moore, 1898–1918) when they were both training for military service. In a letter to Arthur Greeves Lewis describes Paddy as a "good fellow."[82] They undoubtedly became good friends because of their common Irish ancestry. Jack and Paddy made their pact that if either of them should be killed in the war, the survivor would care for the deceased's parent. In Lewis's case, his father Albert Lewis, and in Paddy's case, mother Janie King Askins Moore.

Lewis saw Mrs. Moore frequently because she had come to Oxford to be near Paddy. She was estranged from her husband and although never divorced, remained separated from him for the rest of their lives. George Sayer, a former student who became a trusted Lewis friend, reached the conclusion that Lewis was "infatuated" with Mrs. Moore.[83] She was perhaps the nurturing mother that Lewis had lost when he was nine. Lewis had a month's leave before being sent into active service. Rather than going home to visit his father, Lewis spent his time in Bristol with Paddy and Mrs. Moore. Missing letters (Sayer suggests they were destroyed) between Lewis and his close confidant and perhaps confessor, Greeves, may have shed light on the Moore-Lewis relationship. But Sayer concludes, "The letters that are left make it quite clear that he loved Mrs. Moore."[84] Despite their 25-year age difference, there seemed to be a deep and enduring emotional bond between them.

Paddy was killed in battle in 1918. Lewis had been wounded by shrapnel in the Battle of Arras at Mount Bernenchon (which, in reality, is a flat plain rather than a mountain),[85] shrapnel that killed the Sergeant standing next to him. He was sent to a hospital and eventually returned to Oxford. He helped Mrs. Moore move from her home in Eastbourne to Bristol, and then later in the summer of 1919 to Headington, a village two miles to the northeast of Oxford City Center. By this time, Lewis and Mrs. Moore, along with her daughter Maureen, were inseparable. Lewis moved in with them, although he kept his living arrangements quiet. Lewis was expected to live in college, not out. The trio lived in several rental flats in Oxford before they bought The Kilns in 1930, a house about three miles from Oxford City Center. It was the house in which Lewis would write his best-known works and the house in which he would die. Lewis, Maureen and Mrs.

Moore lived together until Maureen left to be married in 1940 and Mrs. Moore moved into a nursing home in 1950. Mrs. Moore died on January 12, 1951.

What was the true relationship between Mrs. Moore and C. S. Lewis? Most (but not all) Lewis biographers speculate that Lewis and Mrs. Moore had a brief, sexual relationship early in their association.[86] No one will know for certain.

Lewis biographer and personal friend, George Sayer, revised the third edition of his biography to add this conclusion:

> I have had to alter my opinion of Lewis's relationship with Mrs. Moore. In chapter eight of this book I wrote that I was uncertain about whether they were lovers. Now after conversations with Mrs. Moore's daughter, and a consideration of the way in which their bedrooms were arranged at The Kilns, I am quite certain that they were. They did not share a room, but Lewis had a room which, until an outside staircase was built some years later, could be entered only by going through Mrs. Moore's bedroom. Even close friends such as Owen Barfield did not know much of their relationship. Lewis had to be secretive because if the university authorities had found out about Mrs. Moore he would have been sent down and his academic career at Oxford would have been over.[87]

Others strongly argue that theirs was strictly a mother/son relationship and that evidence of their platonic relationship may be found in Lewis's letters.[88] What is clear is that Mrs. Moore was an important fixture in Lewis's life until her death in 1951. It is a relationship shrouded in mystery that evokes varying opinions. Warnie writes that Jack never discussed the nature of their relationship with him. Jack's close friend, Owen Barfield, describes Mrs. Moore as "a sort of baleful stepmother."[89] Although Sayer revised his conclusion suggesting that there was a sexual relationship, he also writes, "Some of those who have written about C.S. Lewis regard his living with Mrs. Moore as odd, even sinister."[90] Yet, as one of Lewis's students at the time, Sayer adds, "This was not the view of those of us who visited his home in the thirties. Like his other pupils, I thought it completely normal that a woman, probably a widow, would make a home for a young bachelor. We had no difficulty accepting her, even when we came to realise that she was not his mother."[91] John Tolkien, one of J. R. R. Tolkien's sons, said that Mrs. Moore was like a "Great Aunt" and that Edith Tolkien, John's mother and J. R. R. Tolkien's wife, had a very good friendship with her.[92]

Janie Moore could be demanding, sometimes summoning Jack home to run errands. Nonetheless, he remained a faithful adopted son. When illness forced Mrs. Moore to move into a nursing home in 1950, Lewis would visit her daily, usually walking the two miles from Magdalen College to her nursing home on the Woodstock Road, and then back again. His relationship with her remained important throughout her life.

What does Lewis's relationship with Mrs. Moore have to do with Lewis as communicator? As a highly educated Oxford scholar, and Oxford tutor and lecturer, Lewis lived in a world of rich intellectual privilege, with well-educated colleagues, and talented and motivated students striving for success. His close association with the Moores gave him a mooring (literally and figuratively) in communicating with the average, non-Oxford-educated person. Lewis was learning how to express ideas to those who would be his audience for his popular works—not the Oxford intelligentsia but the everyman and everywoman who would find his messages about Christianity useful. Lewis's writing appeals not only to the well-educated and well read, but also to those without the benefits of an elite education. His war experiences, although not explicitly discussed in his work, coupled with his new and enduring relationships with Janie and Maureen Moore, played an important role in helping Lewis understand his audience—one of his hallmarks as a communicator.

Besides her lack of education, Mrs. Moore was an atheist. After Lewis's conversion, when he and his brother would head to Holy Trinity Church in Headington Quarry, she would chide them, describing communion as a "blood feast."[93] Lewis's own season of atheism and Mrs. Moores' constant presence as an atheist gave him an ever-present reminder of his audience as skeptical or outright non-believing in God. But Lewis had other companions, including J. R. R. Tolkien, who ultimately influenced his beliefs, writing, and life philosophy.

J. R. R. Tolkien: Oxford Friend and Colleague

Lewis and Tolkien met at Oxford in 1926 and remained friends for the rest of their lives. After meeting him for the first time, Lewis wrote in his diary that Tolkien was, "a smooth, pale fluent little chap ... no harm in him: only needs a smack or so."[94] Although their contact diminished in later years when Lewis began teaching at Cambridge in 1955, both men attest to the importance their relationship had on their writing and thought. As evidence of their continued friendship and affection, Tolkien's son John said he drove his father weekly to see Lewis during the last six months of Lewis's life in the summer and fall of 1963 after Lewis had left Cambridge and returned to Oxford to live full time.[95]

Tolkien started a study group called the Kolbitar (an Icelandic word that means "coal-biters"), which Lewis attended and greatly enjoyed. Tolkien and

Lewis shared an affinity for Norse mythology and enjoyed spirited conversations about all things Norse, which led them to other areas of mutual interest, including the power of stories in general and myth in particular. They were good for each other's creative sparks. Tolkien was a literary perfectionist. (It is perhaps because of his perfectionism and focus on *The Lord of the Rings* that the book *Language and Human Nature* was never written.) Diana Pavlac Glyer, in her insightful book, *The Company They Keep: C. S. Lewis and J. R. R. Tolkien as Writers in Community* (the book that helped me identify the *Language and Human Nature* manuscript), speaks of how these two literary giants influenced and strengthened each other.[96] Glyer describes several collaborative writing projects among the Inklings, including projects by "Lewis and [Owen] Barfield, Lewis and Tolkien, Lewis and Williams, Lewis and [J. A. W.] Bennett, [Nevill] Coghill and Christopher Tolkien, Lewis and [Humphrey] Havard."[97] She also describes the book the Inklings wrote as a group in tribute to their friend Charles Williams, *Essays Presented to Charles Williams*, started before Williams's death but completed after his death on May 15, 1945.

Lewis and Tolkien agreed that more books about science fiction needed to be written. Lewis agreed to write about space travel and Tolkien about time travel. Lewis wrote his space trilogy (also known as the Random trilogy because of the protagonist in all three stories) *Out of the Silent Planet*, *Perelandra*, and *That Hideous Strength*. Tolkien, however, did not fulfill his side of the bargain, but instead steadfastly worked on *The Lord of the Rings*. Although they encouraged each other, they were not always enamored with each other's work. Tolkien did not have a positive response to the Narnia books. He thought them too much a hodgepodge jumble of myths patched together from disconnected mythical genres.[98] Tolkien also did not have praise for Lewis's *Studies in Words*. In a letter dated September 12, 1960, to his son Christopher Tolkien, after reading Lewis's *Studies in Words* J. R. R. Tolkien wrote, "I have just received a copy of C. S. L.'s latest *Studies in Words*. Alas! His ponderous silliness is becoming a fixed manner. I am deeply relieved to find I am not mentioned."[99]

This letter and other similar comments made about each other provide evidence that lead some biographers to conclude that their friendship may have cooled during the last 15 years of Lewis's life.[100] (Some have speculated that Tolkien may have been jealous of Lewis's close friendship with Charles Williams, an editor for Oxford University Press, who admired Lewis.)[101] Tolkien wrote to his son Michael a few days after Lewis's death noting that although he [Tolkien] and Lewis were not "intimates" he further explained, "We were separated first by the sudden apparition of Charles Williams, and then by his marriage" but, in admiration. adds, "… we owed each a great debt to the other, and that tie with the deep affection that is begot, remains. He was a great man of whom the cold-blooded official obituaries only scratched the surface, in places with injustice."[102] There is additional evidence that their friendship remained strong throughout their lives and was important to each of them.[103] Correspondence provides proof that Tolkien was instrumental in Lewis's receiving the prestigious Chair in Medieval and Renaissance Literature at Cambridge University in 1954.[104] Lewis's relationship with and eventual marriage to Joy Davidman seems to have had an effect on the relationship between Lewis and Tolkien. (Lewis did not disclose his "first" marriage to Davidman to Tolkien.) Davidman's sometimes perceived as brash "American style" assertiveness did not always wear well among many of Lewis's friends. (Tolkien called her "That woman" and explicitly mentioned the marriage as a source of "separation" between Tolkien and Lewis.)[105] Lewis and Tolkien's strong bond of friendship nonetheless provided a context for Lewis's conversion or return to Christianity. Without Lewis's conversion and the books and essays that flowed from his pen about Christianity, he may have remained an obscure Oxford tutor. But Lewis's conversion gave him something to communicate about.

A Most Reluctant Conversion

Early in his academic career Lewis's primary goal was to be a poet—a published poet. He achieved that goal in 1919 with the publication of his collection of poems *Spirits in Bondage*. Few have read it, and most would not recognize it as Lewis's work if one saw a first edition on a bookshelf in an old bookshop. Lewis used the pseudonym Clive Hamilton (Hamilton was his mother's maiden name). Because of lackluster sales and the pseudonym, it is one of the rarest of Lewis's books to find in first edition. It is scarce not only because it did not sell well, as well as languish on a dusty shelf because it not immediately recognized as by Lewis, but also because the publisher had the unsold books destroyed. His poetry, although having flashes of exceptional insight, was not well received by readers. Scholars point to Lewis's pre-conversion, compared with his post-conversion, writing productivity as evidence that his conversion gave him intellectual fuel that would make him one of the most widely-read authors in multiple literary genres.

Lewis's conversion to Christianity was evolutionary rather than revolutionary; it evolved over a period of years. The key purpose of Lewis's autobiography, *Surprised by Joy*, was to tell the story of his conversion. People wanted to read the story of how a person raised in a Christian home became an atheist, then became a theist, and eventually a Christian. Lewis's autobiography and numerous biographies describe the story in detail.[106] His parents were religious, his grandfather Hamilton a clergyman in the Church of Ireland, and Lewis was baptized and attended services with his family in Belfast at St. Mark's, Dundela. But his unanswered prayers for his mother and her devastating death, followed by his being sent to boarding schools he hated, left Lewis feeling there was no God—at least not the God he was led to believe in.

Lewis had role models who showed him that a life without God could be a good life. Several influential tutors, including "The Great Knock" Kirkpatrick, were atheists whom Lewis admired for their intellectual talents. Yet after attending Oxford, he found himself surrounded by believers as well as atheists. His close friend J. R. R. Tolkien was a Catholic and Owen Barfield, a theosophist. Lewis had read the Bible primarily as myth; yet when he was confronted with the observation that he believed myth and stories in all forms except the Bible, it jolted him to reconsider the significance of the Bible as a true myth.

Most biographies published before 2013 describe Lewis's belief in God occurring in the spring of 1929, based on Lewis's own description in his autobiography. After a careful reading of Lewis's letters, however, biographer Alister McGrath thinks Lewis got the date wrong.[107] It was actually the spring of 1930 when his belief in God occurred. Lewis scholar Andrew Lazo also confirms that the date was 1930, based on an early draft of Lewis's autobiography.[108] Lewis acknowledged in his published autobiography, "I am troubled by doubts about chronology" when he was describing his home life, so it is understandable that he may have been foggy on the date of his conversion.[109] Although it should be noted that Lewis scholar Brendan Wolfe suggests that Lewis could have been referring to the *academic* year that spanned 1929–1930, rather than the calendar year 1929.[110]

George McDonald's *Phantastes,* randomly purchased from a bookseller's train station stall while Lewis was still a student of William T. Kirkpatrick, was an important discovery early in his drift away from atheism toward Christianity. Lewis would later say about the influence of *Phantastes,* "That night my imagination was, in a certain sense, baptized; the rest of me[,] not unnaturally, took longer. I had not the faintest notion what I had let myself in for by buying *Phantastes.*"[111] G. K. Chesterton's 1926 *The Everlasting Man* was another literary influence on his ultimate conversion. He writes in his autobiography about being confronted with a choice: "The odd thing was that before God closed in on me, I was in fact offered what now appears a moment of wholly free choice." He remembers that moment:

I was going up Headington Hill on the top of a bus. Without words and (I think) almost without images, a fact about myself was somehow presented to me. I became aware that I was holding something at bay, or shutting something out. Or, if you like, that I was wearing some stiff clothing, like corsets, or even a suit of armor, as if I were a lobster.[112]

He also writes, "Really, a young Atheist cannot guard his faith too carefully. Dangers lie in wait for him on every side."[113] In a letter dated February 3, 1930 Lewis wrote to his friend Owen Barfield, "Terrible things are happening to me. The 'spirit' or 'Real I' is showing an alarming tendency to become much more personal and is taking the offensive, and behaving just like God. You'd better come on Monday at the latest or I may have entered a monastery."[114]

Lewis describes his conversion to a belief in God in this often-quoted passage from his autobiography:

You must picture me alone in that room in Magdalen, night after night, feeling, whenever my mind lifted even for a second from my work, the steady unrelenting approach of Him whom I so earnestly desired not to meet. That which I greatly feared had at last come upon me. In the Trinity Term of 1929 [1930] I gave in, and admitted that God was God, and knelt and prayed; perhaps, that night, the most dejected and reluctant convert in all England.[115]

More than a year later, Lewis's conversion to Christianity took a major leap forward. He spent the night of September 19, 1931 in spirited conversation with Hugo Dyson and J. R. R. Tolkien about myth and Christianity. He tells the story to his friend Arthur Greeves in a letter dated September 22, 1931:

He [Dyson] stayed the night with me in College—I sleeping in in order to be able to talk far into the night as one cd.[could] hardly do out here. Tolkien came too, and did not leave till 3 in the morning ... Dyson and I found still more to say to one another, strolling up and down the cloister of New Building, so that we did not get to bed till 4. It was really a memorable talk. We began (in Addison's walk just after dinner) on metaphor and myth—interrupted by a rush of wind which came so suddenly on the still, warm evening and sent so many leaves pattering down that we thought it was raining. We all held our breath, the other two appreciating the ecstasy of such a thing almost as you would. We continued (in my room) on Christianity: a good long satisfying talk in which I learned a lot: then discussed the difference between love and friendship—then finally drifted back to poetry and books.[116]

In *Surprised by Joy* Lewis reports planning an outing to the Whipsnade Zoo during which he rode in the sidecar of Warnie's motorcycle on September 28, 1931. He succinctly describes his final conversion to Christianity: "I know very well when, but hardly how, the final step was taken. I was driven to Whipsnade one sunny morning. When we set out I did not believe that Jesus Christ is the Son of God, and when we reached the zoo I did. Yet I had not exactly spent the journey in thought."[117]

Just a few days after his zoo epiphany, in a letter of October 1, 1931 Lewis tells Greeves, "I have just passed on from believing in God to definitely believing in Christ—in Christianity. I will try to explain this another time. My long night talk with Dyson and Tolkien had a good deal to do with it."[118]

Lewis's description in both his letters and in his autobiography provides a window into how Lewis thought and made decisions. He mulled things over. He took in a bit of information, processed an experience and then thought about it further. Then he tested the idea. Sometimes he shared his idea with friends. After additional thought he announced his conclusion. He talked about his ideas with others or in a lecture. And finally he wrote about it. This cycle of experience, think, mull, talk, and write is how he gave birth to some of the most enduring classics of the twentieth century. One of his virtues as a communicator is his season of pre-writing. Prior to penning his thoughts on paper, he cogitated. His ideas sat on the stove simmering before being served to others.

During the Summer of 1932, Lewis wrote his first book following his conversion. He dashed off *The Pilgrim's Regress* between August 15 and 29th while staying with Arthur Greeves—just across the road from Lewis's childhood home, Little Lea, which had recently been sold following the death of Lewis's father, Albert. The publication of *The Pilgrim's Regress* began a prolific writing career that would produce some of the best-known classics of the twentieth century.

As an author and educator Lewis had many friends and acquaintances, but there is scant record of Lewis's interest in a romantic relationship. In some respects, he was married to his work. But fast forwarding to the 1950s, his relationship with Joy Davidman, first by correspondence and then in person, eventually converted him to marriage. Not unlike his conversion to Christianity, his marriage(s) to Joy evolved slowly over time.

Surprised by Marriage: Finding Joy and Observing Grief

Lewis's relationship with and marriage to Joy Davidman, spanning a ten-year period during the zenith of Lewis's career (she first wrote to him in 1950 and died in 1960), had a significant role in Lewis's literary output. Joy influenced his life and work in ways that Lewis could not have imagined when he received his first letter from her in January 1950.[119] At that time she was married to film writer William Gresham and had two sons, David (1944–2014) and Douglas (1945-). Her early activism in the communist party was compatible with her then disbelief in God. Joy was intellectually restless and exceptionally bright; she was searching for another sense-making paradigm for her life. She became a Christian in 1946.[120] Her conversion to Christianity was greatly influenced by Lewis's books (especially *The Great Divorce* and *The Screwtape Letters*), and eventually prompted her to write to Lewis in 1950. Lewis enjoyed her letters immensely; of the hundreds of letters that he received each year, her letters stood out for their wit and insightful questions.[121]

When Joy made a trip to England in 1952, she wrote asking to meet Lewis. He agreed. Her erotic love poems (discovered by others 60 years after she wrote them) suggest that she was infatuated with Lewis and sought a romantic relationship with him.[122] The excellent biography *Joy: Poet, Seeker, and the Woman who Captivated C. S. Lewis*, by Abigail Santamaria, provides a fascinating description of Joy's life and eventual marriage to Lewis.[123]

By one account, Jack and Joy's first meeting occurred in September. George Sayer writes that they first met at the Eastgate Hotel in Oxford[124] (although clues from Lewis's letters and other artifacts suggest they may have met a few days earlier or briefly earlier in the day).[125] Their first visit went well with good conversation. Lewis must have enjoyed it because, according to George Sayer, he asked her to have lunch with him in his Magdalen College room along with Phyllis Williams, her London friend.[126] Lewis liked to have "chaperones" when dining with women. (Warnie, or other colleagues and friends, often served this function.) When Warnie was not able to join them for the Magdalen luncheon Sayer was invited.[127] After being served a single glass of sherry before lunch, Sayer recalls Joy proclaiming, "I call this civilized. In the States, they give you so much hard stuff that you start the meal drunk and end with a hangover."[128]

Jack and Joy met again in London on December 6th when Lewis invited Joy to spend Christmas at The Kilns with him and Warnie.[129] While visiting at Christmas, she received a letter from her husband Bill, informing her that he was in love with Renee Pierce, a cousin of Joy's. Joy realized that their marriage was over. During the first Christmas that Joy and Jack celebrated together, Joy gave Jack a first edition copy of Ray Bradbury's *The Illustrated Man*. She signed it and included a quote, "And men may grow weary of green wine and sick of crimson seas," a slightly altered line from G. K. Chesterton's poem "The Ballad of the White

Horse." (Who knows? Perhaps they had visited the White Horse chalk etching on a hillside not far from Oxford.) Lewis reciprocated by giving Joy George McDonald's *Diary of an Old Soul*.[130] She also asked Lewis to inscribe her personal copy of *The Great Divorce*—her favorite Lewis book, which had been instrumental in her conversion to Christianity. He obliged and wrote, "There are three images in my mind which I must continually forsake and replace by better ones: the false image of God, the false image of my neighbours, and the false image of myself. C. S. Lewis 30 December 1952 (from an unwritten chapter on Iconoclasm)."[131] Directly under this inscription, he wrote another related message: "Satire is a glass in which the reader commonly sees every face except his own.' Swift, quoted from memory."[132] I know these are the exact quotes because both the Ray Bradbury book Joy gave to Lewis and her copy of *The Great Divorce* are now nestled side by side in my private collection as bibliophilic symbols of the beginning of this great twentieth century love story.

Joy separated from her husband and moved to England with her sons, David, age 9, and Douglas, age 8, in November 1953. The divorce was finalized in 1954.[133] Jack and Joy saw each other infrequently at first and then more often in the mid-1950s and spent the Christmas holidays of 1954 at The Kilns Joy and her sons moved to Headington, just outside Oxford in August of 1955. By that time, Lewis had accepted a position at Cambridge but still resided at his home, The Kilns, on long weekends during the eight-week term time and when the terms were concluded. Even though Lewis was employed by "the Other Place"—the phrase Oxonians use for Cantabrigians (and Cantabrigians reciprocally used by Oxonians)—Joy's being in Headington put her in much closer proximity to him. (Unlike today, in the 1950s and early 60s, there was direct train service between Oxford and Cambridge that made the commute efficient.)

After Lewis's employment at Cambridge, he had no new ideas for books. His close friend George Sayer said, "No pictures came into his mind, he had nothing to say, and this is where Joy gave him invaluable help."[134] Sayer and his wife Moira and invited Jack and Warnie to dinner and Lewis wrote back in an April 2, 1954, letter, "By bad luck Mrs. Gresham (our queer, Jewish, ex-Communist, American convert) and her two boys will be here all next week. So we can't come and dine."[135] But still wanting to have a visit with is friend George asked, "But cd. [could] you both come in on the Tue. or Wed. and meet at the Eastgate at 11 for an hour or more's talk?"[136] Lewis added, "She's a queer fish and I'm not at all sure that she's either yours or Moira's cup of tea (she is at any rate not a bore). But it wd. be a v. bright spot for W. [Warnie] and me. Do."[137] Jack and Joy eventually did have dinner with George and Moira; Jack commented to Sayer at the end of the evening, "And, by the way, I've at last got a really good idea for a book."[138] Whether it was by coincidence or, more probably, the influence of Joy, Lewis's creative juices were flowing again.

In 1955, when Joy and her sons were living at 10 Old High Street, Headington, (with rent paid by Jack) less than two miles from The Kilns Jack and Joy began to see each other more frequently. She helped type and edit *Till We Have Faces*, a novel based on the Greek myth of Cupid and Psyche that was also tellingly dedicated to Joy.[139] By September Jack had talked with Arthur Greeves about the possibility of marrying Joy in a civil ceremony so that he could extend his citizenship to her and she and the boys could remain in England.[140] That ceremony took place on April 23, 1956, at the Oxford Registry Office, then located just a couple of doors down from the Eagle and Child pub in a building that today is a Quaker "Friends" meeting house. Although it was only a "technical" marriage, it soon became more than technical, moving from friendship to affection and finally to romantic love—mirroring the relational escalation described in *The Four Loves*—a book that Joy also helped Lewis develop.

Joy had been experiencing some health issues—leg pains first diagnosed as merely fibrositis.[141] On October 18, 1956, while reaching for a phone call from Katharine Farrer, Davidman fell and broke her leg. X-rays revealed more than just a broken leg—there was cancer.

With the news of Joy's illness Lewis realized that his relationship with Joy had become much more than a marriage of convenience—it had fully morphed into romantic love. As a first step in publicly acknowledging his feelings for Joy, he placed this simple announcement on Christmas Eve 1956 in *The Times* of London: "A marriage has taken place between Professor C. S. Lewis, of Magdalene College Cambridge, and Mrs. Joy Gresham, now a patient in the Wingfield Hospital, Oxford. It is requested that no letters be sent."[142] Once aware of his love for Joy, Lewis began quietly seeking someone who could provide a proper ecclesiastical marriage ceremony. Because of Joy's previous marriage, he was initially unsuccessful in securing permission of an Anglican clergyman to perform the ceremony. Eventually his friend Peter Bide performed the service on March 21, 1957, at the Wingfield Hospital in Oxford.[143]

Joy returned home to The Kilns in April, not expected to live much longer—perhaps weeks. But with what Lewis believed to be a miracle, she regained strength and her cancer went into remission. They enjoyed their time together, especially as she showed signs of improvement. They traveled to Ireland and planned a longed-for trip to Greece with their friends Roger Lancelyn Green and his wife, June. Weeks before they were to leave for Greece, Joy and Jack learned that her cancer had returned. Notwithstanding the severe state of her health, the trip proceeded as planned in April 1960.

Tolkien called Jack and Joy's relationship a "very strange marriage."[144] Yet this "strange" marriage worked. During the time of their relationship, Lewis gained renewed inspiration and wrote *Till We Have Faces* and *The Four Loves* (both greatly influenced by Joy), and *Reflections on the Psalms*. Joy gave Lewis's writing a shot in the arm. Reports from those who knew them were that she helped Lewis by sometimes critically challenging his ideas; she could be blunt. But her refreshing directness, as well as helping Lewis experience the joy of an intimate human relationship, significantly enriched his life and was a muse for his communication productivity. Cancer finally claimed Joy's life on July 13, 1960.

A Well-Read Mind Awake

The making of C. S. Lewis as a master communication craftsperson involves not only the people who influenced him but also the books he read. In preparing his work *English Literature in the Sixteenth Century: Excluding Drama,* Lewis endeavored to read every piece of English literature he could find that existed in the Sixteenth Century.[145] Lewis had a life-long voracious appetite for reading. Remember, Lewis said that not only could he find "a cup of tea large enough" but also "a book long enough" to suit him.[146] Besides walking, and talking with friends by the fire with a drink at his elbow, reading remained one of his favorite pastimes. It was also a necessary task for his work as a tutor and author.

Which of the books did he read that influenced him the most? The editors of *The Christian Century* asked him, "What books did most to shape your vocational attitude and your philosophy of life?" Lewis's answer was published in the June 6, 1962 issue of the magazine.[147] The question was well timed, given that Lewis had only a year and a half to live and had already written the bulk of his literary output. Here is his list, published in rank order:

1. *Phantastes* by George MacDonald
2. *The Everlasting Man* by G. K. Chesterton
3. *The Aeneid* by Virgil
4. *The Temple* by George Herbert
5. *The Prelude* by William Wordsworth
6. *The Idea of the Holy* by Rudolf Otto
7. *The Consolation of Philosophy* by Boethius

8. *Life of Samuel Johnson* by James Boswell
9. *Descent into Hell* by Charles Williams
10. *Theism and Humanism* by Arthur James Balfour

In one of his last interviews, conducted by *Decision* magazine, Sherwood Wirt asked Lewis, "What Christian writers have helped you?" His answer was *The Everlasting Man* by Chesterton, *Symbolism and Belief* by Bevan (a book not on his earlier top-ten list), *The Idea of the Holy* by Otto, and the plays of Dorothy Sayers.[148]

A few months before his death, Lewis was asked what he thought about the Christian books being written in 1963. Lewis did not mince words: "A great deal of what is being published by writers in the religious tradition is a scandal and is actually turning people away from the church."[149] Lewis further explained, "The liberal writers who are continually accommodating and whittling down the truth of the Gospel are responsible. I cannot understand how a man can appear in print claiming to disbelieve everything that he presupposes when he puts on the surplice."[150] Then to make sure his feelings were clear he added, "I feel it is a form of prostitution."[151]

With today's vast resources of the Internet, if we want to know something, we just Google it. Lewis did not have the Internet, but he had the uncanny ability to remember what he read, saw, and heard. A communicator, especially a public speaker or teacher, without the ability to recall information, data, examples, and stories would be considerably less effective than one who can effortlessly retrieve anecdotes and ideas from memory. Memory is one of the classical canons of rhetoric identified by the ancient Romans. C. S. Lewis had the gift of a photographic memory. He was a devoted reader who would read and re-read his favorite books. As he noted in *Experiment in Criticism*, re-reading a good book is a hallmark of a sophisticated reader.

Not only did he read and subsequently re-read books, but he could apparently quote large passages from books in his library from memory. Although some suggest it may be apocryphal, the story is told of Lewis having someone randomly pluck a book from his library shelf and then asking the person to randomly open a page in the book, Lewis could begin quoting from the book from memory.[152] Whether that anecdote is apocryphal or not, other evidence shows that Lewis could recite long passages of poems from memory.[153] In the preface to his biography of Lewis, Sayer relates his first meeting with Lewis in Lewis's rooms at Magdalen College, Oxford.[154] When asked what long poems Sayer liked, Sayer mentioned *The Prelude*. After inviting Sayer to quote from it, Lewis quickly joined him. Lewis soon quoted other lengthy poems from memory.

Lewis had a consummate liberal arts education. He was not trained to *do*, but educated to *be* and to *think*. In a letter to Lewis's father, Lewis's teacher, Kirkpatrick, confirmed that C. S. Lewis was well suited to be an educator. Kirkpatrick wrote, "You may make a writer or a scholar of him, but you'll not make anything else. You may make up your mind to *that*."[155] Lewis's extensive reading tastes coupled with his required reading from tutors and lecturers, gave his communication a depth of insight and ability to draw on centuries-old ideas as well as contemporary thought.

One of Lewis's famous quotes from *The Abolition of Man* is "The task of the modern educator is not to cut down jungles but to irrigate deserts."[156] Lewis scholar Joel Heck elaborates on this metaphor: "He contended that education was not so much a matter of pulling out the weeds of false knowledge and ways of thinking but a matter of encouraging learning, stimulating their thinking, helping them to add to their knowledge and to broadening their ways of thinking."[157] This was the kind of education Lewis received and the kind he believed should be experienced by others. He loved being an educator. It was his depth and breadth of reading that gave him insights that cannot be faked by having the resources of the Internet in our pockets. It is one thing to have information, but quite another to use information by placing it in context and framing it within the great ideas, past and present. Lewis's classic liberal arts education was less about simply acquiring facts, but about synthesizing ideas, principles, and knowledge of literature, history, philosophy, and the arts to illuminate, integrate, and inspire.

The title of Clyde S. Kilby's anthology of Lewis quotations, *A Mind Awake,* describes one of the perceptions that make Lewis, Lewis. More than just the ability to be aware of feelings and thoughts, or to retain information, it is the intellectual skill in actively integrating those ideas, feelings, and thoughts in a way that makes sense. As noted in Chapter 1, Communication is the process of making sense out of the world and sharing that sense with others through creating meaning with verbal and nonverbal messages.[158] Lewis had a mind awake to discover and subsequently communicate sense—not just for himself but also for others. Although his ideas did not resonate with everyone, his legacy suggests he was nonetheless a popular, professional, and prolific communicator. His curiosity, passion for reading, skill in learning languages, keen memory, and innate talent for using words—both spoken and written—all interacted to enhance his communication skill. As chronicled here, Lewis's life provided the education and experience for him to help others make sense of their own lives.

Notes

1. C. S. Lewis, January 19, 1948, letter to Roy W. Harrington, *The Collected Letters of C. S. Lewis, Vol. II: Books, Broadcasts, and the War 1931-1949*, ed. Walter Hooper (San Francisco: HarperCollins, 2004), 830–831.

2. George Bailey, "In the University," *C. S. Lewis: Speaker & Teacher*, ed. Carolyn Keefe (London: Hodder and Stoughton, 1971).

3. C. S. Lewis, Letter to a Fifth Grade Class in Maryland, May 24, 1954. The *Collected Letters of C. S. Lewis, Vol. III: Narnia, Cambridge, and Joy 1950-1963*, ed. Walter Hooper (San Francisco: Harper San Francisco, 2007), 479–480.

4. Lewis, January 19, 1948, letter to Roy W. Harrington, *Collected Letters II*, 830.

5. C. S. Lewis and E. M. W. Tillyard, *The Personal Heresy: A Controversy* (Oxford: Oxford University Press, 1939).

6. See: E. M. W. Tillyard, *The Miltonic Setting, Past and Present* (Cambridge: Cambridge University Press, 1938).

7. Lewis and Tillyard, *The Personal Heresy*, 31–48.

8. Lewis and Tillyard, *The Personal Heresy*, 5.

9. Lewis and Tillyard, *The Personal Heresy*, 11.

10. Lewis and Tillyard, *The Personal Heresy*, 11.

11. Jerry Root, *C. S. Lewis and a Problem of Evil: An Investigation of a Pervasive Theme* (Eugene: Pickwick Publications, 2009), xii.

12. Douglas Gresham, Lewis's stepson explains that he was called Jack because "… of a small dog that he was fond of that he picked the name Jacksie, which was what the dog was called. It was run over (probably by a horse and cart as there were almost no cars in the time and place where he was a child), and Jack, as he later become known just took the name for himself." Douglas H. Gresham, *Lenten Lands: My Childhood with Joy Davidman and C. S. Lewis* (San Francisco: HarperSanFrancisco, 2005), 2. Another explanation: Personal conversation with Walter Hooper (May 17, 2019), Lewis's literary executor and secretary, indicated that Lewis's mother said it was because Lewis liked trains and the train engineer Lewis knew was called Jack.

13. Harry Lee Poe, *Becoming C. S. Lewis: A Biography of Young Jack Lewis (1898–1963)* (Wheaton: Crossway, 2019), 17.

14. See: George Sayer, *Jack: A Life of C. S. Lewis* (Wheaton: Crossway Books, 1994), 41.

15. George Sayer, *Jack*, 41.

16. C. S. Lewis, *Surprised by Joy: The Shape of My Early Life* (London: Geoffrey Bles, 1955), 13.

17. Lewis, *Surprised by Joy*, 13.

18. Lewis, *Surprised by Joy*, 13.

19. Lewis, *Surprised by Joy*, 13.

20. For an excellent discussion of the life of Albert Lewis see: Crystal Hurd, "*The Pudaita Pie*: Reflections on Albert Lewis," *VII Journal of the Marion E. Wade Center* 32 (2015), 47–58.

21. Sayer, *Jack*, 26.

22. See: Alister McGrath, *C. S. Lewis: A Life* (Carol Stream, IL: Tyndale House Publishers Inc., 2013), 8.

23. W. H. Lewis. "Memoir of C. S. Lewis," *Letters of C. S. Lewis*, ed. W. H. Lewis (London: Bless, 1966), 6.

24. Lewis, *Surprised by Joy*, 42.

25. Lewis, *Surprised by Joy*, 42.

26. Lewis, *Surprised by Joy*, 42.

27. Lewis, *Surprised by Joy*, 42.

28. Lewis, *Surprised by Joy*, 43.

29. Lewis, *Surprised by Joy*, 43.

30. Lewis, *Surprised by Joy*, 121.

31. Michael McCrary, "The Failure to Communicate: The Communicative Relationship Between C. S. Lewis and His Father," Into the Wardrobe: A C. S. Lewis Website http://cslewis.drzeus.net/papers/failure-to-communicate/ accessed March 12, 2016.

32. McCrary, "The Failure to Communicate."

33. Lewis, *Surprised by Joy*, 38.

34. Lewis, *Surprised by Joy*, 38.

35. Lewis, *Surprised by Joy*, 38.

36. C. S. Lewis, *A Grief Observed* (London: Faber & Faber, 1961), 1.

37. C. S. Lewis, *The Magician's Nephew* (London: Geoffrey Bles, 1955), 27.

38. Lewis, *Surprised by Joy*, 38.

39. A. N. Wilson, *C. S. Lewis: A Biography* (London: HarperCollins, 1990), 15.

40. Joel D. Heck, *Irrigating Deserts: C. S. Lewis on Education* (St. Louis, MO: Concordia Publishing House, 2005), 67.

41. Lewis, *Surprised by Joy*, 175.

42. Allen Jacobs, *The Narnian: the Life and Imagination of C. S. Lewis* (New York: HarperSanFrancisco, 2005), 27.

43. Sayer, *Jack*, 123.

44. Sayer, *Jack*, 88.

45. Harry Lee Poe, *Becoming C. S. Lewis: A Biography of Young Jack Lewis (1898–1963)* (Wheaton: Crossway, 2019), 55.

46. Lewis, *Surprised by Joy*, 175.

47. Lewis, *Surprised by Joy*, 232.

48. Lewis, *Surprised by Joy*, 232.

49. For a discussion of Arthur Greeves's sexual orientation and Lewis's reaction see: Will Vaus, "C. S. Lewis & Homosexuality Revisited," *The Lamppost: C. S. Lewis, Narnia &*

Mere Christianity (August 26, 2013), http://willvaus.blogspot.com/2013/08/c-s-lew-is-homosexuality-revisited.html Accessed July 23, 2019.

50. C. S. Lewis, *The Four Loves* (London: Geoffrey Bles, 1960), 65.
51. Lewis, *The Four Loves*, 65.
52. Lewis, *Surprised by Joy*, 65.
53. Lewis, *Surprised by Joy*, 155.
54. Lewis, *Surprised by Joy*, 153.
55. Lewis, *Surprised by Joy*, 134.
56. Lewis, *Surprised by Joy*, 134.
57. Lewis, *Surprised by Joy*, 134.
58. See: Heck, *Irrigating Deserts,* 72.
59. Lewis, *Surprised by Joy*, 131.
60. Lewis, *Surprised by Joy*, 166.
61. Lewis, *Surprised by Joy*, 141.
62. Lewis, *Surprised by Joy*, 131.
63. C. S. Lewis, Letter to Eliza Marian Butler, September 25, 1940, *Collected Letters II*, ed. Walter Hooper (San Francisco: Harper San Francisco, 2004), 444.
64. Lewis and Tillyard, *The Personal Heresy*, 69.
65. Heck, *Irrigating Deserts*, 88.
66. Heck, *Irrigating Deserts*, 82.
67. Heck, *Irrigating Deserts*, 88.
68. C. S. Lewis, Letter to Albert Lewis July 19, 1951, *The Collected Letters of C. S. Lewis, Vol. I: Family Letters 1905–1931*, ed. Walter Hooper (San Francisco: Harper San Francisco, 2004), 137.
69. Lewis, *Collected Letters I,* 137.
70. Bruce L. Edwards, "Language/Rhetoric," *The C. S. Lewis Readers' Encyclopedia*, ed. J. D. Schultz & J. G. West (Grand Rapids: Zondervan, 1998), 231–232.
71. Edwards, "Language/Rhetoric," 231–232.
72. Lewis, *Surprised by Joy*, 173–183.
73. K. J. Gilchrist, *A Morning After War: C. S. Lewis and WWI* (New York, NY: Peter Lang, 2005).
74. Gilchrist, *A Morning After War*, 1.
75. Gilchrist, *A Morning After War*, 1.
76. For a discussion of reading between the lines see: Jerry Root, *C. S. Lewis and the Problem of Evil* (Eugene: Pickwick, 2009), 118.
77. C. S. Lewis, *Christian Reflections*, ed. Walter Hooper (Grand Rapids: Eerdmans, 1967), 157.
78. Root, *C. S. Lewis and the Problem of Evil*, 118.
79. Gilchrist, *Morning After War*, 9.
80. See: Heck, *Irrigating Deserts*, 84.
81. Clive Hamilton [C. S. Lewis], *Spirits in Bondage* (London: Heinemann, 1919).

82. As reported in: Sayer, *Jack,* 126.

83. Sayer, *Jack*, 126.

84. Sayer, *Jack*. 128.

85. I thank Jerry Root for this observation based on his personal visit to "Mount" Bernechon.

86. See: Sayer, *Jack* (1997 edition), xvii; For a review of Lewis several biographer's conclusions about the relationship between Lewis and Mrs. Moore also see: Harry Lee Poe, *Becoming C. S. Lewis: A Biography of Young Jack Lewis (1898–1963)* (Wheaton: Crossway, 2019), 250–252.

87. Sayre, *Jack* (1997 edition), xvii

88. See: William O'Flaherty with additional contributions by Jerry Root, "Lewis and Mrs. Moore Were Secret Lovers," Mrs. Moore and Jerry Root http://www.essentialcslewis.com/2017/06/10/cmcsl-3-lewis-and-mrs-moore-were-secret-lovers/ Accessed December 11, 2017.

89. Owen Barfield, *Owen Barfield on C. S. Lewis*, ed. G. B. Tennyson (Middletown: Wesleyan University Press, 1989).

90. Sayer, *Jack* (1997 edition), xvii.

91. Sayer, *Jack* (1997 edition), xvii.

92. As reported to Jerry Root based on a personal conversation with John Tolkien, J. R. R. Tolkien's son.

93. Sayer, *Jack*, 128.

94. C. S. Lewis, *All My Road Before Me: The Diary of C. S. Lewis 1922–1927*, ed. Walter Hooper (San Diego: Harcourt Brace Jovanovich, 1991), 393.

95. Personal conversation reported by Jerry Root based on his conversation with John Tolkien, Oxford.

96. Diana Pavlac Glyer, *The Company They Keep: C. S. Lewis and J. R. R. Tolkien as Writers in Community.* (Kent: Kent State University Press, 2007).

97. Glyer, *The Company They Keep*.

98. For a discussion of Tolkien's commentary about *The Chronicles of Narnia* see: Michael Ward, *Planet Narnia: The Seven Heavens in the Imagination of C. S. Lewis* (Oxford: Oxford University Press, 2008).

99. J. R. R. Tolkien, *Letters of J. R. R. Tolkien,* ed. Humphrey Carpenter with Christopher Tolkien (London: George Allen & Unwin, 1981), 302.

100. See: Humphrey Carpenter, *The Inklings: C. S. Lewis, J. R. R. Tolkien, Charles Williams and Their Friends* (London: HarperCollins, 2006).

101. See: Carpenter, *The Inklings*.

102. J. R. R. Tolkien, Letter draft to Michael Tolkien November or December 1963, *The Letters of J. R. R. Tolkien,* ed. Humphrey Carpenter with Christopher Tolkien (Boston: Houghton Mifflin, 1995), 341.

103. Conversation reported by Jerry Root with J. R. R. Tolkien's son, Fr. John Tolkien; J R. R. Tolkien would visit C. S. Lewis weekly during the last few months of Lewis's

life; Correspondence reveals J. R. R. Tolkien was instrumental in Lewis being appointed to the newly created Chair at Cambridge. See: Roger Lancelyn Green and Walter Hooper, *C. S. Lewis: A Biography: Fully Revised and Expanded Edition* (London: HarperCollins, 2002), 341–343; Tolkien, *Letters of J. R. R. Tolkien*, 341.

104. See: Roger Lancelyn Green and Walter Hooper, *C. S. Lewis: A Biography*, 341–343.

105. Tolkien, *Letters of J. R. R. Tolkien*, 341.

106. Lewis, *Surprised by Joy*; McGrath, *C. S. Lewis;* Sayer, *Jack*; also see: Joel Heck, *Irrigating Deserts.*

107. McGrath, *C. S. Lewis*. Although it should be noted that Brendan Wolfe suggests that Lewis could have been referring to the *academic* year of 1929–1930, rather than the calendar year 1929. See: Brendan Wolfe, "A Note on the Date of C. S. Lewis's Conversion to Theism." *Journal of Inklings Studies*, 9 (1), 2019, 68–69

108. Andrew Lazo, "Early Prose Joy': A Brief Introduction," *VII: An Anglo-American Literary Review* Volume 30 (2014). Also see: "'Early Prose Joy': C.S. Lewis's Early Draft of an Autobiographical Manuscript" by C.S. Lewis (a previously unpublished manuscript transcribed by Andrew Lazo) *VII: An Anglo-American Literary Review* Volume 30 (2014).

109. Lewis, *Surprised by Joy*, 41.

110. See: Brendan Wolfe, "*The Inklings* of C. S. Lewis's Conversion to Theism." *Journal of Inklings Studies*, 9 (1), 2019, pp. 68–69

111. Lewis, *Surprised by Joy*, 171.

112. Lewis, *Surprised by Joy*, 211.

113. Lewis, *Surprised by Joy*, 213.

114. Lewis, Letter to Owen Barfield February 3, 1930, *Collected Letters II*, 882.

115. Lewis, *Surprised by Joy,* 215.

116. Lewis, Letter to Arthur Greeves, September 22, 1931, *Collected Letters I, 970.*

117. Lewis, *Surprised by Joy*, 223.

118. Lewis, Letter to Arthur Greeves, October 1, 1931, *Collected Letters I, 974.*

119. Sayer, *Jack*, 351.

120. See: McGrath, *C. S. Lewis*, 322.

121. See: Abigail Santamaria, *Joy: Poet, Seeker, and the Woman Who Captivated C. S. Lewis* (New York: Houghton Mifflin Harcourt Publishing Company, 2015), see: 193 and 215.

122. Don W. King, *Love Sonnets to C. S. Lewis and other Poems* (Grand Rapids: Eerdmans, 2015); also see: Santamaria, *Joy* Chapter 9 and 10.

123. Santamaria, *Joy.* Also see: Patti Callahan, *Becoming Mrs. Lewis* ((Nashville: Thomas Nelson, 2018).

124. Sayer, *Jack*, 352.

125. I thank Andrew Lazo for noting that there is a copy *Mere Christianity* inscribed to Joy Davidman from C. S. Lewis at the Wade Center, Wheaton College, Wheaton, Illinois dated September 16, which suggests the date of the meeting at the Eastgate hotel reported by Sayer may have been in error.

126. Sayer may have misunderstood the name since there does not seem to be a "Phyllis Williams." I thank Andrew Lazo for this research conclusion.

127. Sayer, *Jack,* 352.

128. Sayer, *Jack,* 352.

129. Sayer, *Jack,* 354.

130. Walter Hooper, *C. S. Lewis: A Companion and Guide* (London: HarperCollins, 1996), 61.

131. Hooper, *C. S. Lewis: A Companion and Guide,* 61.

132. Hooper, *C. S. Lewis: A Companion and Guide,* 61,

133. McGrath, *C. S. Lewis,* 525.

134. Sayer, *Jack,* 219.

135. Sayer, *Jack,* 220.

136. Sayer, *Jack,* 220.

137. Sayer, *Jack,* 220.

138. Sayer, *Jack,* 230.

139. Joy's son and Lewis's stepson, Douglas Gresham, suggests that Joy should be credited as a co-author given her extensive work on the manuscript. Personal conversation with Douglas Gresham, November 7, 2019. Also see: Abigail Santamaria, *Joy: Poet, Seeker, and the Woman Who Captivated C. S. Lewis* (New York: Houghton Mifflin, 2015).

140. Santamaria, *Joy,* 297.

141. McGrath, *C. S. Lewis,* 333.

142. *The Times,* Marriage Announcement, December 24 (London, 1956). Also see McGrath, *C. S. Lewis,* 334.

143. For a description of Bide's role in performing the Davidman and Lewis marriage ceremony see: Peter Bide, "Marrying C. S. Lewis," ed. Roger White, Judith Wolfe and Brendan N. Wolfe, *C. S. Lewis & His Circle: Essays and Memoir's from the Oxford C. S. Lewis Society* (Oxford: Oxford University Press, 2015), 187–191.

144. White, Wolfe and Wolfe, *C. S. Lewis,* 340.

145. C. S. Lewis, *English Literature in the Sixteenth Century: Excluding Drama* (Oxford: Clarendon Press, 1954).

146. C. S. Lewis, as quoted by Walter Hooper, *Of Other Worlds: Essays and Stories* (London: Geoffrey Bles, 1966), v.

147. C. S. Lewis, "*Ex Libris,*" *The Christian Century* (June 6, 1962), 719.

148. C. S. Lewis and Sherwood Wirt, "Cross-Examination," *Undeceptions: Essays on Theology and Ethics,* ed. Walter Hooper (London: Geoffrey Bles, 1971), 215–217.

149. Lewis and Wirt, "Cross-Examination," 215–217.

150. Lewis and Wirt, "Cross-Examination," 215–217.

151. Lewis and Wirt, "Cross-Examination," 215–217.

152. See: Heck, *Irrigating Deserts,* 16–17.

153. Sayer, *Jack, xxxiv.*

154. Sayer, *Jack, xxxiv.*

155. Lewis, *Surprised by Joy*, 174.

156. C. S. Lewis, *The Abolition of Man* (Oxford: Oxford University Press, 1943), 27.

157. Heck, *Irrigating Deserts*, 12.

158. Steven A. Beebe, Susan J. Beebe, and Diana K. Ivy, *Communication: Principles for a Lifetime* (Boston: Pearson, 2019), 3.

3

C. S. Lewis's Big Ideas

"Somehow what Lewis thought about everything was secretly present in what he said about anything."[1]

- Owen Barfield

"You'll never get to the bottom of him."[2]

- J. R. R. Tolkien

In a 1931 letter to Arthur Greeves, Lewis confessed that he did not always like his students. He admitted, "In every given year the pupils I really like are in a minority." But he also added, "… but there is hardly a year in which I do not make some real friend. I am glad that people become more and more one of the sources of pleasure as I grow older."[3] For Lewis, "older" meant 33. One of his students who was to become a "real friend" was George Sayer.

Sayer, whose biography of Lewis is considered among the best because he knew Lewis over a span of many years as both teacher and friend, writes of his first experience in meeting Lewis, as well as a chance encounter with one of Lewis's life-long friends, J. R. R. Tolkien. Sayer relates arriving at Magdalen College and searching for Lewis's room in New Building (built in 1734—new for Oxford).[4]

He first sees "Tollers" whom Sayer describes as "a neat, gray-haired man with a pipe in his mouth and a puckish face." Tollers asks, "Are you a pupil come for a tutorial?"

"No," replies Sayer. "But Mr. Lewis is going to be my tutor next term. I've come to find out what he wants me to read during vacation."

"You're lucky in having him as your tutor," Tolkien says.

Sayer goes on to describe how, after he finds Lewis's room up staircase three, Lewis rattles off several poems from memory with gleeful gusto. Then, ever the dutiful professor, Lewis prescribes a list of books for Sayer to read to prepare him for his upcoming studies. As Sayer leaves New Building, he again bumps into "Tollers" who asks, "How did you get on?"

"I think rather well. I think he will be a most interesting tutor to have."

Then "Tollers" responds, "Interesting? Yes, he's certainly that. You'll never get to the bottom of him."[5]

Most people who read Lewis agree with Tolkien: It is unlikely that you will get to the bottom of Clive Staples Lewis. Several compilation books, *A Year with C. S. Lewis, The Wisdom of Aslan, Preparing for Easter: Fifty Devotional Readings from C. S. Lewis* and *The C. S. Lewis Bible* offer bite-sized, edited portions of Lewis for daily reading. Owen Barfield, another of Lewis's friends, legal executor of Lewis's finances, and lifetime intellectual sparring partner, once declared that "Somehow what Lewis thought about everything was secretly present in what he said about anything."[6] To read Lewis is to discover recurring ideas and themes that permeate his books and essays. Lewis had both great depth and breadth of thought, yet several recurring "big" ideas are present, as Barfield suggests, in everything Lewis wrote.[7]

The primary objective of this book is to examine *how* Lewis communicated and *what* he said about communication, language, meaning, and rhetoric. But in addition to his techniques and methods of communication, the question arises, "What did C. S. Lewis communicate *about*?" Before presenting a detailed review of Lewis's principles of communication (HI TEA) introduced in Chapter 1, this chapter distills four themes that can be found in virtually every Lewis book or essay. The "big ideas" surveyed here are not intended to be comprehensive.[8] Lewis had much to say on many topics. Yet four major themes are evident in almost everything he wrote or said, including his correspondence with friends, colleagues, and admiring strangers; and his books, essays, speeches and poems. The big ideas, summarized succinctly, are: (1) Longing, (2) the Tao, (3) Christianity, and (4) Language.

Longing: The Quest to Find Home

Most people, if they had learned to really look into their own hearts, would know that they do want, and want acutely, something that cannot be had in this world. There are all sorts of things in this world that offer to give it to you, but they never quite keep their promise. The longings which arise in us when we first fall in love, or first think of some foreign country, or first take up some subject that really excites us, are longings which no marriage, no travel, no learning, can really satisfy.[9]

These words from *Mere Christianity* express one of the fundamental ideas that permeate Lewis's speaking and writing. There is "something," suggests Lewis, a longing that resides in each person, that is an inherently unquenchable thirst for something more fulfilling than what meets one's senses. Lewis believed that one's heart's desire, an unfulfilled longing, is never completely satisfied, at least not in this realm. He called this yearning *Sehnsucht* (pronounced *Sehn-Zuckt,* which is German for "yearning" or "craving").[10]

Lewis's notion of longing is rooted in Plato's philosophy that in this life one sees only metaphorical shadows appearing on a cave wall. Although one may see only shadows now, a real fire, real people, true events, and authentic objects are in fact the sources of the presently visible shadows. Lewis suggests that people sometimes confuse the shadows on the cave wall for the ultimate "reality" that they cannot see that lies beyond the horizon, that is inherently ineffable. What they long for cannot be cogently articulated because they have not yet seen it. For Lewis, this world is not the ultimate destination. People are each on a quest to find home. They long for their final destination—to be united with The Source of all Truth.

Lewis poignantly captures the notion of longing in his final Narnia book *The Last Battle*. In the last chapter, titled "Farewell to the Shadowlands," he writes about the New Narnia: "The difference between the old Narnia and the new Narnia was like that. The new one was a deeper country: every rock and flower and blade of grass looked like it meant more."[11] And then he puts his key point in the mouth of the unicorn who exclaims,

I have come home at last! This is my real country! I belong here. This is the land I have been looking for all my life, though I never knew it till now. The reason why we loved the old Narnia so much is because it sometimes looked a little like this. Bree-hee-hee! Come further up, come further in![12]

To come "further up" and "further in" is the quest for our true home. From Lewis's perspective, the objects or experiences people may *think* they want are not what their hearts truly desire. In moments of reflection on the pleasantries of our past, they may sometimes call this longing "nostalgia," or the "good old days." But these warm memories of nostalgic, days-of-yore beauty are not the object of their longing. In his sermon *The Weight of Glory* delivered at St. Mary the Virgin, a centuries-old gothic structure in the heart of Oxford; tourists still climb its tower to get a panoramic view of the city. On June 8, 1941, the church was packed as Lewis suggests,

> Wordsworth's expedient was to identify it [longing] with certain moments in his own past. But all this is a cheat. If Wordsworth had gone back to those moments in the past, he would not have found the thing itself, but only the reminder of it; what he remembered would turn out to be itself a remembering. The books or the music in which we thought the beauty was located will betray us if we trust to them; it was not *in* them, it only came *through* them, and what came through them was longing.[13]

Dysfunction occurs, suggests Lewis, when people start to believe that the shadows are real—that what they see is the only reality there is. But according to Lewis, believing that one can obtain what one sees is an error that limits opportunities for true happiness. Continuing with his observations from *The Weight of Glory*, Lewis eloquently describes what humans truly seek:

> These things—the beauty, the memory of our own past—are good images of what we really desire; but if they are mistaken for the thing itself they turn into dumb idols, breaking the hearts of their worshippers. For they are not the thing itself; they are only the scent of a flower we have not found, the echo of a tune we have not heard, news from a country we have never yet visited.[14]

This "news from a country ... never yet visited" is one's ultimate destiny. What one longs for is to be reconnected to the place of one's dreams—the best recollections of the past and the most optimistic hopes for the future. It is this ever-present longing that Lewis believes is an implicit constant in one's life, a yet-to-be-experienced condition.

People's ultimate desire is not for what is evident in this world. They long to be in the presence of God and all that is Holy. For Lewis, another way of expressing longing or desire was embodied in what he described as *Joy* (which he typically spelled with a capital "J"). Lewis titled his autobiography *Surprised by Joy*, taking the phrase from the opening line of a sonnet by Wordsworth:

> Surprised by joy—impatient as the wind[15]

Lewis placed this quotation underneath his title on the title page. The subtitle of his autobiography, *The Shape of My Early Life,* provides documentation that this sense of Joy came early in his life.

Lewis describes seeing the hills outside his window from his childhood home as a metaphor for longing. He recalls, "And every day there were what we called 'the Green Hills'; that is, the low line of the Castlereagh Hills which we saw from the nursery windows. They were not very far off but they were, to children, quite unattainable. They taught me longing—*Sehnsucht* …"[16]

Not only Jack, but also his brother Warnie, links the longing for the distant and unobtainable hills outside the boys' nursery window as a springboard for the brothers' creative powers of imagination: "We would gaze out of our nursery window at the slanting rain and the grey skies, and there, beyond a mile or so of sodden meadow, we would see the dim line of the Castlereagh Hills—our world's limit, a distant land, strange and unattainable."[17]

The fact that people have unquenched longing is evidence, says Lewis, that there is something more. One of Lewis's key arguments for the existence of something, beyond what is empirically evident is the "argument from desire." The essence of the argument, as articulated in *The Problem of Pain,* is this: People desire only that which exists. When they are thirsty, they seek water to quench their thirst. When people are hungry, they seek food. Would people have these needs, desires, and longing for sustenance if these substances did not exist? Theologian and philosopher Peter Kreeft paraphrases the argument from desire with a syllogism, two succinct premises and a conclusion:

Premise 1:   Every natural, innate desire in us corresponds to some real object that can satisfy that desire.

Premise 2:   But there exists in us a desire which nothing in time, nothing on earth, no creature can satisfy.

Conclusion: Therefore there must exist something more than time, earth and creatures, which can satisfy this desire.[18]

In his own words from *Mere Christianity,* here is Lewis's operational definition of the argument from desire:

The Christian says, 'Creatures are not born with desires unless satisfaction for these desires exists. A baby feels hunger; well, there is such a thing as food. A duckling wants to swim; well, there is such a thing as water. Men feel sexual desire; well, there is such a thing as sex. If I find in myself a desire which no experience in this world can satisfy, the most probable explanation is that I was made for another world.[19]

For Lewis, the argument from desire acknowledges that longing itself is evidence that something more exists to satisfy what one seeks—whether one is able to articulate the object of that desire or not. He adds, "If none of my earthly pleasures satisfy it that does not prove that the universe is a fraud. Probably earthly pleasures were never meant to satisfy it, but only to arouse it, to suggest the real thing."[20] From the forests and castles of Narnia to the far-flung vastness of outer space, as described in his Random trilogy (*Out of the Silent Planet, Perelandra, That Hideous Strength*), Lewis's notion of longing or desire permeates both his plots and his characters. Not just Lewis, but his fictional characters, too, are looking for "the real thing." Lucy longs for Aslan. Ransom longs to return home. But like Edmund, who craved Turkish Delight, what people think will satisfy them ultimately does not meet their needs. In Edmund's case, once he came to his senses, Aslan was what he sought.

Within the first five pages of *Surprised by Joy* Lewis adds to his description of experiencing longing by seeing the hills outside his window with another story that describes his "first beauty" which provided an early brush with Joy. He recalls that Warnie showed him the lid of a biscuit tin that was covered with moss, twigs and flowers. Lewis said, "That was the first beauty I ever knew. What the real garden had failed to do, the toy garden did. It made me aware of nature ... As long as I live my imagination of Paradise will retain something of my brother's toy garden."[21]

A few pages later in *Surprised by Joy*, Lewis describes an additional early evocative experience of Joy (what he calls a "memory of a memory") that gave him insight into the "something more" that we seek. As it did for Lewis, longing sometimes catches people unaware. After seeing his brother's toy garden Lewis recalls standing beside a flowering currant bush on a summer day when "there suddenly arose in me without warning, and as if from a depth not of years but of centuries, the memory of that earlier morning at the Old House when my brother had brought his toy garden into the nursery."[22] It was an intense feeling. Lewis adds,

> It is difficult to find words strong enough for the sensation which came over me; Milton's 'enormous bliss' of Eden (giving the full, ancient meaning to "enormous") comes somewhere near it. It was a sensation, of course, of desire, but desire for what? Not, certainly, for a biscuit tin filled with moss, nor even (though that came into it) for my own past ...[23]

Although Lewis's early memories of longing were fleeting and surprising, he remembered them for the rest of his life.

Why is it important to realize that one's longing is not for something that can be satisfied in this life? Lewis believed that if people fail to understand what it is they truly desire, they may seek substitutes for what they *think* will make them happy. Yet earthly pleasures only momentarily appease. People miss the true appreciation for what they ultimately seek if they place their hopes and desires in fleeting, temporary things. Using a memorable metaphor, Lewis explains how weakness for instant gratification often keeps peoples from experiencing Joy. Again from *The Weight of Glory* Lewis explains,

> We are half-hearted creatures, fooling about with drink and sex and ambition when infinite joy is offered us, like an ignorant child who wants to go on making mud pies in a slum because he cannot imagine what is meant by the offer of a holiday at the sea. We are far too easily pleased.[24]

Throughout his works, both fiction and non-fiction, Lewis speaks of the power and importance of longing for that which ultimately satisfies individual needs. In one of his early books, *The Problem of Pain* he invites us to notice,

> … that the books you really love are bound together by a secret thread. You know very well what is the common quality that makes you love them, though you cannot put it into words … That something which you were born desiring, and which beneath the flux of other desires and in all the momentary silences between the louder passions, night and day, year by year from childhood to old age, you are looking for, watching for, listening for.[25]

Again, for Lewis, that "something," often difficult to put into words, is the quest for our true home. (Lewis's idea of a "secret thread" that binds ideas together will be explored later in this book, in a discussion of Lewis's technique of evoking an emotional response from his readers and listeners.)

Here is yet another description of that for which people long. Lewis uses the metaphor of an amplified echo to describe his feelings of Joyful pleasure:

> Tantalizing glimpses, promises never quite fulfilled, echoes that died away just as they caught your ear. But if it should really become manifest—if there ever came an echo that did not die away but swelled into the sound itself—you would know it. Beyond all possibility of doubt you would say, 'Here at last is the thing I was made for.'[26]

What we are made for, believed Lewis, is to ultimately realize that which truly satisfies—God. Lewis further suggests the centrality and importance of this "thing" people were made for, "We cannot tell each other about it. It is the secret signature of each soul ..."[27] Note that this "thing" is "secret" or incommunicable. One may not be able to use words to describe the "thing" for which one longs; perhaps the best one can come up with are metaphors for heaven, but longing is an ever-present echo in people's lives, even when they are unaware of it. One of Lewis's gifts as a communicator is being able to express ineffable ideas in a memorable way.

Lewis links longing and Joy when he defines Joy as "the longing for that unnamable something ..."[28] Joy is sometimes beyond human consciousness, but Lewis believed it an ever-present longing in varying degrees of intensity. Joy is always about the quest for something else, rather than the sensation of Joy itself. As Lewis suggests, "All Joy reminds. It is never a possession, always a desire for something longer ago or further away or still 'about to be'."[29] Joy is embodied in longing: "Only when your whole attention and desire are fixed on something else—whether a distant mountain, or the past, or the gods of Asgard—does the 'thrill' arise. It is a byproduct. Its very existence presupposes that you desire not it but something other and outer."[30] The longing for the "something other and outer" that is ever-present, even when we are not aware of it, is a key theme in Lewis's speaking and writing.

The Tao: Universal Truth

A second big idea for C. S. Lewis is the existence of Natural Law. Lewis believed that a set of objective values or Natural Laws govern the universe in general, and human behavior in particular. Although observations and statements about perceived reality are by nature subjective, that which truly exists is not subjective but objective, embodied in a universal set of values that affirm what is right and what is wrong. As Lewis explains at the beginning of *Mere Christianity*, Natural Law exists, and all of us break the law—doing so is the essence of being human. He explicitly makes two key points, "First, that human beings, all over the earth, have this curious idea that they ought to behave in a certain way, and cannot really get rid of it."[31] His second point, "[human beings] do not in fact behave in that way. They know the Law of Nature; they break it. These two facts are the foundation of all clear thinking about ourselves and the universe we live in."[32]

Lewis's most comprehensive discussion of objective reality appears in *The Abolition of Man*. Here Lewis makes his initial argument for objectivism by pointing to the power of language in challenging the conclusion of what he calls *The Green*

Book by "Gaius" and "Titius." "*The Green Book*" is actually titled *The Control of Language* by Alex King and Martin Ketley.[33] (Lewis's personally annotated copy of *The Control of Language* is in the archives of The Wade Center in Wheaton, Illinois.) Because Lewis was critical of King and Ketley, he decided not to use their names, but to use their example to illustrate his point. "Gaius" and "Titius" suggest that when someone describes a waterfall as "sublime," the utterance is really a statement about the person's feelings rather than a description of the waterfall.[34] Lewis vehemently disagrees. He argues, "If the view held by Gaius and Titius were consistently applied it would lead to obvious absurdities. It would force them to maintain that *You are contemptible* means *I have contemptible feelings*: in fact that *Your feelings are contemptible* means *My feelings are contemptible.*"[35]

"Gaius" and "Titius" claim that the sublime resides only in our mind as a perceived *feeling*. Again, Lewis disagrees. For him the feeling of sublimity is not a mere mental or emotional state; there really is beauty and things are truly sublime. Lewis argues for the existence of "the doctrine of objective value, the belief that certain attitudes are really true, and others really false."[36] Our thoughts are the way we access what is true. "Truth," suggests Lewis scholar Jerry Root, "is what we think about reality."[37]

Lewis calls Natural Law the *Tao*. As defined by Lewis, the Tao "… is Nature, it is the Way, the Road. It is the Way in which the universe goes on, the Way in which things everlastingly emerge, stilly and tranquilly, into space and time"[38] Lewis further spells out what he means by "The Tao" or Natural Law by explicitly describing it for his readers:

> The Tao, which others may call Natural Law or Traditional Morality or the First Principles of Practical Reason or the First Platitudes, is not one among a series of possible systems of value. It is the sole source of all value judgments. If it is rejected, all value is rejected. If any value is retained, it is retained. The effort to refute it and raise a new system of value in its place is self-contradictory. There has never been, and never will be, a radically new judgment of value in the history of the world.[39]

What are examples of universal Natural Laws? In the Appendix to *The Abolition of Man*, Lewis nominates eight Natural Laws or Duties common to all cultures and people for all time. He describes each Law or Duty with illustrations from a wide range of books and sacred sources from diverse cultures and traditions, spanning several millennia. Here is a brief summary of Lewis's operationalization of Natural Law:

1. *The Law of General Beneficence*: Do not murder, do not be dishonest, or take from others what does not belong to you.
2. *The Law of Special Beneficence*: Value your family members.
3. *Duties to Parents, Elders, and Ancestors*: Especially hold your parents, those who are a generation older than you, and your ancestors with special honor and esteem.
4. *Duties to Children and Posterity*: Respect the rights of the young, and value those who will come in later generations.
5. *The Law of Justice*: Honor the basic human rights of others; each person is of worth.
6. *The Law of Good Faith and Veracity*: Keep your promises, and do not lie.
7. *The Law of Mercy*: Be compassionate to those less fortunate than you are.
8. *The Law of Magnanimity*: Avoid unnecessary violence against other people.[40]

Lewis does not claim that all people and all cultures abide by these laws, only that they are standards or enduring values that serve as the framework for what is right and what is wrong. The eight Natural Laws that Lewis identifies are also not meant to be comprehensive, but illustrative. Lewis modestly notes the following in his preamble to the description of the eight Natural Laws:

> [T]he Natural Law is collected from such sources as come readily to the hand of one who is not a professional historian. The list makes no pretense of completeness … But (1) I am not trying to *prove* its validity by the argument from common consent. Its validity cannot be deduced. For those who do not perceive its rationality, even universal consent could not prove it. (2) The idea of collecting *independent* testimonies presupposes that "civilizations" have arisen in the world independently of one another; or even that humanity has had several independent emergences on this planet. The biology and anthropology involved in such an assumption are extremely doubtful.[41]

This fundamental belief in the nature of right and wrong permeates all of Lewis's writing. Four works in particular describe his belief in objective reality and the enduring Natural Laws that shape human thought. In addition to *The Abolition of Man*, his essay "The Poison of Subjectivism" explains his view of the nature of objective truth. Third, he titled Book I of *Mere Christianity* "Right and Wrong As A Clue to the Meaning of the Universe," and Chapter 1 as "The Law of Human Nature."[42] Fourth, Lewis notes in the preface to *That Hideous Strength* that the novel is yet another effort to illustrate the ideas he made explicit in *The Abolition of Man*. The notion of Natural Law (the Tao) is also evident in his poems, fiction, and non-fiction. As Lewis scholar Jerry Root confirms, "… additional evidence for his position [about objectivism] is scattered throughout his work."[43] Whether in his Narnia stories, correspondence between devils in *The Screwtape Letters*, or his letters to his friends, acquaintances, and admirers, Lewis consistently refers to an enduring sense of right and wrong—a big idea for Lewis, who also hopes it will be a big idea for his readers. Lewis's sense of right and wrong is anchored in his Christian beliefs. Once he embraced Christianity, the existence of the Tao influenced his worldview, including his focus as a speaker and author.

Christianity: Lewis's Primary Sense-Making Lens

Christianity is the third big idea that percolates through all of Lewis's post-Christian conversion work. For Lewis, Christianity eventually became the best possible explanation for making sense out of the world in which he lived. Christianity is practical. One of Lewis's most famous quotations—the one that appears on his memorial stone in Westminster Abbey—is: "I believe in Christianity as I believe that the sun has risen not only because I see it but because by it I see everything else."[44] For Lewis, Christianity helped him view the world as less bewildering. As noted in the previous chapter, communication is "The process of making sense out of the world and sharing that sense with others by creating meaning through the use of verbal and nonverbal messages."[45] For Lewis, his belief in Christianity was his primary sense-making lens that influenced how he shared his message with others.

Although Lewis was born into a Christian home, as chronicled in Chapter 2, he drifted to atheism in his teens and twenties after leaving the comforts of home following the death of his mother. Of his Atheist days he writes, "I was at this time living, like so many Atheists or Antitheists, in a whirl of contradictions. I maintained that God did not exist. I was also very angry with God for not existing. I was equally angry with Him for creating a world."[46] He was angry at many things: his mother's death, being shuttled off to boarding school, and a deteriorating relationship with his father. He also had several tutors who were role-model Atheists, including his influential tutor Kirkpatrick "The Great Knock." Life's hard knocks provided *prima facie* evidence that there was no mythic Grand Story, only the story he experienced.

Following his conversion at age 32 (almost 33), a gradual process that took years to unfold, Lewis's writing and speaking, both his productivity and substance, was transformed. In *Surprised by Joy*, Lewis summarizes his journey to faith as a struggle noting

> The two hemispheres of my mind were in sharpest conflict. On the one side, a many-islanded sea of poetry and myth; on the other, a glib and shallow rationalism. Nearly all that I loved I believed to be imaginary; nearly all that I believed to be real I thought grim and meaningless.[47]

The contrast between the image of "a many-islanded sea of poetry and myth" and "a glib and shallow rationalism" is clear. Lewis's own description of his conversion experience provided the link between his Christian worldview and his life's vocation. He admits he was not certain others would find his come-to-faith story of interest and advises in the preface of *Surprised by Joy*, "I have tried to so write the first chapter that those who can't bear such a story will see at once what they are in for and close the book with the least waste of time."[48] Vintage Lewis: If it doesn't interest you, just skip it.

Lewis's Christian faith illuminated his thought and works. From his first novel, *Pilgrim's Regress*, written shortly after his conversion, to his last book, *Spencer's Images of Life*, compiled from lecture notes by Alastair Fowler and published four years after his death, Lewis's Christian worldview was a dominant theme. In one of the last interviews he gave before his death, he was asked about his conversion by journalist and author Sherwood Eliot Wirt:

Wirt: I believe it was Chesterton who was asked why he became a member of the church, and he replied, "To get rid of my sins." At this point I was surprised by the suddenness of Professor Lewis' reply.

Lewis: It is not enough to want to get rid of one's sins. We also need to believe in the One who saves us from our sins. Not only do we need to recognize that we are sinners; we need to believe in a Savior who takes away sin. Matthew Arnold once wrote, 'Nor does the being hungry prove that we have bread.' Because we know we are sinners, it does not follow that we are saved.

Wirt: In your book *Surprised by Joy* you remark that you were brought into the faith kicking and struggling and resentful, with eyes darting in every direction looking for an escape. You suggest that you were compelled, as it were, to become a Christian. Do you feel that you made a decision at the time of your conversion?

Lewis: I would not put it that way. What I wrote in *Surprised by Joy* was that 'before God closed in on me, I was offered what now appears a moment of wholly free choice.' But I feel my decision was not so important. I was the object rather than the subject in this affair. I was decided upon. I was glad afterwards at the way it came out, but at the moment what I heard was God saying, 'Put down your gun and we'll talk.'

Wirt: That sounds to me as if you came to a very definite point of decision.

Lewis: Well, I would say that the most deeply compelled action is also the freest action. By that I mean, no part of you is outside the action. It is a paradox. I expressed it in *Surprised by Joy* by saying that I chose, yet it really did not seem possible to do the opposite.[49]

Lewis made a decision not only to convert to Christianity but also what he would believe about Christianity. What was Lewis's credo? In his autobiography, in the chapter titled "Checkmate," he quotes George MacDonald saying, "The one principle of *hell* is—'I am my own.'"[50] Or, as he suggests in *The Problem of Pain*, the doors of Hell are locked on the inside.[51] He further clarified in *The Great Divorce*, "There are only two kinds of people in the end: those who say to God, 'Thy will be done,' and those to whom God says, in the end, 'Thy will be done.' All that are in Hell, choose it. Without that self-choice there could be no Hell."[52] A fundamental Christian principle for Lewis is that one should focus on God, not on oneself. Self focus results in pride—which Lewis labels "the great sin."[53]

Lewis's *Mere Christianity* is a good place to find his credo; there he presents ideas about Christianity that he hopes all Christians can support. "Mere" Christianity, as noted in Chapter 1, refers to what all Christian denominations have in common throughout the history of Christianity. Although he was a member of the Anglican Church, Lewis was not concerned about proselytizing a non-believer to join a specific denomination. He would rather someone find a Christ-centered church community that was meaningful to that individual, than engage in debates about which denomination is "the best." He makes this point clear when he says, "You will not learn from me whether you ought to become an Anglican, a Methodist, a Presbyterian, or a Roman Catholic." For Lewis, mere, or essential Christianity

... is more like a hall out of which doors open into several rooms. If I can bring anyone into that hall I shall have done what I attempted. But it is in the rooms, not in the hall, that there are fires and chairs and meals. The hall is a place to wait in, a place from which to try the various doors, not a place to live in.[54]

Lewis's belief was not something that only influenced his church-going habits on Sundays. He lived his faith. According to Walter Hooper, "Most Christians seem to have two kinds of lives, their so-called 'real' life and their so-called 'religious' one. Not Lewis."[55]

Lewis opens book two of *Mere Christianity*, "What Christians Believe," by clarifying what Christians should *not* believe. He states, "If you are a Christian you do not have to believe that all the other religions are simply wrong all through. If you are an atheist you do have to believe that the main point in all the religions of the whole world is simply one huge mistake."[56] Christians, suggests Lewis, "are free to think that all these religions, even the queerest one, contain at least some hint of the truth."[57]

Lewis's core beliefs start with the concept of God. He opens his discussion of "What Christians Believe" with the chapter title "The Rival Conceptions of God." He notes, "When you are arguing against Him you are arguing against the very power that makes you able to argue at all."[58] Lewis often admits that some of his ideas about God are "only guesses" and frequently reminds his readers that he is not a member of the clergy. He views God as not some formless force like "tapioca pudding," but a real person, "God Himself, alive, pulling at the other end of the cord, perhaps approaching at an infinite speed, the hunter, king, husband …"[59] God, according to Lewis, is "beyond personality"—the title of his third volume of BBC talks, published in 1944 and included in *Mere Christianity* in 1952.

Lewis believed in the existence of the Trinity and described the persons of God as eternally existent in God the Father, God the Son, and the Holy Spirit. He also believed that Jesus Christ has special significance as savior. In *The Lion, The Witch and the Wardrobe*, Mr. and Mrs. Beaver describe Aslan, the Christ figure. Mrs. Beaver explains,

> "If there's anyone who can appear before Aslan without their knees knocking, they're either braver than most or else just silly."
>
> "Then he isn't safe?" said Lucy.
>
> "Safe?" said Mr. Beaver, "Don't you hear what Mrs. Beaver tells you? Who said anything about safe? 'Course he isn't safe. But he's good. He's the King, I tell you."
>
> "I'm longing to see him," said Peter, "even if I do feel frightened when it comes to the point."
>
> "That's right, Son of Adam," said Mr. Beaver, bringing his paw down on the table with a crash that made all the cups and saucers rattle. "And so you shall …"[60]

Mr. Beaver's explicitly noting that "He's the King, I tell you" makes it clear that Aslan, as the Christ figure, is a significant and powerful force in Narnia. (Also note that Peter is "longing to see him," which exemplifies the first of Lewis's big ideas discussed in this chapter.)

A key element of Lewis's faith was his belief in life after death. Many of his beliefs about death are summarized in his last Narnia book, *The Last Battle*. Lewis's depiction of death and the eternal nature of the soul, from the final chapter, "Farewell to Shadowlands," is often used at funerals to describe death metaphorically:

> "There was a real railway accident," said Aslan softly. "Your father and mother and all of you are–as you used to call it in the Shadowlands–dead. The term is over: the holidays have begun. The dream is ended: this is the morning."

> And as He spoke He no longer looked to them like a lion; but the things that began to happen after that were so great and beautiful that I cannot write them. And for us this is the end of all the stories, and we can most truly say that they all lived happily ever after. But for them it was only the beginning of the real story. All their life in this world and all their adventures in Narnia had only been the cover and the title page: now at last they were beginning Chapter One of the Great Story which no one on earth has read: which goes on forever: in which every chapter is better than the one before.[61]

This passage is in stark contrast to Lewis's understanding of death as a nine-year-old boy grieving the loss of his mother. His description of life being nothing but "sea and islands now,"[62] and his and his father's and brother's operatic despair, certainly a normal and natural response to the loss of a cherished wife and mother, was dramatically different from his discussion of death after he became a Christian. Once when bidding farewell to his good friend, Sheldon Vanauken, on leaving each other at the Eastgate Hotel in Oxford, Lewis shouted across the road, "Christians never say goodbye."[63] The implication is clear: Death is not the end.

Another illustration of Lewis's transformative, Christian view of death is powerfully presented in the last chapter of *The Silver Chair*. Eustace and Jill discover the dead body of their friend Prince Caspian beneath the water of a stream, looking as pale and withered as one might expect. Aslan tells Eustace to grasp a thorn and force it into his paw. A drop of blood mingles with the water over the dead prince. And then something most unusual occurs:

> The dead King began to be changed. His white beard turned to gray, and from gray to yellow, and got shorter and vanished altogether; and his sunken cheeks grew round and fresh, and the wrinkles were smoothed, and his eyes opened, and his eyes and lips both laughed, and suddenly he leaped up and stood before them—a very young man or a boy. (But Jill couldn't say which, because of people having no particular ages in Aslan's country ...) And he rushed to Aslan and

flung his arms as far as they would go round the huge neck; and he gave Aslan the strong kisses of a King, and Aslan gave him the wild kisses of a Lion.[64]

As with the depiction of the Pevense family in the "Great Story," the resurrection scene of Prince Caspian is a far different encounter with death than what Lewis had with his mother, or what he would experience with the death of his wife Joy on July 13, 1960.

For Lewis, to be a Christian does not mean to doubt the existence of evil in the world. To the contrary, in a chapter in *Mere Christianity* entitled "The Shocking Alternative," Lewis describes his belief in "the dark power" or evil. Each person has free will to make his or her own decisions about what is right and wrong.[65] His well-loved *Screwtape Letters* is fiction, but based on his belief that Satan exists, that there is an evil presence in the world, and we have a choice to make.[66] We experience pain—a problem that exists, memorably described in Lewis's book *The Problem of Pain*, because we have free will to make a choice between good and evil.[67]

Lewis re-asserts a rational argument, known as the "Liar, Lunatic, Lord Trilemma," to make a case for the divinity of Jesus as Christ. This argument has a long Christian tradition that can be traced to St. Augustine. Some of Lewis's critics find "the Trilemma" argument to be overly reductionist and simplistic; others deride the argument for logically omitting other possibilities.[68] Yet other believers have found it helpful in boiling down the idea of Jesus's divinity to its essence. We should not say that Jesus was merely a great moral teacher. As Lewis framed the argument, "A man who was merely a man and said the sort of things Jesus said would not be a great moral teacher. He would either be a lunatic—on the level with the man who says he is a poached egg—or else he would be the Devil of Hell. You must make your choice. Either this man was, and is, the Son of God, or else a madman or something worse."[69]

Lewis suggests people have a choice to make: Jesus was either a liar, crazy, or who he said he was—the son of God.

Because Lewis believed that truth does not go out of fashion, he also rejected the idea that newer is always better and "the assumption that whatever has gone out of date is on that count discredited."[70] As a Christian, he believed that God is the same yesterday, today, and forever.[71] He suggested that the latest thinking, newest theory, or most contemporary idea is not evidence for its superiority. He explains, "All that is not eternal is eternally out of date."[72] As he learned from his friend Owen Barfield, the tendency to favor the new over "the classic" is pejoratively labeled "chronological snobbery."[73] Lewis was not against an idea because it was contemporary, but he did not believe that "new" always trumped being true. Lewis realized his disdain for chronological snobbery did not always make him popular with those who were enamored with the modern world. In his 1954 inaugural lecture at Cambridge, he self-deprecatingly labeled himself a dinosaur and as someone more comfortable with the Old World Order.[74] In his closing line he urged his audience to learn from their elders using himself as an example: "Speaking not only for myself but for all other Old Western men whom you may meet, I would say, use your specimens while you can. There are not going to be many more dinosaurs."[75]

Lewis's popularity as an apologist, a defender of the faith, is a testament to his skill in using language. As noted in Chapter 1, it is Lewis's talent for writing about language and meaning that makes him a Professor of Communication.

Language: Metaphorical Shaper of Thought and Meaning

A fourth big idea of C. S. Lewis comes from his insights about the power, importance, and centrality of language in helping people make sense out of what they experience. Lewis loved language. His interest in language is the cornerstone of the ideas presented in this book. He understood language's power and significance. Both Jack and Joy relished a competitive game of Scrabble—played in multiple languages![76] Some of his clearest memories about his education were recalling tutors who taught him how to think and speak.

Lewis's ideas about longing, Natural Law, and Christianity are connected with how he viewed language. For Lewis, language (symbols that help people make sense of the world) and the assumptions people have about that which is good, beautiful, and true are related. It is through language that one articulates longing, and acknowledges objective truth—infused with a Christian belief in grace and eternity.

Lewis scholar and rhetorician James Como powerfully summarizes how often the nature of language and the use of words played a significant role in Lewis's works, both fiction and non-fiction:

> Not only did Lewis indulge in speech always and everywhere, he viewed it as fundamental to our human nature, our redeemable nature. 'Talking too much is one of my vices, by the way,' he wrote to a correspondent in 1956. But they are the Talking Beasts of Narnia who know Aslan; it is the uttering of nonsense

that effects the demise of the N.I.C.E. in *That Hideous Strength*; it is the hearing of a voice that alters the destiny of John the Pilgrim in *The Pilgrim's Regress*; and Ransom is a philologist whose training and skill enable him to speak with—and thus to dwell among and befriend—the creatures of Malacandra in *Out of the Silent Planet*, creatures who thereafter no longer seem as strange as their mere appearance first suggested.[77]

Lewis's trio of science fiction books offers clues as to the importance of language. In *Out of the Silent Planet* the planet is silent because it does not communicate with its creator—in this instance, lack of communication is a bad thing that leads to disastrous consequences. Ransom, the protagonist of *Out of the Silent Pla*net, is a philologist (one who studies the cultural importance and historical context of words). As the late Bruce Edwards, a renowned Lewis scholar has noted, "Ransom … discovers much of what it means to be human—and by contrast, inhuman—in his exploration of the language and contrasting roles and means of communication among sorns, hrossa, and pfifltriggi on Malacandra."[78]

In *Perelandra*, the second book in the trilogy, the role and importance of language is also evident. Edwards suggests, "Ransom discovers to his horror the limitations of words and the end of mere reason when he reluctantly obeys the command to kill the Unman with an act of physical courage."[79]

The title of Lewis's last book in his Ransom trilogy, *That Hideous Strength*, comes from a line in a 1555 poem *The Monarche*, by Scottish herald Sir David Lyndsay, that refers to the miscommunication that occurs at the Tower of Babel. Lewis's fictional institute Belbury "disintegrates into a Babel of violence, as language ceases to 'mean,' and cacophonous evil is conquered in a reversal of Pentecost."[80]

Lewis remained interested in words and meaning throughout his academic career. His essay "The Death of Words" provides an indication of his ideas about the evolving nature of words and meaning. "When," suggests Lewis toward the end of the essay, "you have killed a word you have also, as far as in you lay, blotted from the human mind the thing that word originally stood for."[81] To make certain his point is explicitly clear, he adds, "Men do not long continue to think what they have forgotten how to say."[82] Words, Lewis suggests, are central to helping people frame what to think, say, experience, remember, and forget.

It is unfortunate that Lewis and Tolkien did not finish their collaboration on a book about the nature of language and its link to human behavior. If completed, it might have provided a more comprehensive view of Lewis and Tolkien's insights about words, language, and meaning. Lewis told Chad Walsh, who visited him in the summer of 1948, that this book was to be called *Language and Human Nature* and was to be published the following year by the Student Christian Movement Press. But this plan never came to fruition. Readers will have to be content gleaning what they can from the fragment that exists as well as mining Lewis's writing for insights about and applications of language.

Lewis's belief in Natural Law impacts not only his theological ideas, but also his assumptions about the nature of meaning, and how meaning is discovered by the words people use. Although each person may have a particular point of view, meaning is *discovered*, just as truth is discovered. Lewis notes that subjectivism, the "belief that can invent 'ideologies' at pleasure ..." impacts human communication. He suggests that such a subjective point of view "begins to affect our very language."[83]

Meaning does not occur randomly or accidently. Lewis rejected well-known linguist and rhetorician I. A. Richards's view of language and meaning, which, in essence, suggests that people *associate* meaning with a given word based on their experience. Richards and his colleague, Charles Kay Ogden, believed that words take on meaning as the words of others are (mostly) arbitrarily associated with the thing the word represents. For Lewis, however, meaning was not happenstance or subjective. Meaning is *discovered* based on what exists. Influenced by his close friend Owen Barfield, Lewis believed that because there *is* objective reality, there is also a true meaning that words metaphorically reflect. All language about supersensibles (Lewis's term for those things beyond sensory experience) is metaphorical rather than indiscriminately associated with meaning. As Lewis makes clear, ". . . if we are going to talk at all about things which are not perceived by the senses, we are forced to use language metaphorically."[84] The symbols we used are metaphorically rather than randomly linked to that which the symbol refers.

The story is told that when I. A. Richards came to Oxford to give a lecture, his host for the evening was C. S. Lewis. Richards stayed at rooms in Magdalen College and asked for a book to read upon retiring to bed. The book Lewis brought for Richards to read was Richards's own *Principles of Literary Criticism*, along with Lewis's sarcastic reverie, "Here's something that should put you to sleep." Because the margins of Lewis's copy of Richards's authored book were filled with Lewis's biting criticism, Richards did not have a restful evening.[85]

In addition to debunking the arbitrary association theory of language and meaning, Lewis also rejected the philosophy of logical positivism, which suggests that only knowledge that can be verified by direct, empirical observation is meaningful. Logical positivists believe that if one cannot see, hear, taste, touch, or smell it—measure it with empirical methods—then there is no evidence that "it," whatever it is, exists. If logical positivists had a bumper sticker, it might well be: *What you see is what you get.*

The philosophy of logical positivism has implications for the use of language. For Lewis, language could indeed refer to that which may not have tangible referents but still expresses important, intangible ideas. God exists although God may not be visible. It is through metaphor, comparison, stories, supposal, and myth that people can communicate about that which may not be scientifically verifiable.

Several Lewis literary scholars see Lewis's use, application, and description of language as a central element in his work. As Bruce Edwards notes, "Lewis saw language as a gift bequeathed to humans by a Creator-God whose own defining attributes include an ability to speak and create through speech."[86] Language, especially human speech that Lewis bestowed on the talking animals of Narnia, is a consistent topic in his work.

Lewis knew that language has limits. There are times when language simply will not get a reader or listener where he or she needs to be. Sometimes a gap exists between that which one wishes to express and the inherent restrictions of language to express those ideas to others. Philosopher Ludwig Wittgenstein famously says, "The limits of my language are the limit of my world."[87] Lewis would agree that language has its limitations. But he would not agree with the logical positivists that language can refer only to that which is sensory or observable. In a passage explicitly commenting on the role of language as a medium for communication, Lewis notes,

> Language exists to communicate whatever it can communicate. Some things it communicates so badly that we never attempt to communicate them by words if any other medium is available ... For precisely what language can hardly do at all, and never does well, is to inform us about complex physical shapes and movements.[88]

Lewis believed that limiting language only to observables and things that can be empirically verifiable restricts what language can communicate.

Arguing that language is, for the most part, inadequate to describe God and things eternal, Lewis suggests that metaphors of Jesus "coming down from heaven" and the image of the Son "sitting at the right hand of the Father" are sometimes the best that humans can do, although they need to be aware that these are metaphors. After describing his ideas about resurrection and the last judgment in *Letters to Malcolm*, Lewis emphasizes that his metaphors and descriptions of the divine are "Guesses, of course, only guesses. If they are not true, something better will be."[89] Metaphorical language is sometimes the best (or only) possible way to describe something that transcends literal description. Lewis also addresses the inadequacy of language to describe the Divine in his essay "Horrid Red Things": "To say that God 'enters' the natural order involves just as much spatial imagery as to say that he "comes down"; one has simply substituted horizontal (or undefined) for vertical movement ..."[90] For Lewis, language, inherently inadequate to describe some experiences, must rely on metaphor to express the ineffable. Lewis notes,

> All language, except above objects of sense, is metaphorical through and through. To call God a 'force' (that is, something like a wind or a dynamo) is as metaphorical as to call Him a Father or a King. On such matters we can make our language more polysyllabic and duller: we can not make it more literal.[91]

In supporting Lewis's assumptions about the importance of metaphor and comparisons to communicate, Lewis scholar Kath Filmer confirms, "By means of metaphor, Lewis engages in imaginative sub-creation and maintains the traditional links between reality and fantasy, between what is known and what is unknown."[92] It is metaphor that makes the link between the known and the unknown. Filmer further elaborates on Lewis's technique:

> When language is used to describe insensibles such as causes, relations, mental states and thoughts, that language, of necessity, is deeply metaphorical. Metaphor instructs, argues, and persuades by analogy, but because of its imaginative function it gives the reader delight and pleasure as well as fulfilling its function of widening his experiential perception of unseen realities.[93]

In his essay "The Language of Religion," another example of Lewis's interest in communication, Lewis discusses the advantages and disadvantages of three kinds of language: Ordinary, Scientific, and Poetic. Each kind of language has its place. Ordinary or everyday language is a fine style to express the basic, day-to-day aspects of life. In other instances, however, more precise, scientific language is needed, not only for scientists, but for those who need to provide a specific, detailed, and accurate summary of facts and events. Poetic language uses metaphor and other figurative words to express sensations or implicit meaning that may lie in "between the words."[94] Whereas ordinary or scientific language *describes*, poetic language *evokes* meaning.

Poetic language was of special interest to Lewis. He would sometimes compose a poem for pleasure, as he did when I discovered this poem written on the back of the manuscript of "The Language of Religion" in the Oxford University Bodleian Library. Just as he was writing about the function of poetic language on page 6, Lewis apparently turned his manuscript page over and wrote a poem, which until 2016 was unknown and unpublished.[95] Here, published for the first time, is the "poem doodle," that Lewis dashed off, displaying his delight in language.[96] It showcases Lewis's playful application of language—in this case, how the prefixes "dis" and "un" can dramatically and with good humor change the meaning of words:

Patruae Verbera Linguae

Dear me, how different you are,
Penelope, from Grandmamma!
Words with the prefix *Dis-* or *Un-*
Alone describe the course you run.
While grandmamma from early youth
Was shevelled, gainly, kempt, and couth.
No sudden crisis ever caught
Her otherwise than turbed and traught;
She suffered fools with modest dain
And sent them gruntled home again,
And then—however long they'd stayed—
Some paraging remark she made,
Nay, even for prettiest female friends
Foretold, and wished, more astrous ends.

If you, dear Pen, prove such as she,
Oh how appointed I shall be!

The poem is in the style of Horace, and the title, *Patruae Verbera Linguae,* is derived from Horace's Ode XII. Lewis's knowledge of Greek poets and poetic forms is not surprising. He knew many languages. He was especially skilled in Greek and Latin, as evidenced by his receiving a First (exceptionally high honors) in "Greats"—that included the study of Greek and Latin.

His interest in languages paralleled his interest in poetry. His early career aspirations were to be a poet. The commemoration of Lewis with a plaque in Poet's Corner in Westminster Abbey is not primarily for his contributions to poetry *per se*, but for his contribution to the canon of ideas expressed in poetic language. In the sermon preached at Lewis's memorial service in November 2013, exactly fifty years after Lewis's death, former Archbishop of Canterbury, The Right Reverend Dr. Rowan Williams suggested that one of Lewis's greatest legacies was his shining a light on the importance of words to both illuminate and confuse. As Williams noted, "The liberation of words is essential to the liberation of our human nature. Indeed … as Lewis says in his last and perhaps greatest fictional work, *Till We Have Faces*. We uncover ourselves to the truth. Because God sees us in the face, we discover we have a reality, a truth, a face, and words to speak."[97] Literary critic Perry Bramlett accurately paraphrases Lewis's assumptions about the role of poetic language when he notes, "… poetic language is remarkable and becomes religious [because it] … points us toward something outside our own experience, like a road map."[98]

Language, whether Ordinary, Scientific or Poetic, and its power both to reveal and to obfuscate are themes running throughout Lewis's writing. The nature of words and language is a big idea that is central to Lewis's thought and messages. C. S. Lewis believed that words, used well, can help us cut through the babble and confusion to reflect the true nature of this life and beyond. A misunderstanding about the nature of words and meaning—the control of language—can ultimately result in one's own abolition. Yet when used effectively, words can help one describe what is out of sight beyond the horizon and imagine new and future events.

Summary: Lewis's Big Ideas

Lewis wrote in a variety of genres (seventeen by one count)[99] and on a wide range of topics, including the history of language, the allegorical nature of love, the evolving nature of language and meaning, and prayer. Although Lewis wrote in numerous styles and formats on a variety of topics, what he wrote and spoke about had consistent, recurring themes. The four big ideas discussed in this chapter—(1) longing, (2) the Tao, (3) Christianity, and (4) language—are certainly not his only big ideas, but they are evident in virtually all of his writing, from fiction to poetry to his academic work.

Longing

Sehnsucht—a yearning and craving for one's true home which is not completely attainable in this life. Here people only catch a glimpse of the ultimate Joy they seek. Lewis describes the notion of longing in several works, including early childhood memories of a view out his nursery window, as well as phrased poetically as the longing for "news from another country we have never yet visited."[100] Humans were made for another world. That people desire more than meets their senses is evidence that there is something more than they see at the present time. Whether that "something" is a desire to return to Narnia once experienced, or a realization, in quiet moments, that there is more to life than what one sees, longing is one of Lewis's key themes in virtually everything he wrote. "Joy" is a response to catching a glimpse for the "unnamable something" that we desire—but Joy is not what we ultimately seek. As Lewis eloquently stated,

> "If we find ourselves with a desire that nothing in this world can satisfy, the most probable explanation is that we were made for another world."[101]

The Tao

Lewis was consistent in his belief in the existence of Natural Law—an enduring, set of values that intuitively provide a universal "Magna Carta," guiding assumptions proclaiming what is true, good and beautiful. His most comprehensive summary of arguments in favor of Natural Law appears in *The Abolition of Man*. Yet throughout all of his writing, in his fiction (such as *That Hideous Strength*) as well as non-fiction (*Mere Christianity*), his belief in the existence of enduring principles of what is right and wrong inform his work.

Christianity

Lewis's Christian belief was a "big idea" that influenced all other ideas and paradigms in both his professional and personal life. His closest friends and eventually the person he would marry were Christians. Arguably, Lewis may have made his professional mark without being a Christian, but his pre-Christian books were not widely hailed as masterpieces. His Christian beliefs and Christian writing and speaking are what made him the memorable person he has become. Lewis's Credo, his statement of what he believed about Christianity is summarized in *Mere Christianity*.

Language

Lewis was a scholar of words and their meanings. His second degree at Oxford was in English Literature and *Language*. He spoke multiple languages. So it is not surprising that his interest in language influenced his writing, speaking and teaching. His students uniformly recall his precision in demanding that they use the right word to express their ideas. Although he would probably not describe himself as a professional philologist (a person who studies the history of word meaning within a cultural context), he made the study of words his hobby. His friend and colleague, J. R. R. Tolkien, was a philologist and the book (*Language and Human Nature*) that they were to have written together likely would have taken a philological focus.

Lewis's "big ideas" were what he communicated about. But it is the way he communicated that occupies the focus for the rest of this book. Drawing upon his own words, the chapters ahead identify what made C. S. Lewis a skilled communication craftsperson that make his ideas so enduring.

Notes

1. Owen Barfield, *Owen Barfield on C. S. Lewis*, ed. G. B. Tennyson (Middletown: Wesleyan University Press, 1989), 121–122.
2. J. R. R. Tolkien, as quoted by George Sayer, *Jack: A Life of C. S. Lewis* (Wheaton: Crossway Books, 1994), xvii
3. C. S. Lewis, Letter to Arthur Greeves December 6, 1931, *They Stand Together: The Letters of C. S. Lewis to Arthur Greeves 1914–1963*, ed. Walter Hooper (London: Collins, 1979), 434.
4. George Sayer, *Jack: A Life of C. S. Lewis* (Wheaton: Crossway Books, 1994), xvii.
5. Sayer, *Jack*, xvii
6. Owen Barfield, *Owen Barfield on C. S. Lewis*, 121–122.
7. For a detailed summary of key Lewis ideas see: Walter Hooper, "Key Ideas," *C. S. Lewis: Companion & Guide* (San Francisco: Harper SanFrancisco, 1996), 549–613
8. Hooper, "Key Ideas." Also see: Jeffrey D. Schultz and John G. West Jr. ed. *The C. S. Lewis Readers' Encyclopedia* (Grand Rapids: Zondervan, 1998).
9. C. S. Lewis, *Mere Christianity* (London: Geoffrey Bles, 1952), 135.
10. Lewis, *Mere Christianity*, 135.
11. C. S. Lewis, *The Last Battle* (London: Geoffrey Bles, 1956), 181.
12. Lewis, *The Last Battle*, 172.
13. C. S. Lewis, "The Weight of Glory," *Theology: A Monthly Review* 43, No. 257 (November 1941), 265–266.

14. Lewis, "The Weight of Glory," 266.

15. William Wordsworth as printed in, *Surprised by Joy*, Also see: William Wordsworth, The Poetry Foundation http://www.poetryfoundation.org/poem/180628 Accessed March 14, 2016.

16. Lewis, *Surprised by Joy*, 14.

17. Warren Lewis, as cited by Devin Brown, *A Life Observed: A Spiritual Biography of C. S. Lewis* (Grand Rapids: Brazos Press, 2013), 21.

18. Peter Kreeft, *Handbook of Christian Apologetics and Argument from Desire*. http://www.peterkreeft.com/topics/desire.htm. Accessed March 14, 2016.

19. Lewis, *Mere Christianity*, 108.

20. Lewis, *Mere Christianity*, 108.

21. Lewis, *Surprised by Joy*, 14.

22. Lewis, *Surprised by Joy*, 16

23. Lewis, *Surprised by Joy*, 16.

24. Lewis, "The Weight of Glory," 263.

25. C. S. Lewis, *The Problem of* Pain (London: Centenary Press, 1940), 133.

26. Lewis, *The Problem of Pain*, 133.

27. Lewis, *The Problem of Pain*, 134.

28. C. S. Lewis, *The Pilgrim's Regress: An Allegorical Apology for Christianity, Reason and Romanticism* (London: J. M. Dent and Sons, 1933).

29. Lewis, *Surprised by Joy*, 89.

30. Lewis, *Surprised by Joy*, 195.

31. Lewis, *Mere Christianity*, 21.

32. Lewis, *Mere Christianity*, 21.

33. Hooper, *Companion and Guide*, 332.

34. Hooper, *Companion and Guide*, 332.

35. C. S. Lewis, *The Abolition of Man or Reflections on Education with Special Reference to the Teaching of English in the Upper Forms of Schools* (London: Oxford University Press, 1943), 4.

36. Lewis, *The Abolition of Man*, 4.

37. Jerry Root, "Setting Forth the Argument of the Abolition of Man & Evaluating It," lecture presented at C. S. Lewis Conference and Faculty Forum T*hrough the Window to the Garden: C. S. Lewis & the Recovery of Virtue*, Kellogg West Conference Center, California State University, Pomona, California, February 23, 2019.

38. Root, "Setting Forth the Argument of the Abolition of Man."

39. Lewis, *The Abolition of Man*, 22–23.

40. See: Lewis, *The Abolition of Man*, 41–48.

41. Lewis, *The Abolition of Man*, 23.

42. Lewis, *Mere Christianity*, 1.

43. Jerry Root, *C. S. Lewis and a Problem of Evil: An Investigation of a Pervasive Theme* (Eugene: Pickwick Publications, 2009).

44. C. S. Lewis, "Is Theology Poetry," *They Asked for a Paper* (London: Geoffrey Bles, 1962), 165.

45. Steven A. Beebe, Susan J. Beebe and Diana K. Ivy, *Communication: Principles for a Lifetime* (Boston: Pearson, 2019), 5.

46. Lewis, *Surprised by Joy*, 113.

47. Lewis, *Surprised by Joy*, 170.

48. Lewis, *Surprised by Joy*, viii.

49. C. S. Lewis and Sherwood Wirt, "Cross-Examination," *Undeceptions: Essays on Theology and Ethics*, ed. Walter Hooper (London: Geoffrey Bles, 1971), 215–217.

50. Lewis, *Surprised by Joy*, 201

51. Lewis, *The Problem of Pain*, 115.

52. Lewis, *The Great Divorce*, 66–67.

53. Lewis, *Mere Christianity*, 121.

54. Lewis, *Mere Christianity*, xi.

55. Walter Hooper, "C. S. Lewis: Oxford's Literary Chameleon of Letters," *Behind the Veil of Familiarity: C. S. Lewis (1898–1963)*, ed. Margarita Carretero Gonzalez and Encarnacion Hidalgo Tenorio (Bern: Peter Lang, 2001), 25.

56. Lewis, *Mere Christianity*, 35.

57. Lewis, *Mere Christianity*, 35.

58. Lewis, *Mere Christianity*, 38.

59. C. S. Lewis, *Miracles. A Preliminary Study* (London: Geoffrey Bles, 1947), 114.

60. C. S. Lewis, *The Lion, the Witch and the Wardrobe* (London: Geoffrey Bles, 1950), 64–65.

61. C. S. Lewis, *The Last Battle* (London: Geoffrey Bles, 1956), 183–184.

62. Lewis, *Surprised by Joy*, 27.

63. Sheldon Vanauken, *A Severe Mercy* (London: Hodder and Stoughton), 1977.

64. C. S. Lewis, *The Silver Chair* (London: Geoffrey Bles, 1953), 238–239.

65. Lewis, *Mere Christianity*, 38.

66. C. S. Lewis, *The Screwtape Letters* (London: Geoffrey Bles, The Centenary Press, 1942).

67. Lewis, *The Problem of Pain*.

68. For a summary of some of the arguments for and against Lewis's trilemma see: Matt Nelson, "Is C. S. Lewis' Trilemma a Good Argument or the Divinity of Christ?" *Word on Fire*, November 16, 2017 https://www.wordonfire.org/resources/blog/is-c-s-lewis-trilemma-a-good-argument-for-the-divinity-of-christ/5639/ Accessed January 24, 2018; Jim Perry, The Secular Web, "The Trilemma—Lord, Liar or Lunatic?" https://www.wordonfire.org/resources/blog/is-cs-lewis-trilemma-a-good-argument-for-the-divinity-of-christ/5639/ Accessed January 24, 2018.

69. Lewis, *Mere Christianity*, 52.

70. Lewis, *Surprised by Joy*, 205.

71. Lewis, *Surprised by Joy*, 205.

72. C. S. Lewis, *The Four Loves* (London: Geoffrey Bles, 1960), 156.

73. Lewis, *Surprised by Joy,* 207–208.

74. C. S. Lewis, *De Descriptione Temporum: Inaugural Lecture from the Chair of Mediaeval and Renaissance Literature* (Cambridge: Cambridge University Press, 1954).

75. Lewis, *De Descriptione Temporum,* 21.

76. Douglas Gresham, *Lenten Lands: My Childhood with Joy Davidman and C. S. Lewis* (New York: HarperCollins, 2003).

77. James Como, *Branches to Heaven: The Geniuses of C. S. Lewis* (Dallas: Spence Publishing Company, 1998): 112.

78. Bruce L. Edwards, "C. S. Lewis on Language," *The C. S. Lewis Review* (April 9, 2015)   http://www.cslewisreview.org/2015/04/c-s-lewis-on-language/   Accessed January 28, 2018.

79. Edwards, "C. S. Lewis on Language."

80. Edwards, "C. S. Lewis on Language."

81. C. S. Lewis, "The Death of Words," *The Spectator* CLXXIII (September 1944), 81.

82. Lewis, "The Death of Words," 81

83. Lewis, "The Death of Words," 81.

84. C. S. Lewis, *Miracles,* 88.

85. John Paul Russo, *I. A. Richards: His Life and Work* (Baltimore: Johns Hopkins University Press, 1988), 795, as cited by Greg M Anderson, "A Most Potent Rhetoric: C. S. Lewis, 'Congenital Rhetorician,' " *C. S. Lewis: Life, Works, and Legacy,* Vol. 4, ed. Bruce L. Edwards (Westport: Praeger Perspectives, 2007), 195–228

86. Bruce L. Edwards, "Language/Rhetoric," *The C. S. Lewis Readers' Encyclopedia,* ed. J. D. Schultz and J. G. West (Grand Rapids: Zondervan, 1998), 231.

87. Ludwig Wittgenstein, *Tractatus Logico-Philosophicus,* trans. by D.F. Pears and B.F. McGuinness (London: Routledge and Kegan Paul, 1961).

88. Lewis, *Studies in Words,* 313.

89. C. S. Lewis, *Letters to Malcolm: Chiefly on Prayer* (London: Geoffrey Bles, 1964), 158.

90. C. S. Lewis, "Horrid Red Things" *God in the Dock* (London: Eerdmans, 1970), 71.

91. Lewis, "Horrid Red Things," 71.

92. Kath Filmer, "The Polemic Image: The Role of Metaphor and Symbol in the Fiction of C. S. Lewis," *The Taste of the Pineapple: Essays on C. S. Lewis as Reader, Critic, and Imaginative Writer,* ed. Bruce L. Edwards Bowling Green (Ohio: Bowling Green State University Popular Press, 1988), 154.

93. Filmer, "The Polemic Image,"154.

94. C. S. Lewis, "The Language of Religion," *Christian Reflections* (1967), 129–141.

95. I found this poem in the Bodleian Library in April 2016 while reading the manuscript "The Language of Religion." The poem was written on the back of the manuscript. For a discussion of Lewis's clever use of adding prefixes and suffixes to words as he did in this poem see: Brenton Dickieson, "The Words C. S. Lewis Made Up: Re/Anti/Un/Ness," *A Pilgrim in Narnia* (December 13, 2017), https://apilgriminnarnia.com/2017/12/13/un/ Accessed January 28, 2018.

96. My thanks to C. S. Lewis scholar Charlie Starr for his help in transcribing Lewis's handwriting of this poem and to Lewis scholar Don King for confirming the authenticity of the poem.

97. Rowan Williams, "Address During the Service to Dedicate a Memorial to C. S. Lewis" (Public address, Westminster Abbey, London, November 22, 2013).

98. Perry Bramlett, *C. S. Lewis: Life at the Center* (Macon: Smyth & Helwys Publisher, 1996), 230.

99. Jerry Root and Mark Neal, *The Surprising Imagination of C. S. Lewis: An Introduction* (Nashville, Abingdon Press, 2015).

100. Lewis, "The Weight of Glory," 268.

101. C. S. Lewis, *Mere Christianity*, 108.

4

Holistic

"I use speaker throughout to cover writer as well."[1]

- C. S. Lewis

"Now the great and I think all but unique essential in C. S. Lewis's makeup was a remarkable combination of two qualities normally supposed to be opposites. I mean on the one hand a deep and vivid imagination and on the other hand a profoundly analytical mind."[2]

- Clyde Kilby

"There is no antithesis, indeed no distinction, between Rhetoric and Poetry."[3]

- C. S. Lewis

What would it have been like to be Reepicheep, the mythical mouse from *Voyage of the Dawn Treader*, hiding in a corner to watch C. S. Lewis prepare his first Broadcast Talk for the BBC in August 1941? Unfortunately, Reepicheep left no description of this historic moment—*historic* because eleven years later, the words would become part of *Mere Christianity*, a book heralded by *Christianity Today* readers as the *best* Christian book written in the 20th century.[4] One can only guess what Reepicheep would have seen if he had indeed been in Lewis's room at Magdalen College or Lewis's study at The Kilns, while Lewis wrote the scripts that survived and are now housed in the BBC archives in Reading, England. But Lewis himself did leave clues.

If Lewis followed his usual routine, he would have dipped his nibbed pen in the ink, paused, pondered, and pronounced the words (sometimes silently, at other times with an audible whisper) he was planning to write. Lewis was a *mindful* writer. He had well-developed ideas, liberally used metaphors, knew the power of a story or short illustration to make his points, and used language precisely. But rather than scribbling away, madly trying to capture his first thoughts in his head, evidence suggests that he followed his own advice and intentionally thought about what he would write. Lewis's mental pre-writing strategy explains why, when viewing his extant manuscripts, one notes that although he did make some corrections of his drafts, his edits on the page were relatively few.

Lewis thought before he wrote, and he thought as he wrote. What did he think about? Lewis is often described as one of the 20th Century's most skilled Christian *apologists*.[5] An apologist is not someone who apologizes, or is sorry for Christianity, but rather someone who defends and explains Christian beliefs. As an apologist, Lewis certainly used his reasoning skills. But in addition to developing reasonable, logical, persuasive messages, he drew upon his skills as a poet and storyteller; his words sparkle with both wit and imagination. His stories, illustrations, and application of myth and metaphor trigger images and "movies in the mind" to make his case. He appealed to the eye and the ear, reason and imagination. He was both rhetorician and poet. In essence, he was holistic.

This chapter describes the first of five principles that make Lewis a skilled communication craftsperson. The first principle is: *Effective communicators are holistic*. This chapter explains what it means to be holistic, drawing upon C. S. Lewis's own words to describe his technique. The chapter also provides examples of Lewis's holistic communication approach as evident in his novels, children's stories, and professional works.

Although Lewis explicitly wrote about language, meaning, and communication from time to time, he did not identify these messages as "communication principles." Nowhere in his writing or speaking does he say, "Be holistic when you communicate." Nor does he cogently describe the other four principles that constitute the core of this book. But throughout his writing—both his published work and his letters—Lewis *does* offer considerable advice and recommendations for using words and language. Sometimes he embeds his thoughts about communication in a single sentence tucked away in a passage about medieval literature. And in other instances, he writes extensively and in considerable detail about words, meaning, messages, and communication, as he does in "Bluspels and Flalansferes," "Before We Can Communicate," "The Language of Religion," and books such as *Studies in Words, Miracles: A Preliminary Study* and *A Preface to Paradise Lost.* His letters to his friends, acquaintances, and fans are another rich source of Lewis's ideas about how to communicate effectively.

Then, of course, there is the book that Lewis and J. R. R. Tolkien planned to write, *Language and Human Nature.* As discussed in the Preface and Chapter 3, although the book was never finished and long thought to be nonexistent, Lewis did write the opening portion of the first chapter, where his carefully worded definitions of language and meaning provide a clear glimpse into his thinking about the nature of both. The principles that follow do not derive from a single Lewis article or book; rather, they represent his ideas about communication found throughout many works published over a lifetime.

A second method of identifying Lewis's communication principles is to examine what he *did* that made him one of the best-loved authors of the 20th century. Lewis believed that a written work should be judged on its own merit. He insisted that readers look at the text itself to assess its virtues, catalogue its flaws, and note how readers respond to it. The five principles that form the foundation of a master craftsperson are exemplified in his writing and speaking. The first principle—to be holistic—is evident in everything Lewis wrote and, in part, helps explain his popularity and proficiency as a communicator.

Principle One: Effective Communicators Are Holistic

C. S. Lewis's close friend, Owen Barfield, suggests that someone new to Lewis's writing might perceive not just one but three Lewises:

> A fairly unsophisticated person who had never had any personal contact with Lewis, but who ... had read the whole or most of what has been written about him, might be pardoned for wondering if it were not one writer, but three, with whom he was becoming acquainted: three men who just happened to have the same name and the same peculiar vigor of thought and utterance. Such a reader (I will venture to put myself in his shoes) might, to avoid confusion, adopt the nomenclature L1, L2, and L3, L1 being a distinguished and original literary critic, L2 a highly successful author of fiction, and L3 the writer and broadcaster of popular Christian apologetics.[6]

Barfield's "three Lewises" describe a *holistic* communicator. What does it mean to be holistic? As presented in this chapter, it describes someone who draws on multiple strategies, methods, and techniques to create and craft messages. Another way to describe Lewis as a holistic communicator is with the paradigm "one style, two Lewises, and three methods":

- *One Style*: Whether writing scholarly articles or children's novels, Lewis has a conversational tone. He communicated for both sight and hearing; he holistically wrote for the eye *and* the ear. His style of appealing to both meaning and sound made his writing clear, accessible, personal, and engaging.
- *Two Lewises*: The Lewis of reason and the Lewis who appealed to the imagination appear often in the same paragraph and sometimes in the same sentence. Lewis married logical reasoning with telling imaginative tales, selecting the right illustration, crafting a picture-perfect metaphor, and using other creative literary techniques to make his messages simultaneously substantive and engaging.
- *Three Methods*: Lewis was (1) a skilled *rhetorician* who understood the principles and power of persuasion; (2) a tactical debater who drew on his *dialectical* skill to listen to, respond to, and anticipate arguments; and (3) a *poet* who used metaphorical language creatively to transport readers to new worlds as well as help them better understand their own. Lewis was holistic in that he toggled among these three methods interchangeably.

One Style: Communicating for Both the Eye and the Ear

C. S. Lewis was interested in how words sounded, as well as how they looked on the page. This interest explains why someone watching him write would have seen, and perhaps *heard*, him mouth the words he was penning.[7] Adding to the oral style of his work, many of Lewis's books and articles started as lectures or speeches presented to a group of academics, students, or the public. He was an efficient communicator in that he often got double duty out of his work. His anthology, aptly titled *They Asked For a Paper*, is a collection of papers and addresses he had presented for several different audiences.[8] For Lewis, the creative process was an awareness that the written word needed to have an oral quality as well.

In part because of the orality of his writing, readers often feel a relationship with Lewis while they are reading his work. To read Lewis—especially his material intended for a wider general audience, such as his popular *Mere Christianity* and

The Screwtape Letters—is like being on the receiving end of a conversation. *Mere Christianity*, for example, originated as broadcast talks to a war-weary Britain; these short talks on BBC radio created the sense of an intimate chat between Lewis and those listening on the wireless. Lewis talked directly *to* his listeners, rather than *at* them.

Several of Lewis's books started as oral presentations. *The Four Loves* began as a series of radio lectures commissioned by the Atlanta Diocese of the Episcopal Church. *The Abolition of Man* emerged from the Riddle Memorial Lectures delivered in Newcastle at an outpost of nearby Durham University. The list of written manuscripts that started as oral presentations, either lectures, broadcasts, sermons, or speeches, is long. Lewis knew how to appeal to both the eye and the ear because he had a great deal of practice at transforming his speeches into written text. His "talk-write" strategy gave his prose a remarkable personal, conversational quality. When one reads Lewis, one sometimes feels inclined to talk back—to answer his questions and respond to his ideas. He provokes mental dialogue to engage his readers. To be fair, some people nonetheless struggle with some of Lewis's ideas, especially those embedded in passages of prose that are dauntingly dense. *The Abolition of Man*, although originating as a lecture, is not a breezy, easy-peasy read. Yet Lewis did not think his audience would be 21st Century readers; he wrote it for a specific, well-educated audience that he believed could decode his ideas.

Rather than viewing speaking and writing as separate communication mediums, Lewis saw these two means of human expression as integrated. Given his own practice, it is not surprising that his definition of language placed considerable emphasis upon the *oral* nature of communication. In one of Lewis's most explicit efforts to describe the nature and function of language, the early draft of *Language and Human Nature*, Lewis writes, "A language in the simplest sense, is a system of signs. Thus there is a language of flags (used in the navy) a 'language of flowers' and so forth."[9] He goes on to say, "But one such system of signs so widely used and so much richer than all the others that it generally is called simply 'language.' This is the system in which the signs are the various noises made by a human mouth. It is language in this sense, which is the subject of the present book."[10]

Why is it significant that Lewis describes language as an *oral* process ("the various noises made by a human mouth"), not just a *written* system of signs? Because Lewis knew that although they use different communication channels (light waves and sound waves), the oral and written elements of language are holistically integrated.

Lewis spoke as he wrote. Walter Hooper writes in his preface to *C. S. Lewis Collected Letters Volume I* that Lewis had a keen sense of writing to appeal to the listener as well as the reader. Hooper notes, "When Lewis dictated letters to me, he always had me read them aloud afterwards. He told me that in writing letters, as well as books, he always 'whispered the words aloud.' Pausing to dip the pen in an inkwell provided exactly the rhythm needed. 'It's as important to please the ear,' he said, 'as it is the eye'."[11] Hooper further confirms the importance of Lewis's oral style when he concluded, "I believed his readers came far closer than they imagined to 'meeting' him in his books, and that I knew of no author's works in which the human voice and the written word seemed so inseparably combined as in his."[12] Lewis confirms this practice of deliberately using an oral style when he writes about his own technique: "When I write I pronounce every word aloud. It's important to please the ear as well as the eye."[13] Lewis writes to a schoolgirl in America with advice based on his own practice: "Always write (and read) with the ear, not the eye. You shd. [should] hear every sentence you write as if it was being read aloud or spoken. If it does not sound nice, try again."[14] And in yet another letter, this time to a correspondent named Mrs. Hook, Lewis explains, "I am always playing with syllables and fitting them together (purely by ear) to see if I can hatch up new words that please me."[15] This oral quality of his writing is one of the factors that make Lewis a skilled communicator.

Why did Lewis pay attention to the way words sound? He knew that as readers "hear" the words in their "mind's ear;" these "sounds" have a potent effect on their emotions. But why was he so focused on the precise *sound* of words? He explains, "I want them to have an emotional, not intellectual suggestiveness: the heaviness of *glund* for as huge a planet as Jupiter; the vibrating, titillating quality of *viritrilbia* for the subtlety of Mercury; the liquidity and (as I thought) spirituality of Maleldil."[16] Lewis liked the way the sound of words made the reader feel. He sought an emotional response from his readers in reaction to the sound a word created.

Significant differences exist between oral and written communication styles.[17] First, when people speak, they are more redundant. They repeat themselves because the listener may miss the message the first time they say it, so they find ways to make their point again, sometimes literally repeating words or phrases, or finding new words to express the same idea. Redundancy improves listener comprehension and recall.

Oral style also tends to be less formal than written style. Speakers typically use more contractions, shorter words, and slang than do writers. (One exception is that text messages often mirror the style of casual spoken comments.) Describing how he shifted from the scripts of his BBC broadcast talks to the printed versions, Lewis notes, "A 'talk' on the radio should, I think, be as like real talk as possible, and should not sound like an essay being read aloud. In my talks I had therefore used all the contractions and colloquialisms I ordinarily use in conversation."[18] Lewis also wrote in first person, which adds to the illusion of having a conversation with someone via the printed page.

A third difference between oral and written style is that oral communication sounds more spontaneous than the written word. The spontaneity of an oral message not only results from using more informal language, but also sometimes reflects a stream of consciousness, immediacy, and responses to events and situations happening at the moment the communication occurs. Because written style is less in the moment, a writer has fewer ways to customize a message for a specific reader. Although Lewis's language use was polished and precise, it often appears spontaneous. For example, in *Mere Christianity* he invites the reader to skip a chapter of little interest or use.[19] Or in anticipating a reader's reaction to something he wrote, he would pose a rhetorical question and then answer it. Being able to anticipate and respond to readers' objections or questions is a way of making the written word appear more spontaneous and informal.

Lewis worked hard to develop an easy, informal, first-person relationship with his readers and listeners, especially in his popular works. Yet he also had a clear and accessible style in his scholarly works, such as *The Allegory of Love* or *English Literature in the 16th Century: Excluding Drama*. Readers of Lewis's popular works often feel as if he knows them; he had a rapport with readers and listeners that was reflected in his sometimes informal and immediate tone and style. Speaking the words aloud as he wrote gave his writing *both* an oral and a written style—*at the same time*—which is one of the keys to Lewis's popularity as an author.

Since the time of the ancient Greek rhetoricians, textual analysis (and what was later studied as rhetorical theory) combined written and spoken human expression under one category of analysis, called simply "rhetoric." Lewis most definitely studied rhetoric. The *Trivium*, among the earliest subjects taught by institutions of higher learning, including Oxford, emphasized a three-pronged, essential curricula of (1) grammar (words and word usage), (2) dialectic (logic and debate), and (3) rhetoric (the elegant application of logic, credibility, and emotion to persuade). These three classic subjects were an important part of Lewis's education and his life's work as a literary historian and critic. As Lewis noted, "Everything we should now call criticism belonged either to Grammar or to Rhetoric. The Grammarian explained a poet's metre and allusions: the Rhetorician dealt with structure and style."[20]

As noted in Chapter 2, Lewis explicitly acknowledges how his "greatest teachers" taught him grammar, rhetoric, and dialectic. Lewis writes, "Smewgy [Harry Wakelyn Smith] and Kirk [William T. Kirkpatrick] were my two greatest teachers. Roughly, one might say (in medieval language) that Smewgy taught me Grammar and Rhetoric and Kirk taught me Dialectic."[21] The study of grammar and rhetoric was *both* oral and written. Lewis's definition of language as a *spoken* system of "various noises made by a human mouth"[22] suggests the importance he placed on the spoken word and is consistent with lessons he would have learned about both speaking and writing from his teachers.

Rhetorician and Lewis scholar James Como discovered that Lewis's copy of Aristotle's *Rhetoric*, housed in the Marion E. Wade Center at Wheaton College, contains no marginal annotations or markings.[23] The lack of annotations made Como wonder whether Lewis actually studied this classic work. Greg Anderson, however, another rhetorical and Lewis scholar who examined Lewis's personal library of books at the Wade Center, found that Lewis's 1665 copy of Quintilian's *Institutionum Oratorium* is "heavily underscored"[24] as are Hugh Blair's *Lectures on Rhetoric and Belles Lettres* and I. A. Richards's *The Philosophy of Rhetoric*.[25] Anderson speculates that Lewis's copy of *Rhetoric* deposited at the Wade Center may have been a replacement copy from Lewis's office library at Cambridge.[26] What is most interesting is the fact that in these existing well-annotated books owned by Lewis, oral and written rhetoric were viewed as inextricably linked and not separate applications.

Finally, Lewis's own academic specialty, medieval and renaissance literature, offers another clue to his holistic oral and written style. During medieval and renaissance times, as in ancient Greece and Rome, no clear distinction was made between the study of spoken rhetoric and written rhetoric. Although academic tomes are typically written in a verbose, formal style, Lewis's magisterial scholarly masterpiece *English Literature in the Sixteenth Century: Excluding Drama*, a book with a mouthful of a title not expected to make the bestseller list, has a surprisingly accessible, oral quality.

Lewis made no distinctions between spoken and written rhetoric in his published work. In his definition of *language* in the unfinished *Language and Human Nature* manuscript, his focus on oral communication is consistent with his other published statements about language and meaning. In *Studies in Words* he says, "I use speaker throughout to cover writer as well."[27] In *The Discarded Image* (Lewis's classic Prolegomena Lectures published after his death), he further confirms the importance of spoken rhetoric:

The ancient teachers of Rhetoric addressed their precepts to orators in an age when public speaking was an indispensable skill for every public man—even for a general in the field—and for every private man if he got involved in litigation. Rhetoric was then not so much the loveliest (*soavissima*) as the most practical of the arts.[28]

For Lewis, a university lecturer who also became a broadcaster, the study of rhetoric, and especially public speaking, was indeed indispensable and practical.

Finally, other, more pragmatic, factors may help explain why Lewis wrote while sounding out the words rather than typing them. Although Lewis appreciated his brother Warnie's service as his secretary and typist, Lewis was not fond of the sound of the typewriter. Lewis did not type. In fact, biographer Alister McGrath speculates that Lewis purposely chose not to learn to type.[29] As McGrath explains, "This mechanical mode of writing, he believed, interfered with the creative process in that the incessant clacking of the typewriter keys dulled the writer's appreciation of the rhythms and cadences of the English language."[30] Further confirmation of Lewis's disdain for a clacking typewriter is found in the advice he gave to would-be writers: "Don't use a typewriter. The noise will destroy your sense of rhythm, which still needs years of training."[31] Along with his dislike of the sound of the typewriter, Lewis's unbending thumbs, an inherited condition, may have made typing difficult, if not impossible, for him.

So what would Reepicheep have seen if he had watched Lewis writing? He would have seen Lewis pausing to dip his nibbed pen in the ink, then mouthing or whispering the words, and finally writing. Lewis was a relational writer who spoke and wrote in one style. And that style was oral.

Two Lewises: The Integration of Reason and Imagination

People reason with their minds but, at least from a metaphorical perspective, imagine with their hearts. Lewis holistically appealed to both mind and heart. As a Christian apologist, Lewis is noted for his rational, logical defense of Christianity. But he also appealed to his readers' imaginations, which made his messages colorfully engaging.[32] His use of story, metaphor, and myth also helped make his messages memorable. Lewis readers sometimes *see* colors, *hear* music, or *catch* a glimpse of sparkling sunlight dancing on a pristine lake. Lewis wrote in such a way that his readers feel the fur in the dark as they push through coats in a wardrobe passage, followed by freezing in the bitingly cold winter world of Narnia. They see the vibrant, undulating green islands in Perelandra glisten in the sparkling sunlight. They hear the waves rhythmically lapping at the shore near Cair Paravel. Lewis loved language and loved using it to spark his readers' imaginations to create mental pictures and cue a cerebral sound track to accompany what they are "seeing." He is heralded for his use of metaphor, plucking just the right words from his extensive vocabulary to create a crisp and colorful mind's eye image. Whether with a brief illustration or a novel-length tale, he painted vivid word pictures. *Out of the Silent Planet,* for example, includes decadent, detailed descriptions. The protagonist Ransom imagines a possible scene of what he may discover on Malacandra: "He saw in imagination various incompatible monstrosities—bulbous eyes, grinning jaws, horns, stings, mandibles. Loathing of insects, loathing of snakes, loathing of things that squashed and squelched, all played their horrible symphonies over his nerves."[33] Lewis did not *tell* his readers what to feel; he *described* the scene and let them make sense out of the vision he painted.

Lewis's early teachers fostered his imagination. His fascination with stories told by his nurse Lizzie Endicott, and his extensive reading of authors such as Edith Nesbit and Beatrix Potter (*Squirrel Nutkin* was a special favorite) nurtured the imagination that eventually helped him take his readers and listeners to enchanted places. The collaborative world of *Boxen*, co-written with his brother Warnie when Lewis was about 8, is evidence of his long-standing talent to create new imaginative worlds (although he claimed that the similarities between Boxen and Narnia are slight.)[34]

In addition to educators who nurtured his imagination, Lewis had teachers who harnessed his reasoning and intellectual talents. In his autobiography *Surprised by Joy,* Lewis describes his teacher, William T. Kirkpatrick, as being a "purely logical entity."[35] Lewis speculates, "Born a little later, he would have been a Logical Positivist."[36] The goal of communication, according to Kirkpatrick, was to be rational and logical. Lewis adds, "The idea that human beings should exercise their vocal organs for any purpose except that of communicating or discovering truth was to him preposterous. The most casual remark was taken as a summons to disputation."[37]

A number of Lewis experts have described Lewis's keen ability to fuse reason and imagination, synthesizing both ways of expression to his full advantage. Lewis's combined logical and imaginative thinking added exponentially to the power of each. His training and natural gifts in developing logical arguments, combined with his poetic instincts, enhanced both logical and creative talents for communicating well. In his essay "The Creative Logician Speaking," Clyde Kilby, founder of the Marion E. Wade Center at Wheaton College, points to how Lewis's creative mind enhanced his logical, analytical abilities: "Now the great and I think all but unique essential in C. S. Lewis's makeup was a remarkable combination of two qualities normally supposed to be opposites. I mean on the one hand a deep and vivid imagination and on the other and a profoundly analytical mind."[38]

Chad Walsh, an Episcopalian priest and author of *C. S. Lewis: Apostle to the Skeptics,* the first book written about Lewis, further notes, "The two strands that run through C. S. Lewis's books are 'logic' and 'romance,' to give them the names he [Lewis] chose."[39] Not only did Lewis study logic and argumentation, but he also read classic stories by Homer, Demosthenes, Cicero, Virgil, Euripides, Sophocles, and Aeschylus.[40] From his early educational experiences and throughout his life, Lewis drew upon both his training in logic and his love of romance and story to enhance his communication talents.

Lewis biographer Alister McGrath, is among the most recent group of scholars to make the case that Lewis was a master of both logic and imagination: "Throughout the 1930s and 1940s, Lewis was exploring the relationship between reason and imagination, between 'the true' and 'the real'—in particular the relationship between rational argument and the use of imaginative narratives."[41] This exploration of reason and imagination occurred as Lewis was exploring his theological beliefs. McGrath suggests, "For Lewis, the key issue he wanted to explore was not the personal story 'Lewis meets God,' but the intellectual issue of how reason and imagination may be both affirmed and integrated within a Christian vision of reality."[42] Lewis's gift was in fusing reason with imaginative language *simultaneously*. C. S. Lewis was not the only author to integrate reason and imagination to make his literary point, but, as McGrath concludes, "He did it better than anyone else."[43]

In a letter to the members of the Milton Society of America, Lewis describes why he sometimes preferred to use creative descriptions and appeals to the imagination to clarify and amplify a logical point. He thought his creative and imaginative impulse was simply part of him; as he explains, "The imaginative man in me is older, more continuously operative, and in that sense more basic than either the religious writer or the critic."[44] He further notes that it was the "imaginative man" in him that drew him to use the "mythopoeic form [appeal to imagination], ranging from Screwtape to a kind of theologized science fiction."[45] Communication scholar Terry Lindvall aptly concludes that Lewis's imaginative and creative writing, "are both fictive (*Poeima*) and rhetorical (*Logos*). They establish an engagement of communicator and audience by calling for the suspension of disbelief …"[46] Poetic and imaginative language, coupled with rational and rhetorical language, augments the power of the message. The reader or listener is able to waive the normal way things work (suspend disbelief) and believe that wardrobes do have secret back entrances leading to a new world.

One of his students remembers Lewis's ability to integrate reason and imagination in the way he taught his pupils. When teaching his students to develop their analytical powers the student recalls, "Lewis would always use analogy—the metaphor in syllogistic harness—to solve all problems. He did this sort of things instinctively; it was his method of 'picture thinking' which he used so extensively in his books."[47] Describing Lewis's strategy of using "metaphor in syllogistic harness" is an apt description of the marriage of reason and imagination. Although Lewis was a master in using metaphor while teaching, at least one of his students, famed British theatre critic Kenneth Tynan, found his reliance on metaphor when teaching sometimes tedious. Tynan reportedly said, "He is eternally trotting out his damned figures in tutorials—'Now if you have three apples and I have five bananas …' It's always three apples and five bananas, and no cigar. He's caustic."[48]Although Lewis's use of metaphor to illustrate a logical conclusion may have, at times, been perceived as overused, it nonetheless was a hallmark of both his teaching and writing, and ultimately served him well as a communicator.

Literary scholar Lee Rossi further explores the claim that Lewis used both reason and imagination, noting that Lewis's use of language "oscillates between two poles. We might call them the rational and the romantic, or the didactic and the playful."[49] About Lewis's use of language to describe eldils (angels) in *Out of the Silent Planet*, Rossi notes, "Clearly we have here two kinds of discourse. One is a definition, the other a hypothesis, a metaphor; one is abstract and the other concrete."[50] By holistically combining reason and imagination *at the same time*, often in the same sentence, Lewis is able to augment the power of language to both inform and inspire, persuade and evoke beauty, and appeal simultaneously to the head and the heart.

Lewis's ability to focus on both reason and imagination is anchored in his belief that imagi*native* is not the same thing as imagi*nary*. Imagi*nary* is first seeing a vision and then describing the picture in one's mind; imagi*native* is developing a creative plot to bring the picture to life. A story that is more imaginative has greater potential for meaning as the story unfolds. Lewis explains, "The more imaginative a mythology, the greater its ability to communicate more reality to us."[51] Using the imagination can confirm truth and provide real insights. Lewis provides the intellectual space for readers to insert their own discoveries. He does not smother readers with unnecessary details, but rather, wants readers to join in the creative process and bring their own experiences to the event. As McGrath notes, "Narnia is an imaginative, not an imaginary, world ... The 'imaginary' is something that has been falsely imagined, having no counterpart in reality ... The 'imaginative' is something produced by the human mind as it tries to respond to something greater than itself struggling to find images adequate to the reality."[52] By being *imaginative* (developing a world of possibilities), rather than merely *imaginary* (making up a picture), the Narnia stories allow the reader or listener to participate in the process of creating the images.

What did Lewis do to nurture his own imagination? He stepped away from his desk. He did something he enjoyed. He read a book from his vast personal library of thousands of books pulled from his cram-filled bookshelves or gingerly plucked from the towering stacks in his home or college rooms. He walked on Addison's Walk at Magdalen College or Shotover Hill near The Kilns. He smoked (on walking trips he called it "taking a soak"—both pipes and several packs of cigarettes a day). He swam. Whether at the clothing-optional Parson's Pleasure or in the pond near his home, he loved swimming. (Some of his favorite books from his personal library evidence water stains, perhaps from reading them in or around the water).[53] He took breaks. He would write a bit and then take a stroll to let his ideas marinate. The rhythm of writing and walking (sometimes with friends and sometimes alone) was his *modus operandi* for creativity. He would often walk from his home in Headington Quarry, The Kilns, to Magdalen College, a distance of about three miles. Taking that walk today involves lengthy waits to cross busy roads; noisy streets full of people, shops, and cars; and general hubbub. But a 1932 Ordnance Survey map, published two years after Lewis moved to The Kilns, reveals few houses near his home. In Lewis's day, his eight-acre homestead, which included gardens, an orchard, and a pond (rumored to be also the place where the poet Shelley would sail paper boats), was a distant outpost, not surrounded by other houses. Shotover Hill is easily visible from Lewis's front lounge. Lewis used walking and thinking, taking advantage of his location away from the city center, to help distill his ideas.

A typical workday for Lewis was to write in the morning and take a walk in the afternoon, often after lunch. Then he would return to more writing in the evening. The walks in between writing helped him sort things out, spark new images, and imagine new worlds. Contemporary neurobiological research supports the use of this technique: Taking breaks, getting away from a routine, and taking a vacation are often-suggested methods of fostering creativity and improving one's imagination. Lewis's integration of reason and imagination was more than a reflection of his education. It mirrored his entire life. Lewis's writing habits were an outgrowth of the way he lived, worked, and related to others.

The two Lewises, the Lewis of reason and the Lewis of imagination, can also be seen in the forms Lewis used to present his big ideas. He often presented the same idea in fiction and non-fiction, prose and poetry. His autobiography, *Surprised by Joy*, the non-fiction prose version of his journey to belief, is also told in an allegorical novel: his first major post-conversion work, *A Pilgrim's Regress*. In *The Abolition of Man*, Lewis uses a rational, logical approach to develop his argument for the existence of a universal moral code that he called the Tao; he writes about the same idea in *That Hideous Strength*, a novel. To ensure that the reader makes the connection, he explains in the preface that through the fictional story, he is making the same point earlier developed in his book *The Abolition of Man*.[54]

Although Lewis drew upon both logic and reason in his writing, he did not view these elements as distinctively separate processes. In "Bluspels and Flalansferes," an early scholarly essay essentially about communication, Lewis links the process of reason and imagination as two parts of the same communicative process.[55] For Lewis, reason is the "natural organ of truth," while imagination is the "organ of meaning." One cannot exist without the other, as truth without meaning would serve no purpose, and meaning without truth would result in nonsense. Lewis's full argument clearly illustrates how reason is linked to imagination: "It must not be supposed that I am in any sense putting forward the imagination as the organ of truth. We are not talking of truth, but of meaning: meaning which is the antecedent condition both of truth and falsehood, whose antithesis is not error but nonsense."[56] Lewis then clearly links reason and imagination when he writes, "I am a rationalist. For me, reason is the natural organ of truth; but imagination is the organ of meaning."[57]

Thus, rather than bifurcating reason and imagination as distinct, unrelated processes, Lewis links the two as tandem elements of human sense making. Although Lewis sometimes wrote works that tipped more prominently to reason, and at other times, works that included greater doses of imagination, both reason and imagination were always present to some degree. His imaginative fiction is based upon an underlying logic. His more rationally argued works are liberally punctuated with metaphor, analogy, comparison, and stories to add meaning to the truths he wanted to express. This holistic combination of reason and imagination contributes to Lewis's success as a communicator.

Three Methods: The Integration of Rhetoric, Dialectic, and the Poetic

In addition to developing an oral style in his written messages and integrating reason and imagination, Lewis drew from his formal education a third holistic strategy that merged three classic communication methods of expression: (1) rhetorical (persuasion), (2) dialectical (debate), and (3) poetic (the aesthetic). This three-part integration of thinking and writing is more academic than the eye-ear or reason-imagination holistic strategies. But after all, Lewis was an academic. So it is not surprising that his approach to writing and speaking is based on these three academic traditions. What is especially noteworthy is his ability not only to use each of these academic forms, but, as with reason and imagination, to *integrate* them.

These classic areas of human expression—rhetoric, dialectic, and poetic—are today often housed in different academic departments in the United States. Contemporary university students take classes in persuasion, rhetoric, argumentation, debate, literature, and poetry as separate and distinct areas of study. Courses in persuasion, debate, and argumentation are typically housed in communication departments (formerly known as speech departments or speech communication departments). Communication students often, but not always, emphasize oral messages. Literature and poetry courses are found in English departments. English majors also typically study composition and the written word, yet some English departments have fostered a split between composition and literature. Journalism students also study the written word, but from the perspective of news reporting or public relations. But Lewis holistically blurred distinctions between rhetoric, dialectic, and the poetic.

Rhetoric

Rhetoric, according to Aristotle, whom Lewis studied, is the process of discovering the available means of persuasion in a given case.[58] Stated succinctly, the art of rhetoric is the ability to use symbols to influence or persuade. Aristotle described three methods of persuasion: logic (*logos*), emotion (*pathos*), and the credibility and ethical characteristics of a speaker (*ethos*). A TV spokesperson, for example, may try to convince you to buy a product or service because the new product (1) will solve a problem for you (a logical appeal), (2) will make you happy (an emotional appeal), or (3) has been endorsed by celebrities or other famous people (an appeal to credibility). Lewis scholar Jerry Root describes how Lewis integrated logic into his writing when he noted, "Lewis used logos to develop his content. One never gets the idea that he is fumbling for something to say. His mind was fertile, manifesting fruit whenever he put his pen to paper."[59] Root also affirmed Lewis's use of ethos: "Perhaps the mode most strongly evident is his ethos. He is honest, and he displays in his work that authenticity of character that is full of genuine humility and childlike wonder."[60] Root further adds, "His ethos is exhibited when he wrestles with thorny passages in the Psalms that others tend to avoid because of their difficulty."[61] The rhetorical methods of ethos, logos and pathos were not just theoretical constructs, but essential methods used to express his ideas.

Lewis thought rhetoric a noble art.[62] Though in *A Preface to Paradise Lost* he said, "It [rhetoric] is in itself noble, though of course, like most arts, it can be wickedly used."[63] Although the word *rhetoric* can have a negative connotation (such as the blast of political bombast from bloviating politicians, or the constant distracting pop-up parade of ads on a variety of media), according to Lewis, it is not inherently unethical. The problem lies with rhetoricians, those who may use rhetoric to achieve unethical goals or use unscrupulous means (such as distorting evidence, inaccurately relying on fear appeals, or lying) to achieve their goals.

For Lewis, rhetoric draws on both reason and creative imagination. In *An Experiment in Criticism*, Lewis describes the rhetorical process of expressing literary ideas as "both Logos (something said) and Poeima (something made)."[64] Then contrasting Logos with Poeima he adds, "As Poeima, by its aural beauties and also by the balance and contrast … it is an *objet d' art*, a thing shaped so as to give great satisfaction."[65] In *A Preface to Paradise Lost* he notes: "[Logos] tells a story, or expresses an emotion, or exhorts or pleads or describes or rebukes or excites laughter."[66] What Logos and Poeima have in common is that they are both goal-oriented. He describes their function when he says, "Both these arts, in my opinion, definitely aim at doing something to an audience."[67] To clarify how both of these arts do something to an audience he adds, "And both do it by using language to control what already exists in our minds."[68]

Rhetorical scholar James Como identified the logical structure Lewis employed to develop his logical, persuasive arguments in two of his classic apologetic works, *The Problem of Pain* and *Miracles: A Preliminary Study*. According to Como, Lewis consistently developed his rhetorical arguments by using a seven-step structure:

1. Frame the problem: Identify the problem or concern and make it relevant to the reader.

2. Define the terms: Clarify murky meaning so it is clear to the reader or listener.

3. Address any psychological reservations: Anticipate objections from the audience.

4. Address objections: Provide logical responses to any objections the reader or listener might likely have.

5. Hypothesize an explanation for the problem: Such as explaining the presence of pain in a world created by a loving God, or providing a rationale for the apparent defiance of physical laws in the occurrence of some concrete, spatio-temporal event (miracles)—turning water into wine, or raising Lazarus from the dead).

6. Demonstrate the advantage of the new hypothesis: Clarify how the new point identified is the best possible explanation.

7. Make the new alternative emotionally appealing: Use story or example to illustrate how the persuasive conclusion meets the reader's needs.[69]

As a Christian apologist and skilled rhetorician, Lewis was especially adept at step four in the preceding list: anticipating objections and then refuting them. It is his ability to identify potential objections and then debunking them that gave his writing a dialectical quality.

Dialectic

Dialectic, a communication form closely associated with rhetoric, is the search for truth through the give and take process of debate—an interactive strategy of asking and answering questions in the style of Socrates, further emulated by Plato. In *The Discarded Image*, a book-length posthumous compendium of Lewis's lectures about literature in the Middle Ages, Lewis defines dialectic as "the art of disputation."[70] He adds, "Dialectic is concerned with proving. In the Middle Ages there are three kinds of proof; from Reason, from Authority, and from Experience."[71] In other words, dialectic seeks to solve problems via deliberation and debate using evidence. Lewis continues, "What is really meant is that, having learned from grammar how to talk, we must learn from Dialectic how to talk sense, to argue, to prove and disprove."[72] To see the dialectical process is to experience the thrust and parry of clashing arguments, questions posed, and answers given in response—a point and counter-point debate.

The opening sentence in Aristotle's work *The Art of Rhetoric* provides an important clue to the relationship of dialectic (debate) to rhetoric (persuasion): "Rhetoric," says Aristotle, "is the counterpart of Dialectic."[73] The key word here is *counterpart.* Whereas dialectic strives to *discover* the truth, rhetoric seeks to *convince* others that the problem has been solved and the answer has been provided. While rhetoric is about persuasion, dialectic is about discovery through debate. The give and take process of searching for truth in courtrooms or in Congress draws on the skill and principles of dialectic. Yet, as Aristotle emphasized, they are connected.

It was to his teacher William T. Kirkpatrick that Lewis attributed his dialectical debating skill and his rhetorical logic and persuasion skills. Lewis describes Kirkpatrick as a purely logical person and notes, "If Kirk's ruthless dialectic had been merely a pedagogic instrument I might have resented it."[74] But Lewis did not resent Kirkpatrick's "ruthless dialectic"; he relished the challenge of defending his ideas. It was with Kirkpatrick that Lewis developed skills that he would later apply at the Oxford Union (home of the student debating society), as well as the Socratic Club and other contexts for demonstrating his ability to debate.

Lewis did not shy away from debate and intense discussion. For him, the process of dialectic was equally as important as, if not more so than, rhetoric—persuading someone to act. Jerry Root, who has closely examined Lewis's use of rhetorical strategies suggests "... the key tool in the rhetorician's toolbox is dialectic. Dialectic functions as the art of debate and supplies rhetoric with its power to persuade."[75] Root adds, "Lewis was a brilliant debater, and he was not afraid of opposition; rather he encouraged it."[76]

His close friend Owen Barfield notes that Lewis's dialectical skill, "was greatly furthered by a characteristic, perhaps only one which he seems to have shared with Jeremy Bentham [founder of utilitarian philosophy]. That is, a certain delight in expounding the obvious and in expounding it meticulously more than once."[77] Lewis scholar Greg Anderson goes so far as to suggest that "Lewis was more interested in dialectic than rhetoric."[78] Anderson draws this conclusion from Lewis's own words. As noted in Chapter 2, in *The Personal Heresy*, the book written collaboratively as a literary debate with E. M. W. Tillyard, Lewis notes, "We have both learnt our dialectic in rough academic arenas where knocks that would frighten the London literary coteries are given and taken in good part."[79] Even if Anderson is right, that Lewis is more interested in dialectic than rhetoric, Lewis nonetheless clearly valued the goals of rhetoric—achieving action. In *English Literature in the Sixteenth Century: Excluding Drama* Lewis extols the virtue of rhetoric when he writes,

> Rhetoric is the greatest barrier between us and our ancestors ... In rhetoric, more than in anything else, the continuity of the old European tradition was embodied.

Older than the church, older than Roman Law, older than all Latin literature, it descends from the age of the Greek Sophists. Like the Church and the
law it survives the fall of the empire, rides the renascentia and the Reformation
like waves, and penetrates far into the eighteenth century ... as Dante says,
'the sweetest of all the other sciences'... If ever the passion for formal rhetoric
returns, the whole story will have to be rewritten and many judgments may be
reversed.[80]

By "the whole story," Lewis means the history of literature. Lewis clearly thought
that if classical rhetorical criticism were to come back into style as a form of
literary criticism, readers' understandings and assessments of many texts would
change. He reached his conclusion about the importance of rhetoric using his
dialectic, search-for-truth skill.

Poetic

With rhetoric being primarily about persuasion, and dialectic about debate, the
poetic is about the aesthetic quest for beauty as achieved through the creative use
of literary language. Although "grammar" was one of the original subjects in *The
Trivium*, the poetic is a refined and elevated study of grammar; it is the application of words and word meanings to achieve "certain ends" (Lewis's words)—a
precise use of words' sound, cadence, rhyme and rhythm to evoke a larger aesthetic interpretation.[81] In *The Personal Heresy*, Lewis provides his insight about
how poetry works. "Poetry," he says, "is an art or skill—a trained habit of using
certain instruments to certain ends."[82] Drawing on his classical education, he explains, "By poetry, I mean as the Renaissance critics meant, imaginative literature
whether prose or verse."[83] To Lewis, poetry could occur in any art form (art,
music, theatre, and other fine and performing arts) "using all the extra-logical
elements of language."[84]

In not limiting poetry to be only "verse" and describing its purpose as "imaginative," he is referring to the function of poetry as the quest for the romantic.
In the classical sense, the romantic is about more than love or sexual desire; it is
also—even primarily—about chivalry and bravery. The legend of King Arthur
and the mythic stories of Norse gods, as well as Greek and Roman gods, are tales
of larger-than-life quests for goodness and virtue.[85]

As noted previously, early in Lewis's career, his primary goal was to be a poet.
He loved the long narrative poems of Dante, Virgil, and Spencer, which trans-
ported Lewis to imaginative places he had never been. In addition to lingering on
these stories and images, Lewis wanted to create mythic, poetic places for others

to visit. But, as noted in Chapter 2, his early poetic works *Spirits in Bondage* and *Dymer* were not widely read. Although there was some positive critical response (Owen Barfield thought they were excellent), lackluster response from others (reflected in the lack of sales) helped him realize that he should pursue creative outlets other than poetry.

For Lewis, effective communication is holistic. It includes all three communication applications—to achieve action (rhetoric); to debate and discuss (dialectic); and to provide inspiration, romance, and beauty (poetic) to help us see farther than these forms on their own permit. The element common to all three is *truth*. Dialectic, through debate, is the search for truth. Rhetoric transpires to convince others of the truth. Truth imbued with beauty (poetic) provides the spiritual balance to which humans aspire; Lewis, in fact, referred to the poetic as "spiritual health."[86]

Lewis not only drew on both his rhetorical and dialectical training to inform his approach to communication, but also saw no major distinctions between the applications of rhetoric and the poetic. Describing the historical roots integrating rhetorical and poetical aims, Lewis writes, "By the Middle Ages [rhetoric] has become literary. Its precepts are addressed quite as much to poets as to advocates. There is no antithesis, indeed no distinction, between Rhetoric and Poetry."[87] He adds, "I think the Rhetoricians always have in view a pupil whose medium will be Latin, but their work also affected vernacular practice."[88] In other words, the art of rhetoric is important for all educated people in managing their day-to-day dealings with others, whether in the courts of law, the political arena, or the market. Lewis reminds his reader in *The Discarded Image* of the link between rhetoric and literary criticism, an explicit focus of Lewis's scholarship: "Everything that we should now call criticism belonged either to Grammar or to Rhetoric. The grammarian explained a poet's meter and allusions: the Rhetorician dealt with structure and style."[89] Lewis's holistic instinct is to integrate whereas contemporary academic practice is to segregate, as evidenced by separate academic departments that focus on rhetoric and dialectic from the standpoint of taking action (as studied in academic departments of communication), and the poetic (as studied in English departments).

Rhetoric, dialectic, and the poetic, *working in holistic combination*, are all means of giving a reader or listener new insights. But each of these three methods of communication, with its own rules and forms, illuminates the communication process from a slightly different perspective. Rhetoric uses well-crafted logical arguments to achieve action—something Lewis drew upon as an apologist. Dialectic involves logic and reason, as well as listening, anticipating and responding to an audience, to prove a point. Lewis greatly enjoyed the clash of ideas while listening and responding to others.

Lewis often integrated the poetic in the form of a story to, in his words, "steal past watchful dragons."[90] Lewis's skill as a poet is evident in his non-poetic writing. Literary scholar Kath Filmer observed, "It is not surprising that Lewis should have transferred his poetic techniques to his prose. Indeed, his friend the poet Ruth Pitter writes that 'his poetry … is … most evident in his prose.'"[91] In his essay "Sometimes Fairy Stories May Say Best What's to Be Said," Lewis provides a clear rationale for his use of story (poetic), specifically the Narnia stories, to achieve rational (dialectic) and persuasive (rhetoric) goals. Lewis writes,

> I thought I saw how stories of this kind [Narnia] could steal past a certain inhibition which paralysed much of my own religion in childhood. Why did one find it so hard to feel as one was told one ought to feel about God or about the sufferings of Christ? I thought the chief reason was that one was told one ought to. An obligation to feel can freeze feelings.[92]

Being too reverent or liturgical may create a barrier for the reader. As Lewis notes, "… reverence itself did harm. The whole subject was associated with lowered voices; almost as if it were something medical."[93] Lewis's solution is to smuggle the Christian message as a supposal. He explains,

> But supposing that by casting all these things into an imaginary world, stripping them of their stained-glass and Sunday school associations, one could make them for the first time appear in their real potency? Could one not thus steal past those watchful dragons? I thought one could.[94]

Lewis's use of story was a purposeful strategy to navigate around rational and logical "guard dragons" (as associated with stained-glass and Sunday school) that might keep the message from resonating with the listener or reader.

As Lewis sought to merge the aims of rhetoric and poetic, some of his contemporaries in the United States were carving out the discipline of speech separate from English. Communication scholars point to Herbert A. Wichelns' classic article "The Literary Criticism of Oratory," published in 1925 (when Lewis was seeking employment as a tutor) for making a clear distinction between rhetoric, with its focus on persuasion (to achieve action), and the poetic or aesthetic literary criticism, concerned with imaginative, creative literature. By uncoupling rhetoric from the poetic, speech scholars sought to carve out a disciplinary focus on the persuasive, action-oriented aspects of oratory, separate from literary criticism as practiced by scholars of English literature. Other speech scholars and rhetorical critics mirrored the taxonomy established by Wichelns with a focus on rhetoric as found in speech; thus, oratory evolved as an area of criticism *separated* from literary criticism. As succinctly stated by rhetorical scholar Gordon Bigelow, "poetry is for the sake of expression" and "rhetoric is for the sake of impression."[95] Rhetorician Carol C. Arnold further suggests that literature refers to "imaginative, enduring works."[96]

A twentieth century rhetorical colleague of Arnold's, Wilbur Howell, also made a clear distinction between the rhetorical and literary perspectives: "The poetical utterance differs from the rhetorical utterance by virtue of the fact that the words used in the latter refer directly to states of reality, and the words used in the former refer directly to things that stand by deputy [the symbolic] for states of reality."[97] More recently, former National Communication Association president and rhetorical scholar Kenneth Andersen noted differences between the aims of rhetoric and the poetic from a communication perspective: "One distinction often made within discourse was that between rhetoric which was concerned with persuasion, with public affairs, with our daily affairs in the world of information and 'influence', and poetic which was concerned with the aesthetic, with creative, literary material."[98] Communication scholars have traditionally focused on "influence" while English literature scholars have focused on the "aesthetic, creative, literary material." A contemporary well-respected rhetorical critic, Karlyn Kohrs Campbell, further specifies that "Rhetoric, then, refers to written and oral discourses that are persuasive."[99]

Clear distinctions were made between rhetoric and the poetic in the early and middle part of the 20th century to carve out a distinct rhetorical tradition in speech departments. More contemporary rhetorical scholars from the oral tradition have endorsed greater integration between rhetorical and poetic approaches to criticism. This integration has occurred especially as concepts of "text" and "discourse" encompass more than speeches, but also include the rhetoric of architecture and social media posts. In a contemporary article minimizing distinctions between rhetoric and poetics, rhetorical educators William Benoitt and Kevin Dean suggest that rhetorical theory is appropriate for criticizing rhetorical as well as literary artifacts.[100]

Yet some contemporary rhetorical scholars continue to view rhetoric, with an emphasis on persuasion to achieve a goal (action), separate from the poetic (as evolved from the study of grammar), which focuses on aesthetics and the quest for beauty. But as Rhetorical and Lewis scholar Greg Anderson suggests, "Lewis was spot on as a rhetorical historian when he claims that the distinction between rhetoric and poetry was meaningless until the modern period."[101] At the same time that speech and English educators were seeking to uncouple rhetoric from the poetic, Lewis drew on medieval and renaissance literary tradition to integrate these two forms of expression just as rhetorical scholars did during medieval and renaissance times.

Kenneth Burke was one of the most original rhetorical thinkers of the 20th century. Burke, like Lewis, saw rhetoric and poetic as working together rather than as separate traditions. Burke says he is more interested "in bringing the full resources of Poetics and *Rhetorical docens* to bear upon the study of a text than in trying to draw a strict line of demarcation between Rhetoric and Poetics."[102] Burke is a mainstay of the contemporary study of rhetoric; Lewis's rhetorical ideas, however, are not referenced in the index or table of contents of contemporary rhetoric textbooks even though he predates Burke's integration of rhetoric and poetics. Lewis's rhetorical ideas have much to offer the study of contemporary rhetoric.

While the academic debate about where to draw the line, or even whether a line should be drawn, between rhetoric and poetics, is of interest to academics, what is the implication of this debate for readers of Lewis? Lewis *did* take a side. He saw a very thin line between rhetoric and the poetic. In 1619 Aristotle's *Rhetoric* and *Poetics* were published in a *single volume* reported to be the first time Aristotle's two seminal works were published in England (although the book, which is in my library, is printed in dual columns of Greek and Latin).[103] The fact that these two books were published *together* supports Lewis's notion that rhetoric and the poetic have a united purpose: to seek truth and illuminate meaning with both logic and imagination.

The best examples of Lewis's integration of rhetoric, dialectic, and the poetic are some of his classic works. Each of his novels can be interpreted from the tripartite perspective of considering the persuasive goal, the interactive dialogue, and literary tropes used to express ideas and achieve a goal. His novels also exemplify a marriage of reason and imagination that appeal to the eye as well as the ear. *The Screwtape Letters* offers an imaginative story with a clear persuasive goal (rhetoric), brimming with devilish dialogue (dialectic). There is a clear integration of not only rhetoric, dialectic, and the poetic, but also reason and imagination. And the book is as clever whether read silently or aloud. Another book series often read aloud as bedtime stories or on long car trips, *The Chronicles of Narnia,* offers additional exemplary evidence of Lewis's skill in holistically using the available means of rhetoric, dialectic, and the poetic to present a narrative with underlying rhetorical overtones. His novels also exemplify a marriage of reason and imagination that appeal to the eye as well as the ear. From his allegorical first novel, *The*

Pilgrims Regress, to his last, based on a retelling of the Cupid and Psyche myth, *Till We Have Faces*, C. S. Lewis's appeal as an author can be explained, in part, by his holistic communication strategies.

Summary: The "H" of HI TEA: The Principle of Being Holistic

This chapter identifies Lewis's comprehensive approach to human communication from three perspectives. First, Lewis did not segregate oral communication from written communication in theory or practice, but viewed them as integral processes of using language to express ideas and emotions to an audience—an audience that might either read the words or hear the words.

Second, Lewis used reason and imagination, often in the same paragraph, to express his ideas. Reason and imagination are both needed to make truth meaningful and to make meaning truthful. Reason is the natural organ of truth; imagination is the organ of meaning.[104] Both are required to make sense and share sense with others.

And third, Lewis minimized the distinction between the aims of rhetoric, dialectic, and the poetic. The goal of communication is to "do something to an audience,"[105] whether the "something" is to achieve action (through rhetoric—discovering the available means of persuasion), discover truth (through dialectic), or promote imagination (through the poetic). These communication methods work together to express ideas to a listener or reader. Lewis debunked academic arguments that rhetoric, dialectic, and the poetic were three unrelated means of human expression. He viewed these three communication forms as having similar goals and aims. Learning theorists recognize three domains of learning (cognitive, behavioral, affective). Lewis's integration of rhetoric, dialectic and the poetic mirrors these three learning domains. Rhetoric (stresses behavioral outcomes), dialectic (emphasizes the cognitive domain), and the poetic (which often evokes an affective response) are three related methods of "doing something to an audience," primarily through the use of language.

Lewis holistically blurred distinctions between communication genres. He wrote *The Chronicles of Narnia* for both children and adults. *The Screwtape Letters* are imaginative fiction with an underlying apologetical purpose. His science fiction series (*Out of the Silent Planet, Perelandra, That Hideous Strength*) drew on both his rich imagination and underlying logic to make a theological point. Lewis wrote both popular and scholarly books. His prose incorporates poetic language; his poetry expresses prosaic ideas. He was master of several literary formats, genres, and styles that are often exemplified in a single work. He was holistic not only in his methods of communicating but also in using these methods in multiple genres to achieve his purpose. As will be noted in the next chapter, his purpose was intentional.

In one of Lewis's memorable essays, "Meditation in a Toolshed," he draws a distinction between looking "at" something and looking "along" something. Observing a beam of light in a dark toolshed, Lewis notes, "You get one experience of a thing when you look along it and another when you look at it."[106] When looking only *at* the beam, he observed, "I was seeing the beam, not seeing things by it."[107] When looking *along* the beam he found,

> Instantly the whole previous picture vanished. I saw no toolshed, and (above all) no beam. Instead I saw, framed in the irregular cranny at the top of the door, green leaves moving on the branches of a tree outside and beyond that, 90-odd million miles away, the sun. Looking along the beam, and looking at the beam are very different experiences.[108]

Lewis did not privilege one strategy (looking at) over the other (looking along). He argued for a holistic way of looking at the world when he concluded, "We must, on pain of idiocy, deny from the very outset the idea that looking *at* is, by its own nature, intrinsically truer or better than longing *along*. One must look both *along* and *at* everything."[109] *Both* are vital ways of making sense.

By looking holistically *at* and *along* the communication process, Lewis observed the overall function of rhetoric, dialectic and the poetic—to do something to an audience. He did not dissect speaking from writing; rather, by integrating the two, he looked "along" the process of making meaning and seeking truth, rather than focusing on only one method of expression. Similarly, reason and imagination are not two distinct, unrelated elements, but are both vital to human expression. Lewis is effective because he looked *at* and *along* the communication process, both in principle and in practice.

For C. S. Lewis, communication is a holistic, creative process rather than segmented and fractured. Communication has the most power when the means of speaking and listening, thinking and imagining, and persuading and discovering are united. Lewis biographer Alister McGrath offers an additional conclusion about Lewis's holistic process when he suggests, "Lewis gives us a way of looking at things that bridges the great divide between modernity and postmodernity. Each outlook has its strengths because it is part of the greater whole."[110] Lewis has the power to link these two prevailing ways of looking at the world because of his ability to be holistic—to appeal to head and heart in ways that help readers and listeners make sense out of their world. For C. S. Lewis, communication integrates all forms of human expression. He helps us see, think, and feel holistically.

Notes

1. C. S. Lewis, *Studies in Words* (Cambridge: Cambridge University Press, 1960), 14.
2. Clyde S. Kilby, "The Creative Logician Speaking," in *C. S. Lewis: Speaker and Teacher*, ed. Carolyn Keefe (Grand Rapids: Zondervan, 1971), 24.
3. C. S. Lewis, *The Discarded Image: An Introduction to Medieval and Renaissance Literature* (Cambridge: Cambridge University Press, 1964), 190.
4. *Christianity Today*, "Books of the Century," April 24, 2000. www.christianitytoday. com/ct/2000/april24/5.92html.
5. See: Walter Hooper, *C. S. Lewis: Companion & Guide* (New York: HarperCollins, 1996); Art Lindsley, *C. S. Lewis's Case for Christ: Insights from Reason, Imagination and Faith* (Downers Grove: IPV Books).
6. Owen Barfield, "The Five C. S. Lewises," *Owen Barfield on C. S. Lewis*, ed. Georg B. Tennyson (Middletown: Wesleyan University Press, 1989), 120–121.
7. C. S. Lewis, *The Collected Letters of C. S. Lewis, Vol. I: Family Letters 1905–1931*, ed. Walter Hooper (San Francisco: Harper San Francisco, 2004), x.
8. C. S. Lewis, "Is Theology Poetry," *They Asked for a Paper* (London: Geoffrey Bles, 1962).
9. C. S. Lewis, *Language and Human Nature, VII: An Anglo-American Literary Review* 29 (2010), 25.
10. Lewis, *Language and Human Nature*, 26.
11. Lewis, *Collected Letters I*, x.
12. Walter Hooper, "To the Martlets," *C. S. Lewis: Speaker and Teacher*, ed. Carolyn Keefe (Grand Rapids: Zondervan, 1971), 50.
13. Hooper, "To the Martlets," 50.
14. C. S. Lewis, Letter to Thomasine, December 14, 1959, *Collected Letters, Vol. III: Narnia, Cambridge and Joy 1950–1963*, ed. Walter Hooper (San Francisco: Harper San Francisco, 2007), 1108.
15. C. S. Lewis, Letter to Mrs. Hook, December 29, 1958. *Collected Letters III*, 1004–1005.
16. Lewis, *Collected Letters III*, 1004–1005.
17. For a discussion of the differences between oral style and written style see: Steven A. Beebe and Susan J. Beebe, *Public Speaking: An Audience-Centered Approach* 11th edition (Boston: Pearson, 2021), Chapter 1.
18. C. S. Lewis, *Mere Christianity* (London: Geoffrey Bles, 1952), v.

19. Lewis, *Mere Christianity,* 114

20. C. S. Lewis, *The Discarded Image* (Cambridge: Cambridge University Press, 1964), 190.

21. C. S. Lewis, *Surprised by Joy: The Shape of My Early Life* (London: Geoffrey Bles, 1955), 141.

22. Lewis, *Language and Human Nature*, 25. Also see: Steven A. Beebe, "C. S. Lewis on Language and Meaning," *VII: An Anglo-American Literary Review*, Vol. 27 (2010), 7–24.

23. James Como, *Branches to Heaven: The Geniuses of C. S. Lewis* (Dallas: Spence Publishing Company, 1998), 27.

24. Greg M. Anderson, "A Most Potent Rhetoric: C. S. Lewis, 'Congenital Rhetorician'," *C. S. Lewis: Life, Works, and Legacy*, ed. Bruce L. Edwards (Westport: Praeger Perspectives, 2007), 198.

25. Anderson, "A Most Potent Rhetoric," 198.

26. Anderson, "A Most Potent Rhetoric," 218.

27. Lewis, *Studies in Words*, 14.

28. Lewis, *The Discarded Image*, 190.

29. Alister McGrath, *C. S. Lewis: A Life* (Carol Stream: Tyndale House Publishers Inc., 2013).

30. McGrath, *C. S. Lewis*, 163.

31. Lewis, *Collected Letters III*, Letter to Tomasine, December 15, 1959, 1109.

32. For a discussion of Lewis and imagination see: Jerry Root and Mark Neal, *The Surprising Imagination of C. S. Lewis: An Introduction* (Nashville: Abingdon Press, 2015).

33. C. S. Lewis, *Out of the Silent Planet* (London: Bodley Head, 1938), 37.

34. C. S. Lewis, *Boxen: The Imaginary World of the Young*, ed. Walter Hooper (London: Collins, 1985); also see: Lewis, *Surprised by Joy*, note 1, "… Animal-Land had nothing whatever in common with Narnia except the anthropomorphic beasts," 22.

35. Lewis, *Surprised by Joy*, 135–136

36. Lewis, *Surprised by Joy*, 136.

37. Lewis, *Surprised by Joy*, 136.

38. Kilby, "The Creative Logician Speaking," 24.

39. Chad Walsh, *C. S. Lewis: Apostle to the Skeptics* (New York: Macmillan, 1949), 3.

40. See: Joel D. Heck, *Irrigating Deserts: C. S. Lewis on Education* (St. Louis: Concordia Publishing House, 2005).

41. McGrath, *C. S. Lewis,* 174.

42. McGrath, *C. S. Lewis,* 169.

43. Alister McGrath, "C. S. Lewis" Lecture at Oxford University, Oxford, UK (May 10, 2015).

44. Lewis, *Collected Letters III*, Letter to the Milton Society of America, 1954, 516–517.

45. Lewis, *Collected Letters III*, Letter to the Milton Society of America, 1954, 516–517.

46. Terrence R. Lindvall, *C. S. Lewis' Theory of Communication* (Unpublished dissertation, University of Southern California, 1980), 464.

47. George Bailey, "In the University," *C. S. Lewis Speaker & Teacher*, ed. Carolyn Keefe (London Hodder and Stoughton, 1971), 112.

48. Attributed to Kenneth Tynan by Bailey, "In the University," 112.

49. Lee D. Rossi, " 'Logic' and 'Romance': The Divided Self of C. S. Lewis." *Bloom's Modern Critical Views: C. S. Lewis*, ed. Harold Bloom (New York: Chelsea House, 2006), 66.

50. Rossi, " 'Logic' and 'Romance,' " 67.

51. Letter to Eliza Marian Butler, 25 September 1940, C. S. Lewis, *The Collected Letters of C. S. Lewis, Vol. II: Books, Broadcasts and the War 1931–1949*, ed. Walter Hooper (San Francisco: Harper San Francisco, 2004), 444–446.

52. McGrath, *C. S. Lewis*, 263.

53. See: George Sayer, *Jack: A Life of C. S. Lewis* (Wheaton: Crossway Books, 1994).

54. See: C. S. Lewis, *That Hideous Strength* (London: John Lane, The Bodley Head, 1945), 7.

55. C. S. Lewis, "Bluspels and Flalansferes: A Semantic Nightmare," *Selected Literary Essays*, ed. Walter Hooper (Cambridge: Cambridge University Press, 1969), 251–265.

56. Lewis, "Bluspels and Flalansferes," 265.

57. Lewis, "Bluspels and Flalansferes," 265.

58. Aristotle, *The Art of Rhetoric*, trans. by Hugh Lawson-Tancred (London: Penguin Books, 1991), 66.

59. Jerry Root, *C. S. Lewis and a Problem of Evil: An Investigation of a Pervasive Theme* (Eugene: Pickwick Publications, 2009), xvi.

60. Root, *C. S. Lewis and a Problem of Evil*, xvi.

61. Root, *C. S. Lewis and a Problem of Evil*, xvi.

62. C. S. Lewis, *A Preface to Paradise Lost* (Oxford: Oxford University Press, 1942), 51.

63. Lewis, *Preface to Paradise Lost*, 51.

64. C. S. Lewis, *An Experiment in Criticism* (Cambridge: Cambridge University Press, 1961), 132.

65. Lewis, *An Experiment in Criticism*, 132.

66. Lewis, *Preface to Paradise Lost*, 52.

67. Lewis, *Preface to Paradise Lost*, 52.

68. Lewis, *Preface to Paradise Lost*, 52.

69. James Como, *Branches to Heaven: The Geniuses of C. S. Lewis* (Dallas: Spence Publishing Company, 1998), 154. Also see: James Como, *C. S. Lewis: A Very Short Introduction* (Oxford: Oxford University Press, 2019), 66.

70. Lewis, *The Discarded Image*, 189.

71. Lewis, *The Discarded Image*, 189.

72. Lewis, *The Discarded Image*, 189.

73. Aristotle, *The Art of Rhetoric*, translated by Hugh Lawson-Tancred, (London: Penguin Books, 1991), 66.

74. Lewis, *Surprised by Joy*, 131.

75. Root, *C. S. Lewis and a Problem of Evil*, xv.

76. Root, *C. S. Lewis and a Problem of Evil*, xv.

77. Owen Barfield, "C. S. Lewis in Conversation," *Owen Barfield on C. S. Lewis*, ed. G. B. Tennyson (San Rafael: The Barfield Press in association with Wesleyan University Press, 1989), 34.

78. Anderson, "A Most Potent Rhetoric," 197.

79. C. S. Lewis and E. M. W. Tillyard, *The Personal Heresy* (Oxford: Oxford University Press, 1939), 69.

80. Lewis, *English Literature in the Sixteenth Century*, 61.

81. Lewis and Tillyard, *The Personal Heresy*, 67

82. Lewis and Tillyard, *The Personal Heresy*, 67

83. Lewis and Tillyard, *The Personal Heresy*, 67

84. Lewis and Tillyard, *The Personal Heresy*, 107–108.

85. For an excellent discussion of Arthurian myth in the writing of C. S. Lewis see: *The Inklings and King Arthur: J. R. R. Tolkien, Charles Williams, C. S. Lewis, & Owen Barfield on the Matter of Britain*, ed. Sorina Higgins (Berkeley: Apocryphile Press, 2017).

86. Lewis, *Preface to Paradise Lost*, 53

87. Lewis, *The Discarded Image*, 190

88. Lewis, *The Discarded Image*, 191.

89. Lewis, *The Discarded Image*, 190.

90. C. S. Lewis, "Sometimes Fairy Stories May Say Best What's to Be Said," *On Stories: And Other Essays on Literature* (Harvest Books, 2002), 47.

91. Kath Filmer, "The Polemic Image: The Role of Metaphor and Symbol in the Fiction of C. S. Lewis," *The Taste of the Pineapple: Essays on C. S. Lewis as Reader, Critic, and Imaginative Writer*, ed. Bruce L. Edwards Bowling Green, (Ohio: Bowling Green State University Popular Press, 1988), 163. And see: Ruth Pitter, note with correspondence from C. S. Lewis in Bodleian Library, Oxford, MS Eng. Let C220/3, 63.

92. Lewis, "Sometimes Fairy Stories."

93. Lewis, "Sometimes Fairy Stories."

94. Lewis, "Sometimes Fairy Stories."

95. Gordon E. Bigelow, "Distinguishing Rhetoric from Poetic Discourse," *Southern Speech Journal* 19 (1953), 83.

96. Carol C. Arnold, *Criticism of Oral Rhetoric* (Columbus: Charles E. Merrill, 1974), 4.

97. Wilbur S. Howell, "Literature as an Enterprise in Communication," *Quarterly Journal of Speech* 33 (1947), 418.

98. Kenneth E. Andersen, "A Perspective on Defining the Field of Communication," in *The Association for Communication Administration Bulletin* 48 (1999), 17

99. Karlyn K. Campbell *Critiques of Contemporary Rhetoric* (Belmont: Wadsworth, 1972), 4.

100. William L. Benoit and Kevin W. Dean, "Rhetorical Criticism of Literary Artifacts." *The National Forensics Journal* 3 (1985), 154–162.

101. Anderson, "A Most Potent Rhetoric," 203.

102. Kenneth Burke, *Language as Symbolic Action: Essays on Life, Literature, and Method* (Berkeley: University of California Press, 1966), 307.

103. Prior to the early 1600s most scholarly books were published in Venice, Italy.

104. C. S. Lewis, "Bluspels and Flalansferes: A Semantic Nightmare" in *Rehabilitations and Other Essays* (Oxford: Oxford University Press, 1939): 133–158.

105. Lewis, *A Preface to Paradise Lost*, 51.

106. C. S. Lewis, "Meditation in a Toolshed," *God in the Dock*, ed. Walter Hooper (Grand Rapids: Eerdmans, 1970), 212–215.

107. Lewis, "Meditation in a Toolshed," 212.

108. Lewis, "Meditation in a Toolshed," 212.

109. Lewis, "Meditation in a Toolshed," 213.

110. McGrath, *C. S. Lewis*, 16.

5

Intentional

"Take great pains to be clear. Remember that though you start by knowing what you mean, the reader doesn't, and a single ill-chosen word may lead him to a total misunderstanding."[1]

- C. S. Lewis

"The way for a person to develop a style is (a) to know exactly what he wants to say, and (b) to be sure he is saying exactly that. The reader, we must remember, does not start by knowing what we mean. If our words are ambiguous, our meaning will escape him. I sometimes think that writing is like driving sheep down a road. If there is any gate open to the left or the right the readers will most certainly go into it."[2]

- C. S. Lewis

Lewis's brother Warnie noted in his diary that he traveled with his brother to Durham on February 24, 1943. Riding the train from Oxford to Durham takes about four hours on a "direct" train—it takes longer on a "milk run" train, one that stops at smaller towns and villages to deliver milk and other supplies. According to the weather summary for 1943, Northern England experienced heavy rain on the 24th. The reported fog may have obstructed the Northern Lights that were visible in Northern England and Scotland that night. Yet when the train pulled into Durham station, even heavy fog would likely not have obscured the view of Durham Cathedral—a massive Romanesque and Gothic structure (469 feet long and 218 feet tall) that dramatically presides over the city of Durham on a cliff overlooking the River Wear. Warnie noted in his diary that "its exquisite beauty came upon us with an impact I shall long remember."[3]

After getting settled in their room in Durham, Jack and Warnie traveled another 45 minutes by train to Newcastle-upon-Tyne where that evening Lewis delivered the first of three Riddell Memorial Lectures in the Physics Lecture Theatre, Kings College, Newcastle—which was also a college of the University of Durham.[4] The title of his lecture was "The Abolition of Man: Reflections on Education with Special Reference to the Teaching of English in the Upper Forms of Schools." Lewis sometimes struggled with finding just the right title, and his subtitle for this classic message was one of his longest. There are no audio or video recordings of the lecture. (In fact, it is astonishing that there are no existing video or film recordings of Lewis at all.) Lewis sometimes used a manuscript and read his lectures (although he noted in a letter to his father that "READ lectures send people to sleep and I think I must make the plunge from the very beginning and learn to TALK, not to recite.")[5]; at other times, when presenting lectures to his students, he spoke extemporaneously from an outline. Although the original speech manuscripts for the Riddell Memorial Lectures do not exist, *The Abolition of Man*, a published version of the lectures, has become one of the most important books in the Lewis canon.

On February 8, 1943, a few days before he traveled to Durham and on to Newcastle, Lewis tried out his core message on the Socratic Club, focusing on the question, "If We Have Christ's Ethics Does the Rest of the Christian Faith Matter?" The summary of his paper published in the *Socratic Digest* provides a general overview of his ideas about Natural Law—the topic he developed in full in his Riddell Memorial Lecture series.[6] As introduced in Chapter 3, Natural Law or the Tao was an important and enduring message for Lewis. The topic was also the subject of his first BBC radio broadcast on August 6, 1941, which was eventually to be published as *Mere Christianity*.

Lewis had excellent debating skills and could usually respond quickly on his feet, but he was generally not a speaker who waited until he stood behind the lectern for inspiration. Although he liked responding to impromptu questions from an audience, he would not have dreamed of rising to give a formal talk unless he knew precisely what he wanted to say. As he started his first of the three Riddell lectures, the audience undoubtedly sat in anticipation waiting for what the Great Man would say. His reputation as an author and speaker was rapidly growing, based on his recently published books *The Problem of Pain* and *The Screwtape Letters*. He had already delivered his successful series of broadcast talks on the BBC, which were published as *Broadcast Talks*.

After being introduced, Lewis arranged his papers, then uttered his first words. There may have been quizzical looks as he began talking about a "sublime" waterfall. As noted in Chapter 3, he then indicted both authors of *The Green Book*, "Gaius" and "Titius" (pseudonyms for Alec King and Martin Ketley) for their assumptions that word use says more about the speaker, than it does about what the speaker is talking about.[7]

"Gaius" and "Titius" suggest that when someone describes a waterfall as "sublime," the utterance is really a statement about the person's *feelings,* rather than a description of the waterfall. Lewis disagrees. He notes, "If the view held by Gaius and Titius were consistently applied it would lead to obvious absurdities. It would force them to maintain that *You are contemptible* means *I have contemptible feelings*: in fact that *Your feelings are contemptible* means *My feelings are contemptible.*"[8] Lewis logically argues for the existence of "the doctrine of objective value, the belief that certain attitudes are really true, and others really false."[9] Objective value exists because real objects *are* by their nature beautiful and sublime. Or as Lewis puts it, "certain attitudes are really true."

Because objective value exists, Lewis further reasons that Natural Laws exist. It is one of his "big ideas" that permeate all of his writing and speaking. Natural Laws, according to Lewis, are values and principles inherent in nature that provide the foundation for what is good, beautiful and true in all contexts. Natural Laws supersede the idiosyncratic, ephemeral rules or laws of a given society or culture. What is right and true in one context is universally (or naturally) right and true in all contexts. Thus, Natural Laws are the sub-structure for all that is moral and ethical.

Lewis uses the word *Tao* as shorthand for objective value and Natural Laws. *Tao* is a Chinese word that comes from Taoism, an Eastern religious philosophy embodied in the *Tao Te Ching*, which contains the teaching of the ancient Chinese philosopher Lao Tzu. Lewis is not trying to co-opt the Taoist *religion* in the place of Christianity. He is using the word *Tao* as a description of the universal way or path. For Lewis, the Tao is a cryptic way of describing essential, universal principles of right and wrong behavior. Specifically, Lewis says that the Tao "is Nature, it is the Way, the Road. It is the Way in which the universe goes on, the Way in which things everlastingly emerge, stilly and tranquilly, into space and time."[10] As Lewis stated in his essay "The Poison of Subjectivism": "Unless we return to the crude and nursery-like belief in objective values, we perish."[11] Hence, his title, *The Abolition of Man*, predicts what will occur if humans do not adhere to Natural Law—they will cease to be; they will be abolished. Given that the word *mere* is synonymous with that which is pure or essential, the Tao is the *mere* way, the *mere* path. Not to follow the path or way embodied in Natural Law (the Tao) is to invite ruin, devastation, and ultimately, the abolition of humanity.

In his analysis of Lewis's stance on objective truth, Peter Kreeft crisply summarizes Lewis's position: "The master heresy is subjectivism. It is the parent of all the others, for only after the objective truth is denied are we 'free' to recreate new 'truths' in the image of our own desires."[12] Human values cannot be made up. Truth is not subjective. In agreement with Lewis, Kreeft adds, "Only when we fall asleep to the real world are we 'free' to dream nightmare worlds into being."[13] Lewis wants his listeners and readers to be aware of the distinction between their dreams and reality.

Intentionality, the "I" of HI TEA, incorporates Lewis's understanding of the role and importance of language in communicating objective truth. In addition to the Tao, another "big idea" that permeates all of Lewis's thinking and writing is a link between language (symbols that help us make sense of the world) and the assumptions we have about reality—that which is good, beautiful, and true. In linking subjectivism with language, Lewis notes, "The belief that we can invent 'ideologies' at pleasure" impacts human communication, in that such a subjective point of view, "begins to affect our very language."[14] It is through symbol use that the Natural Laws embodied in ethical principles are expressed.

Literary scholar Doris Meyers confirms that the first six chapters of *The Green Book* are a summary of linguist C. K. Ogden and literary critic I. A. Richards's classic approach to language.[15] Lewis rejects Ogden and Richards, who view meaning as a random association with a specific word. Their word-thought-thing "triangle of meaning," which still appears in many introductory oral and written communication books,[16] suggests that a word takes on a specific meaning primarily by the arbitrary *common association* with the thing or thought linked to the word.[17] Words, according to the association theory of meaning, are (mostly) arbitrary symbols that have no direct connection with the referent to which the words refer. Over time, Ogden and Richards suggest, people simply have learned to associate certain words for certain things. In their view, humans learn language like Pavlov's dog learned to associate a bell with food powder. Lewis disagrees, instead viewing word meaning as anchored in metaphor. *Language is (mostly) metaphorical rather than merely associational.* This claim is important for Lewis because if there is such a thing as objective truth, reality, and value, words are not arbitrarily plucked from possible utterances or formed by a capricious combination of letters, but are metaphorically connected to that which truly exists. Although Lewis would agree that some words that refer to literal objects or actions are not metaphors (such as onomatopoeic words like buzz, snort and burp), most of language is metaphorical.[18]

For Lewis, then, language is not merely a trigger for a learned emotional or intellectual response. Instead, language contains information to be *discovered*. In his essay, "The Language of Religion," Lewis concludes that language is "a real medium of information."[19] His point is clear: Humans write and speak to attempt to express what is real. The real waterfall merits certain descriptive terms that accurately describe the waterfall's attributes (beauty and sublimity). If an author or speaker describes the object well, the reader or listener, seeing the thing in the "mind's eye," responds in turn with a proper "objective" emotion. Language exists to communicate information accurately, to "show us the object"[20] the author is attempting to describe.

In a 1954 essay that appeared in *The Listener*, Lewis quotes poet Robert Conquest to illustrate his point that language includes both "observation of real events" and "the emotional shared by others members of the species ..."[21] Here Lewis suggests that poetry, with its carefully crafted words, is especially effective in evoking an emotional response. Literary and Lewis scholar Zachary Rone summarizes Lewis's approach to language and intentionality by concluding, "Lewis found that, through careful attention to words and context, one could arrive at a better understanding of truth."[22]

In disagreeing with Ogden and Richards that meaning occurs by association between a word, a thought, and a referent, Lewis supports what Meyers calls "a high evaluation of language,"[23] as espoused by Lewis's friend Owen Barfield in his work *Poetic Diction*.[24] In summarizing Barfield's (and Lewis's) theory of language, Meyers notes:

> Instead of viewing the human being as a passive recipient of sensory stimuli, he [Barfield] sees the mind as an active participation in the very nature of the universe. And instead of regarding metaphor as an abstraction, something added on to more precise, more basic expressions, he regards it as the source of both language and knowledge.[25]

In debunking the association theory of the nature of meaning Lewis rejects the strict behaviorist approach to language and meaning in favor of a more elevated, metaphorical, "poetic" approach.[26]

For Lewis, meaning derived from a word that refers to something beyond human sensory experience is not unintentional happenstance, but evocatively metaphorical. As Lewis clarifies in *Miracles*, "The truth is that if we are going to talk at all about things which are not perceived by the senses, we are forced to use language metaphorically."[27]

Lewis scholar Michael Ward agrees that Lewis has a high view of the nature and function of language. Ward notes, "From one perspective, he has the highest possible view: language is a metaphysical reality with a transcendent origin."[28] Yet, Ward also adds, "From another point of view, he sees that it is, in the sublunary world, subject to severe constraints."[29] Language is transcendent, but has limits.

This discussion of Lewis's suppositions about language and meaning may leave you feeling as foggy as the night Lewis delivered his talk, "The Abolition of Man." You may wonder, "What do these abstract theories and assumptions about the nature of language have to do with being an effective communicator—or, more specifically, with the principle of intentionality?" Here is the answer: For Lewis, language is a tool to help humans understand the nature of reality. Effective communicators do their best to express and describe what they experience and think with mindful intent.

C. S. Lewis strongly disagreed with Lewis Carroll's Humpty Dumpty theory of language and meaning, that we can arbitrarily assign meaning randomly:

> When I use a word," Humpty Dumpty said in rather a scornful tone, "it means just what I choose it to mean—neither more nor less."
>
> "The question is," said Alice, "whether you can make words mean so many different things."
>
> "The question is," said Humpty Dumpty, 'which is to be master—that's all.[30]

No, says Lewis in *The Four Loves*: "We had better not follow Humpty Dumpty in making words mean whatever we please."[31] The practical application: Being clear, specific, precise, mindful and *intentionally* aware that language use is vital to effective communication leads to a more comprehensive discussion of principle two: Effective communication is planned, not random nor arbitrary; it is *intentional*.

Principle Two: Effective Communicators Are Intentional

From a communication standpoint, precisely what does it mean to be intentional? Succinctly stated, to be intentional is to *think before writing or speaking*—to be mindfully aware of what one *intends* to communicate before communicating it. With a clear objective in mind, an intentional communicator purposefully selects the right words to achieve the meaning intended. Communication is not a "ready, fire, aim" process but a thoughtful, mindful sequence of encoding messages, one that requires contemplation of the message *before* it is expressed.

How do modern readers know that Lewis was an intentional communicator? First, he wrote about it. "The first qualification for judging any piece of workmanship from a corkscrew to a cathedral," began Lewis in *A Preface to Paradise Lost*, "is to know *what* it is—what it was intended to do and how it is meant to be used."[32] Note Lewis's explicit use of the word *intended*. One only has to read what he wrote to confirm that he practiced what he preached. This statement is not Lewis's only admonition to be intentionally clear. His very definition of language included the importance of *intentionally* communicating ideas to others.[33]

Before capturing his ideas on paper, Lewis would give considerable thought to what he wanted to say. He believed it was important to *think* about a message and its meaning and then express it. A review of his handwritten manuscripts suggests that he made relatively few revisions (although he would sometimes revise manuscripts to clarify new ideas that occurred to him). Before he wrote his ideas, he mentally formulated them.

As noted in the preface of this book, the Lewis manuscript in the Bodleian Library at Oxford University that includes the words "SCRAPS" on the cover contains early drafts of *The Magician's Nephew*, as well as the opening few pages of *Language and Human Nature*—the book that Lewis was to have co-authored with J. R. R. Tolkien. These "SCRAPS" provide evidence that Lewis would think and then write; he then used the writing process to refine his intent and clarify his message. Odds and ends of other ideas as well as bibliography notes are scattered throughout the notebook.

Walter Hooper confirms that Lewis used his writing time for thinking as well. Hooper notes,

> I once asked how he managed to write with such ease, and I think his answer tells us more about his writing than anything he said. He told me that the thing he most loved about writing was that it did two things at once. This he illustrated by saying: 'I don't know what I *mean* till I see what I've *said*.' In other words, writing and thinking were a single process.[34]

Lewis would agree with organizational theorist Karl Wieck who wrote, "How can I know what I think until I see what I say?"[35] Although Lewis used writing as a strategy to develop his thoughts, he put his words on paper as a means of clarifying his communicative intent. He also honed his ideas during conversation and debate with his colleagues, especially during Inkling meetings—weekly meetings with J. R. R. Tolkien, Warnie, and a small group of other trusted stalwarts held on Tuesday at The Eagle and Child pub or in Lewis's rooms at Magdalen College on Thursday evening.[36] Also usually present were Hugo Dyson (who was with him on September 19, 1931, when Lewis began to understand the "true myth"), Humphrey Havard (Lewis's physician), and Owen Barfield (his long-time friend and solicitor) who would sometimes challenge Lewis's thinking.

For Lewis, having a reader or listener understand the intent of a message was the prime goal. As he wrote in his essay "On Criticism," "The author's intention is that which, if it is realized, will in his eyes constitute success."[37] An intentional or deliberate communicator envisions the kind of response desired. Part of being intentional is not only to have in mind the clear objective of what one wishes to communicate, but also to think about the desired *response* from the listener or reader. The reader or listener should be able to discern the communicator's intent based on what he or she said. As Lewis put it, "If all or most readers, or such readers as he chiefly desires, laugh at a passage, and he is pleased with this result, then his intention was comic, or he intended to be comic."[38] The reaction of the reader is the evidence of whether the intent was achieved. The Inkling meetings were also invaluable as a forum for testing ideas and ensuring that what he intended was communicated clearly. He was able to see for himself that the words achieved their intended effect, one of the criteria for any effective message.

Lewis recognized the challenge of selecting just the right words to communicate the author's intent. Meanings are fragile and it takes an effective wordsmith to accurately communicate that which the communicator intended. It is especially challenging to articulate rich experiences involving the senses. As Lewis noted in a letter to one of his correspondents, Ms. Rhona Bodle, "Indeed, in a sense, one can hardly put anything into words … The simple physical pains and (still more) the pleasures can't be expressed in language."[39] The problem in communicating one's intent, according to Lewis, lies in the inexact nature of language to express the nuances of experience. Life occurs in many colors, yet there are not enough words, or precise enough words, to describe the range of colors, phrased metaphorically, to paint an accurate word picture. But just because the right word is not available does not mean that an experience should be devalued. Lewis suggests that the vagaries of language, not the richness of our experiences, are a prime cause of misunderstanding. He continues to develop his idea about the inherent challenge in the use of language in his correspondence with Ms. Bodle: "What goes easily into words is precisely the abstract—thought about 'matter' (not apples or snuff), about 'population' (not actual babies), and so on."[40] Lewis would agree with a conclusion about the challenge of using words to express ineffable ideas that is attributed to actor Martin Mull: "Writing about music is like dancing about architecture."[41] Some experiences just can't be put into words.

Lewis further illustrates the inadequacies of language in a conversation he includes in his novel *Perelandra*. During a conversation between the narrator of the book (who the reader eventually learns is C. S. Lewis), and the protagonist of the story, Elwin Ransom, the narrator says,

> I was questioning [Ransom] on the subject—which he doesn't often allow—and had incautiously said, "Of course I realize it's all rather too vague for you to put into words," when he took me up rather sharply, for such a patient man, by saying, "On the contrary, it is words that are vague. The reason why the thing can't be expressed is that it's too *definite* for language."[42]

Language, believed Lewis, is inherently vague and can lead to misunderstanding and confusion. Being intentional does not guarantee that the message will be interpreted as intended, but it is a necessary first step in crafting a clear message.

In his book *Miracles*, Lewis compares human communication and intentionality with the way God communicates with his creation. Lewis describes God as having purposeful intent: "God who is totally purposive and totally foreseeing acts upon a Nature which is totally interlocked, there can be no accidents or loose ends ... All results are intended from the first."[43] God, suggests Lewis, communicates (and creates) with an intentional, un-accidental goal in mind. So Lewis's reasoning is that if God is intentional as a Creator, humans, as creators of messages, should be too. The application for communication: Think first; speak second.

Lewis explicitly discusses the critical element of *intent to communicate* as inherent in the nature of using language. In specifying the role of intentionality to communication, in the book fragment *Language and Human Nature*, Lewis first defines language as "in the simplest sense ... a system of signs. Thus there is a language of flags (used in the navy) a 'language of flowers' and so forth."[44] He goes on to say, "But there is one such system of signs so widely used and so much richer than all the others that it generally is called simply 'language.' This is the system in which the signs are the various noises made by a human mouth."[45] Lewis then narrows the scope of his definition to include the importance of intent: "We only see language in its full sense when the noises made not only are signs but are intended to be signs by the person who makes them."[46] The key phrase here is "*intended* [emphasis added] to be signs by the person who makes them."[47] Unintended groans or other vocalizations are not included in Lewis's definition of language. Language, for the purposes of Lewis's study of language and human nature, emphasizes oral as well as written expressions that *intentionally* communicate meaning. Effective communication is thoughtful, deliberate, and mindful, as opposed to thoughtless, impromptu, and mindless.

Lewis would not agree that simply because people can infer meaning from human utterances, communication has occurred. He would not support the contemporary communication assumption that one "Cannot *not* communicate," a communication epithet that frequently appears in contemporary communication textbooks to signify the ubiquity of human communication.[48] Not *not* communicating suggests that even our unintentional movements and messages are ripe for interpretation. The phrase implies that all behavior is potentially communicative. Lewis would not deny that our surreptitious "tells" (such as the poker player's unintended nonverbal leakage cues) provide clues about our psychological state, as well as our likes and dislikes. Language, however, is an *intentional* process of communicating meaning to others; simply because someone is making an utterance (or groan or noise) does not result in meaning, as Lewis defines the term. An effective communicator, whether speaking to a friend or colleague, or delivering a speech before an audience, should have a clear idea of what the message is.

The principle of intention is discussed in several places throughout Lewis's works, although Lewis didn't dub it the "principle of intention." Lewis's assumption that intent is important for a clear language style is consistent with his advice to communicators presented in his essay "Cross-Examination," from *God in the Dock*. Lewis suggests:

> The way for a person to develop a style is (a) to know exactly what he wants to say, and (b) to be sure he is saying exactly that. The reader, we must remember, does not start by knowing what we mean. If our words are ambiguous, our meaning will escape him. I sometimes think that writing is like driving sheep down a road. If there is any gate open to the left or the right the readers will most certainly go into it.[49]

To be clear it is important to mindfully ensure that the communicator knows precisely what to say and then says exactly that.

Lewis loved animals. There were almost always pets present at his home The Kilns As an observer of animals, Lewis intentionally made a distinction between human language and animal communication. Animals can and do express their needs and feelings (whether they are sad or happy, starving or pleasantly full). Animals communicate. But Lewis wonders if a dog is *aware* of its barking. It is awareness or intentional mindfulness that gives humans communicative supremacy. As Lewis explains in a letter to Mrs. Frank Jones in 1950,

My dog if shut in a room and calling for his walk never dreams of barking to tell me where he is. [What] looks very much as if his tail [were] wagging, etc., however much it may be a language *to me*, is not language *to him* and he has no idea of using it as a sign. It is spontaneous, unreflective expression of emotion. His bark *tells me* he is excited, but he doesn't bark *in order to tell me*: just as my sneeze may tell you I have a cold, but I didn't sneeze in order to tell you.[50]

It is the *intentional* use of language that differentiates human communication from animal communication. Animals do not typically ponder the intended meeting of a bark, meow, chirp, or moo. Lewis does not doubt that we make inferences from our pets' behavior, but he suggests they are more about "doing" than intentionally "saying" something when communicating with us. Human use of language should be intentional. Shakespeare or the current poet laureate do not become celebrated for their unintentional communication. Effective and desired communication is premeditated and intentional. As Lewis notes, "... sounds (or their graphic equivalent) are words precisely because they carry the mind through and beyond themselves."[51]

Being aware of what one wants to communicate is essential. As Lewis suggests, "Prolonged thought *about* the words which we ordinarily use to think *with* can produce a momentary aphasia. I think it is to be welcomed."[52] We should take our time when selecting a word and not take the meaning of a word for granted. Rather than being on linguistic auto pilot, one should mindfully consider what words mean. He makes his key point in the next sentence: "It is well we should become aware of what we are doing when we speak, of the ancient fragile, and (well used) immensely potent instruments that words are."[53] Here Lewis again emphasizes the importance of being a mindful communicator. To "become aware of what we are doing when we speak ..."[54] is at the core of being an intentional communicator.

Lewis thought that a lot of muddled speaking and writing occurs because the author had not spent enough time pre-writing (thinking before she or he writes). It is during this pre-writing (or pre-speaking), thinking phase that the communicator should be sure that he/she has something to say. Lewis made the importance of having something to say explicit when he wrote in his *English Literature in the Sixteenth Century: Excluding Drama*, "No style can be good in the mouth of a man who has nothing, or nonsense, to say."[55] Lewis took his own advice: One of the sources for his skill as a communicator was that he wrote and spoke about what really interested him. Fortunately, Lewis was interested in many things—from space travel to talking animals.

Did Lewis have a formula or specific template for his writing? Generally, he followed no set formula or pre-determined structure. In Lewis's last interview, Sherwood Eliot Wirt asked if a specific approach would work best with the current generation of writers. Lewis's response is instructive: "There is no formula in these matters. I have no recipe, no tablets."[56]

The Meaning of *Meaning*

Lewis paid considerable attention to the nature of meaning as an intentional process of expressing what one wants to communicate. In *Studies in Words*, Lewis demonstrates his understanding of the function and use of language when he says, "I have an idea of what is good and bad language ... Language is an instrument for communication. The language which can with the greatest ease make the finest and most numerous distinctions of meaning is best."[57] Lewis suggests that for meaning to be clear the words should be selected with "the greatest ease." The right word should not be forced, obtuse, or unusual. A word is "at ease" if it makes sense to the reader without undue effort or stress in decoding its meaning—the meaning is easily accessible by the reader or listener.

The primary point of *Studies in Words* is to pay attention to what a word means and to be aware that the meaning of words can change over time. As literary scholar Scott Calhoun notes, "Lewis knew the difficulties modern readers had when encountering literature from previous historical periods, as he himself was once a modern reader struggling for the first time to make sense of old vocabularies."[58] Lewis wanted to help a reader examine the historical context of words to realize how the meaning of a word has evolved over time.

The meaning of a word is not cast in concrete. In *Letters to Malcolm*, Lewis says, "The ideal of 'timeless English' is sheer nonsense. No living language can be timeless. You might as well ask for a motionless river."[59] Being aware of both the changing and fragile nature of meaning is one factor in helping the communicator select the right word and the receiver making sense of the message. Yet, although meaning changes, Lewis seemed to be able to use words that transcend time. Perhaps because his own reading and scholarship habits spanned centuries, he recognized what meanings would endure. Lewis's intentional use of simple, clear language continues to communicate to most 21st Century readers.

Although he realized that the meanings of words change over time, Lewis expected thoughtful and accurate use of words; he did not like wishy-washy responses to questions. Walter Hooper, Lewis's resident secretary the summer before

Lewis died, once told me that one of the answers Lewis disdained most during conversation was responding "Whatever" to a question. Thinking and responding to specific questions should be intentional rather than aimlessly unclear or non-responsive.

In the seven and one-half page extant manuscript fragment of the planned Lewis and Tolkien book *Language and Human Nature*, Lewis devotes the opening one and one-half manuscript pages to defining language, followed by six pages discussing the nature of meaning. He recaps his previous definition of meaning: "This [the nature of language] is sometimes expressed by saying that language is vocal noise with a meaning. This will do well enough provided that we remember, or distinguish, the different senses of the word meaning. It has at least three."[60] Lewis then presents three ways of looking at the meaning of *meaning*: (1) *evidential*, meaning resulting from inferring cause and effect; (2) *psychological* meaning, which assumes that what someone means is directly inferred from what someone says; and (3) *empirical* (or symbolic), meaning as illustrated by the mathematical equal sign (=); when someone intentionally uses a word or phrase to symbolize an idea.[61]

Evidential Meaning

Evidential meaning is derived when a person attributes meaning based on the *evidence* of what he or she experiences. A listener or reader then relies on evidential meaning when a statement points to evidence from which he or she can infer a cause and effect relationship. Here is Lewis's example of evidential meaning: " 'That sky *means* rain.' By saying this we intend to convey that the state of the sky is a sign of rain, in the sense that it is evidence (whether certain or probable) that rain will presently begin to fall."[62]

In Lewis's example, the meaning does not reside in the experience. A sky has no intent. The sky simply exists. Meaning occurs based upon the evidence present to the senses or one's interpretation of the evidence; meaning occurs when one infers a cause and effect relationship between a stimulus (sky) and the likely result of the stimulus (rain). White smoke wafting from the chimney of the Sistine Chapel is evidence that a new pope has been elected. If while eating at a restaurant, a diner sees someone blow out candles on a cake the diner concludes that it is the candle-blower's birthday. Humans infer meaning based on the surmised cause and effect evidence their senses experience. Evidential meaning involves reasoning from sign. The presence of a sign, such as a lit porch light on the night of October 31, is likely to mean the home's residents are prepared to dole out Halloween candy.

Psychological Meaning

After briefly describing and illustrating evidential meaning, Lewis identifies and exemplifies his second definition of the word *meaning*—psychological meaning. In this iteration of meaning one infers the psychological interpretation of what someone says or does based on that person's stated or implied intent. Here is Lewis's example: "I *mean* to go to London to-morrow." This might be translated—"I intend, propose, am resolved to go to London to-morrow."[63] Lewis interprets the statement based on the stated psychological intent of the speaker. Identifying a speaker's psychological goal based on what the person says is the basis for inferring a speaker's meaning. If someone says, "I am on a diet and I plan to skip lunch today," a listener might rely on the implied intent to lose weight as the psychological explanation for skipping lunch. Announcing what you intend or mean to do is the basis for determining the psychological motivation for a given behavior or announced plans to behave (such as going to London or skipping lunch). A detective seeking to determine someone's psychological meaning would listen to what a person says he or she plans to do as a way of inferring that individual's psychological intent.

Lewis had more than a passing interest in psychology. Several of his books evidence his interest in psychological influences. *The Screwtape Letters* is an insightful psychological study of how humans sometimes struggle to do what is right but can be led off track by devilish internal arguments and external influences. In his sermon "A Slip of the Tongue," Lewis admits making a verbal error when praying. He had mistakenly prayed that he might "pass through things eternal" (he had meant to say "temporal"). Then he notes, "I am not sure that I am even a strict enough Freudian to believe that all such slips, without exception, are deeply significant."[64] Lewis evidentially understood Freud's ideas. His allegorical novel *The Pilgrim's Regress* features a character named Sigismund, who clearly has Freudian characteristics.

Although there is no evidence Lewis and Freud ever met, the well-written play, *Freud's Last Session,* offers speculative dialogue suggesting what C. S. Lewis and Sigmund Freud might have said to each other if they would have met. Their conversations sometimes directly reflect words Freud or Lewis had written. Armand Nicholi's book *The Question of God* compares the worldviews of Lewis and Freud—two great minds with dramatically different perspectives.[65] One believed in the existence and active involvement of God in human lives; the other did not. Despite having a different perspective than Freud's, Lewis did read psychology and appreciated how the study of the psyche could help people better understand themselves. Lewis refers to the "new" psychology, by which he meant Freud and his contemporaries.

There is another Lewis-Freud connection worth noting. June Flewett was one of the young women who lived with Jack and Warnie when she was a teenager during World War II. June later married Freud's grandson, Clement Freud. It has been suggested that June, also known as Jill, was the inspiration for Lucy Pevense in the Narnia stories.[66] June became an actress on the London stage, including a role in the popular movie *Love Actually* as the housekeeper to Hugh Grant (who played the role of the Prime Minister). Lewis and June remained friends during Lewis's lifetime.

Lewis also read Carl Jung, at one time a pupil of and devotee to Freud, but who later parted company with Freud and developed different psychological models. Jung believed there are two parts to the unconscious. First, the "personal unconscious" is similar to Freud's description of the unconscious, a place where all memories of everything that has been experienced are stored. The second part, called the "collective unconscious" consists of archetypes, which have been described as "a psychic mold into which individual and collective experiences are poured and where they take shape, yet it is distinct from the symbols and images themselves."[67] Jung's notion of the collective unconscious and his theory of archetypes account "for similarities in psychic functioning and imagery throughout the ages and across highly diverse cultures."[68] Thus, the collective unconscious is a universal framework for categorizing human experiences, thoughts, and feelings.

What did Lewis think of Jung's ideas? In his essay "Psycho-Analysis and Literary Criticism," Lewis seems uncertain about the soundness of Jung's psychological perspective, yet seems to find some value in the notion of the collective unconscious.[69] Although Lewis appears to be skeptical of the role of psychology in unraveling the mysteries of human nature, he sees value in a perspective that identifies the existence of universal human characteristics—a psychological Tao. As Lewis phrases it with his typical eloquence, "I perceive at once that even if it [the collective unconscious] turns out to be bad science it is excellent poetry."[70]

Empirical (Symbolic) Meaning

After describing the evidential and psychological approaches to meaning, Lewis identifies a third perspective for examining the nature of meaning—empirical or symbolic meaning. In this third instance, meaning occurs when a word symbolizes or is "empirically" linked to something else. Lewis uses the equal sign (=) to make his point:

The two strokes [=] are not "a sign of" equality or the same as being evidence of equality. If we take the expression a = b as evidence that a does in fact equal b, that will be because we believe the writer to [be] a sound mathematician and an honest man. Even if the expression were quite unbelievable (e.g. 5 = 12) we should still say that the sign "meant" equality: indeed we should only know a statement to be untrue because we knew that the sign mean[s] "equals" (if the writer was using it to mean "is less than," his statements would no longer be untrue).[71]

Lewis's notion of empirical meaning is based on connecting a specific word with the intended meaning of the word. Lewis acknowledges that this third definition of meaning is abstract and challenging to describe. He further explains that "the sign = does not only in fact draw our attention to, or offer to the mind, the relation of equality, but is intended to do so. To mean, in this third sense is 'to draw attention to not accidentally but on purpose.'"[72] In this passage, Lewis suggests that meaning occurs when the speaker does more than draw attention to an idea, but uses words in conscious, intentional ways to encode a message. In this third definition of meaning, the speaker uses words and implies an equal sign in which the words themselves are imbued with intentional meaning from the sender's perspective. Words therefore take on a symbolic meaning.

To summarize, C. S. Lewis argues that speakers and writers infer the meaning of a message in multiple ways: evidential, psychological, and empirical (symbolic).

- The evidential meaning of a word results from a reader or listener inferring cause and effect relationships.
- Psychological meaning occurs when an inference about the intent or psychological motivation of the speaker or writer can be made based on what that person says or writes; interpreting the (psychological) intent helps the listener decode the meaning.
- Finally, empirical or symbolic meaning assumes that a word has a direct or corresponding relationship to what the word symbolizes.

What are the practical implications of Lewis's three views of meaning for those who create and interpret messages? Being aware of the different senses of meaning can help a speaker clarify his or her intent, or a listener more accurately decode a message. Knowing that the interpretation of what someone says is based on the assumed cause and effect evidence (evidential meaning), the inferred motivational intent of the speaker (psychological meaning), or an assumed link between a word and meaning (empirical/symbolic meaning) can help communicators better analyze the basis for any conclusion they reach about what someone says or writes.

Lewis's discussion of the three bases for meaning is not his only advice about how to interpret what something means. In *Letters to Malcolm*, the book he finished just before his death, Lewis identifies "two rules for exegetics" or the process of interpreting a passage of scripture. The first rule: "1) Never take the images literally."[73] This advice is in keeping with Lewis's (and Barfield's) belief that most words are metaphorical. Meaning is evoked from the symbol used (as Lewis described in the empirical or symbolic meaning of words) rather than from a literal interpretation. More meaning is packed into a text than what one "literally" sees or experiences. Lewis's advice: Be mindful of the metaphorical nature of words, especially when interpreting Biblical texts.

Lewis's second rule is "2) When the *purport* [purpose] of the images—what they say to our fear and hope and will and affections—seems to conflict with the theological abstractions, trust the purport of the images every time."[74] Lewis invites people to look at the larger meaning embedded in the metaphor or analogy (or image); look for that which is true. He invites people to consider the original purpose or intent of the passage (analogous to identifying the psychological meaning of a word). In addition, people should be aware of the context and then do their best to discern the original intent of the communicator. Lewis's next sentence makes this explicit, as he uses an analogy to describe an analogy: "For our abstract thinking is itself a tissue of analogies: a continual modeling of spiritual reality in legal or chemical or mechanical terms."[75] Lewis invites people to look for clues in the larger context of what a word, phrase, or image may mean when interpreting a scriptural text. Perhaps realizing that his explanation may still be fuzzy, he provides yet an additional visual metaphor to clarify: "The footprints of the Divine are more visible in that rich soil than across rocks or slag-heaps. Hence what they now call 'demythologising' Christianity can easily be 're-mythologising' it—and substituting a poorer mythology for a richer."[76] This passage distills Lewis's third principle of communication, transposition (communicating from the higher to the lower) that will be discussed in the next chapter.

In addition to giving careful thought about how to intentionally interpret the meaning of words, understanding Lewis's approach to creativity or invention provides a framework for understanding Lewis's goal of being intentional. Even as a writer or speaker creates something new, he or she should be mindful of his or her intended purpose.

Master of Invention

To invent is to create. To draw upon the communication skill of *invention*, one of the classic Roman canons of rhetoric, is to develop original, creative ideas. Lewis's ability to invent other worlds, and to express ideas to navigate "past watchful dragons"[77] is one of his most notable communication talents. He can express old ideas in fresh ways. He is imaginatively creative. He used his skill of invention to develop clear and memorable arguments to support his ideas. As Jerry Root observes, "Schooled in the art of invention, he [Lewis] knew how to craft strong argument, looking not only for the main flow of a river of thought but paying attention, as well, to the detailed tributaries and rivulets which support it."[78]

What is Lewis's advice to a writer or speaker who wants to invent or create new ideas? Communicate about what one knows. He recommends, "Write about what really interests you, whether it is real things or imaginary things, and nothing else. (Notice this means that if you are interested only in writing you will never be a writer, because you will have nothing to write about.)"[79] Cultivate a variety of interests. A communicator writes from his or her experience.

Although Lewis believed it is important to be mindful of one's communicative intent based on one's interests and experiences, he suggests that one need not always be aware of the source of an idea or story. What is vital, however, is to know what point the story makes—its intention. In response to a question about the origin of the Narnia story from his editor, he explained that the inspiration came from seeing pictures in his mind's eye. In his essay "It All Began with a Picture …" he writes,

> So you see that, in a sense, I know very little about how this story was born. That is, I don't know where the pictures came from. And I don't believe anyone knows exactly how he 'makes things up.' Making up is a very mysterious thing. When you 'have an idea' could you tell anyone exactly how you thought of it?[80]

Having an idea (the art of invention) is therefore more important than tracing its origin.

What inspired C. S. Lewis to be such a prolific inventor of new ideas, stories, and worlds? In a lecture to Texas State University faculty and students, Walter Hooper suggested that the seminal factor that made Lewis an effective communicator was that "he had something to say."[81] Until Lewis's conversion to Christianity, suggests Hooper, Lewis certainly had the intellect and was a skilled enough linguistic craftsperson to produce publishable poetry, including lengthy narrative poems. In a presentation to the Oxford C. S. Lewis Society, Hooper confirms that Lewis became a better communicator once he found his "voice":

> Before his conversion he could write well, and he was more ambitious then than at any time in his life. But apart from two early volumes of verse, [*Spirits in Bondage* and *Dymer*] nothing happened. I believe the whole thing can be summed up in five words: Lewis had nothing to say. It really does appear that when Lewis cared more about God than being a writer, God gave him things to say.[82]

Lewis biographer Alan Jacobs echoes Hooper's conclusion that Lewis's conversion was instrumental in giving Lewis something to say. Jacobs writes, "The pre-conversion Lewis is, though obviously highly intelligent, neither a particularly likable nor a particularly interesting person—at least in his letters."[83] But then something happened. Jacobs concludes, "But once he 'admitted that God was God,' it is as though the key to his own hidden and locked-away personality was given to him."[84] Based on both his letters and literary output, Lewis becomes an invigorated personality. Jacobs adds: "What appears almost immediately is a kind of gusto (sheer, bold enthusiasm for what he loves) that is characteristic of him ever after."[85]

It was not until his conversion, first to theism, and then to Christianity, that Lewis had a message he simply had to express. From his autobiographical *Pilgrim's Regress* published in 1933, until *Letters to Malcolm*, the manuscript of which was on his desk at home when he died in 1963, the corpus of Lewis's speaking and writing focused on Christianity. Lewis's having something to say, along with an educationally-awakened mind, permitted him to nurture his creativity and channel his intellect. But Lewis is an intentional, master communicator not only because he had something to say, but because he expresses his ideas with clarity.

Clarity

When people are asked, "What makes Lewis an effective communicator?" one of the most frequent answers is: "He is clear." After reviewing scripts of Lewis's early broadcast talks that eventually became *Mere Christianity*, broadcasting executive Eric Fenn wrote, "I have at last had time today to read your scripts. I think they are quite first class."[86] What made them "first class" from Fenn's perspective? Fenn explained, "There is a clarity and inexorableness about them, which made me positively gasp."[87] Clarity was an explicit communication goal of Lewis. In his advice to a schoolgirl who had sought his advice about writing, Lewis wrote about the virtues of clarity when communicating. He said,

> Take great pains to be clear. Remember that though you start by knowing what you mean, the reader doesn't, and a single ill-chosen word may lead him to a total misunderstanding. In a story it is terribly easy just to forget that you have not told the reader something that he wants to know—the whole picture is so clear in your own mind that you forget that it isn't the same in his.[88]

Clarity is using the right words to express the intent of the speaker that is understood by the receiver of the message. Lewis defines clarity as "using words so that we can all understand what is being said."[89] Lewis sought to be clear except when he intentionally wanted to keep a reader or listener in suspense, or withhold information to make a grand reveal later in the story. As Lewis scholar Jerry Root has noted, "Whatever criticisms one might find with Lewis's work, 'lack of clarity' is never a concern. He crafted his imaginative prose with precision and style."[90]

How does one achieve clarity? Offering additional advice, Lewis notes, "Be sure you know the meaning (or meanings) of every word you use."[91] Summarizing Lewis's skill in using language skillfully and artfully, former student, friend, and biographer George Sayer notes that "The combination of his genius for analogy, logical approach, and plain style in which every word is used precisely makes all his religious writing effective. Yet he rarely oversimplifies."[92] And, Walter Hooper adds, "What he is so good at is taking extremely profound thoughts and putting them in everyday language that anybody can understand."[93] Whether a message is a request to pick up apples at the store, or to describe the Big Bang Theory as a way of suggesting the origin of apples, clarity in communication occurs when the right words are used at the right time for the right audience. As Lewis advised, before we can discuss communication on a "grand, philosophical level, ... to talk about the conflicts of *Weltanschauung* [one's worldview] and the predicament of the modern, or crisis consciousness, it is chilling to be told that the first step is simply linguistic in there crudest sense."[94] By "linguistic," Lewis is referring to ensuring that the words selected clearly communicate the writer's or speaker's *intended* meaning. Chad Walsh, who wrote *C. S. Lewis: Apostle to the Skeptics* noted that Lewis was not only clear when writing but also when speaking. Based on his personal interaction with Lewis, Walsh wrote, "When Lewis talks, he often reminds you of his books ... He is straight to the point, never at a loss for the exact word."[95]

It is one thing to make clarity a criterion for effective communication, and quite another to be clear. For Lewis, clarity occurs with the precise use of language. In "The Language of Religion," Lewis draws on John Keats's poem "The Eve of St. Agnes" to develop an example:

> I begin with three sentences: (1) It was very cold. (2) There were 13 degrees of frost. (3) 'Ah, bitter chill it was! The owl, for all his feathers was a-cold; The hare limped trembling through the frozen grass. And silent was the flock in woolly fold: Numb'd were the Beadsman's fingers'.[96]

With this passage Lewis clearly illustrates his point before he makes it. He wants his reader to *experience* the three different types of language. Only then does he go on to make his point: "I should describe the first as Ordinary language, the second as Scientific language, and the third as Poetic language."[97] He clarifies his definitions: "Of course there is no question here of different languages in the sense in which Latin and Chinese are different languages. Two and three are improved uses of the same language used in one."[98] Then, comparing scientific and poetic language with ordinary language he adds, "Scientific and Poetic language are two different artificial perfections of Ordinary: artificial, because they depend on skills; different, because they improve Ordinary in two different directions."[99] One direction goes "higher" in providing poetic, metaphorical descriptions and the other goes "lower" because it uses the precise language of science to literally describe and categorize.

To talk about religion, one of Lewis's most frequent topics, a person does not need a special kind of language. As Lewis sees it, "the language in which we express our religious beliefs and other religious experiences, is not a special language, but something that ranges between the Ordinary and the Poetical."[100] In discussing the communication problems he thinks are unique to communicating clearly about Christianity Lewis says, "And this means that the thing we are really talking about can never appear in the discussion at all. We have to try to prove that God is in circumstances where we are denied every means of conveying who God is."[101] Although there may not be a proprietary "language of religion," it is nonetheless a challenge to express the ineffable.

For Lewis, clarity, regardless of whether talking about religion or other topics, is best achieved not by relying on only one kind of language, but by using all three (Ordinary, Scientific, and Poetic). The specific type of language used depends on both the speaker's intent and the audience's experiences and background, similar to his idea that a message receiver should look both *at* and *along* what one sees.

Ordinary language may be best; yet at other times Scientific or Poetic language is called for. Lewis notes the value in matching the kind of language to the speaker's goal when he says that "there is a special region of experiences which can be communicated *without* Poetic language, namely, its 'common measurable features', but most experience cannot. To be incommunicable by Scientific language is, so far as I can judge, the normal state of experience."[102]

Why is using precise Scientific language not always the best language to describe certain events or feelings? It can be tedious and unnecessary. When meeting a dear friend after some absence, verbalizing the precise location of the reunion (using scientific language to say, "We are at 29.993 North latitude and 97.944 West longitude.") is less important than using Poetic language ("My, but you are a sight for sore eyes!" or "I love you to pieces!") to describe the joy in being reunited with a loved one. Poetic language is especially useful to evoke an emotion in someone else. Sometimes it is useful to be precise (Scientific language), yet at other times, especially to describe an experience or emotion, Poetic language is needed. During an interview Lewis was asked "As the authority on *The Allegory of Love*, Mr. Lewis, what is your attitude to the detailed, non-allegorical description of the act of love in literature?"[103] After thinking about the question for only a moment, Lewis responded: "To describe the act of love in detail without resorting to allegory [Poetic language] one is restricted to three choices: the language of the nursery, the language of the gutter, or the language of science—all are equally unsatisfactory."[104]

Lewis's ideas about language categories are consistent with those of other linguists. For example, S. I. Hayakawa develops the concept of a "Ladder of Abstraction" in his classic book *Language in Thought and Action*.[105] Hayakawa's "Ladder of Abstraction" visually describes how language ranges on a continuum from concrete to abstract. Abstract words are at the top of the ladder; concrete terms are at the bottom. A word is *concrete* when it has a tangible referent, when what the word refers to can be experienced with one of the senses. If one can see a word's referent, or touch it, smell it, taste it, or hear it, then the word is concrete. If not, then the word is abstract. The word *tree* is concrete, whereas the word *freedom* is more abstract. There are times when being abstract is desirable. Poetry, metaphors and global abstractions may be the best ways to express what's on one's mind or in one's heart. The goal is not always to linger at the bottom of the abstraction ladder (to use concrete words or scientific language), but to be aware of how concrete or abstract that one's words are and to be other-oriented—think about how words or phrases will be interpreted by others.[106]

To be linguistically flexible is to use or combine Ordinary words that may have Poetic or Scientific interpretations. Lewis offers an example of linguistic flexibility in his conversation with E. M. W. Tillyard in *The Personal Heresy*:

> Thus if we take the sentence 'this is cold' we can make it more precise either by saying, 'This is twice as cold as that', or by saying, "Ugh! It's like a smack in the face'. The first proceeds by turning a qualitative sensation into a quantity; the second, by communicating with the aid of an emotive noise and a simile just that quality which the other neglects … The vast majority of human utterances fall between the two extremes.[107]

Words, when artfully combined with other words (whether ordinary, scientific or poetic), can add nuance to clarify intended meaning.

An artist may have a varied-hue palette of paint; it is what the artist uses from the palette rather than the colors that are on the palette that affects the image painted. Before reaching for a paint color (or word), it is important to have in mind an intentional image of the outcome. Lewis's seminal advice on being clear is to understand one's intended meaning before communicating a message to others.

> If, given patience and ordinary skill, you cannot explain a thing to any sensible person whatever (provided he will listen), then you don't really understand it yourself. Here too it is very like doing Latin prose; the bits you can't get into Latin are usually the bits you haven't really grasped in the English.[108]

He further clarifies his point by saying, "And our private language may delude ourselves as well as mystifying outsiders. Enchanted words seem so full of meaning, so illuminating. But we may be deceived."[109] And finally, in drawing distinctions between cognitive and affective (or emotional) understanding, Lewis concludes his essay by saying, "'we understand one another' often means 'we are in sympathy'. Sympathy is a good thing. It may even be in some ways a better thing than intellectual understanding. But not the same thing."[110]

Brevity is an additional hallmark of Lewis's skill in being intentionally clear. One of the best ways to muddle the clarity of a message is to add too many words (much as the Austrian Emperor reportedly critiqued a Mozart opera for having "too many notes.") Lewis had an excellent vocabulary and was well versed in a number of languages. Yet he didn't litter his writing or speaking with extraneous words. Lewis explicitly advocated brevity: "In the very process of eliminating from your matter all that is technical, learned or allusive, you will discover, perhaps for the first time, the true value of learned language: namely, brevity."[111] Being brief can enhance the intentional meaning of a word or phrase. One advantage of a large vocabulary, according to Lewis, is that one can select just the right word, rather than pile on more words than needed to make the point. A well-chosen word, rather than a word-cluttered description, can make one's intention clear. Lewis's skill as a poet at being able to pluck just the right word was one of his best communication assets in giving his writing a clear and memorable style.

Lewis was, at times, pithy. After writing a lengthy narrative or explanation, he would sometimes summarize his point using a minimum of words. For example, when writing about how inspiration works in his essay "The Vision of John Bunyan," he simply wrote, "It came."[112] He then added, "I doubt if we shall ever know more of the process called 'inspiration' that those two monosyllables tell us."[113] Here's another example: "For most of us the prayer in Gethsemane is the only mode." Then he adds a four-word punch line. "Removing mountains can wait."[114] Combining brevity with an apt metaphor (a stylistic technique that will be discussed in detail in the chapters ahead), Lewis economically writes: "Anger is the fluid that love bleeds when you cut it."[115] In using just a few words, coupled with a visual metaphor, he makes his definition memorable.

Style

Jonathan Swift described language style as "proper words in proper places."[116] In addition to communicating clearly and with brevity, C. S. had a stylistic flair for putting words in proper places that gave his messages both immediate and lasting impact. He *intentionally* used words to craft memorable phrases to ensure that his words were in their proper places. As Lewis explains, "There is no class of books which can be 'good in their own way' without bothering about style."[117] C. S. Lewis bothered about style. He also knew that developing an effective style is more than just tinkering with a word here and there. As Lewis notes, "It is always dangerous to talk too long about style. It may lead one to forget that every single sentence depends for its total effect on the place it has in the whole."[118] For Lewis, style is focusing on individual words as well considering their (holistic) "total effect" on the message.

C. S. Lewis is one of the most quoted authors of the 20th century. Wayne Martindale and Jerry Root's meticulously-researched book *The Quotable Lewis*, an encyclopedia of Lewis quotations, remains popular for a reason.[119] Lewis's style has both "eye appeal" and "ear appeal." One marketing-communication specialist noted, " 'Ear appeal' phrases can be like the haunting sounds of a musical that the members of the audience find themselves humming on the way home. Even if people want to forget them, they can't."[120] Lewis knew how to make his readers and listeners "hum" his message long after they put down the book, turned off the radio, or left the lecture hall. Lewis paid attention both to how words look on the page and to how words sound. In a letter to his father, Lewis notes that when learning new languages (in this instance Latin and Greek) it was important to "get the sound and savour of the language" into his head to help him remember what he was reading.[121] He paid attention to how words sound not only when he read and studied but also when he wrote.

Not only is C. S. Lewis one of the most quoted 20th century writers, he is also among the most misquoted authors. Lewis scholar William O'Flaherty is the editor of "Essential C. S. Lewis," a popular, daily email post that features a Lewis quotation, as well as the host of the well-produced podcast *All About Jack*. O'Flaherty has also written *The Misquotable C. S. Lewis: What He Didn't Say, What He Actually Said and Why it Matters*.[122] The book identifies a multitude of phrases and sayings that are attributed to Lewis (most notably on the Internet or sometimes appearing on posters or paperweights) but are inaccurate misquotes. In some instances, just a word or two is added or missing; in other instances, the entire quote includes words Lewis never wrote or uttered. For example, although it frequently appears on the Internet and in Facebook posts, Lewis did not say, "There are far, far better things ahead than any we leave behind." Two extra words ("far, far") are added.[123] Nor did Lewis say, "Experience is the most brutal of teachers. But you learn, my God, do you learn." Not Lewis. It is similar to a phrase spoken by actor Anthony Hopkins portraying C. S. Lewis in the movie *Shadowlands*. But even this phrase, attributed to Lewis, is a misquote from the movie.[124]

In addition to writing for both the eye and the ear, what other strategies did C. S. Lewis intentionally use to make his ideas "sing"? He skillfully used such stylistic techniques as antithesis and repetition.

Antithesis is the use of a two-part sentence in which the second part of the sentence contrasts with, or mirrors, the first. Antithesis gives a message rhythm as well as symmetry. Here are a few classic Lewis examples:

- "All that is not eternal is eternally out of date."[125]
- "Only the courteous can love, but it is love that makes them courteous."[126]
- "Precisely because we cannot predict the moment, we must be ready at all moments."[127]

- "You can't get second things by putting them first; you can get second things only by putting first things first."[128]
- "I believe in Christianity as I believe that the sun has risen not only because I see it but because by it I see everything else."[129]

Repetition, yet another stylistic technique, repeats key words in a sentence for emphasis. Here is an example of doubling up on the word *joy*: "The whole man is to drink joy from the fountain of joy."[130] Another example repeats the words *growth* and *change*: "Mere change is not growth. Growth is the synthesis of change and continuity, and where there is no continuity there is no growth."[131] Whether writing for the eye and ear, or using stylistic techniques such as anthesis or repetition, C. S. Lewis intentionally sought to make his ideas both interesting and memorable.

Summary: The "I" of "HI TEA": The Principle of Being Intentional

According to Lewis, effective communicators should be consciously aware of the intent of their message. Ineffective communicators are mindless communicators. If an idea cannot be clearly expressed to oneself and then to others, the idea is underdeveloped and needs further thought. The link between clear thought and clear communication is inextricable.

The principle of being intentional is more than just wishing to be clear and taking a stab at accuracy. To be intentional is, in fact, to mindfully and artfully select the right words, the most precise words, to clearly achieve your purpose. And, Lewis suggests, the fewer words that can communicate what is to be said, the better. He was a skilled communication craftsman who effectively used a variety of stylistic techniques including omission (brevity), antithesis and repetition.

This chapter uses Lewis own words to make the point that the effective communicator is intentional. Applications of that general admonition include the following advice:

1. Take time to develop your thoughts and ideas before you start speaking or writing.
2. Find ways to stimulate your creativity and clarify your thinking. (For Lewis it was walking, smoking, swimming, and reading).
3. Know what you want to say before you say it.

4. Think it and say it (to yourself) *before* you write it or say it to others.

5. Don't speak or write until you understand what you want to say: If you can't express what you want to say to yourself using complete sentences, then you probably don't yet know what you mean. Stop. Think. Write. Speak.

6. Visualize the final communication goal. Know what you want the reader or listener to be able to *do* when you finish your message.

7. Select the right word—whether from your own vocabulary or by consulting a dictionary or thesaurus.

8. Be linguistically flexible by considering whether you need to be Scientific (literal and precise), Ordinary (the common vernacular), or Poetic (through metaphor, simile or other comparison) to express your idea or emotion.

9. Consider whether the word you need should be abstract or concrete.

10. Pay attention to how words sound.

11. Used appropriately, stylistic techniques such as antithesis or repetition can add cadence to a message.

12. Be brief.

Notes

1. C. S. Lewis, Letter to Thomasine, December 14, 1959, *Collected Letters, Vol. III: Narnia, Cambridge and Joy 1950–1963*, ed. Walter Hooper (San Francisco: Harper San Francisco, 2007), 1108.

2. C. S Lewis, "Cross-Examination," *God in the Dock: Essays on Theology and Ethics,* ed. Walter Hooper (Grand Rapids: Eerdmans, 1970), 263.

3. As quoted by Walter Hooper, "The Abolition of Man or Reflections on Education with Special Reference to the Teaching of English in the Upper Forms of Schools," *C. S. Lewis: A Companion and Guide* (London: HarperCollins, 1996), 331.

4. Hooper, *Companion and Guide*, 330.

5. C. S. Lewis, Letter to Albert Lewis, August 28, 1924, *The Collected Letters of C. S. Lewis, Vol. I Family Letters 1905–1931*, ed. Walter Hooper (London: HarperCollins, 2000), 633.

6. C. S. Lewis, "If We Have Christ's Ethics, Does the Rest of the Christian Faith Matter?" *Socratic Digest* 1 (1943), 23.

7. Hooper, *Companion and Guide*, 331.

8. C. S. Lewis, *The Abolition of Man or Reflections on Education with Special Reference to the Teaching of English in the Upper Forms of Schools* (Oxford: Oxford University Press, 1943), 4.

9. Lewis, *The Abolition of Man*, 11.
10. Lewis, *The Abolition of Man*, 11.
11. C. S. Lewis, "The Poison of Subjectivism," *Christian Reflections* ed. Walter Hooper (London: Geoffrey Bles, 1967), 81.
12. Peter Kreeft, *C. S. Lewis for the Third Millennium: Six Essays on the Abolition of Man* (San Francisco: Ignatius Press, 1994), 69.
13. Kreeft, *Third Millennium*, 69.
14. Lewis, *The Abolition of Man*, 81.
15. Doris T. Meyers, "The Context of Metaphor," *C. S. Lewis in Context* (Kent: The Kent State University Press), 13.
16. For example, see: Steven A. Beebe, Susan J. Beebe and Diana K. Ivy, *Communication: Principles for a Lifetime* (Boston: Pearson, 2019), 49–68.
17. C. K. Ogden and I. A. Richards, *The Meaning of Meaning* (San Diego: A Harvest/HBJ Book, 1989/1923).
18. These ideas are held in common with Owen Barfield: Owen Barfield, *Poetic Diction: A Study in Meaning*. 2nd Revised edition (Middletown: Wesleyan Paperback, 1984). Also see: *C. S. Lewis, Miracles: A Preliminary Study* (London: Geoffrey Bles, 1947).
19. C. S. Lewis, "The Language of Religion," *Christian Reflections* ed. Walter Hooper, (London: Geoffrey Bless, 1967), 134.
20. Lewis, "The Language of Religion," 134.
21. C. S. Lewis, "The Language of Religion," 134, quoting Robert Conquest, "Excerpts from A Report to the Galactic Council," *The Listener* 52 (October 14. 1954), 612.
22. Zachary A. Rhone, *The Great Tower of Efland: The Mythopoetic Worldview of J. R. R. Tolkien, C. S. Lewis, G.K. Chesterton, and George MacDonald* (Kent: The Kent State University Press, 2017), 19.
23. Meyers, "The Context of Metaphor," 13.
24. Barfield, *Poetic Diction*, 7.
25. Barfield, *Poetic Diction*, 13.
26. This is discussed further in: Steven A. Beebe, ""C. S. Lewis on Language and Meaning: Manuscript Fragment Identified," *VII: An Anglo-American Literary Review* 27 (2010), 7–24.
27. C. S. Lewis, *Miracles: A Preliminary Study* (London, 1947), 88.
28. Michael Ward, *Planet Narnia: The Seven Heavens in the Imagination of C. S. Lewis* (Oxford: Oxford University Press, 2008), 151.
29. Ward, *Planet Narnia*, 151.
30. Lewis Carroll, *Alice's Adventures in Wonderland*, "Chapter 6 Humpty Dumpty," (New York: Millennium Publications, 2014).
31. C. S. Lewis, C. S. Lewis, *The Four Loves* (London: Geoffrey Bles, 1960), 10.
32. C. S. Lewis, *A Preface to Paradise Lost* (Oxford: Oxford University Press, 1942), 1.
33. C. S. Lewis, *Language and Human Nature* (Manuscript Fragment), *VII: An Anglo-American Literary Review* 27 (2010), 15; also see: Beebe, "C. S. Lewis on Language and Meaning," 7–24.

34. C. S. Lewis, *Collected Letters III*, xvi.

35. Karl E. *Weick, Karl E. Sensemaking in Organizations (Thousand Oaks: Sage, 1995)*, 25.

36. See: Diana Pavlac Glyer, *The Company They Keep: C. S. Lewis and J. R. R. Tolkien as Writers in Community* (Kent: Kent State University Press, 2007).

37. C. S. Lewis, "On Criticism," *Of Other Worlds: Essays and Stories*, ed. Walter Hooper (London: Geoffrey Bless, 1966), 43.

38. Lewis, "On Criticism," 56.

39. C. S. Lewis, Letter to Rhona Bodle June 24, 1949, *Collected Letters, Vol. II: Books, Broadcasts and the War 1931–1949*. ed. Walter Hooper (San Francisco: Harper San Francisco, 2004), 947.

40. Lewis, *Collected Letters II*, 947.

41. As quoted by Bob Talbert's "Quotebag," *The Detroit Free Press*, 1979, 19C.

42. C. S. Lewis, *Perelandra* (London: The Bodley Head, 1943), 33.

43. Lewis, *Miracles*, 138.

44. Lewis, *Language and Human Nature*, (Fragment) 25; also see: Beebe, "C. S. Lewis on Language and Meaning," 12.

45. Lewis, *Language and Human Nature*, 25.

46. Lewis, *Language and Human Nature*, 25.

47. Lewis, *Language and Human Nature*, 25.

48. Paul Watzlawick, Janet Beavin Bavelas and Don D. Jackson, *The Pragmatics of Human Communication: A Study of Interactional patterns, Pathologies and Paradoxes*. (New York: WW. Norton & Company, 1967), 275.

49. Lewis, "Cross-Examination," *God in the Dock*, 263.

50. Lewis, Letter to Mrs. Frank L. Jones, April 4, 1950. *Collected Letters III*, 22.

51. Lewis, *Experiment in Criticism*, 27.

52. Lewis, *Experiment in Criticism*, 27.

53. C. S. Lewis, *Studies in Words* (Cambridge: Cambridge University Press, 1960), 6.

54. Lewis, *Studies in Words*, 6.

55. C. S. Lewis, *English Literature in the Sixteenth Century: Excluding Drama* (Oxford: Clarendon Press, 1954), 315.

56. C. S. Lewis and Sherwood Wirt, "Cross-Examination," ed. Walter Hooper, *Undeceptions: Essays on Theology and Ethics* (London: Geoffrey Bles, 1971), 215–217. Originally appearing in: Sherwood Eliot Wirt "The Final Interview of C. S. Lewis," *Decision magazine*, Sept 1963 Billy Graham Association. <http://www.cbn.com/special/narnia/articles/ans_lewislastinterviewa.aspx≥ accessed January 29, 2015.

57. C. S. Lewis, *Studies in Words*, 6.

58. Scott Calhoun, "C. S. Lewis as Philologist: *Studies in Words*," *C. S. Lewis: Life, Works, and Legacy*, ed. Bruce L. Edwards (Westport: Praeger, 2007), 81.

59. C. S. Lewis, *Letters to Malcolm: Chiefly on Prayer* (London: Geoffrey Bles, 1964), 6.

60. Lewis, *Language and Human Nature* (manuscript fragment), 26.

61. Lewis, *Language and Human Nature* (manuscript fragment), 26.

62. Lewis, *Language and Human Nature* (manuscript fragment), 26; For additional commentary see: Beebe, "C. S. Lewis on Language and Meaning," 7–24.

63. Lewis, *Language and Human Nature* (manuscript fragment), 26.

64. C. S. Lewis, "A Slip of the Tongue" in *The Weight of Glory: And Other Addresses* (New York: HarperCollins, 1980), 184.

65. Armand Nicholi, Jr. The *A Question of God: C. S. Lewis and Sigmund Freud Debate God, Love, Sex, and the Meaning of Life.* (New York: Free Press, 2002). For a thorough explanation of the factors leading Lewis into atheism and then out of it to theism and Christianity, see: Joel D. Heck, *From Atheism to Christianity: The Story of C. S. Lewis* (St. Louis: Concordia Publishing House, 2017).

66. Paul Bond, "Jill Freud, Inspiration for Lucy in 'Narnia,' Revels C. S. Lewis Memories," REX USA/Associated Newspapers, https://www.hollywoodreporter.com/news/jill-freud-inspiration-lucy-narnia-726145 accessed January 22, 2018.

67. R. H. Hopcke, *A Guided Tour of the Collected Works of C. G. Jung* (Boston: Shambhala, 1999), 15.

68. Hopcke, *A Guided Tour*, 14.

69. C. S. Lewis, "Psychoanalysis and Literary Criticism," *Essays and Studies*, 27 (1942).

70. Lewis, "Psychoanalysis and Literary Criticism," 7.

71. Lewis, *Language and Human Nature*, 26.

72. Lewis, *Language and Human Nature,* 26.

73. Lewis, *Letters to Malcolm*, 52.

74. Lewis, *Letters to Malcolm*, 52.

75. Lewis, *Letters to Malcolm*, 52.

76. Lewis, *Letters to Malcolm*, 52

77. C. S. Lewis, "Sometimes Fairy Stories May Say Best What's to be Said," *Of Other Worlds: Essays and Stories*, ed. Walter Hooper (London: Geoffrey Bles, 1966), 36.

78. Jerry Root, *C. S. Lewis and a Problem of Evil: An Investigation of a Pervasive Theme* (Eugene: Pickwick Publications, 2009), xv.

79. Lewis, *Collected Letters III*, Letter to Thomasine, December 14, 1959, 1108.

80. C. S. Lewis, "It All Began with a Picture," *Of Other Worlds: Essays and Stories,* ed. Walter Hooper. (London: Geoffrey Bles, 1966), 42.

81. Walter, Hooper "C. S. Lewis as Communicator," Lecture, presented at Texas State University, March 27, 2007.

82. Walter Hooper, "The Inklings," *C. S. Lewis & His Circle: Essays and Memoirs from the Oxford C. S. Lewis Society,* ed. M. Roger White, Judith Wolfe and Brendan N. Wolfe (Oxford: Oxford University Press, 2015), 204.

83. Alan Jacobs, *The Narnian: The Life and Imagination of C. S. Lewis* (San Francisco: HarperSanFrancisco, 2005), 131.

84. Jacobs, *The Narnian*, 131.

85. Jacobs, *The Narnian*, 131.

86. See: Phillips, *C. S. Lewis at the BBC*, 141 and *Collected Letters II*, 499.

87. Phillips, *C. S. Lewis at the BBC*, 141 and *Collected Letters II*, 499.

88. Lewis, *Collected Letters III*, 1108.

89. Lewis, *Mere Christianity*, 11.

90. Jerry Root, *C. S. Lewis and a Problem of Evil: An Investigation of a Pervasive Theme* (Eugene, Oregon: Pickwick Publications, 2009), xv.

91. Lewis, *Mere Christianity*, 11.

92. George Sayer, *Jack: A Life* (Wheaton: Crossway Books, 1994), 271.

93. Walter Hooper, "All About Jack: A C. S. Lewis Podcast" with William O'Flaherty, July 16, 2016 <allaboutjack.podbean.com>. Accessed July 16, 2016.

94. C. S. Lewis, "Before We Can Communicate," *God in the Dock*, 255.

95. Chad Walsh, *C. S. Lewis: Apostle to the Skeptics* (New York: Macmillan, 1949), 13.

96. C. S. Lewis, "The Language of Religion," *Christian Reflections,* ed. Walter Hooper (London: Geoffrey Bles, 1967), 129.

97. Lewis, "The Language of Religion," 129.

98. Lewis, "The Language of Religion," 129.

99. Lewis, "The Language of Religion," 129.

100. Lewis, "The Language of Religion," 129.

101. Lewis, "The Language of Religion," 136.

102. Lewis, "The Language of Religion," 138.

103. Reported in George Bailey, "In the University," *C. S. Lewis: Speaker & Teacher* ed. Carolyn Keefe (London: Hodder and Stoughton, 1971), 114.

104. Bailey, "In the University," 114.

105. S. I. Hayakawa, *Language in Thought and Action* 5th edition. (New York: Harcourt, Inc., 1991).

106. For a discussion of the nature of words and meaning and the impact on others see: Steven A. Beebe, Susan J. Beebe and Mark V. Redmond. *Interpersonal Communication: Relating to Others* (Boston: Pearson, 2020).

107. E. M. W. Tillyard and C. S. Lewis, *The Personal Heresy: A Controversy* (Oxford: Oxford University Press, 1939), 69.

108. C. S. Lewis, "Before We Can Communicate," *God in the Dock*, 257.

109. Lewis, "Before We Can Communicate," 257.

110. Lewis, "Before We Can Communicate," 257.

111. Lewis, "Before We Can Communicate," 256.

112. C. S. Lewis, "The Vision of John Bunyan," in *Selected Literary Essays* (Cambridge: Cambridge University Press, 1969)," 147.

113. Lewis, "The Vision of John Bunyan," 147.

114. C. S. Lewis, *Letters to Malcolm: Chiefly on Prayer* (London: Geoffrey Bles, 1964), 63.

115. Lewis, *Letters to Malcom*, 126.

116. Jonathan Swift, First published in Dublin as: *Letter to a Young Gentleman Lately Entered into Holy Orders* (9 January, 1720).

117. C. S. Lewis, "High and Low Brows," in *Selected Literary Essays*, (Cambridge: Cambridge University Press, 1969), 271.

118. Lewis, "The Vision of John Bunyan," 151.

119. Wayne Martindale and Jerry Root, *The Quotable Lewis: An Encyclopedia Selection of Quotes from the Complete Published Works of C. S. Lewis* (Wheaton: Tyndale House Publishers, 1990).

120. Michael M. Kleppter, *I'd Rather Die than Give a Speech* (New York: Carol Publishing Group, 1994), 45.

121. C. S. Lewis, Letter to Albert Lewis, December 22, 1918 in *Collected Letters I*, 422.

122. William O'Flaherty, *The Misquotable C. S. Lewis: What He Didn't Say, What He Actually Said and Why it Matters* (Eugene: Wipf and Stock, 2018); Also see: William O'Flaherty, "Top 10 Lines Falsely Attributed to C. S. Lewis," *Christianity Today* (November 22, 2017), https://www.christianitytoday.com/ct/2017/november-web-only/top-10-misquoted-lines-from-cs-lewis.html.

123. The original phrase "There are better things ahead than any we leave behind." appears in a letter to Mary Shelburne, June 17, 1963, *Collected Letters, III*, 1430.

124. William O'Flaherty, "Top 10 Lines Falsely Attributed to C. S. Lewis," https://www.christianitytoday.com/ct/2017/november-web-only/top-10-misquoted-lines-from-cs-lewis.html.

125. C. S. Lewis, *The Four Loves* (London: Geoffrey Bles, 1960).

126. C. S. Lewis, *The Allegory of Love: A Study in Medieval Tradition* (Oxford: The Clarendon Press, 1936), 2.

127. C. S. Lewis, "The World's last Night," *The World's Last Night and Other Essays* (New York: Harcourt, Brace, 1959), 107.

128. C. S. Lewis, "First and Second Things," *God in the Dock: Essays on Theology and Ethics* (Grand Rapids: Eerdmans, 1970), 281.

129. C. S. Lewis, "Is Theology Poetry," *They Asked for a Paper* (London: Geoffrey Bles, 1962), 165.

130. C. S. Lewis, "The Weight of Glory," *Transposition and Other Addresses* (London: Geoffrey Bles, 1949), 32.

131. C. S. Lewis, "Hamlet: The Prince or the Poem," *Selected Literary Essays*, (Cambridge: Cambridge University Press, 1969), 105.

6

Transpositional

"If the richer system is to be represented in the poorer at all, this can only be by giving each element in the poorer system more than one meaning. The transposition of the richer into the poorer must, so to speak, be algebraical, not arithmetical."[1]

- C. S. Lewis

"The very essence of our life as conscious beings, all day and every day, consists of something which cannot be communicated except by hints, similes, metaphors …"[2]

- C. S. Lewis

On December 4, 1916, Lewis took his first steps in Oxford, a city that was to be his primary home until his death 47 years later. When writing about his first visit to Oxford in his autobiography *Surprised by Joy*, he admits he made no prior arrangements for lodging; rather, he planned to spontaneously see what he could find when he arrived. When he left the Oxford railroad station on foot, luggage in hand, he had high anticipation of seeing the famous Oxford domes and spires. As he later recalled, he was "all agog for 'dreaming spires' and 'last enchantments'."[3] But he was soon puzzled and even disappointed at what he saw. Approaching Oxford from the South, Lewis would have arrived at the train station on platform 2, just as he would have if he arrived in Oxford from the South today. As he started walking, he saw no grand town, tall spires, or beautiful parapets, but what he described as a dilapidated town with rundown buildings and "mean shops." He nonetheless trudged on until he had come to the edge of town. Now he was really stymied. Had he missed the city? Was this Oxford? And then he disclosed, "Only when it became obvious that there was very little town left ahead of me, that I was in fact getting to open country, did I turn around and look." Breathtaking beauty. "There behind me, far away, never more beautiful since, was the fabled cluster of spires and towers."[4] He had left the station from the side on which he arrived and gone in the opposite direction toward Botley—away from the city. As he insightfully put it: "I did not see to what extent this little adventure was an allegory of my whole life."[5]

After realizing his error, he hired a horse-drawn hansom (taxi) to take him to a rooming house where he could get rooms for a week—he told the hansom driver that any rooming house near city center would do. He admits this method of finding a room might now be hazardous, yet on this first visit it "was a complete success, and I was soon at tea in comfortable surroundings."[6] That house still stands at 1 Mansfield Road—just steps away from where he was to explain one of his most captivating ideas about communication.

Twenty-eight years later, and within a few yards of where he had spent his first night in Oxford (exactly 338 steps away), he was reportedly overcome when delivering a sermon, say those who were in the chapel of Mansfield College the morning of May 28, 1944. In the middle of delivering his message, he had to stop. It was reported that he was so overcome with emotion as he talked about the power and the presence of the Holy Spirit that he momentarily left the platform. But in 1963 he told Walter Hooper, when Hooper inquired about his "spiritual experience," that he stopped to leave the platform because he simply had to use the loo.[7] Regardless of the reason for its interruption, the title of his memorable sermon *Transposition*, is also the third principle of Lewis's approach to communication.

Principle Three: Effective Communicators Are Transpositional

At first glance this principle may seem the least intuitively clear. What is transposition? What does it mean to be transpositional? Lewis may have been a master at this skill, but precisely what is it? The term *transposition* is a metaphor. According to language scholar David Tracy, a metaphor's purpose is to tap "the surplus of meaning" that is embedded in language.[8] For Lewis, *transposition* is a process that seeks to unlock this surplus of meaning, especially emotional meaning, that resides in words to describes an experience. Just as *glossolalia* is the phenomena of "speaking with tongues," which Lewis discussed when delivering his sermon to commemorate the Day of Pentecost, *transposition* is the process of making that which is beyond description, clear or at least clearer.

If a person tried to sing a piece of music pitched too high for his or her vocal range, the music would need to be transposed from the out-of-range higher key to a more accessible lower key. To transpose a piece of music from one key (say, the key of G Major) to a lower key (the key of C Major) is to perform the same tune but moved down the scale five whole tones, using an F natural in the scale instead of F sharp. The melody and harmony would be recognizable from the original key, but heard at a five-note lower pitch. *Transposition*, according to C. S. Lewis, metaphorically characterizes the process of communicating a richer, "higher," emotionally-rich experience "in a lower key" so that the intended receiver of the message can discover the intended meaning (to continue the metaphor—the melody) in a new key.

Lewis's description of his first glimpse of Oxford transposes his experience into a story—explicitly suggesting that his walking in the opposite direction of his destination was an allegory of his life's journey from atheist to Christian. What better way to express his mindful observation that in life he realized he had been heading the wrong direction and consequently had missed the beautiful view? Heading the wrong direction was, acknowledged Lewis, an allegory of his entire life.[9]

For Lewis, one's perspective, or vantage point when experiencing an event greatly influences how the event is perceived. In noting the importance of perspective Lewis notes, "What you see and what you hear depends a good deal on where you are standing. It also depends on what sort of person you are."[10] But how does transposing an experience to an accessible "lower key" change the perspective? It gives the reader or listener a new point of view.

Before considering the principle of transposition in greater detail, it is first useful to understand a precursor to the transposition process—*translation*. Lewis viewed both translation and transposition as distinct communication processes. Understanding the process of translation will help clarify the second process, transposition.

Translation: A Prelude to Transposition

To *translate* a message is to paraphrase, decode, decipher, or convert one language to another—to make the ideas of one person understandable and meaningful to another person.[11] Given Lewis's talent for learning languages, he was intimately familiar with the challenge of translating one language to another. Lewis was multilingual; one of his triple firsts was in "Greats" which, in addition to classical history and philosophy, includes the study of Latin and Greek. He was not only skilled in translating Latin and Greek, but also French, German, and Italian as well. He had the ability to make a "foreign" language clear to someone who did not speak that language.

In a number of places in his writing, Lewis describes *translation* as his original primary communication goal (especially translating ideas about Christianity to a broader audience). In his essay "Rejoinder to Dr. Pittenger," Lewis describes his role as an apologist or defender of the faith this way: "My task is simply that of a translator—One turning Christian doctrine ... into the vernacular, into language that unscholarly people would attend to and understand."[12] The translator's paramount twin goals are accuracy and clarity—to use words in a language different from the listeners while communicating the speaker's intent in ways that the listener can understand. What does a translator do? The translator clarifies by using one symbol that has meaning to the message source (such as saying, "*hola*") to substitute for another symbol that has meaning for the receiver ("*hello*"). A translator turns nonsense into sense.

Lewis's motive for serving as a translator was that he had not found others who had translated Christianity effectively. Lewis explains, "One thing at least is sure. If the real theologians had tackled this laborious work of translation about a hundred years ago, when they began to lose touch with the people (for whom Christ died), there would have been no place for me."[13] Translation is not just clarifying the thoughts of obtuse theologians; the passion for sharing the "good news" needs translation as well.

When translating ideas, Lewis believed it is important to pay attention to individual words as well as the overall style of the message. Lewis also thought that it was vital to first have a clear sense of the intended meaning of a message before expressing the idea. So the second of Lewis's principles, being intentional, is linked to the principle of transposition by purposeful and accurate translation. As Lewis argues, "I have come to the conviction that if you cannot translate your thoughts into uneducated language, then your thoughts were confused. Power to translate is the test of having really understood one's own meaning."[14] Note his explicit reference to translating thoughts into clearer, more familiar "uneducated" language.

Lewis was aware he had the talent to translate Christian theology effectively. In a letter to The Rev. John Beddow, Lewis said: "People praise me as a 'translator', but what I want is to be the founder of a school of 'translation'."[15] He apparently doesn't want the burden of being the only person to translate Christian ideas to a larger audience. Lewis's motivation for seeking others to help in translating the Christian message stems from his belief that his time as a translator may be running out, that he is past his prime. He continues, revealing his technique:

> I am nearly forty-seven. Where are my successors? Anyone can learn to do it [translate] if they wish. It only involves first writing down in ordinary theological college English exactly what you want to say and then treating that just as you treated a piece of English set for Greek prose at school ...[16]

In further encouraging others to become translators Lewis says,

> It is inconceivable that there is no one among you [the clergy] who can do this quite as well as I could; and it is far better that it should be done by those who know at first hand what needs to be said. So my advice is that you get on with it at once ...[17]

Lewis, always the educator, concludes his letter to Rev. Beddow with additional tips about how to be a translator:

> (Remember that in the Vernacular *creature* mans 'beast', a *being* means a 'person'. *Personal* often means 'corporeal', *Primitive* means 'crude' or 'barbarous', and avoid words like *Challenge*, *Tribute* and all newspaper clichés). I feel I'm talking rather like a tutor—forgive me. But it is just a technique and I'm desperately anxious to see it widely learned.[18]

Lewis thought his translation technique was a skill others could learn and he was hopeful others would join him in this communication task.

In another essay explicitly about communication, titled "Before We Can Communicate," published relatively late in his career in 1961 when his ideas about communication were mature, Lewis begins by framing the communication task: "I have been asked to write about 'the problem of communication'; by which my inquirer meant 'communication under modern conditions between Christians and the other world.'"[19] Lewis states that his "ideas about 'communication' are purely empirical ...".[20] As noted in the last chapter (and found in Lewis's not-to-be-completed book *Language and Human Nature*, which he planned to co-author with Professor Tolkien), Lewis describes communication as a mathematical equation (hence the term *empirical*) in which one set of symbols equals the meaning intended by the message source.[21] He is describing the process of translation.

Given Lewis's interest in language translation, it is not surprising that he would use *translator* as a metaphor for his role as apologist. His purpose, he said, was not to add to the Christian ideas he translated, but to clarify and explain the Christian message to his intended listener. He had similar goals as an educator. In his tutorial role he wanted his students to summarize or translate the content of their lessons accurately so that the idea would be understood and remembered. Adding to his ideas about translation in "Before We Can Communicate," Lewis describes his tutorial instructional objective: "What we want to see in every ordination exam is a compulsory paper or (simply) translation ..."[22] He clarifies that the goal of translation is to make the meaning clear to the receiver when he advised, "Instead of saying 'How would Cicero have said that?', you have to ask yourself 'How would my scout or bedmaker have said that?"[23] At the weekly tutorial meetings with his students, either one on one or in small groups, students would read their weekly essays to him. Their task was to read books assigned by Lewis and then synthesize or, when applicable, explain, debate, or refute ideas. Lewis knew that "None can give to another what he does not possess."[24] As an assessment measure, the ability to correctly translate a message is evidence that the message was clearly understood.

Lewis also discusses the challenge of accurately translating a message to ensure accurate meaning. He notes that changing a word in a passage (such as *indifferently* to *impartially*) may make sense "to the man in the pew" but may create linguistic confusion for someone who understands the original meaning of the term "indifferently."[25] An effective translator selects words and symbols that have meaning *to the listener*. Lewis notes that as clearly as possible, one should express ideas to the listener or reader so that the message of person A is the message that person B understands.[26] As he put it in his essay "God in the Dock," one needs to translate a message in the language of the listener "just as a missionary learns Bantu before preaching to the Bantus."[27] Yet, he notes that this seemingly obvious principle is not always put into practice. In his letter to Rev. Beddow, he parenthetically notes, "(It has always seemed to me odd that those who are sent to evangelise the Bantus begin by learning Bantu while the Church turns out annual curates to teach the English who simply don't know the vernacular language of England)."[28] His communication lesson is clear: To be an effective translator one has to know the language of the reader or listener. But there is more to communication than mere translation. A more sophisticated process, transposition, has an augmented ambitious objective.

Transposition: Communicating from Higher to Lower, Richer to Poorer

As noted earlier, *Transposition*, is the process of communicating a "higher," emotion-rich experience so that the intended receiver of the message can discover the intended meaning in a in a more accessible "lower key." Transposition is a metaphor for extracting meaning from life experiences so that others make sense of the experience. Lewis makes a distinction between *translation* (a symbolic word-for-word exchange) and *transposition* (moving from "higher" to "lower") in his sermon *Transposition*, published as given on May 28, 1944, "Whit-Sunday" (Pentecost) at Mansfield College Chapel (which today serves as the college's dining hall).[29] (Although there is convincing evidence that the actual date of the sermon was likely June 9, 1946 rather than the published May, 1944 date.)[30]

Regardless of the actual date of his sermon, the concept of transposition was important to Lewis as evidenced by the fact that he continued to develop his ideas by adding new examples in a later publication.[31] Lewis scholar Arend Smilde has meticulously documented how Lewis revised his original 1949 published version of his sermon by inserting seven paragraphs when it was republished in the 1962 anthology of Lewis papers and addresses *They Asked for A Paper*.[32]

In this seminal sermon Lewis notes that substituting one symbol (translation) for another symbol does not always get the communication job done:

> It is of some importance to notice that the word *symbolism* is not adequate in all cases to cover the relation between the higher medium and its transposition in the lower. It covers some cases perfectly, but not others. Thus, the relation between speech and writing is one of symbolism.[33]

There is a need for something more than translation; transposition is needed. Lewis makes a metaphorical distinction between *translation*, which he suggests is an "arithmetic," symbolic process, and *transposition*, an "algebraic" richer to poorer process.[34] His use of the metaphor "algebraic" when discussing transposition suggests that the same symbol ("X," for example) could be used to substitute for a variety of different numbers (or, in the case of words, different interpretations).

In distinguishing between translation and transposition he clarifies differences between the communication channels of speaking (auditory) versus writing (visual) when he notes, "… written characters exist solely for the eye, the spoken words solely for the ear. There is complete discontinuity between them."[35] Although in *Studies in Words* he said he makes no distinction between speaking and writing as a *function* of communication, he notes that sounds and images nonetheless use different processes or channels to communicate information. In *Transposition* he explicitly says, "They [speaking and writing] are not like one another, nor does the one cause the other to be. The one is simply a sign of the others and signifies it by a convention."[36] Further adding to the distinction between one form of communication and another, he clarifies the differences between pictures and the "real world" when he notes, "But a picture is not related to the visible world in just that way. Pictures are part of the visible world themselves and represent it only by being part of it."[37] In his vintage style of communicating, he then provides an example: "The suns and lamps in pictures seem to shine only because real suns or lamps shine on them: That is, they seem to shine a great deal because they really shine a little in reflecting their archetypes."[38] In additional clarification of the differences between words and images as a way of distinguishing between translation and transposition he says,

> The sunlight in a picture is therefore not related to real sunlight simply as written words are to spoken. It is a sign, but also something more than a sign: and only a sign because it is also more than a sign, because in it the thing signified is really in a certain mode present.[39]

He indicates transposition is more than a mere symbolic process, in which one symbol equals (=) another symbol. Lewis adds, "If I had to name the relation I should call it not symbolical but sacramental. But in the case we started from—that of emotion and sensation—we are even further beyond mere symbolism."[40] He has made an important point: Transposition is more "sacramental" than symbolic in the sense that there is a connection to be made between the richer, higher experience of Holy Communion and the verbal description of that experience. Bread and wine are transpositional emblems; they are more than flour, water, yeast and grape juice. When these ingredients are used as the Eucharist or Communion they become transpositional, representing something more meaningful than just bread and wine; they are a conduit from the Divine.

The first clue that the entire focus of Lewis's message is communication occurs in his second sentence, where he begins discussing what "the learned call *glossolalia*."[41] He defines *glossolalia* as that which is uttered by a speaker "under the spirit" and assumed to have meaning for listeners. Contemporary Christians call this phenomenon "speaking in tongues." However, Lewis admits, "It is, to be frank, an embarrassing phenomenon. St. Paul himself seems to have been rather embarrassed by it …"[42] Placing his message in the context of Pentecostal speaking in tongues cleverly identifies the purpose of his message—to describe how a person communicates rich, emotion-laden, challenging-to-communicate experiences to others through the process of *transposition*—the title of his sermon.

After briefly discussing speaking in tongues, Lewis introduces his foundational idea: People may have different interpretations of the same sensation or stimulus, depending on time and circumstance. This observation, that people may interpret the same phenomenon differently, provides the underlying explanation for transposition. Lewis offers an example from *Pepys's Diary* in which the sensations of (1) being sick and (2) hearing music result in the same *biological* reaction. Lewis says, "Now it may be true that not many of us have fully shared Pepys's experience; but we have all experienced that sort of thing."[43] The "sort of thing" he is talking about is having the same physiological reaction (e.g. a quiver in the stomach) interpreted in different ways (it could signify grief, or as he famously noted in his opening line of *A Grief Observed*, fear). Lewis continues, "For myself I find that if, during a moment of intense aesthetic rapture, one tries to turn around and catch by introspection what one is actually feeling, one can never lay one's hand on anything but a physical sensation."[44] Then he provides a personal example: "In my case it is a kind of kick or flutter in the diaphragm."[45] Then he adds, "But the important point is this: I find that this kick or flutter is exactly the same sensation which, in me, accompanies great and sudden anguish."[46] He clinches his point by noting how different experiences can have the same neurological effect: "Introspection can discover no difference at all between my neural response to very bad news and my neural response to the overture of *The Magic Flute*."[47]

Lewis's insight is that he has *identical* physiological reactions to two *different* stimuli. Neurologically, the brain triggers the same physiological response to bad news (a negative experience) and *The Magic Flute* (a positive experience) *but not the same meaning*. He further explains, "If I were to judge simply by sensations I should come to the absurd conclusion that joy and anguish are the same thing, that what I most dread is the same with what I most desire."[48] Lewis's intuition is that different kinds of "higher" emotional experiences may result in a similar ("lower") physiological response.

Lewis then unpacks what he means by *higher* and *lower*: "... our emotion life is 'higher' than the life of our sensations—not, of course, morally higher, but richer, more varied, more subtle."[49] He further adds, "the senses compensate for this by using the same sensation to express more than one emotion ..."[50] In other words, *there is not a one-for-one (translational or symbolic) relationship between a person's emotional experience and his or her physiological response to the emotional experience*. Lewis concludes that there needs to be another term besides *translation* (in which one symbol equals another symbol) to explain how different emotional experiences can result in the same physiological response. He calls this process *transposition.*[51]

Although the preceding, detailed distinction between translation and transposition may seem unnecessarily tedious and unimportant, Lewis's understanding and application of transposition is one of his hallmark communication strategies. It is worth the effort to distinguish between the two processes. It is through transposition that Lewis helps us see and feel "higher" experiences and communicate ineffable ideas.

What are the steps of transposition? Transposition occurs by first thinking about the image or experience and then crafting a metaphor to express the idea or emotion. A person communicates (transposes) best when he or she first recalls, then visualizes a rich experience to express to a listener. Lewis notes that having an experience, in this instance he is talking about his military experience, is a precursor to transposing the experience:

> Ever since I served as an infantryman in the First World War I have had a great dislike of people who, themselves in ease and safety, issue exhortations to men in the front line. As a result I have a reluctance to say much about temptations to which I myself am not exposed.[52]

Selecting the best metaphor to describe an emotion-rich experience requires some personal experience on which the metaphor is based. A person cannot effectively describe an experience that is not first clearly remembered.

According to Lewis, transposition always goes from the "higher," richer experience to a "lower" message that can be understood by the receiver. Transposition does not work in reverse. A transpositional communicator starts with contemplating the rich (higher) emotional experience and then transposes to the lower, using words. Lewis describes transposition as a type of enriched translation process whereby, "The lower medium can be understood only if we know the higher medium"[53] and adds that "the highest does not stand without the lowest."[54] For example, attempting to describe the emotional impact of Rembrandt's masterpiece *The Return of the Prodigal Son* to a six-year-old who has never seen the painting or experienced the emotions of the woebegone prodigal, would involve considerable transposition. In order to help the six-year-old discover the emotional meaning of the painting, the painting itself represents the higher medium. A transpositional, metaphorical example (such as suggesting it would be like being reunited with a long-thought-lost teddy bear) is needed to express the painting's meaning to a youngster.

Facts without meaning have limited potential for clear communication. Facts ("lower") make sense if they are linked to the emotional meaning of an anecdote or story ("higher"). It is the function of facts to stimulate meaning. Lewis clarifies, "I have tried to stress throughout the inevitableness of the error made about every transposition by one who approaches it from the lower medium only … He sees all the facts but not the meaning. Quite truly, therefore, he claims to have seen all the facts. There *is* nothing else there; except the meaning."[55] Lewis then explains his meaning with a transpositional metaphor. Although his prosaic description uses explicit language to make his point, his use of metaphor in the example that follows, clarifies his explanation: "You will have noticed that most dogs cannot understand *pointing*. You point to a bit of food on the floor: the dog, instead of looking at the floor, sniffs at your finger. A finger is a finger to him, and that is all. His world is all fact and no meaning."[56]

In viewing communication as first, a word-for-word symbolic process of translation, and then a more emotionally nuanced process of transposition, Lewis suggests that perfect communication, in either case, is not likely. A communicator must accept that some meaning will be lost, whether the goal is translation or transposition. Acknowledging the imperfect nature of communication is consistent with Lewis's philosophy that all humans live, work, and play in the "Shadowlands."[57] A rational communicator recognizes the existence of "shadows" that obscure the intended meaning of messages.

To help his readers further grasp the notion of transposition, Lewis next uses an example of someone who experiences life in three dimensions, yet may attempt to describe those three dimensions to a person who sees only two dimensions: "… when we pointed to the lines on the paper and tried to explain, say, that 'This is a road,' would he not reply that the shape which we were asking him to accept as a revelation of our mysterious other world was the very same shape which, on our own showing, elsewhere meant nothing but a triangle?"[58] Trying to communicate an emotionally rich idea to another person who does not have the same set of symbols or who has completely different referents is frustrating for both communicator and receiver.

One of the additions Lewis made to the 1962 republished version of *Transposition* includes what he calls "a fable" to further illustrate the "algebraic" process of transposition.[59] He adds a story about a woman who bears a son while she was in a dungeon. Because her son has seen nothing but prison walls, straw on the floor, and just a sliver of the sky viewed through the grating in the prison ceiling, his view of the outside world was severely limited. His mother, an artist, in attempting to communicate what the outside world actually looks like, drew pencil images of rivers, towns and a beach. The dutiful and wanting-to-be-faithful son does his best to believe his mother's visual depictions of the outside world. She learns, however, that the boy thinks that outside the prison walls are actually pencil lines just like the ones she has drawn in her pictures. He thinks an actual river is only a smudged line on white paper. The wavy lines, she comes to realize, are only a crude attempt to describe the real river as well as "waving tree-tops" and "the light dancing on the weir ..."[60] The best one can do to describe something that another person has never seen or has no concept for is to use a representation for the unseen object—in this instance, pencil lines to depict rivers and trees. In this added "fable" Lewis provides yet another illustration to explain transposition as the process of trying to communicate something for which the intended receiver of the message has no clear referent. The mother uses lines on paper as a transpositional strategy. After describing the mother's attempt at transposition substituting the real world for pencil lines, Lewis makes his key point explicit:

> So with us. "We know not what we shall be"; but we may be sure we shall be more, not less, than we were on earth. Our natural experiences (sensory, emotional, imaginative) are only like the drawing, like penciled lines on flat paper.[61]

Now people only see "lines on paper" or as Apostle Paul put it "we see through a glass darkly" and only know "in part."[62] Yet, when like the boy in the dungeon, a person does his or her best to understand what can't yet be seen. A savvy message receiver realizes the inherently imperfect process of communicating something "higher" and "richer" (and often ineffable) to the "lower."

In describing transposition as moving from "higher" to "lower," Lewis foreshadows a contemporary communication theory called Media Richness Theory. The originators of the theory suggest that the communication channels through which one communicates range from media rich to media lean.[63] An example of a media-rich channel is a live, face-to-face conversation with another person; it is "rich" because of all the subtleties of vocal tone, body language, and other senses such as smell that are involved when communicating in person. Nonverbal communication (e.g. facial expression, vocal tone, and the intensity of gestures) is the primary way a person communicates feelings and emotions.[64] Feedback is immediate and continuous.

A media-lean communication channel, by comparison, appeals to fewer senses and has limited or no opportunities for feedback. The written word is a leaner medium than a face-to-face conversation because only sight is involved, and the author is not present so it is not possible to give or receive in-the-moment feedback. Tacking a poster on a bulletin board written by a forlorn pet owner searching for a lost cat is a media-lean method of communicating. Media lean messages are efficient and asynchronous. An asynchronous message is one in which there is a time delay between when the message is sent and when it may be read or heard. Most email, as well as voice mail messages, are asynchronous. The cat-seeking poster-writer's media-lean message could have been posted several months ago—the cat could now be snugly curled by the fire at home.

Media-rich channels include the possibility of instant feedback (such as interrupting, frowning or laughing during the conversation). Media-rich communication is synchronous. As in a face-to-face conversation the communicators respond to one another immediately in real time. During media-rich communication both verbal and nonverbal cues are in play, language tends to be more informal, and messages are tailored to a specific individual or individuals. A phone call uses a richer channel than a text message, but a text (with the possibility of a more immediate response) is richer than a letter sent via regular "snail mail." According to Media Richness Theory, certain types of messages are best delivered using more media-rich methods of communication. Proposing marriage or firing someone—very personal messages—demand a media-rich channel. Searching for lost cats or announcing a garage sale is more appropriate for leaner media channels.

The process of communication ranges from expressing media-rich to media-lean messages. Transposition is necessary when life experiences are simply too rich to be expressed without using metaphor, simile, allegory or other comparisons. Describing the birth of a son or daughter, seeing a multi-hued sunset fill an evening sky, or explaining what it is like to hear Handel's *Hallelujah Chorus* calls for more than literal, "scientific" translations of what is seen or heard in the emotional moment. Rich, sensual experiences brim with light, sound, movement, taste, and touch. Such opulent experiences are best expressed metaphorically to communicate the full range of fragrances, flavors, colors, sounds, and textures. Words are sometimes (often) inadequate to communicate the depth of the emotion being experienced. For example, when comedian Billy Crystal learned of the sudden death of his close friend and fellow comedian Robin Williams, Crystal simply tweeted this message: "No words."

Lewis, who often juxtaposes metaphors on other metaphors, further illustrates the process of transposition in his sermon *Transposition* by using yet another metaphor. He describes the process of transposing an orchestral score into a piano score: "If you are making a piano version of a piece originally scored for an orchestra, then the same piano notes which represent flutes in one passage must also represent violins in another."[65] Transposition is needed to take the higher orchestral score into the lower piano score. The piano score is lower because there are fewer possible sounds and notes that can simultaneously be played on the piano. Lewis further amplifies,

> The piano version means one thing to the musician who knows the original orchestral score and another thing to the man who hears it simply as a piano piece. But the second man would be at an even greater disadvantage if he had never heard any instrument but a piano and even doubted the existence of other instruments.[66]

Transposition seeks to help the message receiver comprehend that which has never been experienced.

Transposition can take many forms. It can be a simple, brief metaphor or simile (such as when Lewis described *Lord of the Rings* as "like lightning from a clear sky"),[67] or it can take a longer form, using story (the tales of Narnia, which describe the death and resurrection of Aslan on the Stone Table) or myth (retelling the Greek myth of Cupid and Psyche in *Till We Have Faces*).

Why is transposition necessary? Because spiritual experiences and other peak or intense emotional moments cannot be translated literally. This is especially true of numinous, mystical, metaphysical, or holy experiences. Lewis suggests, "… the concept of Transposition may have some contribution to make to the theology—or at least to the philosophy—of the Incarnation."[68] Lewis believes that the incarnation actually happened. Myth became fact. Transposition, suggests Lewis, helps people understand the essence of theology: "that humanity, while remaining itself, is not merely counted as, but veritably drawn into, Deity …"[69]

In his 1936 scholarly work *The Allegory of Love*, Lewis describes how the process of translation is different from using more metaphorical or allegorical means of expressing an emotionally rich idea. Although he doesn't use the term *transposition*, he describes the unique role that allegory, in comparison with *translation*, has in expressing certain ideas or experiences. A simple translation, although accurate, may miss some of the intended meaning. Lewis explains, "If the story, literally told, pleases as much as the original, and in the same way, to what purpose was allegory employed? For the function of allegory is not to hide but to reveal, and it is properly used only for that which cannot be said, or so well said, in literal speech."[70] Allegory or metaphor can uncork a "surplus of meaning" not expressed in a literal description.

Literary scholar P. H. Brazier views transposition as Lewis's quintessential communication skill: "Transposition lies at the heart of Lewis's understanding of revelation and is the key to his theology and apologetics: it permeates all of his work, theological, philosophical, literary and apologetic, even the analogical-symbolic narratives."[71] To understand transposition is to grasp one of Lewis's key skills which make him a master communication craftsperson.

It may help to think of translation as a horizontal process—one word substituting for another word, while transposition, by comparison, is a vertical process that always moves from the higher to the lower. An emotion or other meaning-rich "high" experience is expressed, typically using metaphor, or a word picture, so that the ineffable experience can be understood at a "lower" level of communication.

Visual Metaphor: The Technique of Transposition

The discussion of transposition may seem abstract, theoretical and leave one wondering "What does all of this have to do with being an effective communicator?" Here is the answer: The master communication craftsperson applies the principle of transposition by skillfully using metaphor and other types of comparisons to make "higher" and "richer" experiences, emotions and ideas accessible to a reader or listener.

In the 2005 musical *Billy Elliot* that bears his name, Billy is a teenager from a poor mining family in County Durham, England who secretly aspires to be a ballet dancer.[72] At first Billy's father, a widower and seasoned coal miner on strike in the 1970's Margaret Thatcher era, was strongly opposed to the idea when he discovered his son's ballet interests. Billy's dad thought ballet dancers were all "poofs" (gay) and unmanly. Nor did his father have the financial resources to invest in ballet lessons, a further reason for his reluctance to embrace Billy's ballet interests. But, as the story progresses, Billy's father eventually supports his son's quest to receive an education from the Royal Ballet School. During Billy's audition for the school, in the climactic scene of the show, Billy is asked, by those assessing his talent, "What does it feel like when you are dancing, Billy?" At first Billy haltingly stammers, "I . . . I don't know." He pauses and searches for words. Finally, with a quizzical facial expression, he admits he just doesn't have the words. Then, after additional thought, he offers several metaphors to explain what dancing feels like. It's like: forgetting, music, a fire, flying like a bird. After further fumbling for just the right words he finally captures his feeling by exclaiming, "It's like electricity!" He then erupts in an exuberant, breathtaking dance sequence that leaves his judges speechless. That's transposition. Metaphors and wordless expressions are needed when mere words are inadequate to describe a peak, ineffable emotional experience.

Transposition occurs primarily through the use of metaphor, but for C. S. Lewis it is often a specific kind of metaphor: a *visual* metaphor ("like lightening from a clear sky" when describing the impact of *The Lord of the Rings*, which is similar to Billy Elliot's description of dancing as "like electricity!"). Images are evoked. Lewis reveals that his stories often begin with pictures. He *saw* the story before he wrote it. To express what he saw his writing is liberally sprinkled with visual metaphors that appeal to one's senses (especially the sense of sight). Lewis reveals that even his prayers were often imbued with images. In *Letters to Malcom: Chiefly on Prayer*, Lewis discloses, ". . . mental images play an important part in my prayers. I doubt if any act of will or thought or emotion occurs in me without them."[73] Lewis further noted, "I ... think prayer without words is the best."[74] Yet he also admits the challenge of using images rather than words: "To pray successfully without words one needs to be 'at the top of one's form.'"[75] Although Lewis was a talented wordsmith, sometimes something more than a literal description of events or an experience is the best way to communicate. Therefore a *visual* metaphor may be needed to express ineffable ideas and feelings.

Using two visual metaphors, Lewis describes the process of how mental pictures come to him; they come effervescently or in a flourish: "But they [mental images] seem to help me most when they are most fugitive and fragmentary—rising and bursting like bubbles in champagne or wheeling like rooks in a windy sky: contradicting one another (in logic) as the crowded metaphors of a swift poet may do."[76] Lewis then offers his advice for capturing the essence of these fleeting images: "Fix on any one, and it goes dead. You must do as Blake would do with a joy; kiss it as it flies. And then, in their total effect, they do mediate to me something very important. It is always something qualitative—more like an adjective than a noun."[77] He transpositionally embellishes his point with yet another metaphor; "If a musical phrase could be translated into words at all it would become an adjective."[78]

Some educational theorists define a person's learning style as his or her preferred way of processing or making sense out of information.[79] People with an auditory style learn best by hearing information in the form of lectures, podcasts, or stories. Other students, as prescribed by the theory, learn best by actively participating when learning. Still others learn best visually; they remember best what they see. Although learning style theory is controversial, there is evidence that C. S. Lewis may have a preference for visual learning. Lewis's description of how he learned best, his photographic memory, his uncanny ability to remember what he had read (or seen), and his reliance on mental images to prime his creative pump for his stories, are all evidence of his visual learning style preference. Visual learners are at an advantage when it comes to learning to read and remember languages. Lewis was a voracious reader and a master at learning languages.

Although he had skills as a visual learner by remembering what he had read, there is also evidence that he had a keen memory for also remembering what he *heard*. In a 1967 letter to William Luther White, in response to White's question about how the Inklings came into being, J. R. R. Tolkien extolls Lewis's virtues in being able to recall what he heard. Tolkien notes, "C. S. L. had a passion for hearing things read aloud, a power of memory for things received in that way, and also a facility in extempore criticism, none of which were shared (especially not the last) in anything like the same degree by his friends."[80] Lewis apparently had a quick grasp of what he saw and heard.

At the heart of any metaphor, visual or not, is comparison—linking one idea, image, emotion, or experience to another. Specifically, a metaphor is figurative language that makes a comparison without using the words "like" or "as"—which, if used, would make the comparison a simile (e.g. in the opening sentence of this paragraph, describing an important idea as being "at the heart" of the process is a metaphor). Whether the comparison is literal (such as noting similarities between a computer hard drive and a portable flash drive) or figurative (the flowers drank deeply from the rain), metaphors derive their power from associating one concept or experience with another. As discussed in the previous chapter, for Lewis, meaning occurs not through the random association of a word with an idea or object, but through the meaning-rich metaphorical nature of language. As Lewis explains in *The Allegory of Love*, "We cannot speak, perhaps we can hardly think, of an 'inner conflict' without a metaphor; and every metaphor is an allegory in little."[81]

Lewis's metaphors, often inspired by visual or mental images, are liberally sprinkled throughout each of his books and essays. For example, in *Mere Christianity*, Lewis admonishes his readers to correct errors once a mistake has been made. He could have simply stated, "Once you find out you have made a mistake, it is better to correct it than to ignore it." But he makes the point memorably and irrefutably by appealing to the "mind's eye" with two metaphors:

> … if you have taken a wrong turning, then to go forward does not get you any nearer. If you are on the wrong road, progress means doing an about-turn and walking back to the right road; and in that case the man who turns back soonest is the most progressive man. We have all seen this when doing arithmetic. When

I have started a sum the wrong way, the sooner I admit this and go back and start again, the faster I shall get on.[82]

In a well-crafted passage in *Miracles*, Lewis provides another classic transpositional metaphor, using the imagery of ponies and horses to express the ultimate freedom that will occur in another realm: "These small and perishable bodies we now have were given to us as ponies are given to schoolboys. We must learn to manage: not that we may some day be free of horses altogether but that some day we may ride bare-back, confident and rejoicing, those greater mounts, those winged, shining and world-shaking horses ..."[83]

Another classic visual image from *Mere Christianity* helps readers understand the nature of the incarnation. The tin-soldier-into-life metaphor is juxtaposed with the slug-and-crab metaphor:

Imagine turning a tin soldier into a real little man. It would involve turning the tin into flesh. And suppose the tin soldier did not like it. He is not interested in flesh: all he sees is that the tin is being spoilt. He thinks you are killing him. He will do everything he can to prevent you. He will not be made into a man if he can help it.[84]

Lewis then unpacks the metaphor: "What you would have done about that tin soldier I do not know. But what God did about us was this. The Second Person in God, the Son, became human Himself: was born into the world as an actual man ..."[85] Then, in characteristic Lewis style, he adds another metaphor, "If you want to get the hang of it, think how you would like to become a slug or a crab."[86]

Lewis scholar Michael Ward has cataloged nearly thirty similes and comparisons, most of which are visual images or examples, that Lewis used in just one book, *Mere Christianity*, to describe what it is like to become a Christian. For Lewis, becoming a Christian it is like:

- joining a campaign of sabotage
- falling at someone's feet
- putting yourself in someone's hands
- taking on board fuel or food
- laying down your rebel arms and surrendering
- saying sorry
- laying yourself open
- turning full speed astern
- killing part of yourself

- learning to walk or to write
- buying God a present with his own money
- a drowning man clutching at a rescuer's hand
- a tin soldier or statue becomes alive
- waking after a long sleep
- getting close to someone
- becoming infected
- dressing up or pretending or playing
- emerging from the womb
- hatching from an egg
- a compass needle swinging to north
- a cottage being made into a palace
- a field being plowed and re-sown
- a horse turning into a Pegasus
- a greenhouse roof become bright in the sunlight
- coming around from anesthetic
- coming in out of the wind
- going home.[87]

Ward explains Lewis's technique: "Rather than saying, 'come to Jesus,' Lewis is saying, 'This is what it is like to come to Jesus …'"[88] Each of these comparisons illustrates the principle of transposition—making an ineffable, hard-to-describe experience effable. Chad Walsh noted Lewis's liberal inclusion of metaphor and comparisons, explaining their purpose as, "… little poems interspersed in the prose text bringing to full life the ideas that otherwise would smack of the scholar's study."[89] Transposition, then, uses "metaphorical poems" to express emotions and rich experiences.

When transposing experiences and emotions, details and subtleties are inevitably omitted. The transpositional process works by having the reader or listener actively participate by mentally filling in the gaps, drawing upon his or her own experience, to make sense of something not personally witnessed. While connecting the dots, the listener or reader assumes an active role in the situation by recalling a similar moment as a way of making sense of what is described.

"God whispers to us in our pleasures, speaks in our conscience, but shouts in our pain: it is His megaphone to rouse a deaf world."[90] In this classic quotation, pain is likened to a megaphone—a visual metaphor. For C. S. Lewis, influenced by his friend Owen Barfield, who wrote extensively about the metaphorical, poetic nature of language, metaphor holds the key to expressing the "higher" aspects of a person's life experiences—not only higher, richer experiences but, in some respects, all experiences that people perceive through their senses. As Lewis explains in *Miracles*,

> But it is a serious mistake to think that metaphor is an optional thing which poets and orators may put into their work as a decoration and plain speakers can do without. The truth is that if we are going to talk at all about things which are not perceived by the senses, we are forced to use language metaphorically. Books on psychology or economics or politics are as continuously metaphorical as books of poetry or devotion. There is no other way of talking as every philologist is aware ... All speech about supersensibles is, and must be, metaphorical in the highest degree.[91]

Lewis further explains the significance and importance of metaphor in his first scholarly book, *Allegory of Love,* a book devoted to literary applications of allegory, comparison, and metaphor. Lewis notes that many metaphors rely on classic visual comparisons that poets have used for centuries: "What is good or happy has always been high like the heavens and bright like the sun. Evil and misery were deep and dark from the first. Pain is black in Homer, and goodness is a middle point for Alfred no less than for Aristotle."[92]

Lewis scholar Lyle Smith observes that Lewis's use of metaphor provides important clarifying power. Smith observes, "Lewis held that, far from producing meaningless pseudo-statements, metaphors—rightly understood for what they are—keep us equally from meaningless tautologies on the one hand and self-contradiction on the other."[93] When used effectively, metaphors can help readers better understand the mystical and murky. Yet not all metaphors may be clarifying or accurate. In *Miracles,* Lewis relates the story of a girl, "brought up by 'higher thinking parents to regard God as a perfect 'substance'; in later life she realised that this had actually led her to think of Him as something like a vast tapioca pudding."[94] It is important, therefore, to use an accurate metaphor to clarify and express concepts and emotions.

Many readers found Lewis's 1933 allegorical book *The Pilgrim's Regress* puzzling. Lewis wrote this commentary about *The Pilgrim's Regress* in a letter to Belle Allen, who was having difficulty decoding the meaning of some of his allegorical references:

> ... *Pilgrim's Regress* was my first religious book and I didn't then know how to make things easy. I was not even trying to very much, because in those days I never dreamed I would become a "popular" author and hoped for no

readers outside a small "highbrow'" circle. Don't waste your time over it any more.[95]

In a 1943 revised edition of *The Pilgrim's Regress,* Lewis added more detailed annotations to make his early allegorical allusions clearer. His transpositional movement from the higher to the lower in his 1933 version had apparently been too obtuse for many readers. Literary scholar Doris Myers draws clear parallels between the main character and Lewis himself: "… the main character in *The Pilgrim's Regress* is called "John," another form of "Jack," Lewis's nickname. "John" is also a common word to designate an unspecified man, as in "John Doe." Allegorically, then, John is both C. S. Lewis and Everyman."[96]

Lewis suggests that a "good" metaphor is invaluable in making things clear and communicating that which is true. Metaphors, not prosaic explanations, do the most important work of convincing a reader that something is true. Lewis notes, "… all our truth, or all but a few fragments, is won by metaphor. And thence, I confess, it does follow that if our thinking is ever true, then the metaphors by which we think must have been good metaphors."[97]

Lewis's skill as a visual rhetorician, his ability to use visual metaphor to help his readers and listeners see what he saw, is a hallmark of his transpositional communication success. As a visual learner, Lewis had pictures in his head that needed to be transposed to, as he put it, "induce other people to build for themselves pictures in their own minds which may be roughly similar to ours."[98] Painting pictures in one's mind is the work of transposition. Metaphor does more than express emotion—it is the prime method for communicating *any* meaning. As literary scholar Edward Uszynsky notes, "Lewis utilizes metaphorical language not to solicit an emotional response primarily from his readers, but as a vehicle for communicating meaning. Language does not simply convey ideas, but constructs images that correspond with realities defying literal verbal description."[99] Lewis said it best: "The very essence of our life as conscious beings, all day and every day, consists of something which cannot be communicated except by hints, similes, metaphors, and the use of those emotions (themselves not very important) which are the pointers to it."[100] Author George Marsden concludes that one of the key reasons *Mere Christianity* remains popular is because Lewis, "… is a poet at heart, using metaphor and the art of meaning in a universe that is alive."[101] Transposition is a process of using metaphorical "hints" to glimpse what is beyond a person's senses.

Despite its virtues, metaphor has limitations. A metaphor is not a substitute for the "real thing." As Lewis reminds his readers in *Mere Christianity*: "All the scriptural imagery (harps, crowns, gold, etc.) is, of course a merely symbolical attempt to express the inexpressible ... People who take these symbols literally might as well think that when Christ told us to be like doves, He meant that we were to lay eggs."[102] Being aware of the process of transposition, one can avoid taking a metaphor too literally.

Summary: The "T" of "HI TEA": The Principle of Transposition

C. S. Lewis described his role as a communicator from the perspective of two related processes: translation and transposition. The first process, translation, involves converting a message to a different language. Primarily a word-for-word, symbol-for-symbol, "horizontal" process, translation seeks to make the language used by one communicator accurate and clear to another. It is an "arithmetic" process whereby one symbol corresponds to another symbol. Lewis viewed his communication role as an apologist primarily as a translator—someone who encodes the meaning and uses words that the listener can accurately decode.

But the second process, transposition, is the primary focus of this chapter and a hallmark of Lewis's skill as a communicator. *Transposition* is the process of expressing meaning, especially emotional meaning, in ways that move from "higher" or richer experiences to "lower," more easily understood, language. Transposition is "algebraic," not "arithmetic" because one symbol or word stands for multiple concepts. Transposition is needed because literal, prosaic descriptions are inadequate to express ineffable emotional experiences. Whereas the goal of translation is clarity, a horizontal process of selecting one word or idea for another word or idea, the process of transposition is vertical, expressing that which is emotionally rich in words that make the "higher" experience accessible to a reader or listener.

It is through transposition that a person is able to glimpse the ultimate source of beauty or "hear" the music that he or she longs to hear. Lewis memorably exemplifies transposition as a way to express the longing humans experience (one of his major themes as presented in Chapter 2) in his sermon "The Weight of Glory": "The books or the music in which we thought the beauty was located will betray us if we trust to them; it was not in them, it only came through them, and what came through them was longing."[103] Lewis then explicitly makes his key point, "These things—the beauty, the memory of our own past—are good images of what we really desire; but if they are mistaken for the thing itself they turn into dumb idols, breaking the hearts of their worshipers."[104] Then, he provides memorable transpositional metaphors to vivify his point when he adds, "For they are not the thing itself; they are only the scent of a flower we have not found, the echo of a tune we have not heard, news from a country we have never yet visited."[105] Transposition helps people experience the aroma of a fragrance beyond their senses, hear a unique melody composed for their ears only, or receive news for which they have been longing their entire lives.

Notes

1. C. S. Lewis, "Transposition," *Transposition and Other Addresses*, (London: Geoffrey Bles, 1949), 13.
2. C. S. Lewis, "The Language of Religion," *Christian Reflections,* ed. Walter Hooper (London: Bles, 1967), 140.
3. C. S. Lewis, *Surprised by Joy: The Shape of My Early Life* (London: Geoffrey Bles, 1955), 174–175.
4. Lewis, *Surprised by Joy*, 175.
5. Lewis, *Surprised by Joy*, 175.
6. Lewis, *Surprised by Joy*, 175.
7. Walter Hooper, personal conversation, April 28, 2015.
8. David Tracy, *The Analogical Imagination* (New York: Crossroad, 1981); also see: Marcus J. Borg, *Speaking Christian* (New York: HarperOne, 1989), 29; For a comprehensive discussion of the rhetorical function of metaphor see: Michael Osborn, "The Metaphor in Public Address," *Michael Osborn on Metaphor and Style* (East Lansing: Michigan State University Press, 2018), 6–26.
9. Lewis, *Surprised by Joy,* 175.
10. C. S. Lewis, *The Magician's Nephew* (London: The Bodley Head, 1955), 123.
11. See: C. S. Lewis, "God in the Dock," *God in the Dock: Essays on Theology and Ethics,* ed. Walter Hooper (Grand Rapids: Eerdmans, 1970), 242.
12. C. S. Lewis, "Rejoinder to Dr. Pittenger," *God in the Dock: Essays on Theology and Ethics,* ed. Walter Hooper (Grand Rapids: Eerdmans, 1970), 183.
13. Lewis, "Rejoinder to Dr. Pittenger," 183.
14. C. S. Lewis, "Christian Apologetics," *God in the Dock: Essays on Theology and Ethics,* ed. Walter Hooper (Grand Rapids: Eerdmans, 1970), 98.
15. C. S. Lewis, Letter to John Beddow, October 7, 1945, *The Collected Letters of C. S. Lewis, Vol II: Books, Broadcasts, and the War 1931-1949,* ed. 674.
16. C. S. Lewis, Letter to John Beddow, October 7, 1945, *Collected Letters II,* 674.
17. C. S. Lewis, Letter to John Beddow, October 7, 1945, *Collected Letters II,* 674–675.
18. C. S. Lewis, Letter to John Beddow, October 7, 1945, *Collected Letters II,* 675.

19. C. S. Lewis, "Before We Can Communicate," *God in the Dock: Essays on Theology and Ethics,* ed. Walter Hooper (Grand Rapids: Eerdmans, 1970), 254.

20. Lewis, "Before We Can Communication," 254.

21. C. S. Lewis, *Language and Human Nature* (Manuscript Fragment) *VII: An Anglo-American Literary Review 27* (2010), 25.

22. Lewis, "Before We Can Communication," 256.

23. Lewis, "Before We Can Communicate," 256.

24. Lewis, "On the Transmission of Christianity," *God in the Dock*, 116.

25. Lewis, "Before We Can Communicate," 254.

26. Lewis, "Before We Can Communicate," 254.

27. Lewis, "God in the Dock," *God in the Dock*, 243.

28. Lewis, Letter to John Beddow, October 7, 1945, *Collected Letters II*, 674.

29. Lewis, "Transposition," 9–20.

30. Arend Smilde, "C. S. Lewis's 'Transposition': Text and Context," *Sehnsucht: The C. S. Lewis Journal* 13, 2019, 1–28.

31. Smilde, "C. S. Lewis's 'Transposition'," 1–28.

32. Smilde, "C. S. Lewis's 'Transposition'," 1–28. Also see: C. S. Lewis, *They Asked for A Paper* (London: Geoffrey Bles, 1962).

33. Lewis, "Transposition," 15.

34. Lewis, "Transposition," 13.

35. Lewis, "Transposition," 15.

36. Lewis, "Transposition," 15.

37. Lewis, "Transposition," 15.

38. Lewis, "Transposition," 15.

39. Lewis, "Transposition," 15.

40. Lewis, "Transposition," 15.

41. Lewis, "Transposition," 9.

42. Lewis, "Transposition," 9

43. Lewis, "Transposition," 12.

44. Lewis, "Transposition," 12.

45. Lewis, "Transposition," 12.

46. Lewis, "Transposition," 12.

47. Lewis, "Transposition," 12.

48. Lewis, "Transposition," 12.

49. Lewis, "Transposition," 12.

50. Lewis, "Transposition," 13.

51. Lewis, "Transposition," 13.

52. Lewis, *Mere Christianity*, ix.

53. Lewis, "Transposition," 14.

54. Lewis, "Transposition," 14.

55. Lewis, "Transposition," 15.

56. Lewis, "Transposition," 19.
57. See: C. S. Lewis, *The Last Battle* (London: The Bodley Head, 1956), 14.
58. Lewis, "Transposition," 14–15.
59. See: Smilde, "C. S. Lewis's 'Transposition'," 1–28; Also see: C. S. Lewis, "Transposition," *They Asked for a Paper* (London: Geoffrey Bles), 178.
60. Lewis, "Transposition," *They Asked for a Paper*, 178.
61. Lewis, "Transposition," *They Asked for a Paper*, 178–179.
62. I Corinthians Chapter 13, verse 12.
63. For a discussion of media richness theory see: Richard L. Daft and Robert H. Lengel, "Organizational Information Requirements, Media Richness and Structural Design," *Management Science* 32, 5 (May 1986), 554–571.
64. See: Steven A. Beebe, Susan J. Beebe and Mark V. Redmond, *Interpersonal Communication: Relating to Others*, Chapter 7 "Nonverbal Communication Skills," (Boston: Pearson, 2020), 180.
65. Lewis, "Transposition," 13.
66. Lewis, "Transposition," 13.
67. C. S. Lewis, *Time and Tide* 35 (August 14, 1954), 1082.
68. Lewis, "Transposition," 19.
69. Lewis, "Transposition," 19.
70. C. S. Lewis, *The Allegory of Love: A Study in Medieval Tradition* (Oxford: Oxford University Press), 166.
71. P. H. Brazier, "C. S. Lewis: A Doctrine of Transposition," *The Heythrop Journal* (2009), 685.
72. The musical *Billy Elliot* is based on the book and lyrics written by Lee Hall with music by Elton John, *Billy Elliot* (Milwaukee: Hal Leonard, 2009).
73. C. S. Lewis, *Letters to Malcom: Chiefly on Prayer* (London: Geoffrey Bles, 1964), 20.
74. Lewis, *Letters to Malcolm*, 20.
75. Lewis, *Letters to Malcolm*, 20.
76. Lewis, *Letters to Malcolm*, 20.
77. Lewis, *Letters to Malcolm*, 20.
78. Lewis, *Letters to Malcolm*, 20.
79. See: S. J. Alcock and J. A. Hulme, "Learning Styles in the Classroom: Educational Benefit or Planning Exercise?" *Psychology Teaching Review 16* (2010), 67–79.
80. J. R. R Tolkien, Letter to William Luther White, September 11, 1967, *The Letters of J. R. R. Tolkien,* ed. Humphrey Carpenter and Christopher Tolkien (Boston: Houghton Mifflin Company, 1995), 388.
81. Lewis, *Allegory of Love,* 60.
82. Lewis, *Mere Christianity*, 22.
83. Lewis, *Miracles*, 266.
84. Lewis, *Mere Christianity*, 141.
85. Lewis, *Mere Christianity*, 142.

86. Lewis, *Mere Christianity*, 142.

87. Michael Ward, "Escape to Wallaby Wood: Lewis's Depictions of Conversion," *C S. Lewis: Lightbearer in the Shadowlands: The Evangelistic Vision of C. S. Lewis* ed. Angus J. L. Menuge (Wheaton: Crossway Books, 1997), 151.

88. Ward, "Escape to Wallaby Wood," 151.

89. Chad Walsh, *The Literary Legacy of C. S. Lewis* (New York: Harcourt, Brace, Jovanovich, 1979), 205.

90. C. S. Lewis, *The Problem of Pain* (London: The Centenary Press, 1940), 81.

91. Lewis, *Miracles*, 88.

92. Lewis, *Allegory of Love*, 44.

93. Lyle W. Smith, "C. S. Lewis and the Making of Metaphor," *Word and Story in C. S. Lewis: Language and Narrative in Theory and Practice,* ed. Peter J. Schakel and Charles A. Hutar (Eugene: Wipf and Stock, 1991), 18.

94. Lewis, *Miracles*, 90.

95. Lewis, Letter to Belle Allen, January 19, 1953, *Collected Letters III*, 282

96. Doris T. Meyers, "The Context of Metaphor," *C. S. Lewis in Context* (Kent: Kent State University Press), 13.

97. C. S. Lewis, "Bluspels and Flalansferes," *Selected Literary Essays,* ed. Walter Hooper (Cambridge: Cambridge University Press, 1969), 265.

98. Lewis, *Miracles*, 42.

99. Edward Uszynsk, "C. S. Lewis as Scholar of Metaphor, Narrative, and Myth," *C. S. Lewis: Life, Works, and Legacy*, ed. Bruce L. Edwards, Vol. 4 (Westport: Praeger Perspectives, 2007), 236.

100. C. S. Lewis, "The Language of Religion," *Christian Reflections* (London: Bles, 1967), 140.

101. George M. Marsden, *C. S. Lewis's Mere Christianity: A Biography* (Princeton: Princeton University Press, 2016), 176.

102. Lewis, *Mere Christianity*, 108.

103. C. S. Lewis, "The Weight of Glory," *Transposition and Other Addresses* (London: Geoffrey Bles, 1949), 24.

104. C. S. Lewis, "The Weight of Glory," 24.

105. C. S. Lewis, "The Weight of Glory," 24.

7

Evocative

"Do you think your readers [or listeners] will believe you just because you say so? You must go quite a different way to work. By direct description, by metaphor and simile, by secretly evoking powerful associations, by offering the right stimuli to our nerves (in the right degree and the right order), and by the very beat of vowel-melody and length and brevity of your sentences, you must bring it about that we, we readers [and listeners], not you, exclaim 'how mysterious!' or 'loathsome' or whatever it is."[1]

- C. S. Lewis

"Don't tell us the jewels had an 'emotional' glitter; make us feel the emotion. I can hardly tell you how important this is."[2]

- C. S. Lewis

"Let the pictures tell you their own moral. For the moral inherent in them will rise from whatever spiritual roots you have succeeded in striking during the whole course of your life."[3]

- C. S. Lewis

"All seven of my Narnia books, and my three science fiction books, began with seeing pictures in my head."[4] These words from C. S. Lewis's essay "It All Began with A Picture …" describe Lewis's version of how he came to write some of his most celebrated stories. *The Lion, the Witch and the Wardrobe* started with an image of a faun carrying an umbrella with packages under his arms while walking in a snowy wood. Other images also appeared to him. Lewis thought he would connect the images and try to make a story out of them. Lewis admits he did not know where the pictures came from. "But then suddenly," writes Lewis, "Aslan came bounding into it."[5] Lewis adds, once the Lion was there, "He pulled the whole story together, and soon He pulled the six other Narnian stories in after him."[6]

Lewis loved stories. He loved to tell stories; he loved to listen them; thankfully for his readers, he loved to write them. From his earliest days listening to his nurse Lizzie Endicott tell him and his brother Warnie Irish folk tales of swashbuckling adventure, Lewis was enchanted with the power of narrative. It is Lewis's ability to use story, as well as other literary techniques, such as metaphor and simile, that supports the fourth Lewis communication principle: *Effective communicators evoke emotion.*

Lewis viewed stories as a way to communicate (transpose) truth that was not possible using other methods. Stories are meaning-rich. Lewis would undoubtedly have agreed with author Daniel Quinn, who writes, "No story is devoid of meaning, if you know how to look for it. This is as true of nursery rhymes and daydreams as it is of epic poems."[7] Lewis cherished the evocative power of both nursery rhymes and epic poems. He understood the power of a story, as well as the relationship of story to myth, to evoke life experiences. A story has power because the reader or listener enters it, vicariously participates in it, and experiences emotions that spring from the plot and characters. Stories evoke emotions.

But it is not just stories that evoke emotions. C. S. Lewis uses a variety of strategies to induce emotions in his readers and listeners. A well-chosen word, an apt comparison, placing his readers or listeners in the middle of things (using the literary technique *in medias res*), as well as drawing upon the power of myth are strategies Lewis skillfully used to arouse an emotional response.

Principle Four: Effective Communicators Evoke Emotions

Principle four is best summarized by the communication maxim: *It is better to get a message out of someone than to put one in them.* People are more likely to believe, respond to, and remember their *own* messages rather than messages received from others. The ancient Greek philosopher Socrates's primary education method was to ask questions rather than provide answers. Socrates wanted to get messages out of his students rather than put messages in them. Lewis, in emulating his own tutors, used the Socratic method skillfully. Instead of waxing on about a point he wanted to make, he was more likely, according to his tutorial students, to invite a defense of a position by posing well-crafted questions. As one of Lewis's students, W. Brown Patterson, remembers, "In all his criticism he sought to lead me to strengthen an argument, to express an idea more clearly, or to anticipate a difficulty ... Unless I asked him directly he would not elaborate on his own views, let alone try to impose them on me."[8] Lewis was a Socratic-get-messages-out-of-others teacher.

Additional evidence for Lewis's interest in Socratic instructional strategies is that Lewis was the first president of Oxford's aptly named Socratic Club in 1942 and served in that role until 1954 when he started teaching at Cambridge in 1955. Established by Stella Aldwinckle, the Socratic Club was an Oxford society where ideas, especially ideas about Christianity, were discussed and debated. Using questions to seek answers was the primary debating format.

In addition to using questions to evoke a response, Lewis was especially keen to evoke emotions from his readers and listeners through story. Lewis believed that the emotions a story arouses within people are based on our previous experiences. A story has the power to open the magic bottle and to let emotions bubble to the surface. Lewis writes that an author "should never conceive himself as bringing into existence beauty or wisdom which did not exist before, but simply and solely as trying to embody in terms of his own art some reflection of eternal Beauty and Wisdom."[9] Truth and beauty are already there. The job of the communicator is to uncork emotional meaning. Communication is less about transmitting an idea or emotion than about discovery and exploration.

An effective communicator is like a rhetorical Michelangelo who chisels the stone to find that the perfect form had been embedded there all along. Humans are sense-making creatures who look for meaning-infused designs in human experience; to be human is to search for meaning. As Lewis describes this process, "It is not at all surprising that those who stare at it [history] too long should see patterns. We see pictures in the fire ... To the naked eye there is a face in the moon ..."[10] But sometimes if people become too analytical and try to "peek behind the curtain," a story may lose some of its magic. Or, as Lewis suggests about finding the face in the moon, "it vanishes when you use a telescope."[11]

So how does one evoke emotional meaning? Lewis did it primarily by *describing* a situation for the reader or listener to experience; he did not prescribe how to respond; he explained a situation and let his readers or listeners bring their feelings to the story. In other instances, he described how *he* felt (such as his opening sentence of *A Grief Observed*: "No one ever told me that grief felt so like fear."[12]) The key is not to tell someone what to feel, but to create a word picture, or describe a situation so that the reader or listener has his or her own emotional reaction. Here is Lewis's specific advice for painting emotion-evoking mental images: "Don't use adjectives which merely tell us how you want us to feel about the things you are describing. I mean, instead of telling us a thing was 'terrible,' describe it so that we'll be terrified. Don't say it was 'delightful.' Make us say 'delightful' when we've read the description."[13] Lewis thought it was important to invite the reader or listener to conjure their own images in their mind's eye. He noted, "You see, all those words (horrifying, wonderful, hideous, exquisite) are only saying to your readers 'Please will you do my job for me.'"[14] Lewis was consistent in his advice about how to evoke meaning and emotion. In letter to a friend he advises,

> Never use adjectives or adverbs which are mere appeals to the reader to feel as you want him to feel. He won't do it just because you ask him: you've got to make him. No good telling us a battle was 'exciting.' If you succeed in exciting us the adjective will be unnecessary; if you don't it will be useless.[15]

For Lewis it was important that the reader or listener experience an emotion based on the description. In offering advice to another friend, Lewis had this recommendation for evoking emotions: "Don't tell us the jewels had an 'emotional' glitter; make us feel the emotion. I can hardly tell you how important this is."[16]

His proficiency in describing a scene to evoke an emotional response was such a signature skill that those who knew him best remembered him for this communication talent. At C. S. Lewis's funeral, his close friend, Rev. Austin Farrer, offered these words, praising Lewis for his skill in describing an event to evoke emotions: "But his real power was not proof, it was depiction. There lived in his writings a Christian universe which could be both thought and felt, in which he was at home, and in which he made his reader at home."[17]

Ultimately, when evoking emotion, Lewis believed that one should not show one's hand, lest the listener or reader become aware of the technique. To maintain the element of surprise one must keep the listener guessing, using suspense to catch her or him unaware. Lewis makes this point explicit: "If my books are sometimes permitted by God to deliver to particular readers a more perceptible challenge than Scripture itself, I think this is because, in a sense, they catch people unprepared."[18] Lewis thought it was vital that the author manage the expectations of the reader or listener so that they discover what there is to discover. In noting how our expectations can hinder a response he noted, "We approach the Bible with reverence and with readiness to be edified. But by a curious and unhappy psychological law these attitudes often inhibit the very thing they are intended to facilitate."[19] He further adds, "You see this in other things: many a couple never felt less in love than on their wedding day; many a man never felt less merry than at Christmas dinner; and when at a lecture we say 'I must attend' attention instantly vanishes."[20]

Lewis did not think the listener or reader should have to work too hard to discover the author's meaning. As noted in Chapter 6, Lewis acknowledged that *The Pilgrim's Regress*, originally published in 1933, was flawed in that the reader had to toil to figure out his embedded allegorical message. His added commentary in the 1943 edition helped the reader decode the allegory. The best emotional responses emerge without strain. Lewis's advice to readers and listeners is to be aware of what one wants to express (be intentional), but not to force a response. Lewis especially liked a music analogy used by his spiritual mentor George McDonald. McDonald writes, "The best way with music, I imagine, is not to bring the forces of our intellect to bear upon it, but to be still and let it work on that part of us for whose sake it exists. We spoil countless precious things by intellectual greed."[21] The reader or listener should be able to catch the evocative meaning by simply waiting, listening, and letting the emotions percolate.

Lewis's recommendation to describe a scene rather than prescribe an emotional response for the reader or listener could be overdone for some readers. Lewis biographer Alan Jacobs found Lewis sometimes provided too much expository detail, especially in Lewis's novels. Jacobs observes:

> … more likely [Lewis's] fiction, which is indeed marred at times by a tendency to explain what should simply be shown. (I have always found the dominance of Lewis's "expository demon" to be the downfall of *Perelandra*; this was his favorite among his novels—at least until he wrote *Till We Have Faces*—and indeed is the favorite of many other readers, but I find it nearly unreadable because of its ceaseless exposition and explanation.)[22]

Yet, as Jacobs notes, both *Perelandra* and *Till We Have Faces* were on Lewis's list of his favorite works. And, although Lewis may have had an "expository demon" at times, many readers continue to find his novels enjoyable, in part, because of their rich, detailed descriptions of other worlds.

Lewis sometimes became frustrated when words were inadequate to evoke the emotion he wished to provoke. He expresses his impatience with the inadequacy of words in a letter to Ms. Rhona Bodle. His comments also speak to the need for transposition because of the limitations of language when expressing ineffable experiences:

No, one can't put these experiences into words: though all writing is a continual attempt to do so. Indeed, in a sense, one can hardly put anything into words: only the simplest colours have names, and hardly any of the smells. The simple physical pains and (still more) the pleasures can't be expressed in language. I labour the point lest the devil shd. [should] hereafter try to make you believe that what was wordless was therefore vague and nebulous. But in reality it is just the clearest, the most concrete, and the most indubitable realities which escape language: not because they are vague but because language is.[23]

The previous chapter presented Lewis's ideas about transposition—the use of metaphor (especially visual metaphor), comparisons and poetic language to describe experiences and emotions that cannot be adequately expressed prosaically. This chapter explains *why* transposition is needed: It is necessary to evoke emotion in readers and listeners in situations where a literal description is inadequate. The chapter also unmasks *how* Lewis does it, through five specific emotion-evoking strategies.

- *Lewis uses words well*: Drawing on his skill as a poet, Lewis knew the power of a well-chosen word to evoke an emotion. Given Lewis's belief (based on the influence of Owen Barfield) that words are (mostly) metaphorical, even a single, aptly-chosen word, has the potential to evoke powerful feelings within us. Like many gifted writers, he was also a voracious reader. As Lewis scholar Jerry Root notes, "Lewis wrote well, in part, because he read often."[24]
- *Lewis skillfully uses comparisons*: Lewis liberally uses similes, metaphors, analogy, and allegory to evoke specific feelings in his readers. Not only does he generously use these tropes, but he discusses how and why they evoke feelings within us.
- *Lewis uses the technique In Medias Res* (Latin for in the middle of things): Lewis sometimes plops his readers in the middle of a situation and lets them figure out where they are and what is happening. He uses uncertainty and the reader's own bewilderment to gain attention and evoke tension, then eventually resolves the mystery, pointing the reader in the right direction.
- *Lewis is a master storyteller*: Lewis's use of story, a communication strategy that both he and Tolkien explicitly discuss in their writing, is one of his most effective emotion-evoking techniques. Some stories are brief and others elaborately detailed, yet regardless of length, Lewis's stories evoke emotional responses based on the reader's own experiences.

- *Lewis draws upon the power of myth*: Lewis knew the potency of myth to illuminate shadows and discover truth.[25] *Myth* in this instance does not refer to fictitious stories or that which is untrue, but rather to large-scale symbolic narratives imbued with meaning that unlock an emotional response within the reader or listener. Lewis the apologist persuaded by having the reader inductively reach his or her own conclusion about what Lewis called "the true myth"—Christianity.

Evoke by Selecting the Right Word

Lewis was a stickler for using just the right word. As noted in Chapter 5, several of his students have commented about his scrutiny of their weekly tutorial papers, questioning their precise use of a word or phrase.[26] George Sayer recalls what it was like to be a student in one of Lewis's tutorials: "He was … insistent on the accurate use of words. Questions like 'What exactly do you mean by "sentimental"? or "How are you using the word 'romantic"? What do you suppose it meant 200 years ago?' were common questions from Lewis. Perhaps mirroring the teaching strategy of his old tutor Kirkpatrick, 'The Great Knock.' "[27] Sayer remembers Lewis saying, "Wouldn't it be rather better, Sayer, if you're not sure of the meaning of that word, not to use it at all?"[28] Yet, Lewis could offer lavish praise when a student used a word effectively. One of Lewis's students remembers, "He spent five minutes praising one word I had used to describe Dryden's poetry (the word was 'bracing')."[29] According to George Bailey, when providing feedback to students Lewis apparently had three levels of comment: "If the essay was good: 'There is a good deal in what you say.' If the essay was middling: 'There is something in what you say.' If the essay was bad: 'There *may* be something in what you say.' "[30] Other standard comments, which make effective use of metaphors, were "Too much straw and not enough bricks" or "Not with Brogans [heavy work boots], please, slippers are in order when you proceed to make a literary point."[31] Lewis expected his students to be precise; he let them know when they hit the mark, or when they missed it.

Lewis focused on selecting just the right word because of the power of language to evoke emotions. He writes, "One of the most important and effective uses of language is the emotional."[32] The evocative emotional power of words lies not with prescribing how the reader or listener should feel. Emotions do not emerge because the author tells the reader what to feel, but when the reader draws his or her own conclusions from what the author describes. "It is the facts," says Lewis, "not the language, that arouse the emotion."[33] It is how the facts are presented in the form of words that evoke emotions within us.

To be maximally effective, Lewis wanted his reader to be unaware of his technique. As he explained, being too explicit weakens the effect: "What expresses or stimulates emotion directly, without the intervention of an image or concept, expresses or stimulates it feebly."[34] The speaker or writer should select words that imply and hint, but let the listener fill in the gaps by imagining, hearing, seeing, smelling, tasting, and touching to evoke meaning and emotion.

Using the right word has positive, long-lasting benefits. Lewis writes,

> [An] utterance, besides entertaining, charming or exciting us for the moment, should have a desirable permanent effect on us if possible—should make us either happier, or wiser, or better … The only two questions to ask about a poem, in the long run, are, firstly, whether it is interesting, enjoyable, attractive, and secondly, whether this enjoyment wears well and helps or hinders you towards all the other things you would like to enjoy or do, or be.[35]

For Lewis, the test of a good poem is that it (1) is interesting or enjoyable and (2) has a lasting impact.

In *Letters to Malcolm*, Lewis discusses the comparative merits of a prepared-by-others prayer and a self-authored, extemporaneous prayer. Although he is explicitly discussing prayer, his commentary also reflects his ideas about the nature and function of words, regardless of whether spoken to pray or to curse. Lewis explains that whether a prayer is "ready-made" or "one's own words" does not really matter to him. Both methods are ways of evoking meaning. He explains, "For me words are in any case secondary."[36] Lewis's sentiments invoke the General Semantics mantra: *Meanings are in people not in words.*[37] General Semantics, which emerged during the 1920s, is the study of words and their meaning, developed by Polish-American Alfred Korzybski.[38] According to General Semanticists, meaning does not reside in a word: rather, meaning, from a Lewisian perspective, is evoked at the intersection of reason and imagination. People ultimately discover what something means. (Although, as Lewis explained in *The Abolition of Man*, a waterfall truly can be inherently sublime.)

Lewis employs a metaphor to describe the function of words when he notes, "They [words] are only an anchor."[39] Then he piles on another metaphor adding: "Or, shall I say, they are the movements of the conductor's baton: not the music."[40] Words function to anchor thoughts and focus the mind on the meaning of a word; words help people discover the metaphorical "surplus of meaning" resident within them. Lewis's key point: Words *evoke* rather than carry meaning. Meaning is *discovered*.

In addition to the evocative power of words, Lewis also knew the limitations of words as a means of expressing feelings. He advises that the power of communicating emotion does not come from labeling something as "mysterious" or "loathsome" or "awe-inspiring" or "voluptuous." Emotions are triggered not when an author tells others how to feel, but when the author sets the stage for emotions to be evoked. Here is Lewis's classic advice for evoking emotions. He first asks, "Do you think your readers [or listeners] will believe you just because you say so? You must go quite a different way to work."[41] He then answers the question by giving explicit instructions,

> By direct description, by metaphor and simile, by secretly evoking powerful associations, by offering the right stimuli to our nerves (in the right degree and the right order), and by the very beat of vowel-melody and length and brevity of your sentences, you must bring it about that we, we readers [and listeners], not you, exclaim 'how mysterious!' or "'loathsome' or whatever it is.[42]

The writer or speaker should set the stage and let the drama happen as the listener uses the descriptive spark of a word to evoke emotions.

Words would not be words if they did not evoke meaning or an emotional response. Consistent with the ideas Lewis included in *Letters to Malcolm*, he writes in *An Experiment in Criticism*, "A word which simply 'was' and didn't 'mean' would not be a word."[43] By definition, according to Lewis, a word evokes *something else*. Even nonsense language fits this category. Lewis illustrates this point: "*Boojum* in its context is not a mere noise. Gertrude Stein's 'a rose is a rose' if we thought it was 'arose is arose,' would be different."[44] He recognizes that an unintended meaning may be evoked, but even if the word is on the surface nonsense, if the reader derives meaning from it, then it is, in fact, a word.

Because of Lewis's holistic principle of appealing to the eye and the ear as described in Chapter 4, he was acutely interested in the *sound* of a word as well as its meaning. He describes this technique in his writing of *The Screwtape Letters*: "I fancy that Scrooge, screw, thumbscrew, tapeworm and red tape all do some work in my hero's name, and that slob, slobber, slubber, and gob have all gone into slubgob."[45] In a letter to a friend, he further describes his technique of making sure words have the right sound to them: "I am always playing with syllables and fitting them together (purely by ear) to see if I can hatch up new words that please me. I want them to have an emotional, not intellectual, suggestiveness …"[46] Although, as suggested in Chapter 6, there is evidence that Lewis was a visual learner who often used visual metaphors, he did not dismiss the power of sound to stimulate meaning.[47] In confirming Lewis's skill in writing for the ear Jerry Root suggests, "His early practice of reading poetry and his lifetime love of poetry composition enabled him to develop a rhythm to his writing that makes it a delight to read out loud and easy to read in silence. Not only did he write for the ear, but he wrote visually, too."[48]

Words, especially those embedded within stories, that poetically express beauty, or unlock truth with an apt metaphor, are the prime emotion-evoking tools. Lewis's book *Studies in Words* makes emotional meaning a central concept. His discussion of language and meaning is consistent with his observations in "At the Fringe of Language," the concluding chapter found in *Studies in Words*. Interestingly, in the original manuscript, held in the Bodleian Library in Oxford, Lewis originally titled this final chapter "The Language of Emotion," but crossed this title out in favor of the more metaphorical "At the Fringe of Language." Here Lewis discusses the power and use of less-literal language to evoke ineffable emotional experiences, especially religious experiences that arouse one's emotions.

Poetic, metaphorical language is best when attempting to communicate experiences, emotions, and events that the listener may not have witnessed, but can experience vicariously. Lewis explains, "Poetry I take to be the continual effort to bring language back to the actual."[49] Lewis literary scholar Perry Bramlett accurately paraphrases Lewis's theoretical assumptions about the role of poetic language: "Poetic language is remarkable (and becomes religious [because it] … points us toward something outside our own experience, like a road map."[50]

Evoke by Using Comparison

A hallmark of Lewis's communication skill is his ability to use finely-crafted comparisons—analogies, both literal and figurative, as well as metaphors and similes to evoke emotion. One can open any of his books or essays at random and find a well-crafted comparison. For example, in *Preface to Paradise Lost* Lewis uses a musical instrument analogy: "The reader is the organ and Milton as the organist. It is on us he plays, if we will let him."[51] He continues noting that Milton did not write *Paradise Lost* to give us "new ideas about the lost garden but to make us know that the garden is found, that we have come home at last and reached the centre of the maze—our centre, humanity's centre, not some private centre of the poet's."[52]

In a letter offering advice to a young writer, Lewis explains how to develop an appropriate allegorical comparison: "A strict allegory," says Lewis, "is like a puzzle with a solution: a great romance is like a flower whose smell reminds you of something you cannot quite place. I think the something is 'the whole quality of life as we actually experience it.'"[53] Lewis's use of comparisons, allegory, metaphor, and simile were integral to his communication skill. Lewis says, "We can make our language duller; we cannot make it less metaphorical."[54]

Lewis also used metaphors, especially *visual* metaphors, as noted in the previous chapter, to paint pictures from images he had seen in his head. In his essay "C. S. Lewis as a Student of Words" (which includes an excellent summary of *Studies in Words*), Lewis scholar Michael Covington concludes that Lewis's "acknowledgement of the power of images is one of the strengths of Lewis's work. He recognizes, as others do not, that informing someone means equipping him with appropriate mental images."[55] Lewis not only exemplifies this technique in his writing, but describes the importance of using images to communicate: "Images, I must suppose, have their use or they would not have been so popular. (It makes little difference whether they are pictures and statues outside the mind or imaginative constructions within it.)"[56]

How did the images that inspired Lewis come to him? Lewis was not always aware of where his stories originated, explaining that: "a man writing a story is too excited about the story itself to sit back and notice how he is doing it."[57] Lewis's stories emerged without a clear pedigree of their origin. Lewis describes the creative process as simply being quiet, still, and mindful:

> With me the process is much more like bird-watching than like either talking or building. I see pictures. Some of the pictures have a common flavor, almost a common smell, which groups them together. Keep quiet and watch and they will begin joining themselves up. If you were very lucky.[58]

By "bird watching" Lewis was able to discover the moral truth (the Tao, the path or way). The pictures in his mind were not intended only to entertain, but also to teach. Lewis suggests, "Let the pictures tell you their own moral."[59] He wants the reader or listener to identify the moral value of a story based on his or her own experiences.

Images that spark metaphor and description, however, may become too powerful when the reader or listener substitutes the image for the real thing. General semanticists have a slogan that admonishes "The map is not the territory" which is to suggest that a word is a symbol but is not the thing it symbolizes.[60] The road drawn on a map years ago may be different than the actual road that is traversed today; new roads may be added and others may be closed. A Golden Calf had the power to misdirect the Israelites attention to the image itself, rather than what the image represented. In discussing the problem of a disconnect between the symbol and the actual object Lewis says: "To me, however, their [images'] danger is more obvious. Images of the Holy easily become holy images—sacrosanct. My idea of God is not a divine idea. It has to be shattered time after time. He shatters it Himself. He is the great iconoclast."[61] For Lewis, all reality *is* iconoclastic.[62] Our understanding of God is dynamic. Fresh experiences often dismantle older, longer-held beliefs or ways of viewing the world. Life performs a chiropractic function in that it realigns and readjusts human perceptions and ways of making sense out of the world. Reality is iconoclastic.[63]

In clarifying his perspective of iconoclasm, as discussed in Chapter 2, Lewis wrote the following inscription in Joy Davidman's copy of *The Great Divorce*: "There are three images in my mind which I must continually forsake and replace by better ones: The false image of God, the false image of my neighbour, and the false image of myself. C. S. Lewis Dec 30th, 1952 (from an unwritten chapter on iconoclasm)."[64] Again, Lewis is noting that reality, including our own image of ourselves, is iconoclastic. Although Lewis suggests he needs to change his own "false image of God," what does not change is the nature of God and that which is eternal. Or, as he succinctly put it, "All that is not eternal is eternally out of date."[65] Our use of symbolic language may confuse us into worshiping the symbol (the word) rather than that for which the symbol stands.

Although both rhetoric and poetry use metaphor to stimulate action and evoke emotions, each has its own unique purpose and function. The goal of rhetoric, says Lewis, is to "produce in our minds some practical resolve ... and it does this by calling the passions to the aid of reason."[66] Rhetoric uses reason to evoke passion, which then spurs action. On the other hand, poetry aims at "producing something more like vision than it is like action,"[67] although vision, in this sense, also includes the passions. As Lewis explains, drawing upon metaphor to make his point: "When we try to rouse someone's hate of toothache in order to persuade him to ring up the dentist, this is rhetoric."[68] In the classic use of the term *rhetoric*, Lewis acknowledges the potential power of using fear appeal in an effort to arouse emotion to, in turn, induce action.

Evoke by Placing Us in the Middle of Things

In medias res ("in the middle of things") is a literary device, attributed to the ancient poet Horace, that plunges the reader into the central plot of the story without exposition or backstory. The reader is likely to be confused for a time, but eventually the past becomes clear.

The effectiveness of *in medias res* can be explained by a contemporary communication perspective called Uncertainty Reduction Theory. Uncertainty Reduction Theory predicts that when someone experiences uncertainty, the person becomes uncomfortable.[69] Metaphorically speaking, we are "allergic" to uncertainty.[70] To manage the discomfort of uncertainty a person asks questions and seeks information to help reduce the uncertainty. Just as in one's life, a reader or listener may sometimes feel bewildered (in the middle of things), not knowing what will happen next. But viewed from a different vantage point, an experience comes to make sense.

Lewis's Narnia stories exemplify this "in the middle of things" technique. In *The Lion, the Witch and the Wardrobe* (LWW), for example, the backstory of Professor Kirk and the White Witch is never told; it is revealed in the prequel book—*The Magician's Nephew*. Lewis scholars disagree as to the order in which one should read *The Chronicles of Narnia*. The publisher currently labels *The Magician's Nephew* as first in the series and plasters a "1" on the spine of the book. Other purists suggest that a new Narnia reader should start with *The Lion, the Witch and The Wardrobe*; it was published first, so it should be read first. (*The Lion, the Witch and the Wardrobe* was published in 1950; *The Magician's Nephew*, the sixth book in the series, was not published until 1955). Part of the charm of *The Magician's Nephew* derives from it being the prequel to Lucy's first foray into Narnia. It is as if Lewis is implicitly communicating to his readers that what his characters are experiencing at any given moment will make more sense when viewed from a broader perspective—the perspective of what has transpired *prior to* the events that are currently happening. Perhaps he is suggesting a method for interpreting a person's own story, believing that what happens to someone in the present moment can be better understood in the context of a larger framework over the expanse of time. Lewis's theological beliefs (e.g. about creation, and Jesus's birth, life, resurrection—the "true myth") provide a larger context in which to view everyday problems, worries, and concerns. Lewis himself offered contradictory advice about in what order to read the Narnia books. He once suggested that they be read in chronological order (the order in which events occur, meaning starting with *The Magician's Nephew*). Then, on another occasion, he recommended reading the Narnia book in the order in which they were published.[71]

Lewis's views about the nature of time and how people use their 525,600 minutes a year make his use of *in media res* especially interesting. Most people think of time as arriving moment to moment. As Lewis characterized time in

Mere Christianity, "One moment disappears before the next comes along; and there is room for very little in each. That is what time is like."[72] Even though people "tend to assume that the whole universe and God himself are always moving on from past to future just as we do …,"[73] for Lewis, "God is not in Time."[74] He clarifies with a metaphor: "If you picture Time as a straight line along which we have to travel, then you must picture God as the whole page on which the line is drawn … God, from above or outside or all around, contains the whole line, and sees it all."[75]

Perhaps there was something even more implicit in the Narnia stories than a Christian "supposal" (the term Lewis used to describe the Narnia stories, rather than labeling them an allegory) or the use of the literary technique of *in medias res*. Writing to schoolgirl Sophia Sorr, Lewis explains that the Narnia stories are not allegories but a supposal. Lewis says, "But it [LWW] is not, as some people think, an *allegory*. That is, I don't say 'Let us represent Christ as Aslan.' I say, 'Supposing there was a world like Narnia, and supposing, like ours, it needed redemption, let us imagine what sort of Incarnation and Passion and Resurrection Christ would have there.' See?"[76] He made the same point when writing to a fifth grade class in Maryland. He said, "You are mistaken when you think that everything in the book [*The Lion, the Witch and the Wardrobe*] 'represents' something in this world."[77] He added, "Things do that in *The Pilgrim's Progress* but I'm not writing in that way."[78]

Lewis scholar Michael Ward has convincingly argued that Lewis smuggled a deeper, purposefully hidden state or quality into his seven Narnia stories. As Ward notes in the opening line of the preface to his well-researched *Planet Narnia*, "It is to be hoped that this book reaffirms the worth of implicit communication; not everything that needs to be said needs to be said outright."[79] Ward has insightfully deciphered a hidden code; he suggests Lewis intentionally placed an ineffable idea in each of the seven Narnia stories to communicate that there is something more to this life than meets one's senses. Ward has documented that each Narnia book is embedded with qualities of one of the seven planets (Jupiter, Mars, the Sun, the Moon, Mercury, Venus, Saturn) known during medieval times, the time period of Lewis's literary specialty, to provide an atmosphere for the story.[80] Specifically, *The Lion, the Witch and the Wardrobe* is about Jupiter evoking an air of joviality, with the red spot on the planet symbolizing the merriment of Father Christmas, who appears in the story. J. R. R. Tolkien expressed his disappointment with *The Chronicles of Narnia*, describing them as a hodgepodge of various myths and symbols, pointing to the presence of Father Christmas as especially nonsensical. But understanding the Jupiter symbolism in the book helps to explain Father

Christmas's presence; he helps communicate the Jovial element in LWW. *Prince Caspian* has the hidden battle elements of Mars, also heralded as the "bringer of war" in Gustav Holst's *The Planets* suite. Once one has read *Voyage of the Dawn Treader* and realized the allusions to the sun, one can never read it the same way again. Where does the ship Dawn Treader tread? To the dawn—the rising sun. *The Silver Chair* incorporates several allusions to the moon, including the descriptive term *silver* in the title—a color often associated with the moon. *The Horse and His Boy* is a story of Mercury who was known for being "the messenger." Allusions to messengers including drawings of the protagonist Shasta that evokes a classic image of Mercury are found throughout the book. *The Magician's Nephew*, the prequel that lets readers know they were in the middle of things when they read *The Lion, the Witch and the Wardrobe*, has the quality of Venus. And finally, *The Last Battle*, which tells the story of the end of time, as symbolized by influences from Saturn.[81]

What makes Ward's discovery so powerful and important is that it provides new insights with which to read the Narnia stories and offers further evidence of Lewis's ability to evoke an atmosphere without readers realizing an atmosphere is being evoked. Lewis was subtle, indirect, and implicit—all masterful aspects of evoking and unlocking messages rather than explicitly describing how readers should feel or what they should believe. The feeling emanates from *within* the reader—a more credible source than if presented by someone else.

Lewis placed the reader "in the middle of things," using medieval planetary symbolism to evoke planetary climates. Lewis biographer Alister McGrath suggests, "If Ward is right, Lewis has crafted each novel in the light of atmosphere associated with one of the planets in the medieval tradition."[82] McGrath agrees that evoking a climate or implicit planetary aura does not offer prescriptions as to what happens in each story. McGrath suggests, "This does not necessarily mean that this symbolism determines the plot of each novel, or the overall series; it does, however, help us understand something of the thematic identity and stylistic tone of each individual novel."[83] The "thematic identity" and "tone" provide both depth and breadth, as the reader is placed in the story and experiences the emotions of the characters.

Is there additional evidence that Lewis embedded implicit messages into his stories? Yes. Here is Lewis discussing the use of an implicit literary technique that supports Ward's argument that Lewis implanted a "secret code" in the Narnia stories: "You may have noticed that the books you really love are bound together by a secret thread."[84] The "secret thread" and "common quality" that cannot be put into words could readily apply to Lewis's own writing. He embeds this "thread" or implicitly uses planetary symbolism to evoke an imperceptible, non-linguistic response from his readers.

Evoke by Telling Stories

As noted earlier, Lewis loved a good story. His Narnia stories, Ransom space trilogy adventures, and novels evidence his gifts as a suspenseful storyteller. In his essay "On Stories" he demonstrates his understanding of the use of narrative as an indispensable communication tool, especially in communicating ideas that may be beyond the discernable or explicit elements in the plot.[85] He opens his essay by noting how little has been said about the theory of stories, then cites three examples of authors who have written about the nature of narrative: Aristotle, Boccaccio, and Jung. Lewis goes on to analyze the purpose, function and application of stories and storytelling.

Lewis, his friend J. R. R. Tolkien, and George MacDonald who inspired both Lewis and Tolkien,[86] anticipated the work of contemporary rhetorical scholar Walter Fisher in providing a basis for using narrative analysis to interpret a rhetorical message.[87] It is Fisher's insight that modern-day rhetoricians pay special attention to as they offer a narrative analysis of messages. Yet, prior to Fisher's explication of the role of narrative analysis as a rhetorical method, Lewis, Tolkien and MacDonald spelled out the significance of stories, fairy stories in particular, as a rhetorical method for communicating certain kinds of messages and evoking emotions.[88]

The power of a story rests not only in the suspense and uncertainty that is eventually resolved as the story unfolds, but also in the way the story is told. Embedded within the Narnia stories, for example, is the "deeper magic from before the beginning of time," the magic that implicitly drives the story forward.[89] Even when the reader or listener is familiar with what happens next, a story can delight and surprise. As Lewis notes in a key distillation of his storytelling technique, "The re-reader is looking not for actual surprises (which can come only once) but for a certain surprisingness."[90] Yes, sometimes a person reads or watches a movie to see what happens next; but for Lewis, the plot is secondary to the feeling evoked by the author. A person re-reads books, watches a favorite movie again and again, or attends the same opera many times not because he or she has forgotten the plot, but because of how the book, movie, or opera makes him or her feel. It is, as Lewis says, not the surprise but the "surprisingness" that the reader or listener seeks. When watching the routine of a favorite comedian, the listener may already know the joke, but still seeks the emotional release from the punch line. It is that "punch" that is sought rather than the plot. The plot of the story is the conduit that evokes an emotional response.

It was important to Lewis that the reader be surprised by what is discovered. In making his case for the hidden "Narnia code," Michael Ward offers an insightful analysis about Lewis's use of what Lewis called the "Kappa Element of a story," which evokes an atmosphere or climate. Lewis gave a talk to a literary society in 1940 called "The Kappa Element in Romance." Ward notes, " 'Kappa' he took from the initial letter of the Greek word κρυπτόν, meaning 'hidden' or 'cryptic.' Lewis later reworked the talk as the essay "On Stories," published in 1947, and although he dropped the term "Kappa" from "On Stories," the hidden thing itself was still his main concern."[91] For Lewis, the use of the "Kappa Element in Romance," that which is hidden from plain sight, has tremendous power to evoke emotions and create a narrative climate that provides an implicit rather than explicit atmosphere.

Lewis does not suggest that every author should draw on mental images to create a story; that was his method. His visual images from an unknown source provide his inspiration. Lewis comments directly about this technique in "Sometimes Fairy Stories May Say it Best" when he says,

> In the author's mind there bubbles up every now and then the material for a story. For me it invariably begins with mental pictures. This ferment leads to nothing unless it is accompanied with the longing for a Form; verse or prose, short story, novel, play or what not. When these two things click you have the Author's impulses complete.[92]

The use of the words *ferment* and *bubbling* suggest that the writing process is an evocative process. Continuing his metaphorical description of the creative process Lewis adds, "It is now a thing inside him pawing to get out. He longs to see that bubbling stuff pouring into that Form as the housewife longs to see the new jam pouring into the clean jar."[93] Even when describing how to evoke emotion through storytelling, Lewis's jam-in-the-new-jar metaphor expresses what it feels like to create a new story.

For Lewis, describing the scene in a story is like decorating a house. Writers festoon the plot with "furniture" to set the stage for their imaginations. In describing his technique of writing for children (which was really not that different from writing for adults), Lewis suggests, "Indeed, everything in the story should arise from the whole cast of the author's mind. We must write for children out of those elements in our imagination which we share with children .... The matter of our story should be a part of the habitual furniture of our minds."[94]

Lewis believed that the underlying message of the story, especially the emotional meaning, is within the reader all along; but telling the tale helps the reader become aware of his or her feelings, sometimes just under the surface. A story helps connect the reader with his or her unarticulated feelings. With story, suggests Lewis biographer McGrath when describing Lewis's technique, "A veil is lifted, a door is opened, a curtain is drawn aside—and we are enabled to enter a new realm. Our own story is now seen to be part of a much bigger story, which helps us both understand how we fit into a greater scheme of things and discover and value the difference we can make."[95]

Lewis was not interested in story for its own sake but, as McGrath accurately deduces, he was interested in "our own story" and how an individual's story fits into The Story that helps them discover joy. In the movie *Shadowlands,* which chronicles Lewis's relationship with Joy Davidman, one of C. S. Lewis's students quotes a line from the student's father: "We read to know that we are not alone." (Although often attributed to Lewis, there is no evidence C. S. Lewis said or wrote this line.[96] The quote should actually be attributed to the author of the play and screenplay *Shadowlands*, William Nicholson.) Still, it expresses a Lewisian idea: Stories connect people to a larger community and something bigger than themselves.

Revering stories for their power to unlock messages and especially emotions, Lewis also writes about how stories operate, subliminally, to help the reader or listener see, hear, taste, and touch in fresh and surprising ways. In describing how stories "work" to communicate implicit messages he says, "To be stories at all they must be series of events: but it must be understood that this series—the plot, as we call it—is only really a net whereby to catch something else. The real theme may be, and perhaps usually is, something that has no sequence in it, something other than a process and much more like a state or quality."[97] As Lewis explains in describing the purpose and function of stories, "In life and art both, as it seems to me, we are always trying to catch in our net of successive moments something that is not successive."[98] Lewis's ability to tell stories and embed meaning in "non-successive" and implicit ways is one key to his communicative success. His skill in using the plot of stories as "... a net of time and event for catching what is not really a process at all."[99] is one of the factors making his messages effective and enduring.

Lewis wants the reader or listener to make a personal connection with the story rather than having the communicator explicitly tell the reader or listener the point or moral of a story. In discussing how explicit to be in spelling out the moral of a story, especially a story for children, Lewis had strong opinions. The story should first paint a picture with words; then, let the moral of the story rise organically from the mental image. In his essay, "On Three Ways of Writing for Children" Lewis advises, "Let the pictures tell you their own moral. For the moral inherent in them will rise from whatever spiritual roots you have succeeded in striking during the whole course of your life. But if they don't show you any moral, don't put one in."[100] A good story evokes; the moral rises from the story based on the listener's life experiences and should not be trumpeted too loudly. The storyteller suggests the melody line; the listener embellishes and adds the harmony.

Lewis was not pleased when his editors wanted to reveal a theme in promotional materials or on the dust-jacket blurb. He wanted the story to work its magic without telegraphing the plot. George Sayer describes Lewis's irritation when the editors wanted to make the meaning of one of his space travel novels too explicit:

> Jack wanted the moral and spiritual significance of his works of fiction to be assimilated subliminally, if at all, and he was annoyed when his publisher outlined the theme of *Out of the Silent Planet* in the blurb on the dust jacket. Over and over again in talking about his fiction, he would say, 'But it's there for the story.'[101]

As Lewis says in "On Stories," "The story itself, the series of imagined events, is nearly always passed over in silence or else treated exclusively as affording opportunities for the delineation of character."[102]

In keeping with Lewis's not wanting to reveal too much to a reader too soon, Lewis wrote to Mr. Smoot in January 1947, thanking him for offering to provide an index to the next published edition of *The Screwtape Letters*. But Lewis politely rejects the offer. He explains, "I am delighted with your index, but I think it would be unwise to put it in the book. You see part of the success of that book depends on luring the ordinary reader into serious self-knowledge under pretense of being a kind of joke. A subject index at once gives the bluff away and stamps it as deadly serious."[103] Lewis then says, "Of course this [would] not deter readers like you. But it is the worldly reader I specially want to catch."[104]

Evoke by Using Myth

Myths are seminal stories that draw upon historical and cultural elements within a culture, giving them special power to evoke emotions.[105] In the popular vernacular, the word *myth* is sometimes used to describe something that is false or made up, such as the tooth fairy or leprechauns. From a literary perspective, however, a myth is not false or untrue; it is a cultural narrative with a deeper meaning that becomes clear once the reader or listener understands the underlying truth embedded in the story. A myth is a story that expresses a core idea wrapped in poetic and metaphorical language to evoke a truth that is less accessible by direct description. A myth, by definition, has great potential to evoke a larger theme or message. Stated succinctly, *not all stories are myths, but all myths are stories.*

According to Lewis, myth is "a story where the mere pattern of events is all that matters."[106] Myth, says Lewis, is neither "misunderstood history" nor "diabolical illusion" nor "priestly lyings" but "at its best, a real though unfocused gleam of divine truth falling on human imagination."[107] In his essay "Myth Became Fact," Lewis describes myth as "the isthmus which connects the peninsular world of thought with that vast continent we really belong to. It is not, like truth, abstract; nor is it, like direct experience, bound to the particular."[108] Lewis scholar Charlie Starr amplifies Lewis's ideas when describing Lewis's approach to myth: "Myth is the device that allows us to access the higher reality without reducing it to either abstract thought or mere experiential examples."[109]

For Lewis, myths are inherently true although the events of the story may not have actually happened. When Lewis was still in the process of reconciling the nature of Christianity and myth, Tolkien once said that Lewis described mythic fairy stories as "Breathing a lie through silver."[110] Tolkien, correcting Lewis, emphatically responded: "No, they are not."[111] Rather than being a lie, Tolkien believed a myth expresses truth. Lewis later agreed with Tolkien concluding that myth, rather than being false, has great power to evoke the "unfocused gleam of divine truth."[112] The meaning of the myth is unlocked when it ignites "human imagination."[113] A good myth, said C. S. Lewis in a letter to Father Milward, is "a story out of which ever varying meanings will grow for different readers and in different ages."[114] Also, according to Lewis, myth "is higher than allegory that has been filled with only one meaning in that a human can put into allegory only what he already knows but in myth one puts what he does not yet know and could not come by in any other way."[115] Whether it is the legend of King Arthur, the Black Panther, or the *Star Wars* saga, myth taps into fundamental glimmers of divine truth.[116]

Myth has considerable power because it can sneak past what Lewis called the "watchful dragons" of conscious thought that stand guard to monitor what is experienced.[117] One's rational side, believed Lewis, is always on watch to protect a person from less rational influences. Being rational is not a bad thing unless the "watchful dragon" seeks to skewer that which is true or logical, or to eliminate or deny the presence of beauty and joy. Myth, however, provides a means of stealing past the forces that protect a person from the romantic, the beautiful, and the poetic. According to Lewis, myth "gets under our skin, hits us at a level deeper than our thoughts or even our passions, troubles oldest certainties till all questions are reopened, and in general, shocks us more fully awake than we are for most of our lives."[118] Myth has greater potential to evoke feelings and meaning than allegory because there is richer meaning to be mined from a myth.[119]

In addition to myth and the metaphorical nature of language, how do the fundamental elements in the communication process (source, message, channel, receiver) interact to evoke emotional meaning? For Lewis, the channel of the process or form of the message is not important—it is almost irrelevant. Whether one receives the mythic meaning of a story by text, tweet, sermon, poem, or novel, the source or medium of the message is less important than the mythic meaning itself. Here is one of Lewis's most explicit statements about the nature of communication that explains the power and importance of myth in expressing mythic ideas. Words, Lewis suggests, are the means of communication, but myth is what transcends the words. Lewis provides a detailed explanation for the importance of myth in communicating key ideas:

> Any means of communication whatever which succeeds in lodging those events in our imagination has, as we say, "done the trick." After that you can throw the means of communication away. To be sure, if the means of communication are words, it is desirable that a letter which brings you important news should be fairly written. But this is only a minor convenience; for the letter will, in any case, go into the wastepaper basket as soon as you have mastered its contents and the words ... are going to be forgotten as soon as you have mastered the Myth. In poetry the words are the body and the "theme" or "content" is the soul. But in myth the imagined events are the body and something inexpressible is the soul; the words, or mime, or film, or pictorial series are not even clothes—they are not much more than a telephone. Of this I had evidence some years ago when I first heard the story of Kafka's Castle related in conversation and afterwards read the book for myself. The reading added nothing. I had already received the myth, which was all that mattered.[120]

How the myth is expressed is less important than what a myth evokes. The means (or channel, whether prose or poetry) of expressing the myth may go "into the waste basket" (or deleted from a tweet or Facebook post), but the underlying truth endures. Charlie Starr accurately distills Lewis's ideas about myth: "The myth is not to be found in the language that conveys it, but in the elements of the story itself: the events of the plot, the setting, the kinds of creatures and types of characters that appear in it."[121]

Mythic language, according to Lewis, "arouses in us sensations we have never had before, never anticipated having, as though we had broken out of our normal mode of consciousness."[122] It is the power of myth to arouse sensations that Lewis understands and uses in his writing. From the appearance of Merlin in *That Hideous Strength* to Aslan as a "supposal" Jesus in the Narnia stories, Lewis draws on myth to take his stories to another level. Lewis found that truths "dipped in a story" have augmented power to inspire and motivate by tapping the power of myth to evoke emotions that already reside within people.

Summary: The "E" of "HI TEA": The Principle of Evoking Emotions

The fourth communication principle of C. S. Lewis is this: Language evokes emotions through the use of word, comparison, placing a reader or listener in the middle of things, story or myth. Summarized succinctly, this principle suggests that it is better to get a message out of the reader or listener than to put one in. For Lewis, one of the most important uses of language is to arouse emotional responses that endure long after the book is closed or the speech has ended. Lewis would agree with Carl Buchner (whose quotation is often erroneously attributed to Maya Angelou), "They may forget what you said but they will never forget how you made them feel."[123] Emotion is the Velcro to which meaning sticks.

The current chapter reviews five strategies that Lewis not only used, but also discussed as methods of evoking emotional meaning in listeners and readers.

- First, Lewis was a perfectionist for selecting the right word to evoke a specific emotion.
- Second, as a master craftsperson of comparisons, Lewis knew the importance of a well-chosen metaphor. Not only metaphor, but also simile, allegory, analogy, and the "supposal" have power to evoke emotional meaning.
- Third, when reading Lewis, readers sometimes find themselves in the middle of things not quite sure where they are or what has happened in the past. Lewis's application of the technique of *in media res* was effective in using the reader's uncertainty to point him or her in a fresh direction, especially in *The Chronicles of Narnia*.

- Fourth, Lewis was a master storyteller. For him, stories are plots designed to catch something else, often an emotional response that does more than just surprise, but is imbued with "surprisingness."
- The fifth strategy draws on the power of myth, narratives embedded with larger truths that have meaning to individuals as well as a larger cultural community.

An effective communicator uses implicit communication strategies to help receivers discover the meaning of the message for themselves. Self persuasion is the most effective persuasive method. Rather than relying on what others say, it is a person's own thoughts, emotions and experiences that ultimately result in reinforcing or changing attitudes, beliefs and values that influence behavior. His heralded skill as an apologist (defender of the faith) lies in his ability to get messages out of his readers and listeners. Through the use of words, comparisons, *in media res*, story, and myth, effective communicators evoke emotions that may be lost in translation if communicated more explicitly. Communication, believed Lewis, is about helping the reader or listener discover the meaning of his or her own experiences. It is the personal, internalized meaning and one's emotional responses that ultimately influences a person's actions.

Notes

1. C. S. Lewis, *Studies in Words* (Cambridge: Cambridge University Press, 1960), 218–219.
2. C. S.Lewis, *The Collected Letters of C. S. Lewis, Vol. III: Narnia, Cambridge, and Joy 1950-1963* (San Francisco: Harper San Francisco, 2007), 881.
3. C. S. Lewis, "On Three Ways of Writing for Children," *Of Other Worlds: Essays and Stories,* ed. Walter Hooper (London: Geoffrey Bles, 1966), 33.
4. C. S. Lewis, "It All Began with a Picture," *Of Other Worlds: Essays and Stories,* ed. Walter Hooper (London: Geoffrey Bles, 1966), 42.
5. Lewis, "It All Began with a Picture," 42.
6. Lewis, "It All Began with a Picture," 42.
7. Daniel Quinn, *My Ishmael,* (New York: Bantam Books, 1997), 26.
8. W. Brown Patterson, "C. S. Lewis: Personal Reflections," *C. S. Lewis Remembered: Collected Reflections of Students, Friends & Colleagues,* ed. Harry Lee Poe and Rebecca Whitten Poe (Grand Rapids: Zondervan, 2006), 90.
9. C. S. Lewis, "Christianity and Literature," *Rehabilitations and Other Essays* (Oxford: Oxford University Press, 1939), 192.

10. C. S. Lewis, "Historicism," *Christian Reflections*, ed. Walter Hooper (London: Geoffrey Bles, 1967), 105.

11. Lewis, "Historicism," 105.

12. N. W. Clerk [C. S. Lewis], *A Grief Observed* (London, Faber & Faber, 1961), 7.

13. Lewis, Letter to Joan Lancaster, June 26, 1956, *Collected Letters III*, 766.

14. Lewis, Letter to Joan Lancaster, June 26, 1956, *Collected Letters III*, 766.

15. Lewis, Letter to Jane Gaskell, September 2, 1957, *Collected Letters III*, 881.

16. Lewis, Letter to Jane Gaskell, September 2, 1957, *Collected Letters III*, 881.

17. Austin Farrer, "In His Image: In Commemoration of C. S. Lewis," *The Brink of Mystery*, ed. Charles Conti (London, SPCK, 1976), 45; Also see: Austin Farrer, "In His Image," *Remembering C. S. Lewis: Recollections of Those Who Knew Him*, ed. James Como (San Francisco, Ignatious Press, 2005), 383.

18. Lewis, Letter to Mr. Don Holmes February 17, 1959, *Collected Letters III*, 1022–1023.

19. Lewis, *Collected Letters III*, Letter to Mr. Don Holmes February 17, 1959, 1023.

20. Lewis, *Collected Letters III*, Letter to Mr. Don Holmes February 17, 1959, 1023.

21. George McDonald, *The Complete Fairy Tales* ed. U. C. Knocepflmacher (Penguin Classics, 2000), 10.

22. Alan Jacobs, *The Narnian: The Life and Imagination of C. S. Lewis* (San Francisco: HarperSanFrancisco, 2005), 243.

23. C. S. Lewis, Letter to Rhona Bodle, June 24, 1949, *The Collected Letters of C. S. Lewis, Vol. II: Books, Broadcasts, and the War 1931–1949*, ed. Walter Hooper (San Francisco: Harper San Francisco, 2004), 947.

24. Jerry Root, *C. S. Lewis and a Problem of Evil: An Investigation of a Pervasive Theme* (Eugene: Pickwick Publications, 2009), xiv.

25. See: Zachary A. Rhone, *The Great Tower of Efland: The Mythopoetic Worldview of J. R. R. Tolkien, C. S. Lewis, G.K. Chesterton, and George MacDonald* (Kent: The Kent State University Press, 2017).

26. See: James Como, ed. *C. S. Lewis at the Breakfast Table* (New York: Macmillan, 1979).

27. George Sayer, "Recollections of C. S. Lewis," *C. S. Lewis & His Circle*, ed. Roger White, Judith Wolfe, Brendan N. Wolfe (Oxford: Oxford University Press, 2015), 176.

28. Sayer, "Recollections of C. S. Lewis," 176.

29. George Bailey, "In the University," *C. S. Lewis: Speaker & Teacher*, ed. Carolyn Keefe (London: Hodder and Stoughton, 1971), 108.

30. Bailey, "In the University," 108.

31. Bailey, "In the University," 108.

32. C. S. Lewis, *Studies in Words* (Cambridge: Cambridge University Press, 1960), 215.

33. Lewis, *Studies in Words*, 215.

34. Lewis, *Studies in Words*, 215.

35. E. M. W. Tillyard and C. S. Lewis, *The Personal Heresy: A Controversy* (Oxford, Oxford University Press, 1939), 119.

36. C. S. Lewis, *Letters to Malcolm: Chiefly on Prayer* (London: Geoffrey Bles, 1964), 18.

37. For a discussion of General Semantics and an applications to words and mean-ing see: Steven A. Beebe, Susan J. Beebe and Mark V. Redmond *Interpersonal Communication: Relating to Others*, 9th edition (New York: Pearson, 2020), 157–165.

38. Alfred Korzybski, *Science and Sanity: An Introduction to Non-Aristotelian Systems and General Semantics* (Brooklyn: Institute of General Semantics, 1921).

39. Lewis, *Letters to Malcolm*, 21.

40. Lewis, *Letters to Malcolm*, 21.

41. *Studies in Words*, 218.

42. *Studies in Words*, 219.

43. C. S. Lewis, *An Experiment in Criticism* (Cambridge: Cambridge University Press, 1961), 28.

44. Lewis, *An Experiment in Criticism*, 28.

45. C. S. Lewis, *The Screwtape Letters and Screwtape Proposes a Toast* (London: Beoffrey Bles, 19661), 12.

46. Lewis, *Collected Letters III,* Letter to Mrs. Hook, December 29, 1958, 1005–1006.

47. For an excellent summary and analysis of Lewis's use of visual metaphor see: Alister McGrath, *The Intellectual World of C. S. Lewis* (London: Wiley-Blackwell, 2014).

48. Jerry Root, *C. S. Lewis and a Problem of Evil: An Investigation of a Pervasive Theme* (Eugene: Pickwick Publications, 2009), xv.

49. Lewis, Letter to Ms. Rhonda Bodle, June 24, 1949, *Collected Letters, II, 947.*

50. Perry C. Bramlett, *C. S. Lewis: Life at the Center* (Macon: Smyth & Helwys Publisher, 1996), 230.

51. Lewis, *Preface to Paradise Lost*, 40.

52. Lewis, *Preface to Paradise Lost,* 49.

53. C. S. Lewis, Letter to Lucy, September 11, 1958, *Letters to Children,* ed. Lyle W. Dorsett and Marjorie Lamp Mead (New York: Scribners, 1996), 81.

54. C. S. Lewis, "Is Theology Poetry," *Screwtape Proposes a Toast and Other Pieces* (London: Fontana Books, 1965), 53.

55. Michael Covington, "C. S. Lewis as a Student of Words," *Word and Story in C. S. Lewis: Language and Narrative in Theory and Practice* ed. Peter J. Schakel and Charles A. Huttar (Eugene: Wipf and Stock, 1991), 41.

56. C. S. Lewis [N. W. Clerk], *A Grief Observed* (London: Faber & Faber, 196), 52.

57. Lewis, "It All Began with a Picture …," 53.

58. C. S. Lewis, "On Three Ways of Writing for Children" *Of Other Worlds: Essays and Stories*, ed. Walter Hooper (London: Bles, 1966), 311.

59. Lewis, "It All Began with a Picture…," 42.

60. For a seminal discussion of general semantics see: Alfred Korzybski, *Science and Sanity: An Introduction to Non-Aristotelian Systems and General Semantics* (Institute of General Semantics, 1994).

61. C. S. Lewis, *A Grief Observed*, 52.

62. For an excellent discussion of how, for Lewis, reality is iconoclastic see: Jerry Root, *C. S. Lewis and the Problem of Evil: Investigation of a Pervasive Theme* (Cambridge: James Clarke & Co., 2009, 176–184.

63. See: Root, *C. S. Lewis and the Problem of Evil*, 171–184.

64. Inscription found in the author's copy of Joy Davidman's personal copy of C. S. Lewis, *The Great Divorce* (New York: The MacMillan Company, 1946). Also see: Walter Hooper, *C. S. Lewis: A Companion and Guide,* (London: HarperCollins Publisher), 61.

65. C. S. Lewis, *The Four Loves* (London: Geoffrey Bles, 1960), 137.

66. C. S. Lewis, *A Preface to Paradise Lost* (Oxford: Oxford University Press, 1956), 52.

67. Lewis, *A Preface to Paradise Lost*, 52.

68. Lewis, *A Preface to Paradise Lost*, 52.

69. C. R. Berger and J. J. Bradac, *Language and Social Knowledge* (Baltimore: Edward Arnold, 1982); Mark V. Redmond, "Uncertainty Reduction Theory" (2015). *English Technical Reports and White Papers. 3.* http://lib.dr.iastate.edu/engl_reports/3; Also see: Steven A. Beebe, Susan J. Beebe and Mark V. Redmond, *Interpersonal Communication: Relating to Others* New York: Pearson, 2020, 66.

70. I thank my friend and colleague Dr. Rebecca Fox at Texas State University for this metaphor.

71. See: Andrew Rilstone, "In What Order Should the Narnia Books Be Read," Narniaweb.com accessed April 26, 2016.

72. C. S. Lewis, *Mere Christianity* (London: Geoffrey Bles, 1952), 132.

73. Lewis, *Mere Christianity*, 132–133.

74. Lewis, *Mere Christianity*, 133.

75. Lewis, *Mere Christianity*, 133.

76. Lewis, Letter to Sophia Storr, December 24, 1959, *Collected Letters III*, 1113.

77. Lewis, Letter to a Fifth Grade Cass in Maryland, May 24, 1954, *Collected Letters III*, 479.

78. Lewis, Letter to a Fifth Grade Cass in Maryland, May 24, 1954, *Collected Letters III*, 479.

79. Michael Ward, *Planet Narnia: The Seven Heavens in the Imagination of C. S. Lewis* (Oxford: Oxford University Press, 2008), xi.

80. Ward, *Planet Narnia*.

81. Also see: Michael Ward, *The Narnia Code: C. S. Lewis and the Secret of the Seven Heavens* (Carol Stream: Tyndale House Publishers, 2010).

82. Alister McGrath, *C. S. Lewis: A Life* (London: Hodder & Stoughton, 2013), 299.

83. McGrath, *C. S. Lewis: A Life*, 299.

84. C. S. Lewis, *The Problem of Pain* (London: The Centenary Press, 1940), 133.

85. See: Lewis, "On Stories," ed. Walter Hooper, *Of Other Worlds: Essays and Stories* (London: Geoffrey Bles, 1966).

86. See: C. S. Lewis, ed. *George Macdonald: An Anthology* (London: Geoffrey Bles: The Centenary Press, 1946).

87. Walter Fisher, *Human Communication as Narration: Toward a Philosophy of Reason, Value, and Action,* (Columbia: University of South Carolina Press, 1987). Also see: J. R. R. Tolkien, "On Fairy-Stories," C. S. Lewis, ed. *Essays Presented to Charles Williams* (Grand Rapids: Wm. B. Eerdmans, 1947).

88. Lewis, "On Stories"; J. R. R. Tolkien, "On Fairy-Stories," C. S. Lewis, ed. *Essays Presented to Charles Williams.*

89. C. S. Lewis, *The Lion, the Witch and the Wardrobe* (London: Bles, 1950), 132–133.

90. C. S. Lewis, "On Stories," 17.

91. Michael Ward, "Implicit Communication in C. S. Lewis," Lecture presented at Texas State University, April 5, 1916.

92. C. S. Lewis, "Sometimes Fairy Stories May Say Best What's to be Said,"*Of Other Worlds: Essays and Stories* ed. Walter Hooper (London: Geoffrey Bles, 1966), 35.

93. Lewis, "Sometimes Fairy Stories May Say Best What's to be Said," 35.

94. Lewis, "On Three Ways of Writing for Children," 33.

95. McGrath, *C. S. Lewis,* 279.

96. See: William O'Flaherty "Confirming Quotations," *The Essential C. S. Lewis* http://www.essentialcslewis.com/2015/09/05/we-read-to-know/ accessed May 20, 2017; also see: "7 Things C. S. Lewis Didn't Say," *The Wardrobe Door,* http://thewardrobe-door.com/2014/03/7-things-c-s-lewis-didnt-say.html accessed May 20, 2017.

97. Lewis, "On Stories," 18.

98. Lewis, "On Stories," 20–21.

99. Lewis, "On Stories," 20–21.

100. Lewis, "On Three Ways of Writing for Children," 33.

101. Sayer, *Jack,* 256.

102. C. S. Lewis, "On Stories," 3.

103. Lewis, Letter to Mr. Smoot, January 1947, *Collected Letters II,* 758.

104. Lewis, Letter to Mr. Smoot, January 1947, *Collected Letters II,* 758.

105. For a discussion of Lewis's application of myth see: Zachary A. Rhone, *The Great Tower of Efland: The Mythopoetic Worldview of J. R. R. Tolkien, C. S. Lewis, G.K. Chesterton, and George MacDonald* (Kent: The Kent State University Press, 2017).

106. As quoted by Rhone, *The Great Tower of Efland.*

107. C. S. Lewis, *Miracles: A Preliminary Study* (London, 1947), 161.

108. C. S. Lewis, "Myth Became Fact," *God in the Dock: Essays on Theology and Ethics,* ed. Walter Hooper (Grand Rapids: Eerdmans, 1970), 66.

109. Charlie W. Starr, *The Faun's Bookshelf: C. S. Lewis on Why Myth Matters* (Kent: Black Squirrel Books, 2018), 53.

110. The conversation between J. R. R. Tolkien and C. S. Lewis about myth is reported in: Humphrey Carpenter, *The Inklings: C. S. Lewis, J. R. R. Tolkien, Charles Williams,*

and *Their Friends* (London: George Allen and Unwin, 1978), 146–147. Also see: J. R. R. Tolkien, *On Fairy-Stories: Expanded Edition with Commentary and Notes*, ed. Verlyn Flieger and Douglas A. Anderson (London: HarperCollins, 2008), 65.

111. Carpenter, *The Inklings,* 147.

112. Lewis, *Miracles,* 161.

113. Lewis, *Miracles* 161.

114. Lewis, Letter to Father Peter Milward, September 22, 1956, *Collected Letters III*, 789.

115. Lewis, Letter to Father Peter Milward, September 22, 1956, *Collected Letters III*, 789; Also see: Terrence Lindvall, *C. S. Lewis' Theory of Communication*, Unpublished doctoral dissertation, University of Southern California, 1980.

116. For a discussion of myth and the hero's journey see: Luke Adam Dye, "The Hero's Journey of T'Challa: Marvel's Black Panther as Contemporary Mythmaking," Paper presented at the National Communication Association annual conference, Baltimore, Maryland, November 15, 2019.

117. C. S. Lewis, "Sometimes Fairy Stories May Say Best What's to Be Said," 37.

118. C. S. Lewis, ed. *George MacDonald: An Anthology*, (New York: McMillan, 1948), xxvii-xxviii.

119. For a comprehensive discussion of C. S. Lewis and myth see: Starr, *The Faun's Bookshelf.*

120. Lewis, *George MacDonald*, xxvii-xxviii.

121. Starr, *The Faun's Bookshelf,* 86.

122. Lewis, *George MacDonald*, xxvii.

123. *Quote Investigator*, "Exploring the Origins of Quotations," "They May Forget What You Said, But They Will Never Forget How You Made Them Feel," https://quotein-vestigator.com/2014/04/06/they-feel/ Accessed February 5, 2018.

8

Audience Centered

"We must learn the language of our audience."[1]

- C. S. Lewis

"You must translate every bit of your Theology into the vernacular. This is very troublesome, and it means that you can say very little in half an hour, but it is essential."[2]

- C. S. Lewis

John Lawlor, an officer in the Royal Air Force, was in a bar listening to the radio on August 6, 1941, at 7:45 pm, in the officer's mess of the Royal Air Force base where he was stationed during World War II. Someone ordered a drink. Just as the barman was about to hand the drink back to the customer, Lawlor heard the voice of C. S. Lewis during his first radio broadcast talk: "Suddenly everyone just froze listening to this extraordinary voice. And what he had to say. And finally they end up and there was the barman with his arm still up there and the other man still waiting for his drink. And they all forgot it, so riveting was that."[3] What was it that made Lewis's talk grab the attention of his audience? Here are the opening few sentences of Lewis's first broadcast talk:

> Every one has heard people quarrelling. Sometimes it sounds funny and sometimes it sounds merely unpleasant; but however it sounds, I believe we can learn something very important from listening to the kind of things they say. They say

things like this: "How'd you like it if anyone did the same to you?"—"That's my seat, I was there first"—"Leave him alone, he isn't doing you any harm"—"Why should you shove in first?"—"Give me a bit of your orange, I gave you a bit of mine"—"Come on you promised."[4]

Justin Phillips, who wrote *C. S. Lewis at the BBC,* narrates Lewis's technique: "Lewis's very first sentence and what follows is what journalists would call a 'grabber.' It engages you right away."[5] Using conflict, an age-old element of any good story, Lewis began his message by plunging his listeners in conversation that was both familiar and interesting. He knew that communication is a process of connecting to *individual* listeners. Although a radio broadcast is a form of mass communication, an audience is not a "mass" of people, but rather, a collection of individuals. Phillips suggests that a major part of Lewis's appeal was his skill in speaking "personally" to his listeners. First impressions in a relationship are important when establishing credibility and likeability. As Phillips notes, "Lewis made the connection with the audience as strongly as he could in this first broadcast."[6] He adds, "One of the keys to Lewis's appeal was his willingness to identify wholly with the listener and to reject any sense of preaching or speaking down to people."[7] Speaking on the radio is like having a personal, intimate chat with a friend. Lewis not only adapted to his audience but also to the medium of radio.

Earlier in 1941, Dr. James W. Welch, Director of Broadcasting for the BBC, had written to Lewis to see if he would be interested in speaking to the British people. Welch suggested a couple of ideas including "A series of talks on something like 'The Christian Faith as I see It—by a Layman.' I am sure there is a need of a positive restatement of Christian doctrines in lay language."[8] Welch had read Lewis's *The Problem of Pain* and was impressed with Lewis's skill in making theological ideas clear to the general public. Lewis wrote back: "I would like to give a series of talks as you suggest … I should mention Christianity only at the end, and would prefer not to unmask my battery till then."[9] In this response, Lewis considers the importance of the background of the audience in influencing what he would say. Despite the popularity of the broadcasts, his talks and subsequent books (first published as three separate books, *Broadcast Talks, Christian Behavior,* and *Beyond Personality,* and then slightly revised and combined in 1952 to form *Mere Christianity*) have sometimes been criticized as being too simplistic while glossing over real challenges that Christians face. But simplicity and clarity as means of connecting to his listeners is what made, and continues to make, Lewis's message effective. Lewis biographer Alister McGrath defends Lewis's rhetorical choices: "It is easy to criticize *Mere Christianity* on account of its simple ideas which clearly need to be fleshed out and given a more rigorous philosophical and theological foundation … *Mere Christianity* is an informal handshake to begin a more formal acquaintance and conversation."[10] Lewis was not attempting to write the final word about Christianity, but to provide an invitation, especially to those who already believed, to explore convictions more deeply. After delivering one of his early broadcast talks, he wrote to a friend, "I assumed last night that I was talking to those who already believed. If I'd been speaking to those who didn't, of course everything I'd said would have been different."[11] He knew his audience. *Mere Christianity* seeks areas of common ground among Christians.

No recording of Lewis's first broadcast survives. In fact, there is only one recording of any broadcast talk, an episode of his last series that was pre-recorded (which is why it survives). Why no existing recordings? BBC recordings in those days were made on twelve-inch metal discs cut by a steel needle. Given the high cost and scarcity of metal, the disks were reused unless there was a historic reason to keep the recording.[12] At the peak of this technology's use, more than 7,000 discs were made every week at the BBC. But later the metal was recycled or used for the war effort. In this instance no one thought that there was a historic reason to keep the recordings. Lewis was merely an Oxford don, a layman author, sharing his ideas about Christianity.

There was no premonition when Lewis delivered his first talk that he had a significant message or was a memorable messenger. His first broadcast had a relatively modest audience of 560,000 people. Not bad, especially since the lead-in to his talk was the Norwegian News (in Norwegian),[13] but still not the best, given that the potential listening audience was about 30 million people. Yet after his first broadcast, the audience tripled for his second, August 13th, broadcast, which reached more than 1.7 million people.[14]

Although Lewis was known well enough to have been brought to the attention of James Welch, the head of BBC religious broadcasting, Lewis was not a widely known speaker or notable author to most of his listeners. *The Screwtape Letters* had not yet been published. But although Lewis's listeners did not know much about him, he had thought about them. It is C. S. Lewis's ability to understand and connect with his readers and listeners that inspires the fifth and final Lewis lesson about communication.

Principle Five: Effective Communicators Are Audience Centered

In his classic book, *Rhetoric*, written in 333 B.C.E., Aristotle emphasized the importance of communication as an audience-centered process. Aristotle proclaims,

"For of the three elements in speechmaking—speaker, subject, and person addressed—it is the last one, the hearer, that determines the speech's end and object."[15] Lewis took this advice to heart. One of Lewis's skills as a communicator was being able to relate to his intended audience—whether in his written works (including his voluminous correspondence), his lectures to students, speeches to enlistees in the Royal Air Force, or broadcasts to the British people via his BBC broadcasts. People who heard Lewis on the radio attended to his message because he was skilled in making a personal connection with them. As Phillips notes, "Lewis had found a [broadcasting] style that suited him and the listener. It was direct, colloquial, and intellectually challenging."[16] Phillips's observations refer to Lewis's holistic skill in being both resonating to the ear and "intellectually challenging" to the mind. Readers, too, find a personal quality in his ability to connect with them.

Lewis's close friend Own Barfield recalls a Southwark Cathedral lunch-hour talk for city workers, in which Lewis dazzlingly connected to his audience: "… it seemed to me to be admirably adapted to his heterogeneous audience, and both his phrasing and his delivery retained as much of the sparkle of his private conversation as was compatible with the milieu."[17] Barfield would certainly know what Lewis was like as a conversationalist since Barfield spent considerable time with Lewis as both his solicitor and good friend.

How did Lewis develop such a personal relationship with his audience? This chapter explains how he connected to listeners and readers, using his own words to describe his audience-centered technique. Specifically, the chapter describes Lewis's abilities as an editor of his writing and speaking. He had a talent for establishing a relationship with his readers and listeners, as well as understanding what the readers or listeners bring to what is written or spoken. A good communicator—especially an apologist seeking to persuade, defend, and convince, must know to whom he or she is speaking. As Lewis explicitly advises, "If we are to convert our heathen neighbors, we must understand their culture, language and mental habits."[18] Lewis suggests being audience centered is more than just finding the right words to communicate. Understanding the audience's culture and mental habits—which includes how they make sense out of the world—is of paramount importance in crafting relatable messages.

As noted in Chapter 6, Lewis believed that the primary goal of a Christian communicator was first to translate Christian ideas clearly so that the intended audience would understand the message and then appropriately respond. It is also important to use words and phrases that the listener understands—to keep the language of the reader or listener in mind. In offering specific advice for connecting to an audience, Lewis says the process of translating ideas to a listener or reader should be "Just turned: not adorned, not diluted, not made 'matey'. The exercise is very like doing Latin prose. Instead of saying, 'How would Cicero have said that?' You have to ask yourself, 'How would my scout or bedmaker have said that?'"[19] Scouts and bedmakers are not stupid; they have reasonable intelligence. But they may not have had the benefit of attending a college or university where they would have developed an extensive vocabulary, nor would many of them likely have understood allusions to myths, artists, authors, philosophers, or composers.

The author of a work is often not the best judge of whether the message hits its mark. Whether a message is clear, interesting, and edifying, is determined by the audience. But before a speaker shares information and tries to motivate, the communicator must secure the listener's attention. In a debate with one of his colleagues, Dr. Eustance Mandevill Wetenhall Tillyard, Lewis points out that "… different things interest different people. It cannot be helped. That is the interesting *simpliciter* which interests the wise man."[20] Making a message interesting and capturing the attention of the reader or listener are the first prerequisites for communication success.

As noted in Chapter 2, one influence on Lewis's engaging and conversational communication style that should not be over looked is that of Mrs. Moore. Although Mrs. Moore was not his "scout" or "bedmaker," she was an important presence in his life. As his "adopted mother," she served as a constant, personal presence to remind him to write and speak to those who were not reading a dozen books a week, as he or his students and colleagues were doing. Mrs. Moore, as well as his long-serving gardener Paxford, helped to keep him grounded—to help him understand his audience.

Lewis seemed to have the skill to connect with a wide variety of people, ranging from the humble to the exalted. His driver, Clifford Morris, tells the story of Lewis conversing with lorry (truck) drivers at a truck stop who were captivated by Lewis's charm and wit. After a rousing conversation Lewis had with a group of drivers one of them went up to Morris and inquired who "the gov'nor'" was. When the lorry driver learned that it was famed author and broadcaster C. S. Lewis, the driver, surprisingly exclaimed, "Blimey, he's a toff, he is! A real nice bloke!"[21]

It is Lewis's ability to connect with ordinary people, from Mrs. Moore to truck drivers, that explains why he continues to be read by such a wide and diverse audience. Lewis scholar George Marsden suggests, "At the same time that Lewis was alert to common human traits, he was also alert to how these traits related to ordinary people he encountered every day."[22] Marsden further notes,

That aspect of his common touch suggests that he cultivated a similar approach to those whom he saw around him—whether the hired help at home, the staff at the university, shopkeepers, barkeepers, parishioners at the church, soldiers he met on the train or on RAF visits—as he did to persons from the past, to try to see through their eyes.[23]

Regardless of the goal of the communicator, the primary focus should always be on the intended audience. As described in Chapter 4, Lewis was a holistic communicator, blurring distinctions between rhetoric, dialectic, and poetry. In *A Preface to Paradise Lost*, building on the idea that effective communication is holistic, Lewis offers a distinction between rhetoric and poetry that, regardless of the objective of a message, the focus should be on the listener when communicating to others. He emphasizes, "Both these arts, in my opinion, definitely aim at doing something to an audience. And both do it by using language to control what already exists in our minds."[24] This passage brings into play several of the five principles presented in this book—not only being holistic, but also being intentional, transpositional, evocative, and audience centered. The key words in this passage are *doing something to an audience*. Regardless of whether it is a sonnet or a lecture, the communicator exists to "do something" to those who will read or hear the message. Effective communication is goal directed, and that goal is about achieving an effect with the reader or listener.

Lewis believed that the business of the Christian community is "to present that which is timeless (the same yesterday, today, and tomorrow) in the particular language of our own age."[25] Again, note Lewis's observation that the language should be "of our own age"—it should reflect the vernacular of the time and place. In his essay "Good Work and Good Works," Lewis emphasizes the importance of any artist being audience centered:

When an artist is in the strict sense working, he of course takes into account the existing tastes, interests, and capacity of his audience. These, no less than language, the marble, or the paint, are part of his raw material; to be used, tamed, sublimated, not ignored nor defied.[26]

An audience can be complex and multifaceted; rarely do all audience members have similar backgrounds and goals. The communicator's task is to decide which specific audience members—the primary target audience—are most important. Lewis knew he needed to adapt to different audiences, and a range of personalities in a given audience on different occasions. In a July 16, 1946, letter to Dr. Thomas Riddle, one of many people who wrote to Lewis inviting him to speak to a conference, Lewis declined the invitation, explaining, "I am primarily an arguer not an exhorter and my target is the frankly irreligious audience."[27] In this case, "irreligious" does not only mean non-believer, but also someone who may not regularly participate in religious activities.[28] As further evidence of his awareness of his target audience, Lewis writes: "Speaking in a very large hall with an atmosphere of enthusiasm in it was not my pigeon."[29] His "pigeon" or intended listener was an audience he knew very well, an audience that was a prime motivation for his foray into apologetics—the "irreligious" and non-believer. Looking back, he would have counted himself as a member of that "irreligious" audience in the 1920s. He understood firsthand the critiques, questions, and counter arguments an unbelieving listener would have about Christianity.

Misanalysing His Audience: Learning from Communication Failures

Lewis's Oxford University lectures were hailed as masterpieces; they were logically organized, well-delivered, and interesting. It was said that one could always tell when Lewis was speaking at the Oxford University Examination Hall on the High Street because of the rows and rows of bicycles stacked outside the entrance. Despite evidence that Lewis garnered a large following (and continues to do so, as evidenced by the continuing robust sale of his books), Lewis experienced his share of communication stumbles, especially early on when presenting public lectures. Owen Barfield remembers a specific instance when Lewis gave a lecture in which "both the construction and delivery were rather lifeless ... it is clear that he was learning his craft."[30]

In most cases Lewis's communication failures occurred when he did not accurately analyze or skillfully adapt his delivery or his message content to his listeners. In virtually every situation in which his audience analysis skills eluded him, he learned from his errors and became more aware of the skills he needed to be successful. Although his communication missteps were rare, they helped him better understand and apply principles of being audience centered as his career matured.

Lewis's biographer, former student, walking companion, and good friend George Sayer describes an early speaking assignment of Lewis's that was notably off target. Not mincing words, Sayer called it a flat out "fiasco." Here's the story: Lewis was asked to deliver a university lecture series but, unfortunately, he was scheduled to speak at the same time as a better-known, popular lecturer. But the double scheduling was not the biggest challenge he had to overcome. Because of a misprint in the lecture announcements, instead of speaking at University College, his home college, he was listed as speaking at Pembroke College, which is several blocks away and around the corner in the St. Aldates area of Oxford. As Sayer notes, because of the publishing error, "It was a wonder that anyone turned up at all, but four people did."[31] Apparently, Lewis did not captivate his quartet of listeners. Sayer notes, "By February his audience had dwindled to two, including an elderly parson."[32] Realizing that giving a formal lecture to two people would be odd, Lewis decided to change to a more informal venue. He invited the two faithful audience members, one a clergyman, to come to his room for the "talks." He also suggested that they interrupt him if they had any questions. "It was a great mistake," said Sayer. "The elderly parson interrupted so often that Jack 'could hardly get a word in.' "[33] It was not Lewis's finest rhetorical hour. Although he attempted to adapt to his two-person audience, what had been billed as a "lecture" ended up with Lewis becoming the audience as he listened to the old parson ramble on, offering new points and counter arguments.

During World War II, Lewis was invited to give lectures to Royal Air Force (RAF) recruits. Charles Gilmore, a former student at Oxford, had met Lewis briefly in the 1920s, but now had the task of finding speakers for an RAF lecture series. When he approached Lewis in 1941 about being a speaker for the series, Lewis was, as Gilmore says, "diffident."[34] Lewis thought he was too old (forty-two) to have anything to say to the young recruits. But he relented and finally agreed to give a talk.

His first effort to speak to the RAF occurred at Abingdon, a small market town just a few miles down the River Thames from Oxford. Gilmore charitably described the talk as "neither striking nor startling."[35] But Lewis had a different recollection; he thought it was "a complete flop."[36] Sayer also wrote about the Abingdon lecture, providing additional details: "He considered his first talks, which were at the RAF station near Abingdon, a failure. Fewer than a dozen men turned up, and none of them showed any desire to ask questions at the end."[37] "Perhaps," speculates Sayer, "Many of the men may have been put off by his tendency to lecture (he knew nothing at the time of leading a discussion group), but some were also put off by his cool, rational approach, by the lack of emotional and obvious devotional content."[38] Lewis was admittedly more comfortable developing logical arguments than offering emotion-laden stories. Sayer suggests that, for Lewis, "feelings were unreliable transient things, and there was little to be gained by making people feel better."[39]

Despite these rhetorical misjudgments, Lewis learned to adapt his message to fit the audience and the occasion. Specifically, he learned that spouting theories, quoting scholars and theorists, and providing indirect responses to someone's question are not effective ways of connecting to his listeners. He developed strategies to evoke emotions rather than explicitly emote.

Lewis scholar Bruce Johnson, who has extensively investigated some of Lewis's less-than-stellar talks, describes a speaking event in which Lewis attempted to use strong emotional appeals and a "Come to Jesus" invitation at the end of his talk.[40] But when reflecting later on the occasion, Lewis concludes, "those who, like myself, lack the gift for making it [an emotional appeal] had better not attempt it."[41] Lewis also notes, "I must add that my work has suffered very much from the incurable intellectualism of my approach."[42] In his essay "Christian Apologetics," when discussing the use of strong emotional appeals to evangelize, Lewis admitted, "I have seen it done, precluded by a religious film and accompanied by hymn singing, and with very remarkable effect. I cannot do it."[43] Lewis's emotional appeals were more effective when he was telling a story or using a visual metaphor to evoke emotion, rather than using more explicit emotion-arousing techniques. Lewis also knew that offering his "personal testimony" was not his cup of tea. When broadcasting executive Eric Fenn asked Lewis to consider sharing personal reflections about his faith on the BBC broadcasts Lewis cogently responded, "Not my pigeon, I think."[44] He then added, "Not that personal 'testifying' isn't most important, but it isn't my gift."[45]

In yet another speaking situation with A. W. Goodwin-Hudson (whom Lewis called "Haddon"), Lewis and Haddon were responding to questions from an audience about religion. At this point in his career, Lewis was aware that in addition to offering "personal testimony," emotional messages were also not his forte. Lewis confided to Haddon, "Haddon, I wish I could do the heart stuff. I can't. I wish I could. I wish I could press home to these boys just how much they need Christ … Haddon, you do the heart stuff and I'll do the head stuff."[46] A few years after acknowledging that the "heart stuff" was not his key gift, Lewis wrote in his essay "Modern Man and His Categories of Thought" that the best way to bring people to Christ "is a team of two: one to deliver the preliminary intellectual barrage, and the other to follow up with a direct attack on the heart."[47]

In the early 1940s, Lewis's fame was growing due to his radio broadcasts and successful books. Yet despite his renown in some circles, many in his RAF audiences were not aware of his credentials as a communicator. Lewis reports in a 1942 letter to a correspondent that often when arriving to speak to a military audience, he would find he had no audience. Not a soul was there to hear him.[48]

On one occasion when Lewis did have a sizable audience, he was invited to speak to RAF recruits who were also chaplains. Unfortunately, the group had heard some less-than-mesmerizing lecturers in the past and therefore did not expect much when yet another would-be theologian rose to speak to them. Charles Gilmore, who organized the talk, confides that he was worried that Lewis might not make a good impression on the group because the previous speakers were dull. Gilmore's fears increased when Lewis announced his topic: "Linguistic Analysis in Pauline Soteriology." And then, reports Gilmore, to make matters worse, as Lewis started his talk he stumbled and in halting speech, seemed to be "feeling for words."[49] Gilmore astonishingly adds, "Clive Staples Lewis feeling for words! He hummed, and the ill-mannered coughed."[50] As the listeners' low expectations were confirmed, their attention waned, as evidenced by Gilmore's observation, "A future bishop secretly got on with *The Times'* crossword"[51] instead of listening to C. S. Lewis. Things looked bleak. Lewis was losing his audience. Yet, apparently realizing his misanalysis of his audience's interests, about halfway through the talk, Lewis changed tactics. Gilmore reported,

> He suddenly said something about prostitutes and pawnbrokers being 'Pardoned in Heaven, the first by the throne,' and the rest of the morning was full of the clang of steel on steel and the laughter of good fellows, and answers that belonged to life. The linguistic analysis topic was tossed aside as Lewis switched topics.[52]

What began as an abstract talk about linguistics became a more interesting talk; apparently, prostitutes and pawnbrokers are a sure-fire way to perk up an RAF audience.

Arguably Lewis's worst communication failure occurred with the largest audience (5.5 million people) who ever heard him speak during his lifetime.[53] The BBC had a popular 1940s radio program called *Brains Trust*.[54] The format was simple. A panel of experts responded to questions sent in by listeners. The May 1942 *Brains Trust* program included C. S. Lewis, who was on the panel as an informed layperson, to respond to questions about religion. The transcript of the broadcast confirms that Lewis's responses were surprisingly much too long, and sometimes off topic, as well as esoteric.[55] Johnson notes that a listener who wrote a letter to the editor of the *Catholic Herald* suggested that in the future religious questions should be answered by "a sound Christian layman"—meaning someone other than Lewis.[56] Other reviews were equally unflattering. According to James Welch, Director of Religious Broadcasting for the BBC, who had originally asked Lewis to give his 1941 Broadcast Talks, audience reaction was lackluster, even curt. Welch said Lewis had been "eaten alive."[57] Based on Lewis's poor performance, the BBC Board of Governors ultimately decided that the *Brains Trust* program was "not the appropriate setting for the discussion of religious matters."[58]

Yet again Lewis learned from the experience. He later reported that the question-and-answer approach was a most useful one. He wrote to J. S. A. Ensor: "Now that you mention Questions at the meeting it suddenly occurs to me that the best meetings I've ever had have been all questions i.e. I've announced myself as a one-man's *Brains Trust* on moral and religious questions."[59] Lewis would not have warmed to a Q & A format if he had not learned to make answers short and clear. He adapted. Once during a Q & A session, he was asked, "Would you please give us a simple explanation of the Holy Trinity?" Lewis, after first deferring to someone else, then wittily and metaphorically quipped, "The question that you have asked us is like asking a slug to explain Einstein."[60] He learned that listeners do not want a dissertation in response to their questions. They want a clever, clear, and concise answer.

In another Q & A format session, Lewis was speaking to the Royal School for Daughters of Officers of the Army, with the principal of the school serving as Question Master. Most of the questions were about how best to raise girls. Not a parent, Lewis was certainly no expert. But the questions about raising girls continued, with an exasperated Lewis simply repeating his response: He did not know. Then, blessedly, one of the students changed the subject, asking, "Oh Mr. Lewis, could you perhaps tell us what hell is like?" Lewis quickly quipped, "Yes, very much like what I've just been through."[61]

A common mistake of inexperienced speakers is to be message centered rather than audience centered. A message-centered speaker emphasizes *what* will be said rather than *to whom* it will be said. Extant lecture notes suggest that early Lewis lessons were dense and stuffed with too much information. But with time and experience, he learned to be listener centered. He discovered when the audience paid attention and when they did not.

Yet at the same time Lewis was missing the mark with some audiences, he presented one of his most heralded sermons. Most Lewis scholars point to his June 8, 1941, sermon, "The Weight of Glory," as one of the best rhetorical efforts of his life. It continues to be among his most quoted messages. Although it is not overtly emotional, Lewis painted pictures with words, while using metaphors that resonated with those who heard him in St. Mary the Virgin Church in Oxford that warm Sunday evening, and that still makes an impression on those who read it more than 75 years after the sermon was first delivered. Here is an excerpt as he makes his seminal point:

> The load, or weight, or burden of my neighbour's glory should be laid daily on my back ... There are no ordinary people. You have never talked to a mere

mortal. Nations, cultures, arts, civilizations—these are mortal, and their life is to ours as the life of a gnat. But it is immortals whom we joke with, work with, marry, snub, and exploit—immortal horrors or everlasting splendours ... Next to the Blessed Sacrament itself, your neighbour is the holiest object presented to your senses.[62]

Some Lewis readers may not agree that he was consistently audience centered. When reading *The Abolition of Man*, for example, a reader may wonder, "Is this really the master communicator communicating with simplicity and clarity?" Some of Lewis's writing assumes a significant background in philosophy or literature. Yet he wrote for his *intended* audience. When reading his books or essays 70 or 80 years after they were written, one must remember that he was not writing to a 21st century audience, especially a book that was originally a talk delivered to an academic audience. Lewis's ability to be audience centered stems from several processes—editing for, speaking to, relating to, and understanding his listeners and readers.

Editing for the Audience

Although Lewis's manuscripts typically reflect very little editing, he edited *before* he put the words on paper. Lewis scholar Diana Glyer discovered that when comparing Lewis's first drafts with the final, published version, he changed less than 8 percent of the manuscript; and those changes were primarily changes in word choice.[63] The reason few changes were made was because he pre-wrote. He carefully thought about what he would write. He would then, before writing, mouth or whisper the words, and then, using a dip pen, write. Using a pen that needed to be replenished with ink meant he could write about five or six words before he repeated the process and re-dipped his pen in the ink. The pause in writing as he dipped his pen gave him time to refine his ideas. His sense for knowing what to leave out was one of his pre-eminent communication skills.

He knew what to revise as he sat at his desk to write because his ideas were already percolating. Lewis scholar Bruce Charlton suggests, "Lewis produced scores of first rate essays—done in a few hours each; and their coherence relies upon their being completed in a single burst of inspiration."[64] Whereas J. R. R. Tolkien spent years working on a book, Lewis worked in a shorter time frame. Lewis's longest book, *The Oxford History of English Literature: Excluding Drama* is almost 700 pages; perhaps it was because it took him several years to write he called it "Oh Hell" (from its initials OHEL). Charlton further speculates,

Lewis's strength was also his limitation. Because he wrote quickly and with con-
centration—he was very prolific (and indeed his letters, of which he wrote many
per day, are of an extremely high, publishable, standard)—but when he could
not finish a book satisfactorily in a single burst of rapid writing extending over
not-many-weeks maximum; he was never able to achieve the spontaneity of style
and effortless integration characteristic of his shorter works.[65]

Audience-centered authors edit. They write and revise. They know what to discard
from earlier drafts, as well as what additions to make: sometimes, in the case of
presenting a speech, they make edits while the speech is in progress, based on
discerning cues from listeners. In a written message, it is not possible to delete
paragraphs once they have been printed, yet in anticipating a reader's response,
Lewis did sometimes suggest that a passage, paragraph or chapter be skipped if the
content did not interest the reader.[66]

Lewis used his literary circle, "The Inklings," to help him refine his ideas and
shape his prose. The collaborative writing process, chronicled in two excellent
books by Diana Pavlac Glyer, *The Company They Keep*[67] and *Bandersnatch*,[68] illustrates how Lewis used the reactions from his friends to help him with the classic
communication process of invention. As Glyer explains, the Inklings served as
editors, opponents, collaborators and resonators for one another.[69] These four
collaborative functions mirror the classic four phases of group communication
as found in small group communication research: orientation (reviewing the
agenda), conflict (discovering differing points of view), emergence (reaching con-
sensus) and reinforcement (affirming and celebrating).[70] According to communication researchers, many groups experience these group phases, sometimes in
sequence, sometimes not.[71]

- ORIENTATION (Editing): When people collaborate, they typically first
  become oriented to the task, similar to reviewing a manuscript to assess
  where editing is needed. An editor performs "linguistic triage" to identify the strengths and weaknesses of the material. Most groups, even those
  meeting over several years, as did the Inklings, have an initial period of
  orientation to assess the agenda of the day.
- CONFLICT (Opposing): The second phase of group communication,
  conflict, is captured in Glyer's description of the Inklings as opposers who
  would challenge each other's ideas. The Inklings did not always agree with
  one another. Conflict is an inevitable element in group discussion. The
  fact that the Inklings sometimes challenged one another helped make their
  writing better.

- EMERGENCE (Collaborating): Third, groups eventually experience the phase known as emergence, which Glyer characterizes as collaboration. After becoming oriented and realizing that group members may see things differently, conversation and discussion eventually yields a solution or product. In the case of the Inklings, what emerged was some of the best-loved literature of the 20th Century.[72]
- REINFORCEMENT (Resonating): Finally, there is a sense of celebration and reinforcement for work well done. To be a resonator is to be in positive sync with another person. The Inklings served as resonators as they celebrated their success, confirmed one another's talents, and enjoyed one another's company with beer and boisterousness.

When editing, it is important to select the best word in terms of both precision and clarity. Having to stop a lecture to periodically define terms can be tedious. Lewis notes that "once the lecture or discussion has begun, digressions on the meaning of words tend to bore uneducated audiences and even to awaken distrust."[73]

In another statement about the importance of adapting language to the audience, Lewis offers this explicit advice about being audience centered: "We must learn the language of our audience. And let me say at the outset that it is no use at all laying down *a priori* what the 'plain man' does or does not understand. You have to find out by experience."[74] Here Lewis suggests that an audience-centered speaker does not just guess what the "plain man" understands; it takes editorial trial and error—something Lewis experienced as a speaker—to figure out what works with a specific audience. Lewis's many years lecturing in the university, as well as presenting sermons and speeches to the public (some better received than others), gave him editorial experience to know what his listeners and readers would understand.

Dr. Norman Pittenger was a U. S.-born, theologically liberal colleague who taught at General Theological Seminary in New York, and then at Cambridge, with whom Lewis had several philosophical and theological disagreements. In his essay "Rejoinder to Dr. Pittenger," Lewis complains that his own writings were sometimes inappropriately evaluated, "*in vacuo*, with no consideration of the audience to whom they were addressed or the relevant errors they were trying to combat."[75] Lewis further clarifies, "I was writing *ad populum*, not *ad clerum*. This is relevant to my manner as well as my matter."[76] To evaluate a message without considering its audience in Lewis's case, (a general, "popular" audience rather than "*ad clerum*" or to clergy) effects an injustice. Context, audience, and message purpose are key to developing, editing, and interpreting a message.

The goal of an editor is to prune and polish the message so that it connects with the listener. Although Lewis believed in objective values, the audience ultimately discovers the meaning of a message. Language, according to Lewis, "exists to communicate whatever it can communicate."[77] It takes time, suggests Lewis, to assess the effectiveness of a message and the skill of the editor. It may take multiple readings over a span of time for the reader to catch the "true or right meaning." As Lewis explains,

> The ideally true or right "meaning" would be that shared (in some measure) by the largest number of the best readers after repeated and careful readings over several generations, different periods, nationalities, moods, degrees of alertness, private preoccupations, states of health, spirits, and the like cancelling one another out when (this is an important reservation) they cannot be fused so as to enrich one another.[78]

A message has to stand on its own. Readers or audience members typically do not compare notes among themselves, so it is important to find just the right word to help audience members discover meaning individually.

Additional ideas about Lewis's editorial thought process may be gleaned from the preface of *Mere Christianity*. Although he wrote for both the eye and the ear, he knew the requirements of *both* mediums—the written and spoken word—and he was intentionally mindful of the differences between them. He explains that "A 'talk' on the radio should … be as like real talk as possible, and should not sound like an essay being read aloud."[79]

I have reviewed Lewis's BBC transcripts. Although brief, his handwritten additions to the manuscript suggest that he was aware of the differences between speaking and writing. At the beginning of his third talk, for example, he penned these words as an informal preface to his message: "I must begin by apologizing for my voice. Since we last met I've managed to catch an absolute corker of a cold."[80] Adding a colloquial observation helped him relate to his listeners. He adds, "Should you hear this talk suddenly interrupted by a loud crack you needn't jump to any rash conclusions. It'll probably only be me sneezing or coughing."[81] He had read papers to academic audiences and even published several of his papers in his 1962 compendium *They Asked for a Paper*.[82] Yet he knew that some editorial adjustments were needed to translate the spoken word into the printed word:

> In my talks I had therefore used all the contractions and colloquialisms I ordinarily use in conversation. In the printed version I reproduced this, putting *don't* and *we've* for *do not* and *we have*. And wherever, in the talks, I had made the importance of a word clear by the emphasis of my voice, I printed it in italics.[83]

But in hindsight he had second thoughts about his strategy. He writes:

> I am now inclined to think that this was a mistake—an undesirable hybrid between the art of speaking and the art of writing. A talker ought to use variations of voice for emphasis because his medium naturally lends itself to that method: but a writer ought not to use italics for the same purpose. He has his own, different means of bringing out the key words and ought to use them. In this edition I have expanded the contractions and replaced most of the italics by recasting the sentences in which they occurred: but without altering, I hope, the "popular" or "familiar" tone which I had all along intended. I have also added and deleted where I thought I understand any part of my subject better now than ten years ago or where I know that the original version had been misunderstood by others.[84]

This description of Lewis as editor offers a behind-the-scenes look at Lewis's communication process. The fact that this comment about his writing method is the first paragraph in his preface to *Mere Christianity* underscores the importance he places on the editing process.

Relating to the Audience

A relationship is a *connection* that one person has with another.[85] Lewis's readers often identify his ability to relate to them as individuals as one of the reasons they enjoy reading Lewis. How does an author, who writes to the reader asynchronously (from a different time and place) develop that relationship, especially when the words were sometimes written decades ago? A good writer develops a sense of *immediacy*.

Immediacy is a psychological construct that describes the perceived degree of physical and psychological closeness that exists between people.[86] To be immediate is to experience a warm and friendly relationship with another person. After reading one of his books, those who admire Lewis's writing often say, "It's as if he knows you; he's having a conversation with you." From the standpoint of immediacy, it's as if he is "near" you; if not physically, he is psychologically close—one has a sense that the author anticipates the reader's reaction to what is written. Justin Phillips describes Lewis's informal communication quality when describing his conversational style in his broadcast talks noting, "He carries you along as a good companion walking down a road. It is like listening to a benevolent uncle trying to explain the laws of cricket to his nephew."[87]

Specifically, Lewis uses the technique of *verbal immediacy*, the psychological closeness engendered by words and word choice. Using immediate personal pronouns (such as *we*, *us*, and *our*), including several personal examples (using *I*, *me*, and *my*), self-disclosing personal experiences, posing questions, and speaking *with* readers and listeners rather than *at* them are all means of being verbally immediate. Lewis used these techniques well and often.

When first meeting Arthur Greeves, the across-the-street neighbor who became one of his closest confidants, Lewis discovered that Arthur, like Lewis, had an abiding interest in Norse mythology and "things Northern." On making this connection, Lewis experienced what he called a "What? You too?" connection with Arthur.[88] Immediacy is the ability to make a "you too?" connection with readers and listeners. Lewis's struggles, disappointments, and challenges made him seem a kindred spirit by his readers and listeners. Lewis evoked an immediate "you too?" connection with his readers.

Lewis was comfortable using conversational idioms as he wrote. Lewis's *Letters to Malcolm* was originally planned as a straightforward book about prayer. He wrote to Don Giovanni Calabria on January 5, 1953, "I invite your prayers about a work which I now have in hand. I am trying to write a book about private prayers for the use of the laity …"[89] But he struggled with the format. In a February 15, 1954 letter to Sister Penelope he wrote, "I have had to abandon the book on prayer; it was clearly not for me."[90] He seemed to question whether writing a book of advice about prayer was appropriate coming from an unordained church member. He did not want to put himself in the position of prescribing how others should pray.

It was ten years later when he hit on an idea that was more in his comfort zone; he would write *Letters to Malcolm: Chiefly on Prayer* as a series of letters to a friend. This format, like *The Screwtape Letters*, permitted him to be more verbally immediate. He not only wanted his readers to have a conversation with him as author, but to react to what he wrote, just as if receiving a letter from a friend. Although "Malcolm" was imaginary (several people thought there really was a Malcolm), writing letters allowed Lewis to have a chat with his readers rather than to pontificate as an expert on the subject. When his editor invites him to write a blurb for the book, Lewis responds, "I'd like you to make the point that the reader is merely being allowed to listen to two ordinary laymen discussing the practical and speculative problems of prayer as these appear to them; i.e. the author does *not* claim to be teaching."[91]

Communication scholar Terry Lindvall makes a strong case that Lewis consciously wanted to have a dialogue with his readers. As Lindvall notes, when Lewis was discussing how to communicate with others, "Lewis placed equal emphasis on the role of the audience. Accurate understanding does depend, in part, on the clear expression of the speaker, but it also requires the audience to actively receive and discover the intended meaning of the speaker."[92] For Lewis, Lindvall suggests, "meaning emerges out of the act of encounter, in which the speaker and the audience are united in the attempt for accurate understanding."[93] Lewis involved his listener as active participant in the communication process. He invited them to participate in *discovering* the meaning of a message by asking questions, self-disclosing his own opinions, and using conversational language to evoke a reader or listener response.

Perhaps it is the feeling of having a two-way conversation that explains why so many people felt compelled to write to Lewis; they felt they had a relationship with him. He was their friend. His own revelations about his feelings, doubts, and uncertainties all made him approachable—or at least seem as though he wanted to be approached. Although the letter-writing task was sometimes a burden, he developed close friendships with several people through letters. The book *Letters to An American Lady* chronicles his multi-year correspondence with Mary Willis Shelburne, a woman who frequently sought his advice.[94] Based on the consistency with which he wrote back to her, he apparently enjoyed the continuing conversation, although he also noted how responding to an avalanche of mail could be burdensome. Sheldon Vanauken's book *A Severe Mercy* offers a glimpse of Lewis's friendship with the author when Vanauken experienced the tragic loss of his wife.[95] The letters from Lewis to Vanauken included in *A Severe Mercy* reveal Lewis's tender heart and empathic hand of friendship. His correspondence with former students George Sayer, Dom Bede Griffiths, and many others document his loyalty as a friend, pen pal, and confidant.[96] Letters, written in Latin, between Lewis and Don Giovanni Calabria, published as *The Latin Letters of C. S. Lewis*, chronicle a multi-year friendship.[97] And his life-long friendship and correspondence with Arthur Greeves also evidence Lewis's loyalty as a friend.[98]

The qualities of loyalty, compassion, and enjoyment of relationships, especially through letters, comes across in his books and essays. The massive and magisterial three-volume set of *Collected Letters of C. S. Lewis* meticulously edited by Walter Hooper provides additional evidence of Lewis's skill and interest in sustaining relationships through correspondence. Writing letters is the epitome of audience-centered communication. Lewis did not write form letters. He wrote personalized messages responding to specific questions and requests. Perhaps it was his decades of letter writing that honed his ability to develop a relationship, a *personal* relationship, with others through the written word. Most letters written *to* C. S. Lewis do not exist; he did not keep them. Yet reading his letters offers a true sense of conversation because of Lewis's ability to paraphrase and respond to his correspondents.

Although Lewis had many deep and long-lasting friendships, and wrote about friendship as one of the most cherished categories of relationships, there were some who suggest he could be off-putting. The dichotomy of Lewis as close friend to some, yet disconfirming to others, adds to his perception as a man of many compartments. Some perceived him to be brash. Lewis biographer A. N. Wilson asserts that several of Lewis's colleagues, especially those he worked with in Magdalen College, Oxford, did not like him. Wilson writes about a "backstage" Lewis that could sometimes be obnoxiously loud and boisterous:

> The reasons why many of his Oxford colleagues had disliked him were obvious. He was argumentative and bullying. His jolly, red, honest face was that of an intellectual bruiser. He was loud, and he could be coarse. He liked what he called 'man's talk', and he was frequently contemptuous in his remarks about the opposite sex. He was a heavy smoker—sixty cigarettes a day between pipes— and he liked to drink deep, roaring out his unfashionable views in Oxford bars. This—the 'beer and Beowulf' Lewis—was understandably uncongenial to those of a different temperament.[99]

Lewis apparently did not have patience for unprepared students. George Sayer agrees that Lewis did not always suffer fools politely. He describes what it was like coming to Lewis's room—room 3 on staircase 3 of New Building, Magdalen College, Oxford, for a tutorial: "It was formidable being alone with Lewis. He sat on a sofa at one side of the fireplace and the pupil on the other."[100] Intimidating indeed. Sayer then describes what happened if the student was unprepared: "If the student had not done his essay, he would be sent away at once—Lewis could be quite fierce." Sayer also added, "I remember a delightful but odious, very lazy friend of mine in Magdalen who had to leave the college altogether ... Lewis expected his pupils to work."[101]

Whether there are kernels of truth in Wilson's portrayal of Lewis as loud and bullying or not (and there were several others who report less-than-pleasant encounters with Lewis),[102] Lewis established and maintained many personal, ongoing interpersonal relationships through his letters. His letters evidence a nuanced, thoughtful, and generous Lewis who would take time to write to *anyone* who wrote to him.

The conversational writing style that connected Lewis with his readers and listeners often came through in his books and essays as well as in his letters. In his chapter on faith in *Mere Christianity*, for example, he says, "If this chapter means nothing to you, if it seems to be trying to answer questions you never asked, drop it at once. Do not bother about it at all"[103] Having an author tell a reader to skip a chapter if it does not interest or concern the reader is unusual. Lewis uses the same technique in his autobiography, where he writes in the Preface, "I have tried so to write the first chapter that those who cannot bear such a story will see at once what they are in for and close the book with the least waste of time."[104] A few pages later he adds, "The reader who finds these three episodes of no interest need read this book no further …"[105] Yet, it is this candid conversational written quality that provides immediacy—Lewis connects with his readers.

Speaking to an Audience

Lewis was known not only as a skillful writer but also as an effective public speaker. Former Lewis student George Baily noted, "I count his lectures among the foremost of his intellectual products. Lewis was at his effective best as a lecturer."[106]

Owen Barfield recalls a speaking event in London at which Lewis was especially effective. Addressing a large audience on the topic "The Literary Impact of the Authorized Version," Lewis "spoke without notes, or, if he had any, scarcely bothered to consult them. This time both his voice and his manner were full of life. He was genially in touch with his hearers, as he danced them along through his theme, which was that there was virtually *no* direct literary impact at all."[107]

The metaphor of Lewis "dancing" his audience along aptly describes how others viewed Lewis's speaking talent. Kingsley Amis, a former student at Oxford who became a friend of Lewis's, describes how he and some of his student friends would categorize lecturers on a scale of "hard" to "soft." A "hard" lecturer was one who focused on message content. As Amis notes, "Hard men gave you information, while soft ones offered civilized discourse."[108] Hard lecturers piled on information without regard to the interest or attention level of the listeners. Soft lecturers, on the other hand, provided stories and illustrations—but a too soft lecturer would result in students leaving the lecture hall with nothing written down in the way of principles or information. Amis classifies J.R.R. Tolkien as among the "hardest," even using the word "repulsive" to describe his lecture style. Repulsive, not because he did not have anything to say, but because he had *too much* to say. From Amis's perspective, Tolkien was much too dense and did not give the listener a chance to mentally breathe. Like the anthropomorphized brooms in Walt Disney's *The Sorcerer's Apprentice* relentlessly carrying buckets of water to Mickey Mouse, the information just kept coming without stopping. But because of Tolkien's knowledge of Old English and the likelihood of questions that would appear about his topic on exams, students attended Tolkien's lectures. "The softest of the soft," according to Amis, was Lord David Cecil.[109] He was engaging but less meaty. Then in describing the "golden mean" lecturer, Amis places C. S. Lewis as in between "hard" and "soft." Amis describes Lewis's lecture style as "The only reputable hard-soft merchant" and "the best lecturer I ever heard."[110] Lewis had learned that moving from a "hard," chock-full-of-information lecturer, to a "softer" lecturer who included more illustrations, stories, metaphors and anecdotes along with substantive content, was more appealing to an audience.

Lewis used not only his skill in creating messages with a balance of "hard" and "soft" information to connect to his listeners, but also his skill in delivering those messages. One of his key assets as a speaker was his rich, clear voice. Based upon the few recordings that are in existence, Carolyn Keefe, a speech expert and author of *C. S. Lewis: Speaker and Teacher*, describes his voice this way:

> Perhaps the most outstanding characteristic of Lewis's voice is the resonance. It has a richness of sound, an expansiveness and dimension, the sort of balanced tone you can obtain by regulating the treble-bass dials on a stereophonic instrument. The resonance in combination with the baritone pitch gives an impression of masculinity and strength.[111]

Lewis recalls what it was like hearing his recorded voice for the first time: "The first time I heard my own voice on a record I didn't recognize it and was shocked … If all my critics cd. [could] hear their own voices they'd be very surprised."[112] It was because of Lewis's sometimes loud, booming voice that several scholars suggest J. R. R. Tolkien patterned Treebeard after Lewis.[113]

What would it have been like to be a student hearing one of Lewis's lectures? Former student George Bailey describes Lewis's lecture delivery, both verbal and nonverbal, as skilled, no-nonsense, and intentional:

> Indeed, his delivery in his lectures was entirely straightforward, almost severe. He never noticeably consulted his lecture notes. When he had finished his lecture, he folded up his papers almost as he uttered the last word and walked briskly in a beeline for the door. No one would have dared accost him in his passage. He was blessed with a fine sonorous baritone voice capable of a wide range of intonation and inflection but his delivery was highly disciplined and deceptively easy. He was never dramatic, let alone melodramatic. I cannot remember a single

gesture during his lectures. In appearance at the rostrum he was relaxed, almost deadpan, a study in economy. He was the consummate medium for what he had to say: he gave every word, every phrase, every sentence, every larger passage its full value. He gave full expression to his flashes of humour without obtruding his personality, as it were, between the flash and the audience. His style, I suppose, was low pressure but never conspicuously so. Lewis, I am sure, never "threw away a line" in his life.[114]

Lewis's close friend and solicitor, Owen Barfield, offers another detailed description of Lewis's speaking style:

Lewis not only thought rapidly, but the clothing of his thought in words was equally swift. It was, however, remarkable in him that this rapidity of semantic utterance never gave rise to a corresponding rapidity of vocal utterance. That was always measured, always distinct. I never heard him gabble. Not only so, but I do not believe I ever heard him slur a single sentence. Whatever he was saying, and in whatever mood, his voice flowed evenly on. Once could almost say it was the *kind* of voice one could hardly imagine doing anything else. I think most people found its timbre agreeable, perhaps partly because of the distinctness, but not only because of it … It was low-pitched. It was hollow, rather than sharp. It seemed perhaps to issue from the whole of his head, rather than merely from his throat. An enemy might have characterized it as "booming." It was accompanied by very little movement of the facial muscles.[115]

He liked to connect with his audience using an extemporaneous style, although sometimes he wrote his lectures out verbatim such as when he presented (read) a formal paper at a conference or address.[116] When he was preparing his first philosophy lectures in 1924 he described his speaking strategy to his father:

I am plodding on with my fourteen lectures—I am at number five, or rather have just finished it. I think I said before that I am not writing them IN EXTENSO [full length], only notes. The extemporary element thus introduced is dangerous for a beginner, but READ lectures send people to sleep and I think I must make the plunge from the very beginning and learn to TALK, not to recite. I practice continually, expanding my notes to imaginary audiences, but of course it is difficult to be quite sure what will fill an hour.[117]

Although he told his father he wasn't preparing a full text of his lectures, Walter Hooper has copies of his first lecture notebooks and, as Hooper notes, "Lewis decided in the end to write them *in extenso* …"[118] I have seen these lecture "notes" and they read like a complete manuscript rather than partial speaking notes. Lewis's strategy of practicing his lectures in front of an "imaginary audience" is a technique championed by contemporary public speaking textbooks.[119]

Despite missing the mark on some early occasions, with experience, Lewis learned how to connect with his audience, especially for his Prolegomena lectures—lectures that Owen Barfield had heard early on and thought were overly dense. Walter Hooper noted that Lewis eventually became well known for his Prolegomena lectures that were published as *The Discarded Image* after Lewis's death. These classic lectures, delivered both at Oxford and Cambridge, offer a comprehensive introduction to medieval and renaissance literature. Hooper notes, "A bare summary of *The Discarded Image* cannot possibly convey the impression given to those students who *heard* Lewis. Not even *The Discarded Image* itself can do that."[120] An existing set of lecture notes transcribed by Rodney Hilton, a student who heard Lewis give the lectures in 1935 in Oxford, provide evidence of Lewis's skill in presenting an organized, well-paced, information-packed lecture.[121]

Lewis biographer Roger Lancelyn Green described Lewis's Prolegomena lecture technique, several years after Own Barfield's initial less-than-stellar impression of Lewis speaking on this subject. From Green's observations, Lewis had learned from his previous efforts. Students flocked to his lectures; they learned to arrive early or they would not get a seat. Green notes that Lewis would adapt his written text "during the lectures with additional examples or explanations" and also describes "the lighter moments: good laughs which he timed with all an actor's skill, and knew from previous experience when to expect so that he could build up to them."[122] Green adds that it was evident from Lewis's content that he was "a lover of literature who had read every text he mentioned, had enjoyed most of them, and was eager to share both his knowledge and his enthusiasm with anyone whom he could persuade to do so …"[123]

Lewis preferred to give his audience a full measure of his content. Green corroborates George Bailey's observations about Lewis's leave-taking behaviors at the conclusion of his lecture:

> He lectured for precisely three-quarters of an hour, and he never waited to answer questions. Two minutes before the end of the lecture he would quietly gather his notes together, return the watch which at one time he was in the habit of borrowing from the nearest member of his audience, and prepare to leave— lecturing all the time. Then, as he finished his last sentence, he would step off the dais and stride down the hall at top speed. If he was at all late in arriving at the lecture, he would begin it even before he entered the hall: several times the great

voice came booming up the steps outside the hall door and Lewis would enter in haste, lecturing vigorously.[124]

Lewis not only used his live-and-in-person presentations to good advantage, but also was equally adept at using the broadcast media effectively. He was, however, never completely comfortable speaking on the radio; Justin Phillips suggests that he was more comfortable writing than broadcasting. Phillips concluded, "Writing for radio meant dealing with a host of producers who would suggest changes or improvements that Lewis found tiresome. The BBC had created for him a new audience and transformed him into a national figure. His books had no difficulty in finding their public."[125] In addition to his general discomfort with radio, Phillips suggests Lewis did not spend much time listening to the radio except for a few news bulletins: "The broadcasting medium seemed increasingly trivial to him. In his books and his correspondence, references to radio listening are usually negative."[126] Lest there be no doubt as to Lewis's less-than-positive attitude about the wireless, when a schoolgirl wrote to him for advice about how to be an effective writer, among his first directives: "Turn off the radio."[127]

Despite his needing to be cajoled to speak on the radio, Lewis's broadcast career was successful because he was able to translate his skill in having a conversation on the page with having a conversation with his listeners on the air. It was his holistic ability to write for the ear as well as the eye, his pleasing voice, his precise language style, or a combination of these attributes that helped Lewis connect with his radio listeners. He was successful in finding an audience of people who were eager and interested in his message and the way he presented his message. His friend Owen Barfield thought Lewis's voice was a prime asset for broadcasting: "I was particularly struck by how unexpectedly well that voice recorded. It needed no tiresome artificial sprightliness to give it life … He could, I believe, have become a frequent and popular broadcaster, if he had set out to do so."[128]

Lewis knew that although communication should be audience centered, a listener or reader can never quite catch the complete meaning of a message. As Lewis noted, "Admittedly we can never quite get out of our own skins. Whatever we do, something of our own and of our age's making will remain in our experience …"[129] There is always going to be a difference of perspective between communicator and listener. He further explains with an apt metaphor the challenge of taking another person's perspective: "I can never see anything exactly from the point of view even of those whom I know and love best. But I can make at least some progress towards it … If I can't get out of the dungeon I shall at least look out through the bars. It is better than sinking back on the straw in the darkest corner."[130]

Although Lewis had gained a well-earned reputation as an excellent public speaker, in the last decade of his life he decided to reduce the number of his speaking engagements, especially those related to theology or religious topics. Owen Barfield recalls a specific instance in which Lewis was invited to speak but simply decided not to accept the invitation. An eavesdropping Barfield recalls,

> I happened to be in his rooms at Magdalen, Oxford, on an occasion not long before he left there for Cambridge [1954], when someone rang him up evidently with an invitation to address an audience. He courteously declined it, but it soon became apparent that his caller was being importunate enough to press him for reasons. I heard Lewis reply that there were no particular reasons, but that he had recently come to the decision that talking in public, as distinct from writing, was not what he was cut out for; or words to that effect. I have no idea why this was so. I wondered at the time whether he had been disappointed at the reception accorded to him, but on reflection I doubt very much whether that was it. I got the impression that it was a theological or religious address he was being asked to give, and I dare say it was only from that particular field that he had decided to withdraw. But why? He had by that time preached a fair number of sermons, including at least one university sermon. Some of them have been printed, and I never heard or read an adverse comment on his delivery.[131]

Although Lewis gave fewer public apologetic lectures, he continued to be a prolific author.

Being a Good Audience Member

George Sayer describes how Lewis's ideas about the significance of focusing on readers and listeners, as summarized in *An Experiment in Criticism,* had been germinating for some time. Sayer explains, "He had been discussing the subject [of *An Experiment in Criticism*] for years. As a working schoolmaster, I had often spoken to him of the importance of shielding students from literary criticism until they had made a personal response to the books they were studying."[132] Lewis was concerned that if students, or any reader for that matter, were to hear from a critic *before* reading the book or essay, the reader would rely too much on the critic for interpretation. Sayer recalls Lewis announcing "in some excitement that he had thought of a possible way out—to look at books from the reader's point of view."[133] Sayer notes that *An Experiment in Criticism* was at first not well received, "… but within five years it was referred to as a now classic broadside.

Though the least combative of Jack's critical books—he became notably gentler after Joy's death—it is the most influential."[134] The book was influential because of the importance Lewis placed on the role of the receiver of a message. His key point: The reader is the primary judge of a work's quality and utility, not the critic, nor anyone else. Lewis's ideas echo those of another literary theory known as reader response theory, in which a work is evaluated from the standpoint of the reader's response rather than only the text itself.[135]

Lewis believed the audience or reader has an obligation to be appropriately prepared to receive that which is presented. One preparation strategy is to be mindfully open and "empty" about what will be received. As noted throughout this book, communication, for Lewis, is a process of discovery for the listener. The key to being a good reader or listener (discoverer), according to Lewis, is to have no preconceived ideas about the message. To be open is to clear one's mind, focus on the speaker's or author's intent, and be physically and mentally attuned to receive the intended message. One should avoid prejudice or attempts to look for specific confirmations of suspicions. Here Lewis describes, in his own words, how to be a good receiver of a message:

> … if it is worthwhile listening or reading at all, it is often worth doing so attentively. Indeed we must attend even to discover that something is not worth attention … We must empty our minds and lay ourselves open … No book or person is immune from being rejected; no work or person can succeed without a preliminary act of goodwill on the part of the reader.[136]

Whether attending a lecture or picking up a book, people do so to meet a need—a need for information, entertainment, or confirmation of an already held belief. Listeners and readers seek something. According to Lewis,

> . . . we seek an enlargement of our being. We want to be more than ourselves. Each of us by nature sees the whole world from one point of view with a perspective and a selectiveness peculiar to himself. And even when we build disinterested fantasies, they are saturated with, and limited by, our own psychology. The man who is contented to be only himself, and therefore less a self, is in prison. My own eyes are not enough for me; I will see through those of others. Reality, even seen through the eyes of many, is not enough. I will see what others have invented."[137]

One of the reasons people read and listen to stories is to gain an understanding of how others live, work, relate and learn. In order to receive what a story, or any piece of art has to offer, one must be open to let the words or image work on us.

Lewis suggests that "We sit down before the [object] in order to have something done to us, not that we may do things with it. The first demand any work of art makes upon us is surrender."[138] By surrender Lewis wants readers and listeners to set aside their thoughts, ideas and prejudices. He also wants listeners to avoid the psychological tendency to selectively attend and perceive messages. Rather than hearing what a person wants to hear he suggests, "Look. Listen. Receive. Get yourself out of the way. (There is no good asking first whether the work before you deserves such a surrender, for until you have surrendered you cannot possibly find out.)"[139]

It is readers who bring meaning to the story. As Lewis notes in one of his often-quoted passages,

> In reading great literature I become a thousand men and yet remain myself. Like the night sky in a Greek poem, I see with a thousand eyes, but it is still I who see. Here, as in worship, in love, In moral action, and in knowing, I transcend myself: and am never more myself than when I do.[140]

Being a good audience member (or reader) involves being mindful of and attending to silence. As Lewis suggests *in Surprised by Joy*, "Total surrender is the first step of fruition .... Shut your mouth; open your eyes and ears. Take in what is there and give no thought to what might have been there or what is somewhere else."[141] Be still. Just listen. The simple yet unambiguous suggestion: Close mouth, open eyes and ears. Lewis explains that if a reader or listener does not get out of the way, "We are so busy doing things with the work that we give it too little chance to work on us. Thus increasingly *we meet only ourselves*."[142]

A story is written or told to achieve certain goals. One of those goals could be simply to entertain. Given the options of "receiving" or "using" a work, Lewis suggests a reader or listener simply receive it so as not to get in the way of what the author intended. Lewis phrases it this way: "A work of art can be either 'received' or 'used.' When we 'receive' it we exert our senses and imagination and various other powers according to a pattern invented by the artist. When we 'use' it, we treat it as assistance for our own activities …"[143]

The problem, suggests Lewis, is that one can never completely escape from one's self. As contemporary mindfulness literature admonishes, *wherever you go there you are*.[144] In order to be receptive to the message, just get out of the way. Seek an "enlargement of our being."[145] Lewis explains, "We want to see with other eyes, to imagine with other imaginations, to feel with other hearts, as well as with our own. We are not content to be Leibnitzian monads. We demand windows."[146]

In another of his often-quoted statements, Lewis suggests that his own eyes are not enough. He seeks access to other worlds and even other species through the power of seeing through the eyes of others. He laments,

> Even the eyes of all humanity are not enough. I regret that brutes cannot write books. Very gladly would I learn what face things present to a mouse or a bee; more gladly still would I perceive the olfactory world charged with all the information and emotion it carries for a dog.[147]

Ultimately, the audience determines whether a message has been successful. Just as a communicator can use strategies to express messages that connect with an audience, audience members can employ strategies to be better receivers of the message. Lewis's advice: Be quiet. Listen. Receive.

Summary: The "A" of "HI TEA": The Principle of Being Audience Centered

To be effective, communication should achieve three goals: (1) be understood, (2) achieve the intended effect, and (3) be ethical.[148] The audience, not the speaker, determines whether each of these three goals has been accomplished. Consequently, the audience, or as Aristotle put it, "the hearer," determines "the speech's end and object."[149] Being audience centered is a hallmark of all excellent communicators, and it is a skill that C. S. Lewis possessed, practiced, and wrote about. Woven throughout his work is an emphasis on focusing on the reader or listener.

C. S. Lewis was an especially effective editor of his messages, although someone might not reach this conclusion by reviewing his manuscripts. Much of his editing was done *before* he put pen to paper. He thought intentionally (Principle Two) and made mental edits and changes before he wrote his message.

Lewis's public lectures, sermons, and speeches evidence a similar conversational quality. Although there are no existing recordings of Lewis delivering a speech or sermon in front of a live audience, (although there are recordings of him speaking in a recording studio) his published transcriptions of his messages provide clues to his conversational, oral style.

A key to being audience centered was Lewis's ability to develop a personal relationship with his readers and listeners. Not only his word choice, but his writing style resulted in a conversational style. Although Lewis did not believe he was writing "for the ages" but for a specific audience, his clarity and liberal use of examples, metaphor, and story gave his writing an "evergreen" quality that continues to resonate with readers more than half a century after his death. He was verbally immediate. Using personal pronouns and seemingly talking with, rather than at, an audience added to his conversational, relational quality.

Lewis not only had advice for those who speak or write to an audience, but he also had recommendations for how to be a good audience member; be open and receptive to what a speaker or author has to say. The best readers and listeners are those who realize their own eyes are not enough. Rather, readers and listeners should seek to see through the eyes of others and receive the messages so that they can stop, look, listen, and learn.

Notes

1. C. S. Lewis, "Christian Apologetics," *God in the Dock: Essays on Theology and Ethics* (Grand Rapids: Eerdmans, 1970), 96.
2. Lewis, "Christian Apologetics," 98.
3. John Lawlor, *C. S. Lewis: Memories and Reflections* (Dallas: Spence Publishing, 1998), 119.
4. C. S. Lewis, *Mere Christianity* (London: Bles, 1952), 3.
5. Justin Phillips, *C. S. Lewis at the BBC*, (New York: HarperCollins, 2002), 120.
6. Phillips, *C. S. Lewis at the BBC*, 121.
7. Phillips, *C. S. Lewis at the BBC*, 120.
8. As quoted in Phillips, *C. S. Lewis at the BBC, 120.*
9. As quoted in Roger L. Green and Walter Hooper, *C. S. Lewis: A Biography* (London: Collins, 1974), 202.
10. Alister McGrath, *C. S. Lewis: A Life* (London: Hodder and Stoughton, 2013), 226.
11. C. S. Lewis, Letter to Patricia Thomson, December 8, 1941, *Collected Letters, Vol. II: Books, Broadcasts and the War 1931–1949,* ed. Walter Hooper (San Francisco: Harper San Francisco, 2004), 499.
12. Phillips, *C. S. Lewis in a Time of War* (San Francisco: HarperSanFrancisco, 2002), 121.
13. Phillips, *C. S. Lewis in a Time of War*, 117.
14. See: Bruce R. Johnson, "C. S. Lewis and the BBC's *Brains Trust*: A Study in Resiliency," *VII: An Anglo-American Literary Review*, 30 (2013), 74.
15. Aristotle, *The Art of Rhetoric*, trans. Hugh Lawson-Tancred, (London: Penguin Books, 1991), 101.
16. Phillips, *C. S. Lewis at the BBC*, 121.
17. Owen Barfield, *Owen Barfield on C. S. Lewis*, "C. S. Lewis in Conversation," ed. G. B. Tennyson (Middletown: Wesleyan University Press, 1989), 42.
18. C. S. Lewis, "Christianity and Culture," *Christian Reflections* (London: Bles, 1967), 17.

19. Lewis, "Before We Can Communicate," *God in the Dock* (Grand Rapids: Eerdmans, 1970), 256.

20. E. M. W. Tillyard and C. S. Lewis, *The Personal Heresy: A Controversy* (Oxford: Oxford University Press, 1939), 119.

21. Evan K. Gibson, "Jack Lewis: Scholar, Apologist, Storyteller," *C. S. Lewis: Spinner of Tales* (Eugene: Wipf and Stock Publishers, 2009), 4.

22. George M. Marsden, *C. S. Lewis's Mere Christianity: A Biography* (Princeton: Princeton University Press, 2016), 163.

23. Marsden, *C. S. Lewis's Mere Christianity*, 163.

24. C. S. Lewis, *A Preface to Paradise Lost* (Oxford: Oxford University Press, 1942), 54.

25. Lewis, "Christian Apologetics," *God in the Dock*, 93.

26. C. S. Lewis, "Good Work and Good Works," *The World's Last Night* (New York: Harcourt, Brace and Company, 1960), 80.

27. C. S. Lewis, Letter to Thomas Wilkinson Riddle, July 16, 1946, *The Collected Letters of C. S. Lewis, Vol. II: Books, Broadcasts, and the War 1931–1949*, ed. Walter Hooper (San Francisco: Harper San Francisco, 2004), 718–719.

28. Lewis, Letter to Thomas Wilkinson Riddle, July 16, 1946, *Collected Letters II, 719*.

29. Lewis, Letter to Thomas Wilkinson Riddle, July 16, 1946, *Collected Letters II, 719*.

30. Owen Barfield, *Owen Barfield on C. S. Lewis,* 43.

31. George Sayer, *Jack: A Life of C. S. Lewis* (Wheaton: Crossway Books, 1994), 181.

32. Sayer, *Jack,* 181.

33. Sayer, *Jack,* 181.

34. Charles Gilmore, "To the RAF," ed. James Como, *C. S. Lewis at the Breakfast Table* (San Diego: A Harvest Book Harcourt Brace and Company, 1992), 187.

35. Gilmore, "To the RAF," 187.

36. Sayer, *Jack,* 181.

37. Sayer, *Jack,* 282.

38. Sayer, *Jack,* 282.

39. Sayer, *Jack,* 282.

40. Bruce R. Johnson, "C. S. Lewis and the BBC's *Brains Trust*: A Study in Resiliency," *VII: An Anglo-American Literary Review*, 30 (2013), 74.

41. Lewis, *God in the Dock*, 244. Also see: Johnson, *Brains Trust,* 74.

42. Lewis, *God in the Dock*, 244.

43. Lewis, "Christian Apologetics," 99.

44. Lewis, Letter to Eric Fenn April 12, 1943, *Collected Letters II*, 568-569.

45. Lewis, *Collected Letters II*, 568.

46. Bishop A. W. Goodson-Hudson, "How I Met C. S. Lewis and Why," Sound recording, Wade Center, CSL-Y/SR-166, 1975 as transcribed by Johnson, *Brains Trust,* 82.

47. C. S. Lewis, "Modern Man and his Categories of Though," *Present Concerns: Ethical Essays* ed. Walter Hooper (London: Fount, 1986), 66.

48. C. S. Lewis, Letter to Lewis John Collins, July 12, 1942, *Collected Letters II*, 524.

49. Gilmore, "To the RAF," 189.

50. Gilmore, "To the RAF," 189.

51. Gilmore, "To the RAF," 189.

52. Gilmore, "To the RAF," 189.

53. See: Johnson, "C. S. Lewis and the BBC's *Brains Trust*," 67–92.

54. The discussion of Lewis appearing on the radio program Brains Trust is based on research reported in: Johnson, "C. S. Lewis and the BBC's *Brains Trust*," 67–92.

55. Johnson, "C. S. Lewis and the BBC's *Brains Trust*," 67.

56. As reported by Johnson, "*Brains Trust*," Dorothy Kavanagh, "Religious Brains Trust," *Catholic Herald* (May 22, 1942).

57. Kenneth Wolfe, *The Church and the British Broadcasting Corporation* 1922–1956 (London: SCM, 1984).

58. Wolfe, *The Church and the British Broadcasting Corporation*.

59. Lewis, Letter to J. S. A Ensor, March 13, 1944, *Collected Letters II,* 606.

60. Johnson, "C. S. Lewis and the BBC's *Brains Trust*,"81.

61. Johnson, "C. S. Lewis and the BBC's *Brains Trust*," 81.

62. C. S. Lewis, "The Weight of Glory," *Transposition and Other Addresses* (London: Geoffrey Bles, 1949), 32–33.

63. Research conducted by Diana Pavlac Glyer, shared with an audience at the national conference "Through the Window to the Garden: C. S. Lewis & the Recovery of Virtue," Cal Poly University Pomona, February 23, 2019.

64. Bruce Charlton, "In His Writing Style, C. S. Lewis Was Essentially a Sprinter/Short-Middle-Distance Dasher (But Tolkien was Built for Marathons)," *The Notion Club Papers—an Inklings Blog,* (Wednesday, August 23, 2017), http://notionclubpapers.blogspot.com/2017/08/in-his-writing-style-cs-lewis-was.html.

65. Bruce Charlton, "C. S. Lewis Was Essentially a Sprinter," http://notionclubpapers.blogspot.com/2017/08/in-his-writing-style-cs-lewis-was.html.

66. C. S. Lewis, *Mere Christianity* (London: Bles, 1952), 114.

67. Diana Pavlac Glyer. *The Company they Keep: C. S. Lewis and J. R. R. Tolkien as Writers in Community.* (Kent: Kent State University Press, 2007).

68. Diana Pavlac Glyer, *Bandersnatch* (Kent: Kent State University Press, 2015).

69. Glyer, *Bandersnatch*.

70. For a discussion of group process see: Steven A. Beebe and John T. Masterson, *Communicating in Small Groups: Principles and Practices* 12th edition (New York: Pearson, 2021), Chapter 10.

71. B. Aubrey Fisher, "Decision Emergence: Phases in Group Decision Making," *Speech Monographs* 37 (1970), 60; also see: B. Aubrey Fisher, *Small Group Decision Making: Communication and the Group Process*, 2nd ed. (New York: McGraw-Hill, 1980), 132.

72. Glyer. *The Company They Keep.*

73. C. S. Lewis, "God in the Dock," *God in the Dock: Essays on Theology and Ethics,* ed. Walter Hooper (Grand Rapids: William B. Eerdmans Publishing Company, 1970), 243.

74. C. S. Lewis, "Christian Apologetics," 96.

75. C. S. Lewis, "Rejoinder to Dr Pittenger," *God in the Dock: Essays on Theology and Ethics* ed. Walter Hooper (Grand Rapids: William B. Eerdmans Publishing Company, 1970), 182.

76. Lewis, "Rejoinder to Dr Pittenger," 182.

77. C. S. Lewis, *Studies in Words* (Cambridge: Cambridge University Press, 1960), 214.

78. C. S. Lewis, "On Criticism," *Of Other Worlds: Essays and Stories*, ed. Walter Hooper (London: Geoffrey Bles, 1966), 56.

79. C. S. Lewis, *Mere Christianity* (London: Geoffrey Bles, 1952), v.

80. C. S. Lewis, "Materialism or Religion," British Broadcasting Corporation Transcripts, Archived BBC Reading, England, Wednesday, 20th (August, 1941). Also see: Phillips, *C. S. Lewis in a Time of War,* 128. Phillips notes that originally Lewis planned a more explicit joke wanting to say, "You needn't jump to any rash conclusion that we are being bombed, it's probably only me sneezing and coughing."

81. These handwritten additions are found at the beginning of his third talk on a copy of the original manuscript held in the BBC archives in Reading, England. Wednesday, August 13, 1941.

82. C. S. Lewis, *They Asked for a Paper: Papers and Addresses* (London: Geoffrey Bles, 1962).

83. C. S. Lewis, *Mere Christianity*, v.

84. C. S. Lewis, *Mere Christianity*, v.

85. See: Steven A. Beebe, Susan J. Beebe and Mark V. Redmond, *Interpersonal Communication: Relating to Others* (Boston: Pearson, 2020), 6.

86. For a discussion of immediacy see: Virginia P. Richmond, Marian L. Houser and Angela M. Hosek, "Immediacy and the Teacher-Student Relationship," *Handbook of Instructional Communication: Rhetorical and Relational Perspectives* ed. Marian L. Houser and Angela M. Hosek with Virginia P. Richmond, James C. McCroskey and Timothy P. Mottet (New York: Routledge, 2018), 97–111.

87. Phillips, *C. S. In a Time of War*, 123.

88. C. S. Lewis, *Surprised by Joy: The Shape of My Early Life* (London: Geoffrey Bles, 1955).

89. C. S. Lewis, *The Collected Letters of C. S. Lewis, Vol. III: Narnia, Cambridge, and Joy 1950–1963*, ed. Walter Hooper (San Francisco: Harper San Francisco, 2007), 275. Also see: Walter Hooper, *C. S. Lewis: Companion & Guide* (New York: HarperCollins, 1996), 378.

90. Lewis, Letter to Sister Penelope, February 15, 1954, *Collected Letters III,* 428.

91. Walter Hooper, *Companion & Guide,* 380.

92. Terry Lindvall, *C. S. Lewis' Theory of Communication.* Unpublished doctoral dissertation, University of Southern California (1980).

93. Lindvall, *C. S. Lewis' Theory of Communication*.

94. C. S. Lewis, *Letters to an American Lady* ed. Clyde S. Kilby (Grand Rapids: Eerdmans, 1967).

95. Sheldon Vanauken, *A Severe Mercy: C. S. Lewis and a Pagan Love Invaded by Christ, Told by One of the Lovers* (London: Hodder and Stoughton, 1977).

96. Lewis, *Collected Letters III*.

97. *C. S. Lewis and Don Giovanni Calabria, The Latin Letters of C. S. Lewis,* trans. and ed. Martin Moynihan (South Bend: St. Augustine's Press, 1998).

98. C. S. Lewis, *They Stand Together: The Letters of C. S. Lewis to Arthur Greeves (1914–1963)*, Walter Hooper ed. (New York: Macmillan Publishing Co., 1979).

99. A. N. Wilson. *C. S. Lewis: A Biography* (London: Harper Perennial, 1990), xii.

100. Sayer, *Jack*, xvi.

101. George Sayer, "Recollections of C. S. Lewis," ed. Roger White, Judith Wolfe and Brendan N. Wolfe, *C. S. Lewis & His Circle: Essays and Memoirs from the Oxford C. S. Lewis Society* (Oxford: Oxford University Press, 2015), 175.

102. For a summary of less than flattering perceptions of C. S. Lewis see: Stephanie L. Derrick, *The Fame of C. S. Lewis: A Controversialist's Reception in Britain and America*, (Oxford: Oxford University Press, 2018), 50–80. Although others dispute Derrick's observations noting the excerpts she references are not consistent with his voluminous correspondence and other first-hand reports. See: Andrew J. Spence, *A Book Review from Books at a Glance*, Review published, April 29, 2019. https://www.booksataglance.com/book-reviews/the-fame-of-c-s-lewis-a-controversialists-reception-in-britain-and-america-by-stephanie-derrick/ Accessed June 17, 2019.

103. Lewis, *Mere Christianity*, 114.

104. Lewis, *Surprised by Joy*, x.

105. Lewis, *Surprised by Joy*, 18.

106. George Bailey, "In the University," *C. S. Lewis: Speaker and Teacher*, ed. Carolyn Keefe (Grand Rapids: Zondervan, 1971), 122.

107. Owen Barfield, *Owen Barfield on C. S. Lewis*, 43.

108. Eric Jacobs, *Kingsley Amis: A Biography* (London: Hodder & Stoughton, 1996), 117.

109. Jacobs, *Kingsley Amis*, 117.

110. Jacobs, *Kingsley Amis*, 117.

111. Carolyn Keefe, ed. *C. S. Lewis: Speaker and Teacher* (Grand Rapids: Zondervan, 1971), 172.

112. Lewis, Letter to J. S. A. Ensor, March 13, 1944, Collected Letters II, 606.

113. See: Alan Jacobs, *The Narnia: The Life and Imagination of C. S. Lewis* (San Francisco: HarperSanFrancisco, 2005).

114. George Bailey, "In the University," *C. S. Lewis: Speaker and Teacher*, ed. Carolyn Keefe (Grand Rapids: Zondervan, 1971), 110.

115. Owen Barfield, "C. S. Lewis in Conversation," *Owen Barfield on C. S. Lewis,* ed. G. B. Tennyson, (Middletown: Wesleyan University Press, 1989), 42.

116. C. S. Lewis, *They Asked for a Paper: Papers and Addresses* (London: Geoffrey Bles, 1962).

117. Lewis, Letter to his Father, Albert Lewis, August 28, 1924, *Collected Letters* II, 633.

118. Walter Hooper, "To the Martlets," *C. S. Lewis: Speaker & Teacher*, ed. Carolyn Keefe (London: Hodder and Stoughton, 1971), 70.

119. Steven A. Beebe and Susan J. Beebe, *Public Speaking: An Audience-Centered Approach* (Boston: Pearson, 2021), Chapter 1.

120. Walter Hooper, *C. S. Lewis: Companion and Guide*, "The Discarded Image: An Introduction to Medieval and Renaissance Literature (1964)" (San Francisco: HarperCollins, 1996), 525.

121. These lecture notes are in the author's private collection.

122. Roger L. Green and Walter Hooper, *C. S. Lewis: A Biography* (New York: HarperCollins, 1974) as published in Walter Hooper, *C. S. Lewis: Companion and Guide*, "The Discarded Image: An Introduction to Medieval and Renaissance Literature (1964)," (San Francisco: HarperCollins, 1996), 525.

123. Hooper, *C. S. Lewis: Companion and Guide*, 525–526.

124. Bailey, "In the University," 110.

125. Phillips, *C. S. Lewis at the BBC*, 275.

126. Phillips, *C. S. Lewis at the BBC*, 275.

127. Lewis, *Collected Letters III*, Letter to Thomasine, December 14, 1959, 1108.

128. Owen Barfield, *Owen Barfield on C. S. Lewis*, 43.

129. C. S. Lewis, *An Experiment in Criticism* (Cambridge: Cambridge University Press, 1961), 101.

130. Lewis, *An Experiment in Criticism*, 101. A similar example appeared in the republished essay C. S. Lewis, "Transposition" *They Asked for a Paper* (London: Geoffrey Bless, 1962), 166-182.

131. Owen Barfield, *Owen Barfield on C. S. Lewis*, 42.

132. Sayer, *Jack*, 398.

133. Sayer, *Jack*, 398.

134. Sayer, *Jack*, 398.

135. For a description of reader response theory see: Todd Davis and Kenneth Womack, *Formalist Criticism and Reader-Response Theory* (New York: Palgrave, 2002).

136. Lewis, *Experiment in Criticism*, 116, 131–132.

137. Lewis, *Experiment in Criticism*, 140.

138. Lewis, *Experiment in Criticism*, 18–19.

139. Lewis, *Experiment in Criticism*, 18–19.

140. Lewis, *Experiment in Criticism*, 140–141.

141. Lewis, *Surprised by Joy*, 156.

142. Lewis, *Experiment in Criticism*, 85.

143. Lewis, *Experiment in Criticism*, 81.

144. Jon Kabat-Zinn, *Wherever You Go, There You Are* (New York: Hyperion, 1994).

145. Lewis, *Experiment in Criticism*, 137.

146. Lewis, *Experiment in Criticism,* 137.

147. Lewis, *Experiment in Criticism*, 140.

148. Steven A. Beebe, Susan J. Beebe and Diana K. Ivy, *Communication: Principles for a Lifetime* (Boston: Pearson, 2019), 7.

149. Aristotle, *The Art of Rhetoric*, 101.

9

How to Communicate Like C. S. Lewis

"Always prefer the plain direct word to the long, vague one. Don't *implement* promises, but *keep* them."[1]

- C. S. Lewis

"Never use abstract nouns when concrete ones will do. If you mean 'More people died' don't say 'Mortality rose.' "[2]

- C. S. Lewis

"When you give up a bit of work don't (unless it is hopelessly bad) throw it away. Put it in a drawer. It may come in useful later. Much of my best work, or what I think is my best, is the re-writing of things begun and abandoned years earlier."[3]

- C. S. Lewis

"In seventh grade, when my English teacher asked us to write to some prominent author asking his advice on writing, I naturally wrote to my favourite author …"[4] Warnie thought this letter to his brother Jack from a schoolgirl named Tomasine "a striking example of impudence, not of the charming school child, but of her schoolmistress."[5] Why Warnie thought the question rude is not clear. Perhaps he thought it was just not appropriate for Tomasine's teacher to encourage her to write to a busy author and ask for advice about his craft. But Lewis felt compelled to answer every letter, impudent or not, including Tomasine's. Lewis opens his response, dated December 14, 1959, by acknowledging the challenge of the task: "It is very hard to give any general advice about writing."[6] But then he adds, "Here's my attempt."

(1.) Turn off the Radio.

(2.) Read all the good books you can, and avoid nearly all magazines.

(3.) Always write (and read) with the ear, not the eye. You should hear every sentence you write as if it were being read aloud or spoken. If it does not sound nice, try again.

(4.) Write about what really interests you, whether it is real things or imaginary things, and nothing else. (Notice this means that if you are interested only in writing you will never be a writer, because you will have nothing to write about …)

(5.) Take great pains to be clear. Remember that though you start by knowing what you mean, the reader doesn't, and a single ill-chosen word may lead him to a total misunderstanding. In a story it is terribly easy just to forget that you have not told the reader something that he needs to know—the whole picture is so clear in your own mind that you forget that it isn't the same in his.

(6.) When you give up a bit of work don't (unless it is hopelessly bad) throw it away. Put it in a drawer. It may come in useful later. Much of my best work, or what I think is my best, is the re-writing of things begun and abandoned years earlier.

(7.) Don't use a typewriter. The noise will destroy your sense of rhythm, which still needs years of training.

(8.) Be sure you know the meaning (or meanings) of every word you use.[7]

Lewis, ever the teacher, had definite opinions about how to communicate—both how to write and how to speak. His practical communication lessons about the craft of communication were not restricted to a single letter. As noted throughout this book, Lewis wrote liberally about how to express skillfully ideas to others. He knew communication principles not only in theory but also in practice. He was a teacher by profession, so when someone asked to learn about how to improve his or her communication skill, Professor Lewis seemed happy to oblige.

Here are excerpts from a letter he wrote to Joan Lancaster, June 26, 1956; like the letter to Tomasine, it is full of useful advice about how to be an effective communicator:

Dear Joan–

Thanks for your letter of the 3rd. You describe your Wonderful Night v. [very] well. That is, you describe the place and the people and the night and the feeling of it all, very well—but not the *thing* itself—the setting but not the jewel. And no wonder! Wordsworth often does just the same. His *Prelude* (you're bound to read it about 10 years hence. Don't try it now, or you'll only spoil it for later reading) is full of moments in which everything except the *thing* itself is described. If you become a writer you'll be trying to describe the *thing* all your life: and lucky if, out of dozens of books, one or two sentences, just for a moment, come near to getting it across … What really matters is:–

1. Always try to use the language so as to make quite clear what you mean and make sure your sentence couldn't mean anything else.
2. Always prefer the plain direct word to the long, vague one. Don't *implement* promises, but *keep* them.
3. Never use abstract nouns when concrete ones will do. If you mean "More people died" don't say "Mortality rose."
4. In writing. Don't use adjectives which merely tell us how you want us to *feel* about the thing you are describing. I mean, instead of telling us a thing was "terrible," describe it so that we'll be terrified. Don't say it was "delightful"; make *us* say "delightful" when we've read the description. You see, all those words (horrifying, wonderful, hideous, exquisite) are only like saying to your readers, "Please will you do my job for me."
5. Don't use words too big for the subject. Don't say "infinitely" when you mean "very"; otherwise you'll have no word left when you want to talk about something *really* infinite.

Thanks for the photos. You and Aslan both look v. [very] well. I hope you'll like your new home.

With love
yours
C.S. Lewis[8]

These letters are communication lessons in miniature. They brim with "dos and don'ts" about how to write and speak to others.

The premise of this book is that Lewis was interested in communication, language, and meaning, and wrote extensively about these topics. Throughout the previous chapters, commentary about how to be an effective communicator uses Lewis's own words drawn from a variety of his works. This final chapter culls out specific prescriptions for improving *your* communication with others, based on Lewis's principles and practices of communication.

Although Lewis studied rhetoric, especially classical rhetoric, there is no evidence that he ever took or taught a contemporary course in "communication." The National Association of Academic Teachers of Public Speaking (that was eventually to become today's National Communication Association) was established in 1914 in Chicago, Illinois—about the time Lewis was beginning his academic study. The study of rhetoric was a fixed element in an Oxford education; however, studying public speaking, or other aspects of communication such as interpersonal or group communication, was not required (and is still not included) in the Oxford University curricula.

Lewis uses the word *communication* or *communicate* in several of his works, including "Before We Can Communicate." Other works such as *Studies in Words*, "The Death of Words," "Transposition," "The Language of Religion," "Bluspels and Flalansferes: A Semantic Nightmare," "Four-Letter Words," *A Preface to Paradise Lost*, *The Discarded Image*, and *An Experiment in Criticism* are teeming with suggestions, ideas, principles, and prescriptions for effective communication. A word count of all of Lewis's works, including his letters, reveals that he used the word *communication* 231 times.[9] Although not formally schooled in "communication," Lewis did have instruction in how to write (grammar), speak (rhetoric), and debate (dialectic). His liberal arts education, coupled with his prolific writing and speaking career, gave him credentials to be a communication professor.

The study of communication has its roots in classical rhetoric with contemporary applications that range from public speaking to posting on Facebook. The most elementary model of human communication includes the components of source, message, channel, and receiver. Whether viewed as a linear, interactive, or the transactive perspective, all communication models include references to these four elements of source, message, channel, and receiver.[10]

A linear "Communication as Action" model of communication views communication as an exchange or transmission of messages or ideas. Contemporary communication theorists reject the notion that meaning is "sent" and "received"; communication is not as simple as that. Even when interactive feedback is added to become the slightly more sophisticated "Communication as Interaction" model, merely including feedback does not quite capture the messiness of how communication works. The "Communication as Transaction" model is deemed the most accurate because it includes the notion that meaning is created, simulated, or discovered (Lewis's perspective) based on mutual, concurrent sharing of symbols. Communication is a transactional process in that people send and receive messages *at the same time*. Meaning is not transferred or sent; when communicating in person one does not say something and then wait for a response, but typically responds to nonverbal cues from the other person before the sentence is completely uttered. Meaning is created or discovered based on the context, noise, experience, and culture of senders and receivers.[11]

If you think these three approaches to communication sound like textbook models, you are right. Virtually every introductory communication textbook traces the evolution of communication as *action* (messages are sent), *interaction* (messages are sent with a subsequent response), and *transaction* (a multitude of messages expressed, interpreted, and responded to simultaneously). Yet the question is, "How will chronicling these 'academic' models of communication help someone become a better communicator?"

These three broad perspectives of communication give a communicator frameworks for analyzing and improving his or her own communication. These models can help you determine why "What we have here is failure to communicate,"[12] (a line memorably uttered by character actor Strother Martin as the prison warden "Captain" to "Luke," played by Paul Newman in the classic film *Cool Hand Luke*). For example, when there is a "failure to communicate," did the communication error originate with the source of the communication? Not effectively putting thoughts into words, selecting the wrong time to express an idea (when you may be too tired and stressed at bedtime for contentious issues), or using contradictory nonverbal messages can be a significance source of communication failure. Or was the communication problem in the message itself—was it poorly worded so as to offend the listener? The channel of the message could be yet another source of communication problems. Some messages are best delivered face-to-face (e.g. a marriage proposal) rather than emailed, texted, or tweeted. Finally, the message receiver (the listener or reader) may just not be paying attention. Or the communicator failed to consider the needs and interests of the audience so that the message fell flat, missing its mark. Viewing communication as a complicated transactional process, rather than a simple act or interaction, helps explain why messages can be misunderstood and not achieve their intended effect.

Lewis knew that noise, a prominent element of any basic communication model, was corrosive to appropriate and effective communication. In *The Screwtape Letters,* Screwtape tells his nephew Wormwood that music and silence are both auditory tools of "The Enemy" (God) and therefore should be avoided at all costs. What is the devilish goal of communication? Noise. Rather than clear and accurate communication, Screwtape recommends confused and obfuscated messages:

Music and silence—how I detest them both! How thankful we should be that ever since our Father entered Hell—though longer ago than humans, reckoning in light years, could express—no square inch of infernal space and no moment of infernal time has been surrendered to either of those abominable forces [music and silence], but all has been occupied by Noise—Noise, the grand dynamism, the audible expression of all that is exultant, ruthless, and virile—Noise which alone defends us from silly qualms, despairing scruples, and impossible desires.[13]

Therefore, instead of promoting communication accuracy, "Screwtape's Guide to Communication" advocates creating noise and eliminating silence. It is noise, distraction, and obfuscation that the devil seeks. Lewis, however, advocates intentional clarity.

Although Lewis did not discuss the fundamental elements of the communication model, or explicitly prescribe how to eliminate communication noise, he did offer considerable advice about how to communicate effectively. Sprinkled throughout his writing, are his principles of communication as represented by the acronym HI TEA (Holistic, Intentional, Transpositional, Evocative, and Audience Centered). Although he never cogently compiled these five principles, HI TEA is embedded throughout what he wrote and said. This final chapter reprises these five Lewisian communication principles by identifying practical applications for improving communication with others.

How to Be Holistic

Effective communicators are holistic communicators. As detailed in Chapter 4, to be holistic is to communicate to the whole person, appealing to the auditory (ear) and visual (eye) senses, as well as integrating reason and imagination. In addition, holistic communicators use a variety of methods and strategies to persuade, debate, and beautify. Lewis blurs the distinction between good speaking and good writing; both are outcomes of the same process of expressing ideas to others, regardless of the message channel. He appeals to reason through using logical arguments. He appeals to imagination through using story, metaphor, and myth. In addition, he holistically integrates the processes of rhetoric (using persuasive strategies), dialectic (debating ideas), and the poetic (expressing beauty) through using examples, comparisons, illustrations, and stories Lewis uses multiple methods and approaches to engage his readers and listeners.

What are the specific skills of being holistic? Just as Lewis communicated for the eye and the ear, you too can use this technique. Appealing to reason and imagination involves not only thinking logically and developing sound arguments, but also using interesting and appealing supporting material. Clarifying and then achieving your communication goal—appealing to reader's and listener's "right brain and "left brain" is yet another holistic communication strategy.

Communicate for the Eye and the Ear

In *Studies in Words*, Lewis writes, "I use *speaker* throughout to cover *writer* as well."[14] His technique for both seeing and hearing words was simple: He spoke as he wrote. As noted in Chapter 4, Walter Hooper reports, "Lewis said. 'It's as important to please the ear, as it is the eye.'"[15]

To put this principle into practice, emulate Lewis's five-step technique:

- First, *visualize* the person or people to whom you are writing.
- Second, *think* about what you want to say.
- Third, *talk* to the listener or reader, *speaking the words out loud*.
- Fourth, *write* what was spoken.
- Finally, *review* what was written and, as Lewis has advised, "If it does not sound nice, try again."[16]

Continue to visualize, think, talk, write, and review. Especially when developing a speech, say the words out loud before making notes or while drafting the outline. Test how the words *sound*.

Another technique is to audio record the message, then listen to it. Edit the message for an oral style by making it more informal and personal than the typical written style. Although some communication messages should be more formal than others, Lewis suggests that the default communication style uses simple words, is brief, and is mindful of what someone will hear as well as see when reading the message.

Use Interesting and Varied Supporting Material

You cannot *not* do it. You cannot *not* use supporting material. Supporting material consists of the examples, evidence, stories, definitions, explanations, quotations, statistics, and other material that help you make your point. If someone used no supporting material when talking or writing, it would result in simply asserting conclusions. Conversations with friends would be brief. When meeting friends for dinner, without supporting material, the conversation might go like this: "I had an interesting day today." Period. There would be no amplification. The listener, also using no supporting material, might simply respond, "I did, too." And that would be the end of the conversation. There would be no anecdotes, stories or additional comments. It would be a boring chat.

Supporting material makes a message either interesting or mind-numbing; a viral TED talk becomes viral because it incorporates poignant personal stories and heart-warming illustrations. Supporting material can be visual (a PowerPoint image) or verbal (illustrations, stories, explanations, definitions, descriptions, analogies, statistics and opinions). Chances are, when listening to a professor, politician, or personal friend, if you are bored it is because the speaker is using uninteresting supporting material. And the process works in reverse: If *you* are boring someone, it is probably because *you* are not using interesting supporting material.

Two things make supporting material interesting: (1) appealing to the senses and (2) adapting material to the other person. Lewis knew how to do both.[17] He was a master craftsperson at using examples, illustrations (both real and hypothetical), stories, metaphors, and analogies. He knew that being concrete and personal are the keys to gaining and sustaining interest. To be concrete is to describe something to help your listeners or readers see, hear, taste, touch, and/or smell the scene or example you describe. Rather than saying, "Frito-Lay sells 2.6 billion pounds of snack food each year," make the number something listeners can comprehend. Say this: "2.6 billion pounds is triple the weight of the Empire State Building." The point becomes more dramatic. Or instead of saying, "The flood displaced 60,000 people from their homes," say "Imagine our city's football stadium filled to capacity with 60,000 people—men, women, boys, girls, parents, grandparents; picture them in your mind—that's how many people are homeless tonight." Whether Lewis is describing Cair Paravel in Narnia or what it is like to take a ride in a spaceship heading to Malacandra, his vivid descriptions make his messages interesting. He describes colors, sounds, textures, aromas. He obviously loved food, for many of his passages, especially in *The Chronicles of Narnia*, offer descriptions of mouthwatering cakes, sweet-cherry pies, breakfasts with steaming cups of tea, delectable sweets, and bounteous banquets fit for the Kings and Queens of Narnia.[18]

In addition to being concrete and appealing to the senses, he also knew the proper balance of providing supporting material. Too much "content" without adequate "support" makes a message dull and tedious. Public speaking teachers recommend that an effective and interesting presentation should contain about 70 percent supporting material and only 30 percent new information, key points, or conclusions.[19] (Remember Kingsley Amis's observations that Tolkien was too "hard" where Lewis was just right—he had a proper mix of "hard" and "soft" information.)[20] The 70 percent supporting material makes the talk interesting.

In *The Discarded Image* Lewis makes clear that during the Middle Ages, listeners or readers expected a message to digress from the main point and to be amplified with supporting material. As Lewis notes, "But the most important of all the *morae* is *Diversio* or Digression … For good or ill the digressiveness of the medieval writers is the product not of nature but of art."[21] He further notes that, "the interwoven stories that so incessantly cross and interrupt one another, may be simply one more application of the digressive principle and an offshoot of Rhetoric."[22] Although Lewis says he does not fully accept or embrace rambling digressions, he knew that supporting material (that may at first seem a digression) enhances listener interest—at least if the "digressions" are on point.

Communicate to the Whole Mind

It is vital to use supporting material that appeals to both the metaphorical "right side" and "left side" of the brain.[23] Neuropsychologists explain that the brain is not quite as simple as using the left side exclusively for language, abstract ideas, and cognitive skills, and the right side for visual and sensual information. Using the whole mind is a metaphor for using both *reason* and *imagination*, as Lewis did, often in the same paragraph.[24] Using interesting supporting material at the same time you are developing logical, rational arguments provides a strong one-two punch of (1) stating your point and then (2) making your point interesting. The metaphorical right side of the brain engages the imagination to enable one to see, taste, touch, and hear, while well-chosen words marshaled to develop logical and rational arguments engage the left side of the brain.

Whether in speaking or writing, be mindful that messages include logical ideas, clear language, and rational thought balanced with interesting stories, clever anecdotes, creative metaphors and fresh analogies that appeal to both reason and imagination. Visual images help more abstract ideas stick in one's memory. More than 45 years later I still remember a public-speaking student who wanted her audience to remember the benefits of eating whole wheat bread rather than white bread. She announced that whole wheat bread has twice as much wheat germ as white bread—a nice "left brain" conclusion. Then she said, "Imagine this room is a loaf of whole wheat bread. Next door the room is a loaf of white bread. Now imagine that each of us in this room is a wheat germ. There are twice as many of us in this room as in the next room." The listeners' "left brain" liked the statistics; imagining themselves as wheat germs in a loaf of bread activated the "right brain." The speaker appealed to the whole mind. The prescription: Use logic, data, and statistics, coupled with analogy, metaphor, and story.

Visual images provide glue to help information stick in readers' or listeners' memory. Describe a scene so that a metaphorical movie screen rises into readers' or listeners' minds, and they see, hear, and experience what you vividly describe. Make a mental movie screen more like an IMAX screen than a small smart phone screen. Surround readers or listeners in colorful images. Help them feel the vibrations of the booming bass notes and the tinkling sparkle of bells. Appeal to their whole "right brain" and "left brain" by making sure they hear the bells and whistles. Lewis engaged the whole mind by using both. You can too.

How to Be Intentional

To be intentional is to be mindful of what you are doing while you are doing it. An intentional communicator is aware of both *what* is said and *how* it is said. Intentional communicators also have a clear goal in mind when expressing ideas to others. Ineffective communicators are not clear, even to themselves, about what they wish to say; they are absently, mindlessly on autopilot.

A four-stage model of conscious awareness has been attributed to psychologist Abraham Maslow: unconscious incompetence, conscious incompetence, conscious competence, and unconscious competence.

- Stage 1: *Unconscious incompetence.* **You do not know that you do not know.** You are unaware of your own incompetence. For example, at one point in your life you did not know you wanted to drive a car. You were unconsciously incompetent about car driving behavior.
- Stage 2: *Conscious incompetence.* **You become aware that you are not competent in performing a specific skill.** You know you do not know. You realized you would like to drive a car, but you were also aware that you did not know how to do it.
- Stage 3: *Conscious competence.* **You learn how to do something, but it is not easy; you still mindfully think about each step of performing the skill.** When you first learned to drive, you became consciously competent—you were actively focused on each aspect of shifting, breaking, steering, and all other aspects of car driving behavior. You knew what to do, but you had to think about what to do.
- Stage 4: *Unconscious competence.* **Your performance becomes easy and second nature to you.** If you have been driving for several years you do

not have to think about every aspect of car driving—you just drive. You perform a skill without consciously pondering every detail.[25]

For Lewis, effective communication requires conscious competence before communicating becomes second nature to you (unconscious competence). Be intentional. To be intentional is to thoughtfully have something to say, develop a clear objective, and use language with precision. Do not start writing until you have clarified in your own mind what you wish to express.

Have Something to Say

In one of the last interviews C. S. Lewis ever gave, editor Sherwood Elliot Wirt asked him, "If you had a young friend with some interest in writing on Christian subjects, how would you advise him to prepare himself?" Lewis responded, "I would say if a man is going to write on chemistry, he learns chemistry. The same is true of Christianity."[26] But then Lewis turns to the general nature of writing: "But to speak of the craft itself, I would not know how to advise a man how to write. It is a matter of talent and interest. I believe he must be strongly moved if he is to become a writer."[27] Lewis was a master communication craftsperson because he had something to say and he was highly motivated to say it. "Writing," said Lewis, "is like a 'lust' or like 'scratching when you itch.' Writing comes as a result of a very strong impulse, and when it does come, I for one must get it out."[28]

To have something to say is to draw upon the skill of invention, one of the classic Greek and Roman canons of rhetoric. Invention is the ability to develop original, creative ideas. What was Lewis's inspiration for his creative ideas? As noted in Chapter 5, in a lecture to Texas State University faculty and students, Lewis's secretary, Walter Hooper, suggested that the seminal factor that made Lewis an effective communicator was the fact that "he had something to say."[29] Until Lewis's conversion, explains Hooper, Lewis had the intellect and was a skilled enough linguistic craftsperson to be a published poet. But it was not until he believed, first in God and eventually in Christianity, that Lewis had a momentous message to express. From his first book published after his conversion, the autobiographical *The Pilgrim's Regress,* until the posthumously published, *Letters to Malcolm,* the corpus of Lewis's speaking and writing either directly or implicitly addressed Christianity. Lewis's ability to give his readers and listeners glimpses of other worlds and to express ideas that would navigate "past watchful dragons,"[30] provides evidence that among his chief communication talents was his ability to express old ideas in fresh ways.

Lewis explicitly underscored the importance of having something to say when he offered this admonition to an American schoolgirl: "Write about what really interests you, whether it is real things or imaginary things, and nothing else."[31] He further makes explicit the importance of having something to say when he writes in *English Literature in the Sixteenth Century: Excluding Drama*, "No style can be good in the mouth of a man who has nothing, or nonsense, to say."[32] Lewis took his own advice: He wrote and spoke about what really interested him.

What interests you? What are you *passionate* about? And how do your interests connect with those with whom you communicate? Whether you are writing a novel or talking with a friend, having something to say is a primary requisite. Reflect on your interests, passions, and hobbies, as well as your work, travel, and family experiences for clues to what you are passionate about.

Unless someone assigns you a topic or the occasion dictates what you should talk about (such as making a speech or toast at a wedding), selecting a topic for a speech can be a challenge. Rather than trying to identify only one topic, use this brainstorming technique to help generate ideas:

- Get a piece of paper or open a blank page on your computer, tablet, or phone.
- Find a quiet spot.
- Think about the audience, the occasion, and your own interests.
- Start writing a list of not one but at least fifty topics. The key is not to self-censor as you brainstorm.
- Just write. Edit later. Wild and wacky ideas are welcome.

Here is the key to brainstorming whether practiced individually or in a group: *Separate the generation of ideas from the evaluation of ideas.* Create first, critique later. (It is especially hard to avoid implicit evaluation in a group, whether it is accolades or criticism, which explains why collaborative brainstorming may not be effective.[33]) With your list of fifty or more topics, go back and review what you have written. Considering what interests both you and your audience, select a topic that appeals to you both. Discover your passion. Communicate about that passion.

Develop a Clear Communication Objective

Stop reading this book for a moment and point to where you think north is. Most smart phones have a compass app, so after you have taken a stab at finding north, take a moment and check. Where *is* north? Did you get it right? When you take a trip, you need to know where north is. Communicating with someone is like taking a trip: Where you are now is vital to determining where you go next. If you do not know where you are going, you will not get there.

Lewis always had a goal in mind for whatever he wrote. He knew where he was taking his readers, although sometimes he would keep the destination a secret to be revealed later. When developing a message, whether in speaking with friends, writing a book, or giving a formal speech, it is important to know which way your metaphorical north is—to know your specific communication objective.

Public speaking, a more formal speaking situation, is a goal-directed activity. The goals for giving any speech can be placed in one of three baskets: to inform, to persuade, or to entertain. Of course, a message may encompass two or all three goals. Informative messages should also be enjoyable and hold an audience's attention—they should entertain. Information is necessary to persuade, but rarely does information alone persuade. As you craft a speech, it is important to know in which direction you want to go.

To inform is to teach by defining, describing, or explaining something. To persuade is to change or reinforce attitudes, beliefs, values, and behavior—or some combination of these things. To entertain is to get a reader or listener to enjoy him- or herself. So the first step in finding north—your message goal—is to determine your *general* purpose.

The next step in finding north is to develop a *specific* purpose. Rather than having a vague notion of what you want to accomplish, it is important to have a very precise audience-centered goal in mind. Your specific purpose is a concise statement of *what you want your reader or listener to be able to do when they finish listening your speech or reading what you have written.* When crafting your specific purpose statement avoid using unmeasurable verbs such as *appreciate, understand,* and *know.* Make your objective observable and measurable. Here's my specific purpose in writing this book: *After reading this book, the reader should be able to list, describe, identify and apply C. S. Lewis's five principles of communication (HI TEA) in Lewis's works and in their own communication.* Note the specific verbs used in my purpose statement (list, describe, identify, apply). I have a very clear sense of what you should *do.* And the emphasis is on the word *do.* Can you list the five principles of HI TEA? Can you describe them? In addition, after reading this book and especially this chapter, I want you to be able to *apply* the principles to your own communication.

For every speech, paper, or even informal email message, you should have your precise behavioral objective in mind. Where do you intentionally want to take your listener or reader? If you are leading them and you do not know which way "north" is, they are not likely to get there. Make sure your objective includes a measurable verb (such as *explain, describe, list, purchase, act,* or *perform*) that prescribes what you want the reader or listener to be able to *do* after they receive your message.

Use Language Precisely

Virtually all of Lewis's pupils recall his insistence for using just the right word in the right place. As he recommends to the schoolgirl who wrote to him for communication advice, "Take great pains to be clear."[34] He also notes, "Be sure you know the meaning (or meanings) of every word you use."[35]

Lewis says that people may sometimes *think* they know what they mean, but a learned vocabulary may clutter the clarity of their own thought. Using language precisely requires thinking with clarity. In his essay "Before We Can Communicate," Lewis writes, "If, given patience and ordinary skill you cannot explain a thing to any sensible person whatever (provided he will listen), then you don't really understand it yourself."[36] Lewis concludes his point by explaining that people should not confuse "sympathy" with mere understanding: " 'We understand one another' often means 'we are in sympathy.' Sympathy is a good thing. It may even be in some ways a better thing than intellectual understanding. But not the same thing."[37] To understand someone is to be able to put into words the precise *thoughts* and *ideas* of the other person. Understanding is a cognitive process. To understand is to de-center; to "get" the idea.[38] To have empathy, is to have an emotional, rather than only a cognitive, resonance with someone. To empathize is to feel what someone else is feeling. Both sympathy and empathy are important, but they are different processes. Sympathy is *thinking* about or merely acknowledging what someone is feeling. Empathy is *feeling* their pain, sorrow or joy.

If you have thought, "I know what I mean, I just can't put it into words." Lewis would respond: "No, you really don't know what you mean." If an idea cannot be clearly expressed to others, then the idea is underdeveloped and needs further thought. The link between clear thought and clear, expressed communication is inextricable.

It is important not only to say what we mean but to say it clearly. Being able to speak in words that make sense to the listener is the goal. In a letter to the editor of *The Christian Century*, Lewis writes, "Any fool can write learned language. The vernacular is the real test."[39] In *Studies in Words*, Lewis demonstrates his understanding of the function and use of language: "I have an idea of what is good and bad language … Language is an instrument for communication."[40] Always the effective professor of communication, Lewis further advises, "The language which can with the greatest ease make the finest and most numerous distinctions of meaning is best."[41]

Being clear is also different from using words with style. In his essay "The Vision of John Bunyan," Lewis noted, "It is always dangerous to talk too long about style. It may lead one to forget that every single sentence depends for its total effect on the place it has in the whole."[42] Using the right word, then, depends on the context of the word.

It is one thing to be told to be precise and use the right word, but the question remains, "How do you do that?" It helps to have the mind of C. S. Lewis, including his vocabulary, memory, and knowledge of languages from his lifetime of study. He not only was a master of English, but also was proficient in Latin, Greek, French, German, Italian, and Spanish. Choosing the right word may take patience. It may also involve pondering your own intentions, as well as having a good dictionary and thesaurus (either hardcopy or electronic) handy. A thesaurus can help you find synonyms. But Lewis would recommend using simple rather than esoteric words.

Although Lewis may not have needed to spend much time revising and re-writing, most of us need to review, revise, rewrite, and revise again. We need to consider our audience and the time and context of the message. Here is an example illustrating the point: To save money, someone in the FBI decided to reduce the size of memo paper during J. Edgar Hoover's tenure as director. When Hoover received a reduced-sized memo, he wrote in one of the narrow margins on the page, "Watch the borders." For the next month and a half it was very difficult to enter the U.S. from either Canada or Mexico.[43] The wrong word or a misinterpretation of a word (in this case the word *borders*) may create a problem called *bypassing*—confusion that occurs when the same word has different meanings to different people. The key to avoiding bypassing as a communication problem is to first be aware of the nature of words and the potential for missed meaning. Then, listen, respond, and ask questions to ensure that the meaning you infer is the meaning intended by the sender of the message. When you are the sender, be mindful of words you use that may be misinterpreted by a reader or listener. When in doubt, clarify meanings and provide definitions.

Other language problems occur from what is called *allness language*. To use allness language is to make sweeping, untrue generalizations. Examples of allness language include "All people from England like tea." "You never listen to me." "You are always late." Unless *all*, *every*, *never*, or *always* is the precise and accurate term you want to use, avoid allness terms. Using allness terms can also make others feel defensive. If you do use such terms, own them by adding, "to me" or "from my perspective." Qualifying allness terms enhances accuracy and reflects awareness that your declaration of how you see the world is simply that: a perspective from your point of view, rather than a sweeping generalization that is likely to be inaccurate.

In summary, to use words well, consider these guidelines:

- Use specific words: A specific word refers to an individual member of a general class—for example, say *lilac bush* rather than *plant*, or *orange marmalade* rather than *jam*.
- Use concrete words—words that appeal to one of the five senses.
- Use unbiased words—use gender-neutral words like *flight attendant* rather than stewardess.
- Use vivid words by adding selected adjectives and descriptive terms to add color and interest to your language.
- Use simple words. Lewis would agree with George Orwell: "Never use a long word where a short one will do … Never use a foreign phrase, a scientific word, or a jargon word if you can think of an everyday English equivalent."[44]
- Use the correct word: Use proper grammar and avoid usage errors by consulting a good English handbook.

The key goal in being intentional is to communicate clearly. Communication researcher Joseph Chesebro has summarized several research-based strategies to enhance message clarity and intentionally turn information into communication.[45] These recommendations are especially relevant when giving a speech or lesson:

- Preview your main ideas. Tell the listeners what you are going to tell them.
- Explain how what you present relates to a previous point or to something the listener already understands.
- Frequently summarize key ideas. Sometimes listeners' minds wander.
- Use effective transitions and signposts; enumerate your major ideas by saying "I have three points to make." Then number each idea as you proceed.
- When appropriate, provide a brief visual outline to help listeners follow your ideas.
- When giving a presentation, once you announce your topic and outline, stay on message.

- Conclude your remarks with a cogent summary. Again, enumerate your key points. Tell them what you've told them.

There are no sure-fire strategies to ensure clarity of your message. But thinking about what you want to say and then using strategies to keep your listener focused on your message can enhance message clarity.

How to Be Transpositional

As explained in Chapter 6, to transpose a piece of music is to play the music in a key other than that in which it was written. Lewis describes transposition as a communication process of going from a higher, richer medium to a lower medium. To transpose is to communicate rich experiences by getting "between the words" with pictures, metaphors and comparisons. Three closely related strategic applications of transposition involve (1) using just the right comparison, such as a simile or apt analogy; (2) communicating for the "mind's eye"; and (3) creating well-crafted visual metaphors.

Use Comparisons Skillfully

One of Lewis's communication hallmarks is his ability to use finely-crafted analogies, both literal and figurative, as well as effective metaphors to express his ideas. For example, in *Mere Christianity*, Lewis notes that being "nice" is not the goal of living a full, Christian life. As he puts it, "A world of nice people, content in their own niceness, looking no further, turned away from God, would be just as desperately in need of salvation as a miserable world—and might be more difficult to save."[46] He clarifies his point by noting that people need more than niceness. Here is where his metaphorical skills come into play when he adds, "It is not like teaching a horse to jump better and better but like turning a horse into a winged creature. Of course, once it has got its wings, it will soar over fences which could never have been jumped and thus beat the natural horse at its own game."[47] He further augments his point noting, "But there may be a period, while the wings are just beginning to grow, when it cannot do so: and at that stage the lumps on the shoulders—no one could tell by looking at them that they are going to be wings—may give it an awkward appearance."[48] His skillful use of simile vivifies his point.

To communicate like C. S. Lewis, consider creative ways to use appropriate metaphors, analogies, and similes. As literary and Lewis scholar Dabney Hart has noted, "The right words, according to Lewis, are more likely to be those of the poet than those of the philosopher, because poetic language is closest to original meaning."[49] Rather than describing a scene prosaically, look for ways to include an apt comparison.

How do you use comparisons skillfully? After you have written a message or drafted an outline for a speech, consider where you might add a comparison for clarity. Rather than just saying, "My fingers were cold" consider adding a metaphor or simile such as, "It was so cold I felt like I had been scraping ice off my windshield using a credit card without wearing gloves." Think of comparisons as the spice of communication. Your first draft is the "meat and potatoes" of your message. Roasted meat and boiled potatoes can certainly satisfy. But to turn your message into a culinary feast, add spice. Metaphors and similes add zest. And just as with spice, take care not to use too much. Do not overwhelm the reader or listener with overpowering "flavors."

Communicate for the "Mind's Eye"

When you hear the word "gymnasium," which of the following three responses best describes your reaction? (1) You *imagine* a scene with people exercising, (2) you *see* the word "gymnasium," or (3) you *hear* the sounds of people talking and laughing as they exercise? Your preferred response to a word is linked to your learning style preference. As noted in Chapter 6, some, though not all, learning theorists suggest that there are three fundamental styles of learning: visual, auditory, and kinesthetic.[50]

- *Visual learners* learn best when they *see* what they are supposed to learn. Watching a movie or video, observing a demonstration, and watching an event are ways visual learners learn best.
- *Audio learners* would rather hear a story than watch it unfold on a screen. Hearing someone read a book is preferred over reading it.
- *Kinesthetic learners* like action and movement when they learn. Active participation is the best way to help kinesthetic learners remember what they learn. Even something as simple as inviting learners to walk to a white board to write a brief word or phrase is better than passively sitting in a chair while writing. Movement reinforces learning.

New research suggests that rather than preferring only one learning style, people actually learn best if learning is reinforced both verbally *and* visually.[51] Given

Lewis's penchant for crafting visual metaphors, as well as using pictures in his head as the catalyst for stories, he was most likely primarily a visual learner. Even if visual learning is not your learning preference, your powers of description can be enhanced if you first see what you are describing in your "mind's eye" before you put your vista into words.

Having a clear mental image of what you are describing is especially important when telling a story. In "It All Began with a Picture," in which the title of the essay reveals the key point of the essay, Lewis describes how he came to write *The Lion, the Witch and the Wardrobe.* He indicates, "The *Lion* all began with a picture of a faun carrying an umbrella and parcels in a snowy wood. This picture had been in my head since I was about sixteen."[52] Lewis had the skill to translate the images in his mind into words that created visual rhetoric for readers and listeners. He described the creative process as being like bird watching: Find time to be still and *see* what transpires.[53]

How do you appeal to the "mind's eye"? Become a "bird watcher." Not a literal bird watcher but a metaphorical bird watcher. As you write, be mindful of what you see. Give yourself time to think first about what you want to say, and if possible, *see* what you want to say. Conjuring an image that you can then describe makes you like a journalist describing an event. Imagine, see, observe. Then transpose: Put what you "see" into words.

Craft Effective Visual Metaphors

Aristotle says, "The soul never thinks without a picture." Lewis knew how to communicate with our souls. The use of visual metaphor is especially important to Lewis's ability to transpose experience and emotion. In summarizing Lewis's talent for "visual rhetoric" in his BBC talks, Lewis scholar Jolyon Mitchell concludes that Lewis's skill in converting his visual images to words, "… may further explain the ease with which he made surprising pictorial connections, topical pictorial allusions, and swift pictorial transitions in his broadcast talks."[54] Lewis had the ability not only to see what he wanted to say, but to develop a visual metaphor that captured what he "saw." He used his well-honed "bird watching" skills. To craft a visual metaphor, emulate Lewis's technique. Simply remain quiet. Look. Then transpose what you see using words—a process that typically involves creating a visual metaphor. Although both using comparisons and appealing to the "mind's eye" have been noted, the closely related skill of developing visual metaphors is a special kind of metaphor that Lewis used liberally, so it deserves special attention.

Lewis said he was not always aware of the source of his mental images, including the visual metaphors that he used to create his stories and to illustrate his non-fiction. In response to a question from his editor about the origin of the Narnia story, he explains,

> So you see that, in a sense, I know very little about how this story was born. That is, I don't know where the pictures came from. And I don't believe anyone knows exactly how he 'makes things up.' Making up is a very mysterious thing. When you 'have an idea' could you tell anyone exactly how you thought of it?[55]

But Lewis did know that it all started with a picture.

A visual metaphor depicts an experience or a feeling by using words to express the scene in the author's mind. The image of a door is one of Lewis's often-used visual metaphors. Whether open, closed, or even sometimes in the air, the door becomes a metaphor for change, movement, and a passage to somewhere new. Perhaps it is the presence of so many closed doors and private entrances in Oxford that inspired Lewis to use the door as a frequent metaphor of how the imagination can transport a person from one place to another. Whether it is opening a wardrobe door, closing the door of a spaceship, peering behind the doors of N.I.C.E., or seeing an image of a door in the air in *The Last Battle*, Lewis often describes portals that simultaneously serve as both exits and entrances. In his sermon *The Weight of Glory* he suggests that although the door is shut, God willing, we shall get in.[56] A door for Lewis symbolizes transformation. It connotes both moving away from the past and venturing into an unknown future. Doors keep harm at bay or are flung open to reveal new possibilities. Lewis understood that people's lives are a series of simultaneous comings and goings, doors opening and closing as they routinely cross thresholds and transoms, even when they are not aware they are between rooms. As in the case of Lewis's door metaphor, an apt comparison has the power to move from the" higher to the lower," to stimulate new thought, and memorably express an idea or feeling.

How to Be Evocative

As presented in Chapter 7, "It is better to get a message out of someone than to put one in them." This classic maxim distills the essence of being an evocative communicator. Lewis understood that communication is about helping the reader or listener *discover* meaning and evoke emotion. Meaning is evoked not transmitted. We are ultimately persuaded when we listen to our own inner voice.

Lewis is a master storyteller. His messages are liberally laced with stories and "supposals" (his term for what is sometimes called "allegory"), to vivify his ideas and help readers and listeners discover the meaning of the messages for themselves. Evoking emotion is at the heart of making emotional connections with your readers and listeners. Evocative communicators are able to express ideas and emotions explicitly. Lewis's ability to tell stories and get messages out of others, and his skill in delivering messages, are classic ways to evoke emotional experiences in readers and listeners.

Tell Stories

Don Hewitt, the original producer of the award-winning TV program *60 Minutes* that has been on the air more than a half century, was often asked, "What is the secret of your success as a communicator?" Hewett responded: "Tell me a story."[57] Everyone likes to hear a good story. Hewitt amplified his response. He said the Bible does more than describe the nature of good and evil; it masterfully tells stories about Job, Noah, David, and others. Like the award-winning producer, Lewis knew that everyone likes a well-told story. His Narnia stories, space adventures, novels, and even his epic poem *Dymer* offer evidence of his master storyteller skill. In his essay "On Stories," Lewis advocates the use of narrative and story as indispensable communication tools, especially in communicating ideas that may be beyond the discernable elements in the plot.[58] Readers re-read stories not because they wonder what happens in the story, but because they want to rekindle the feelings and emotions they had when they read the story the first time. As Lewis puts it, "The re-reader is looking not for actual surprises (which can come only once) but for a certain surprisingness."[59]

Describing his approach to stories and storytelling, Lewis says, "To be stories at all they must be a series of events: but it must be understood that this series— usually known as the plot—is only really a net whereby to catch something else."[60] The story, believes Lewis, is only the vehicle for evoking meaning. Lewis adds, "The real theme [of the story] may be, and perhaps usually is, something that has no sequence in it, something other than a process and much more like a state or quality."[61] His Narnia stories are particularly well known for using plot to express "a state or quality." His "supposal" of what would happen if, in another world in another time, Christ would appear as a Lion, is successful in evoking a state or quality that has had a profound impact on readers since the stories were published.

How do you tell a good story? Any good story has a "spine" or general structure that sets the stage, describes the characters, and moves things along to the conclusion. For example, consider using the narrative of the hero's journey three-act structure (situation, complication, resolution). Storyteller Kat Koppett offers this general framework for telling any story:

- Begin by saying where and when the story takes place, "Once upon a time ..."
- Next, set the stage by introducing characters and describing the situation by adding, "Every day ..."
- Then introduce the complication, "But one day ..."
- Elaborate on the complications, "Because of that ..."
- Add additional drama and obstacles by continuing to say, "Because of that ..." (Repeat as needed)
- Then resolve the conflict by saying, "Until finally ..."
- Wrap it up by concluding, "Ever since then ..."
- Optional ending: "And the moral of the story is ..."[62]

With the general structure of the story in place, remember that the heart of any story is *conflict*—the tension between one or more characters or the conflict of seeking a resolution to a problem. Literary scholar Christopher Booker suggests that in all of the stories ever told there are only seven essential narrative archetypes or basic plots. The essence of each plot can be summarized as:

1. The Quest
2. Voyage and Return
3. Overcoming the Monster
4. Rags to Riches
5. Rebirth: From Shadow into Light
6. Comedy: Problem and Solution
7. Tragedy: Solution and Problems[63]

A good story has a classic plot that is about overcoming an obstacle, whether with a specific character or a larger conflict, in achieving a goal or taking a journey. Narnia plots include quests, voyages, monsters, riches, rebirth, and both comedy and tragedy.

Although Booker suggests that there seven basic plots, it is possible that there are not seven plots, but only one. I invite you to consider that all stories really revolve around only one key idea: *All stories are about finding home.* Where does the hero go after finding riches? Home. "Quest" stories are ultimately about questing for what? Home. Voyage and return to where? Home. Where does the protagonist go after the monster has been vanquished? Home. Where do births and re-births happen? Home. Test this conclusion: Note whether the next movie or TV show you see, or novel you read is, in some way, about finding home. The solution to human problems can be found in the utterances of both Oz's Dorothy and E.T.: "There is no place like home" and "Phone home." Conflict, the stuff of all stories, separates people from that which they seek—or, in Lewisian terms, that for which they long. What is the ultimate human longing? For home.[64] And what is the ultimate emotion upon finding home? *Joy* imbued with *Love*. Lewis would have supported his friend Dorothy L. Sayers's sentiment expressed by one of her characters, Peter Wimsey to his wife, Harriet Vance: "And what do all the great words come to in the end, but that? I love you. I am at rest with you. I have come home."[65]

A well-told story includes conflict that delays or keeps the protagonist from finding home. Yet, it is obvious that some stories end before the protagonist arrives home. Some stories end tragically—finding home is denied or never achieved. Home is not necessarily a literal place, but a condition, or metaphorical vision in which those who find home experience joy, hope, peace, and love.

Good stories also have interesting characters. Well-developed details of a character's appearance, personality, and behavior help make the character seem authentic. Complicated, multidimensional characters, like Edmund from the Narnia books, have both virtues and vices, which add interest and hold readers' attention as they wonder what the character will do next.

Additional criteria of a well-told story include the following:[66]

- *The story should be relevant to the point the communicator wants to make.* Although most stories are inherently interesting, telling a story to illustrate a specific point gives the story additional meaning. Parables, for example, make sense when there is a lesson to be learned. But the parable, anecdote, or story should lead the reader or listener to the point of the lesson.
- *The details of the story should be vivid and specific.* A well-told story provides enough details that the listener or reader can be part of the story. But in keeping with the principle of being evocative, do not smother the conjured images with too many details. Let the listener or reader draw upon his or her past experiences to fill in the gaps. Garrison Keillor is a master story-teller who provides just enough details about his fictional Lake Woebegone so that listeners evocatively participate in the story.

- *The listeners or readers should be able to identify with the characters and plot.* The people in the story should be relatable to those listening or reading. Shakespeare's classical characters endure because their actions, thoughts, and motivations mirror readers' own psychological virtues and vices.
- *Something happens: There is movement and action.* A good story is inherently interesting because of what happens to the characters. Whether the story is tragic or comic, the story arc involves a plot in which there are both obstacles and progress.
- *Something does not always happen. Sometimes there is suspense as readers wonder what will happen next.* While stories have action, there are also times of inaction. Characters wait. Readers wonder what will happen next—yet sometimes nothing happens. Just as in life, there is a journey with both interesting mountain vistas and vast deserts. Arrival at an oasis after traversing scorching nothingness adds to the refreshment people find when they arrive.

Lewis knew how to tell a good story and to use a plot to catch something else—an ineffable emotional response. With an understanding of the structure of a story and its overall outcome (finding home), consider using stories to evoke meaning in the hearts and minds of your readers and listeners.

Get Messages Out of People

Lewis knew that it is difficult to refute one's own honest emotional responses. He was able to get his readers and listeners to use their own experiences to evoke emotion. Lewis also knew that information alone is not communication. Communication occurs when there is a response to information.

Lewis was a skilled writer for children. But he also understood how adults are best motivated to learn. Contemporary research suggests that adult learners: (1) prefer to understand why they are learning what they learn; (2) bring their lifetime of experience to what they learn; (3) are usually self-motivated; (4) are more self-reflexive and consequently have a better understanding of what they need to learn than do children; (5) learn best by focusing on problems.[67] What does this have to do with Lewis getting messages out of people? Both Lewis's fiction and non-fiction suggest that he understood what motivated an adult reader to keep on reading. Whether describing the problem of pain, how miracles happen, or the nature of prayer, Lewis used techniques based on principles of andragogy, or adult learning.

What are these specific techniques? In order to know what the readers or listeners want or need, it is important to think like they think, then imagine what they need and feel. Link your desired goal with what your listeners or readers find interesting and desirable. *Communicate for their "in basket."* Do you have an "in basket" on your desk or in your email, where tasks and projects are queued? Or perhaps you have a pile of sticky notes or a digital "to do" list on your smart phone to remind you of what needs to be done. People are interested in the tasks, projects and "to do" lists that are lurking in their "in basket." Ensuring that your communication message relates to the needs and concerns of your listeners or readers is the best way to gain and maintain attention.

Listeners and readers are selfish. They want to know what is in it for them. While developing a story, put yourself in the place of the reader or listener. Consider what their needs, problems, and concerns might be. Then use your prose to remind them of a problem or need; note how what you are proposing or discussing can solve the problem or address the need. You are more likely to get a message out of someone if what you are talking about is important or salient to that reader or listener.

Help your readers or listeners find home. Lewis perceived that his audience, his readers and listeners, longed for something beyond what they could see. His stories and underlying theological message resonated with their unmet need to "find home" and ultimately experience God. Although he sometimes (in fact, quite often) implicitly disguised the underlying motive of longing, he used an unfulfilled desire to drive the arc of a storyline, whether it was children lost in Narnia or a philologist stranded on Mars. The skill of evoking messages out of others is heightened when the communicator has a clear understanding of the unfulfilled needs of the reader or listener.

Master Nonverbal Communication Skills

Because there are no extant films or videos of C. S. Lewis, no one today can see how Lewis physically delivered a lecture, sermon, or speech. We can only rely on eyewitness descriptions. But recordings of Lewis's voice do exist. From those recordings, as well as from descriptions of those who saw Lewis speak in lecture halls and during tutorials, it is clear that Lewis was a master oral communicator. He could deliver a message well. Perhaps, as noted, in Chapter 2, he inherited his speaking skill from his father Albert, who was a solicitor and who, as Lewis describes in his autobiography *Surprised by Joy*, was "fond of oratory" and had "a fine presence, a resonate voice, great quickness of mind, eloquence, and memory."[68]

Lewis also self-reports in his autobiography that he had an early talent for mimicry. Lewis's early tutor, Harry Wakelyn Smith (also known as "Smewgy"), had a considerable flair for dramatically reading poetry aloud and encouraged Lewis to declaim poetry with gusto. Thus, Lewis had early role models to demonstrate effective techniques of expressing ideas with stylish panache. Sayer also reports that Lewis enjoyed good animated conversation, quoting Lewis as saying, "How I like talking!"[69]

One of Lewis's strategies for improving his speaking skill was practice: "He would practice his lecture to an imaginary audience," observed one of his former students.[70] He followed the advice that modern public speaking educators continue to suggest: Rehearse your speech while recreating the speaking environment.

What are research-based and time-tested skills for effectively delivering a speech? Consider the following list of delivery suggestions:[71]

Maximize Eye Contact

- Establish eye contact with the entire audience, including those in the back and corners.
- Connect with *individuals* in your audience one at a time for a few seconds.
- Look into your listeners' eyes, not over their heads.

Use Appropriate Gestures and Movement

- Focus on communicating the message rather than on your gestures; your gestures should naturally support what you are saying.
- Note how you use gestures in normal conversation with family and friends; use gestures in more formal situations that reflect your unique style.
- Vary your gestures.
- Adapt your gestures to fit the situation. Larger audiences expect more formal gestures; smaller groups expect more informal, casual movement and gestures.
- Be definite with your gestures; when you feel the urge to emphasize a point, do so rather than use halting, timid gestures.
- Move closer to an audience when you have a more personal, intimate point to make.
- Beware of random pacing or shuffling.
- Move to signal a new point, or change the tone of the message.

Maintain Effective Posture

- Plant your feet, placing one foot slightly in front of the other (rather than directly side by side)—you will be less likely to sway from side to side if one foot is just a bit in front of the other one.
- Imagine your head is being held up by a string.
- Stand up straight while pulling your shoulders back just a bit.

Use Appropriate Facial Expressions

- Monitor your facial expressions as you rehearse your speech.
- Use facial expressions that are in sync with your verbal message.
- Make a video while rehearsing: Then review the video to ensure your non-verbal message supports your verbal message.

How to Be an Audience-Centered Communicator

A good communicator never loses sight of the reason for communicating with others—to connect with the audience. Word choice, selection of examples and illustrations, and overall organization of a message should all be based on what best helps a communicator express his or her ideas to the listeners or readers. Brevity, clarity, and interest are the means by which an effective communicator evokes messages in others. An effective communicator, believed Lewis, is, above all, audience centered. An audience-centered communicator works to enhance credibility, selects just the right communication channel, and then skillfully analyzes readers and listeners to appropriately adapt to them.

Enhance Your Credibility

Aristotle used the term *ethos* to refer to what contemporary public speaking textbooks describe as a speaker's credibility. To be credible, a communicator should be ethical, possess good character, have common sense, and be concerned for the wellbeing of the audience.[72] Quintilian, a Roman teacher of rhetoric, believed that an effective speaker also should be a good person speaking well. Credibility is based on the listeners' mindset regarding the speaker. The listener, not the speaker, determines whether a speaker is credible.

How do you become credible? There are three phases in which to enhance your credibility:[73]

- *Initial credibility* is the impression listeners have even before the speaker speaks. Consider having someone introduce you with a well-prepared introduction. Look the part. The general rule of thumb is that a speaker should dress just a bit better than the listeners. Begin with eye contact and have an attention-catching opening line.
- *Derived credibility* is the perception listeners or readers have as they read or hear the message. Lewis's skill in communicating clearly and engagingly—as well as his ability to express complex ideas clearly using metaphors, similes, and analogies—helped him establish derived credibility. Presenting a well-organized message, skillfully delivered (good eye contact, gestures, and facial expressions), with credible research to support your points enhances your derived credibility. Lewis's deep, resonant voice helped him garner credibility.
- *Terminal credibility*, is the perception listeners have when a speaker concludes. Lewis's continued popularity in the 21st century provides evidence of his high terminal credibility. End your message with a brief summary, and conclude with a final story, quotation, or anecdote that makes your point in a memorable way.

Not everyone found Lewis a credible communicator—which makes the point that credibility is not something you possess, but something that others give you. I once attended a dinner party in Oxford and sat across from a world famous physician. As he was in his late 80s and had lived in Oxford all of his life, I asked him if he had ever met C. S. Lewis. He scowled, and then bellowed, "I can't stand the man!" He apparently had no use for Lewis's Christian ideas. I was reminded of an important lesson: Credibility rests in the perception of the listener. To some of his academic colleagues, his foray into theological topics and his popular fiction, as well as his broadcasting on the radio, lowered his credibility. Yet his credibility among those who continue to buy his books remains high.

Of the three classical subsets of credibility—competence, trustworthiness, and dynamism—Lewis scores high among his readers and listeners on all three dimensions. His knowledge of his topics, his experiences as writer and Christian thinker, and his skill in speaking contributed to others' perception of him as a credible message source. People still buy Lewis's books because of his credibility. When Billy Graham passed away in 2018, former U.S. President George W. Bush wrote, "Billy Graham was, with C. S. Lewis, one of the 20th century's most influential figures in evangelism."[74] Both Lewis and Graham were perceived as competent, trusted, and dynamic; to credibly communicate like C. S. Lewis and Billy Graham, you should be, too.

Select the Appropriate Communication Channel

As noted earlier, the four elements of any communication are source, message, channel and receiver. Messages need a channel to connect the message source with the receiver. The channel "carries" the message. A communication channel can be auditory, visual, tactile, olfactory, or gustatory. Communication can be mediated electronically via broadcast (radio, TV) or narrowcast (phone, or text message). Of course, Lewis pre-dated the Internet and Facebook by several decades. But even for his time, he was not a heavy user of the media. There was no TV at The Kilns, his Oxford home for almost 40 years. His media of choice? The printed page, especially books rather than newspapers. Books were followed by live and in-person communication, including visits with friends.

Despite Lewis's general discomfort with radio (Justin Phillips concluded that references to listening to the radio in his works are negative),[75] Lewis's broadcast skill was successful because he was able to translate his ability to have a conversation on the page to having a conversation with his listeners on the air. Perhaps it was his ability to write for the ear as well as the eye, his voice, his clear and simple language style, or a combination of these attributes that helped Lewis connect with his radio listeners. What is evident is that he was successful in finding an audience of people who were eager and interested in his message and the way he presented it.

What guidelines can help you match your message with the proper channel? People usually communicate good news with a richer, more immediate channel (such as face-to-face), and bad news with a less immediate channel (like text or email). Introduced in Chapter 6, Media Richness Theory suggests that a channel is "rich" if it (1) has potential for ample feedback (a response), (2) accommodates more rather than fewer cues at a time, (3) can permit various types of languages (such as both verbal and nonverbal) at the same time, and (4) has the potential to convey feelings and emotions.[76] Communicating with someone live-and-in-person is a media-rich method of interacting. Posting a message on a bulletin board is a media-lean communication channel.

Even when Lewis was using a relatively media-lean channel, such as writing a book, he sought to invite feedback by asking the reader questions along the way, telling the reader to skip passages that were of no interest, or using first-person pronouns to emulate a personal conversation with the reader. He sought to enhance the quality of the relationship by adding to the richness of the channel.

The takeaway: Select a media-rich channel when there is a need to express or gage emotional reactions. Making a final decision to hire someone for a job, or announcing a decision to seek a divorce, call for media-rich channels. More perfunctory, routine messages can suffice with leaner media. Even though called for, when an immediate, media-rich channel is not possible, use the best available channel, such as a phone call (more immediate than a text), or an email (rather than a written note), to best effect by emulating an immediate, media-rich channel. At the death of a loved one, there is no substitute for being present to support your friend or family member—the richest media possible. Flowers are sent because they evoke not only beauty but a multitude of senses to express sympathy. Not all message need a media-rich channel. But when communicating important messages, mindfully consider which channel is best when considering the meta-message (the message about the message such as the relational message) you want to express.

Analyze and Adapt to Your Audience

When I meet my public speaking students on the first day of class, I announce, "I'm now going to give you the answer to every question I will ask you this semester about public speaking." That usually gets their attention. Then I add, "No matter what I ask you about how to prepare or present a speech, what I tell you next is probably the best possible answer." They lean forward, ready to write down the all-purpose answer. I pause for dramatic effect, and then I say, "Here is the answer: *It depends on the audience.*" How long should a speech last? It depends on the audience. Should I start my speech with a joke? Again, you have the answer. No matter what question or decision you have to make about giving a talk, the answer depends on the needs, interests, and expectations of your listeners. "Rhetoric," said rhetorical scholar Donald C. Bryant, "is the art of adjusting ideas to people and people to ideas."[77] Yet it is not just public speaking in which the listener is important; *any* communication strategy in *any* situation is dependent upon the receiver of the message for its success. It is the listener or reader that ultimately determines whether a message is effective and appropriate.

Key questions to ask about any speaking situation include the following: Who is the audience? What does the audience expect? What are their interests and needs? Whenever possible, gather as much information as you can about your listener or reader. The more important the situation, the more care that should be given to considering the needs and interests of the audience. Job interviews and formal presentations need extra attention to the message receiver, but every message should reflect the interests, culture, background, and experiences of the audience.

There are three steps to analyzing and adapting to your audience. First, gather information about your audience. You typically do this informally, just by observing them. Some demographic information (such as age and gender) can be inferred by observation, but sometimes you may need more formal detective work. For important speeches, politicians and CEOs of corporations use surveys or focus groups (a group of people who are interviewed to discover their likes, dislikes, attitudes, values, and beliefs about a speaker or topic). In addition to collecting audience demographics, assess their psychological profile. What are their likes and dislikes, as well as attitudes, beliefs, and values related to the topic and to you?

After you have gathered information, you need to make sense of it. The second step is to analyze the information. Specifically, look for similarities among audience members. In addition, are there cultural, ethnic and racial differences among audience members?

After you gather and analyze audience information, you are ready for the most important task: The third step is to ethically and appropriately adapt to the audience. To adapt is to made a decision about a host of things such as word choice, type of supporting material, message organization or the channel of the message.

Adapting to an audience does *not* mean that you tell them only what they want to hear. If you adapt to your audience by abandoning your own sense of right and wrong, you are an unethical speaker rather than an audience-centered one. It was President Truman who pondered, "I wonder how far Moses would have gone if he'd taken a poll in Egypt?"[78] It does mean that even if you have a message with which you know your listeners will disagree, you phrase your message in ways that will be heard rather than ignored or quickly dismissed.

Here's a summary of strategies to use when adapting to three kinds of audiences: receptive, neutral, or unreceptive.

For Receptive Audiences,

- Identify with them: Note what you have in common with your listeners.
- Clearly state your communication goals, since they are also the goals of your listeners.

- Use stories and other forms of emotional support.
- Tell your audience what you are trying to accomplish.

For Neutral or Apathetic Audiences,

- Capture your listeners' attention early in your presentation by using such strategies as a story, apt quotation, hypothetical example, or rhetorical question.
- Identify and discuss beliefs and values that you and your listeners share.
- Relate your topic and goals not only to your listeners, but also to their family and friends.
- Be realistic; with a neutral or apathetic audience, do not be overly optimistic about what you can accomplish.

For an Unreceptive Audience,

- Begin your message by emphasizing areas of agreement before you discuss areas of disagreement.
- Acknowledge opposing points of view.
- Keep listeners listening; Do not expect significant change.
- Do not announce that you plan to change their minds; it may set off a backlash and they may just stop listening.

A skilled communicator realizes that the ultimate outcome of a message does not depend on the speaker, the channel or even the message itself. *It depends on the audience.*

Remember HI TEA

So how do you communicate like C. S. Lewis? Remember "HI TEA." As a communicator, your job is to be

- **H**olistic
- **I**ntentional
- **T**ranspositional
- **E**vocative
- **A**udience Centered

Here's a final look at the five principles and the corresponding "how to" techniques:

Be a Holistic Communicator

- Communicate for the eye and the ear: Write while saying the words out loud.
- Use interesting supporting material: Use a variety of different kinds of supporting material that are concrete and personal.
- Communicate to the whole mind: Use language and logic to appeal to the "left brain" and visual images and metaphors for the "right brain."

Be an Intentional Communicator

- Have something to say: Reflect on your interests and passions for ideas about what to say with genuine enthusiasm and conviction.
- Develop a clear, measurable communication goal: Know which way is "north" by developing your precise objective, specifying what the reader or listener should be able to *do* after receiving your message.
- Use language precisely: Thoughtfully select the right word. You may consult dictionaries and thesauruses, but remember that the best word may be the simplest, shortest word.

Be a Transpositional Communicator

- Use comparisons skillfully: Liberally use appropriate analogies and similes to express your ideas and communicate emotion.
- Move from the "higher" to the "lower" by appealing to the "mind's eye": Start with a mental image of what you want to express. Visualize your message as a picture or series of pictures.
- Create effective visual metaphors: Transpose your emotions and experiences using metaphors, similes, or other comparisons that appeal to the senses, especially sight.

Be an Evocative Communicator

- Tell Stories: Everyone loves a well-told, relevant story that has an interesting plot and memorable characters, and that makes a point to help your readers or listeners "find home."

- Get messages out of people: Tap a reader's or listener's background, culture, or experience so that the receiver participates in discovering meaning. Describe the scene, rather than tell someone what to feel.
- Master nonverbal communication skills: Use effective eye contact, voice, posture, and gesture to gain and maintain favorable attention.

Be an Audience-Centered Communicator

- Enhance your credibility: Through storytelling, skillfully using language, and referencing your own experiences, you can establish yourself as interesting, knowledgeable, and informed.
- Select the appropriate communication channel: Consciously match your message with the channel.
- Analyze and adapt to your audience: The quintessential principle of communication is: *It depends on the audience.* Always keep your reader and listener in mind. Ethically adapt ideas to people and people to ideas.

I have heard the question, "Who is our C. S. Lewis today?" Or, "Is there an author or speaker today who has the same kind of skill and influence as Lewis?" Although there are many skilled contemporary communicators, the simple fact is, there will never be another C. S. Lewis. He had a unique communication style. But you can learn lessons from Lewis about how to communicate effectively. What can you do? Here's the answer condensed in a single sentence: ***Holistically*** **and *intentionally* develop strategies to *transpose* your ideas and *evoke* appropriate emotions from others while keeping your focus on the most important aspect of communication—the *audience.***

Although there will never be another C. S. Lewis, his principles of how to be an effective communicator endure. Being mindful of his communication principles and applications can further enhance the quality of your own communication. If you can put C. S. Lewis's communication principles into communication practice, you, too, will master the craft of communication.

Notes

1. C. S. Lewis, Letter to Joan Lancaster, June 26, 1956, *The Collected Letters of C. S. Lewis, Vol. III: Narnia, Cambridge, and Joy 1950-1963* (San Francisco: Harper San Francisco, 2007), 766.
2. Lewis, *Collected Letters III*, Letter to Joan Lancaster, June 26, 1956, 766.

3. Lewis, *Collected Letters III*, Letter to Thomasine, December 14, 1959, 1108.
4. Lewis, *Collected Letters III*, Letter to Thomasine, December 14, 1959, 1108.
5. Lewis, *Collected Letters III*, Letter to Thomasine, December 14, 1959, 1108; note 256, 1108.
6. Lewis, *Collected Letters III*, Letter to Thomasine, December 14, 1959, 1108.
7. Lewis, *Collected Letters III*, Letter to Thomasine, December 14, 1959, 1108.
8. Lewis, *Collected Letters III*, Letter to Joan Lancaster, June 26, 1956, 765–766.
9. Joel Heck, "Joel Heck's Lewis Site," Joelheck.com accessed April 1, 2016.
10. Steven A. Beebe, Susan J. Beebe and Diana K. Ivy, *Communication: Principles for a Lifetime* (Boston: Pearson, 2019), 5.
11. Beebe, Beebe and Ivy, *Communication*, 9–12.
12. This famous line was spoken by character actor Strother Martin in the role of Captain in the 1967 movie *Cool Hand Luke*.
13. C. S. Lewis, *The Screwtape Letters*, (London: Bles, 1942), 113–114.
14. C. S. Lewis, *Studies in Words*, (Cambridge: Cambridge University Press, 1960), 14.
15. Lewis, *Studies in Words, 14*.
16. Lewis, *Collected Letters III*, Letter to Joan Lancaster, June 26, 1956, 1108.
17. For a discussion of the use and application of supporting material see: Steven A. Beebe and Susan J. Beebe, *Public Speaking: An Audience-Centered Approach*, 11th edition (Boston: Pearson, 2021), 150.
18. See: *The Narnia Cookbook: Food from C. S. Lewis's The Chronicles of Narnia* (New York: HarperCollins, 1998).
19. Beebe and Beebe, *Public Speaking*, 56; Frank E. X. Dance, *Speaking Your Mind: Private Thinking and Public Speaking* (Dubuque: Kendall/Hunt, 1974).
20. Eric Jacobs, *Kingsley Amis: A Biography* (London: Hodder & Stoughton), 117.
21. C. S. Lewis, *The Discarded Image: An Introduction to Medieval and Renaissance Literature* (Cambridge: Cambridge University Press, 1964), 193.
22. Lewis, *The Discarded Image, 193*
23. For an excellent discussion of communicating for the whole mind see: Daniel Pink, *A Whole New Mind: Why Right-Brainers Will Rule the Future* (New York: Riverhead Books, 2006).
24. Pink, *A Whole New Mind*.
25. For a discussion of being consciously competent see: Beebe, Beebe and Ivy, *Communication*, 31.
26. C. S. Lewis and Sherwood Wirt, "Cross-Examination," *Undeceptions: Essays on Theology and Ethics* (London: Geoffrey Bles, 1971), 215–217; also see: http://www.cbn.com/special/narnia/articles/ans_lewislastinterviewa.aspx accessed January 29, 2015. Originally appeared in *Decision Magazine* (Billy Graham Association: September 1963).
27. Lewis and Wirt, "Cross-Examination."
28. Lewis and Wirt, "Cross-Examination."

29. Walter Hooper, "C. S. Lewis: Communicator," Lecture presented at Texas State University, Centennial Hall, Department of Communication Studies, March 27, 2007.

30. C. S. Lewis, "Sometimes Fairy Stories May Say Best What's to be Said."

31. Lewis, Letter to Thomasine, December 14, 1959, *Collected Letters III*, 1108.

32. C. S. Lewis, *Oxford History of the English Language in the Sixteenth Century: Excluding Drama*. (Oxford: Oxford University Press, 1944). 315.

33. See: E. F. Rietzschel, B. A. Nijstad, and W. Stroebe, "Productivity Is Not Enough: A Comparison of Interactive and Nominal Brainstorming Groups on Idea Generation and Selection," *Journal of Experimental Social Psychology* 42 (2006): 244–251; also see: P. B. Paulus and M. T. Dzindolet, "Social Influence Processes in Group Brainstorming," *Journal of Personality and Social Psychology* 64 (1993): 575–586; P. B. Paulus, K. L. Dugosh, M. T. Dzindolet, H. Coskun, and V. K. Putman, "Social and Cognitive Influences in Group Brainstorming: Predicting Production Gains and Losses," *European Review of Social Psychology* 12 (2002): 299–326.

34. Lewis, Letter to Thomasine, December 14, 1959, *Collected Letters III*, 1108.

35. Lewis, Letter to Thomasine, December 14, 1959, *Collected Letters III*, 1108.

36. C. S. Lewis, "Before We Can Communicate," *God in the Dock*, ed. Walter Hooper,(Grand Rapids: Eerdmans, 1970), 257.

37. Lewis, "Before We Can Communicate," 257.

38. For a discussion of social decentering and empathy see: Steven A. Beebe, Susan J. Beebe and Mark V. Redmond, *Interpersonal Communication: Relating to Others* 9th edition (Boston: Pearson, 2020), 108

39. Lewis, Letter to the editor of *The Christian Century*, December, 1958, *Collected Letters III*, 1007. Originally published in *The Christian Century*, "Version Vernacular," 75 (December 31, 1958), 1515.

40. Lewis, *Studies in Words*, 6.

41. Lewis, *Studies in Words*, 6.

42. C. S. Lewis, "The Vision of John Bunyan," *Selected Literary Essays*, ed. Walter Hoooper (Cambridge: Cambridge University Press, 1969), 151.

43. Beebe, Beebe and Redmond, *Interpersonal Communication*, 157.

44. George Orwell, "Politics and the English language," *About Language*, ed. W. H. Roberts and G. Turgeson (Boston: Houghton Mifflin, 1986), 282.

45. Joseph L. Chesebro, "Effects of Teacher Clarity and Nonverbal Immediacy on Student Learning, Receiver Apprehension, and Affect," *Communication Education* 52 (April 2003): 135–147; Scott Titsworth, Joseph P. Mazer, Alan K. Goodboy, San Bolkan, and Scott A. Myers, "Two Meta-analyses Exploring the Relationship between Teacher Clarity and Student Learning," *Communication Education* 64, 4 (2015): 385–418.

46. Lewis, *Mere Christianity*, 215–216.

47. Lewis, *Mere Christianity*, 215–216.

48. Lewis, *Mere Christianity*, 215–216.

49. Dabney Hart, "The Power of Language," In H. Bloom ed. *C. S. Lewis* (New York: Chelsea House Publishers, 2006), 49–62.

50. See: Virginia. P. Richmond and Joan. Gorham, *Communication, Learning, and Affect in Instruction* (Acton: Tapestry Press, 1998); also see: Steven A. Beebe, Timothy P. Mottet and K. David Roach, *Training and Development: Communicating for Success* (Boston: Pearson, 2013), 38–42.

51. For an excellent review of learning styles research and the Duel Coding (verbal and visual) Theory of learning see: I. Choi, S. J. Lee, & J. Kang, "Implementing a Case-Based E-learning Environment in a Lecture-Oriented Anesthesiology class: Do Learning Styles Matter in Complex Problem Solving Over Time?" *British Journal of Educational Technology, 40* (2009), 933–947; J. Cuevas, "An Analysis of Current Evidence Supporting Two Alternate Learning Models: Learning Styles and Dual Coding" *Journal of Educational Sciences & Psychology, 6* (2016), 1–13; Joshua Cuevas, Is Learning Styles-Based Instruction Effective? A Comprehensive Analysis of Recent Research on Learning Styles, *Theory and Research in Education* 13, 3 (October 6, 2015), 303–333.

52. Lewis, "It All Began with a Picture," 529.

53. Lewis, "It All Began with a Picture," 529.

54. J. P. Mitchell, *Visually Speaking: Radio and the Renaissance of Preaching* (Edinburgh, Scotland: T & T Clark, 1999), 96.

55. Lewis, "It All Began with a Picture," 529.

56. C. S. Lewis, "The Weight of Glory," in *Transpositions and Other Addresses* (London: Bles, 1949), 31.

57. Don Hewitt, interview broadcast on *60 Minutes*, CBS Television Network (24 January, 2010).

58. Lewis, "On Stories," 19.

59. Lewis, "On Stories," 18.

60. Lewis, "On Stories," 18.

61. Lewis, "On Stories," 18.

62. Kat Koppett, *Training to Imagine: Practical Improvisational Techniques for Trainers and Managers to Enhance Creativity, Teamwork, Leadership, and Learning* (Sterling: Stylus Publishing, 2013).

63. Christopher Booker, *The Seven Basic Plots: Why We Tell Stories* (London: Bloomsbury, 2004).

64. Henri Nouwen, along with C. S. Lewis, has written eloquently about the universal longing for home. See: Henri J. M. Nouwen. *Finding My Way Home: Pathways to Life and the Sprit* (New York: The Crossroad Publishing Company, 2004); Henri J. M. Nouwen. *The Return of the Prodigal Son: A Story of Homecoming* (New York: Image, Doubleday, 1993).

65. Dorothy L. Sayers, *Busman's Honeymoon* (London: Gollancz, 1937).

66. Beebe and Beebe, *Public Speaking*, 273.

67. For a discussion of adult learning see: Beebe, Mottet and Roach, *Training and Development*, Chapter 2.

68. Lewis, *Surprised by Joy*, 12. Also see: Crystal Hurd, "*The Pudata Pie*: Reflections on Albert Lewis" *VII: Journal of the Marion E. Wade Center* 32 (2015), 47–58.

69. George Sayer, *Jack: C. S. Lewis and His Times* (Wheaton: Crossway, 1994), 123.

70. Sayer, *Jack*, 181, See: Note 15.

71. For a comprehensive discussion of presentational speaking delivery see: Beebe and Beebe, *Public Speaking*, Chapter 11.

72. For a detailed discussion of C. S. Lewis and ethos see: James E. Beitler III, "Preparing the Way: C. S. Lewis and the Goodwill of Advent," *Seasoned Speech: Rhetoric in the Life of the Church* (Downers Grove: IVP Academic, 2009), 25–56.

73. Beebe and Beebe, *Public Speaking*, 307.

74. George W. Bush, "How Billy Graham Changed My Life," *The Wall Street Journal*. February 23, 2018. https://www.wsj.com/articles/how-billy-graham-changed-my-life-1519427900.

75. Justin Phillips, *C. S. Lewis at the BBC* (New York: HarperCollins, 2002), 202.

76. L. K. Trevino, R. L. Draft, and R. H. Lengel, "Understanding Managers' Media Choices: A Symbolic Interactionist Perspective," *Organizations and Communication Technology*, ed. by J. Fulk and C. Steinfield (Newbury Park: Sage, 1990), 71–94.

77. Donald C. Bryant, "Rhetoric: Its Functions and Its Scope," *Quarterly Journal of Speech* 39 (December, 1953), 26.

78. Harry S. Truman, in Robert H. Farrell, ed., *Off the Record: The Private Papers of Harry S Truman* (New York: Harper & Row, 1980), 310.

Index